PEACE, THEY SAY

A History of the Nobel Peace Prize, the Most Famous and Controversial Prize in the World

JAY NORDLINGER

ENCOUNTER BOOKS  NEW YORK • LONDON

First American edition published in 2012 by Encounter Books,
an activity of Encounter for Culture and Education, Inc.,
a nonprofit, tax exempt corporation.
Encounter Books website address: www.encounterbooks.com

Manufactured in the United States and printed on
acid-free paper. The paper used in this publication meets
the minimum requirements of ANSI/NISO Z39.48 1992
(R 1997) (*Permanence of Paper*).

FIRST AMERICAN EDITION

LIBRARY OF CONGRESS CATALOGING-IN-PUBLICATION DATA
Nordlinger, Jay, 1963–
Peace, they say: a history of the Nobel Peace Prize, the most famous and
controversial prize in the world / Jay Nordlinger.
p. cm.
Includes bibliographical references and index.
ISBN-13: 978-1-59403-598-2 (hardcover: alk. paper)
ISBN-10: 1-59403-598-9 (hardcover: alk. paper) 1. Peace—Awards—History.
2. Nobel Prizes—History. I. Title.
JZ5537.N67 2012
920.02—dc23
2011025603

10 9 8 7 6 5 4 3 2 1

To Martha Apgar and Roger Kimball
(in alphabetical order, as the Norwegian Nobel
Committee often, but not always, does)

# CONTENTS

Contents

INTRODUCTION

Is there a higher earthly honor than the Nobel Peace Prize? It's hard to think of one. It represents a summit of human achievement, and goodness. "Mamas, don't let your babies grow up to be cowboys," went an old song. They would certainly want their babies to grow up to be Nobel Peace Prize winners. And if they did not, they would be a very special kind of parent indeed.

When you receive the Nobel Peace Prize, you are crowned a "champion of peace." A former chairman of the relevant Nobel committee, Francis Sejersted, wrote that "the Laureate will symbolise good will and purity of heart all over the world . . . ." If you win the prize, people will recite a Beatitude to you, and about you: "Blessed are the peacemakers." (They don't so often recite the second part of that Beatitude: "for they shall be called the children of God." Perhaps those words seem unfit for secular society.)

A Nobel peace laureate is considered a sage in the world, a moral guide, and an example to all. Desmond Tutu—winner of the prize for 1984—has said, "No sooner had I got the Nobel Peace Prize than I became an instant oracle. Virtually everything I had said before was now received with something like awe." It's true, too, for better or worse.

The title of this book says that the Nobel Peace Prize is the most "famous" award in the world. That is maybe not strictly true. The Academy Award, a.k.a. the Oscar, is probably equally famous, if not more so. But, Hollywood to one side, the Nobel Peace Prize is almost certainly No. 1. Winners of the award are listed in the dictionary—not just encyclopedias, but dictionaries. Open one, and you will find "Menchú, Rigoberta" (who won in 1992). And consider this tidbit: In 2010, Jimmy Carter came out with his *White House Diary*. On the jacket flap, his bio read, "Jimmy Carter, our thirty-ninth president, received the Nobel Peace Prize for 2002." The presidency is mentioned first, but the weight of the sentence, there at the end, is on the Nobel prize.

Of this prize, Henry Kissinger, a 1973 laureate, wrote in his memoirs, "There is no other comparable honor." Accepting the award in 1949, John Boyd Orr confessed "grave doubts" about his worthiness to receive "the greatest honor any man can get." Later, delivering his Nobel lecture, he said, "The award of the Nobel Peace Prize is an international event of the first importance. It arouses the interest of the people of all countries . . . ." Ten years later, Philip Noel-Baker received the award: given, as it always is, in Oslo, Norway, during the month of December. He said,

> There has come to me what I have always counted as the greatest of the honors which men bestow; it has come to me in the lovely capital of a beloved country, mantled now in Christmas snow; it has come by the decision of your Nobel Committee of wise and most distinguished men. What more could any man or woman ask of Fate?

You might expect winners of this prize to talk this way: After all, they have won. And they are grateful, possibly overwhelmed. But others also acknowledge the supremacy of this prize. Presenting the award in 2007, the Nobel chairman cited the Oxford *Dic-*

tionary of Contemporary World History—which describes the award he was presenting as "the world's most prestigious prize."

It was first handed out in 1901, and of course continues to be handed out today. A history of the Nobel Peace Prize gives us a survey of the 20th century—and, at this point, about a decade's taste of the 21st. We will make our history a chronological one, beginning with the beginning, marching on through the decades, and eras, till we get to President Obama, the 2009 winner. (I will touch on the 2010 and 2011 prizes in an afterword.) Each prize relates to another, really. Along the way, however, there will be excursions and pauses—some jumpings ahead, some looks back. I will explore such questions as, What is peace, anyway? and, Who did not win the prize who should have, or might have?

A history of the Nobel Peace Prize is, among other things, a collection of people, a parade of personalities. In 1974, a Nobel chairman said that the roll of laureates had included "statesmen negotiating round the conference table, defenders of human rights, experts on international law, rebels, humanists, idealists, pragmatists, dreamers. They have all been controversial figures." More than one person has noted that this is a prize that Mother Teresa won; and that Yasser Arafat won. That's a strange kind of prize, isn't it? Some winners are famous names, enduringly famous names—even golden, heroic names. Schweitzer. George C. Marshall. Those two men were honored in Oslo on the same day, incidentally (1953). Other winners belong to obscurity: although we will bring them back a little.

Ernesto Teodoro Moneta was an extraordinary Italian, a co-laureate in 1907. Albert John Lutuli is not nearly as well known as Nelson Mandela, or Desmond Tutu, for that matter. But he was an anti-apartheid leader of an earlier day, and a great man. Carl von Ossietzky won the Nobel Peace Prize for 1935, a year he spent in a Nazi concentration camp. Hitler and his government were so upset at the award to him that they forbade German

3

citizens to accept any Nobel prize: whether for peace, chemistry, literature—anything.

Are you acquainted with Fridtjof Nansen? Noel-Baker, in his Nobel lecture, said, "To all his friends and colleagues, Nansen was the most gifted and, in all true elements of human greatness, the greatest of great men."

We will often hurry through this book, barely touching on the laureates, as we march toward 2009 and Obama (with those tastes of 2010 and '11). Entire books could be written on each of these laureates; indeed, entire books *have* been written, on most of them. And the laureates themselves have written books—lots of them. I will provide brushstrokes here. Those full paintings are pretty easily findable by those who want them. What I will offer is a painting of the Nobel Peace Prize in general (warts and all).

The laureates will not get equal time in this book: Some, I will linger over, others, I will give just a brush or two. And the better-known ones will often get the fewest strokes—they are stroked so amply elsewhere. As I was composing this book, some friends said to me, "Just concentrate on the interesting ones"—the interesting laureates. Problem is, they are all interesting. Very, very few dullards have won the Nobel Peace Prize. They tend to be world-beaters, dynamos, supermen. Nansen was a great athlete, on top of everything else that was amazing about him. Noel-Baker won a silver medal at the Olympics. Charles G. Dawes—do you remember Coolidge's vice president?—wrote a piece of music called *Melody in A*. It got turned into a pop standard, "It's All in the Game."

That is hardly important. But is it interesting? I think so.

A history of the prize is not only a collection of people, it's a collection of speeches: by the laureates themselves, and by the Nobel chairmen, explaining the committee's choices. In these speeches, there is a lot of "globaloney," to use Clare Booth Luce's inspired term. But there is gold as well. Great orators in prize history include Martin Luther King (whose Nobel lecture, unfortunately, is marred by a nasty and untrue line concerning Barry Goldwater, defeated in the U.S. presidential election the month before). There are also modest orators who are nonetheless worthy. Many have been forgotten, but we will put them in the spotlight again.

A fair number of these speeches, people will find terribly "relevant." For example, the 1950 winner, Ralph Bunche, spoke of—and condemned—"preventive" war, which later we would call "preemptive" war. Jimmy Carter cited Bunche in his own Nobel lecture, given more than a half-century later. And yet, everything, really, is "relevant": relevant to its own time, and also to ours. Issues of war and peace, and freedom and oppression, change little.

The Nobel Peace Prize is sometimes a weapon. In 1987, the chairman spoke of "placing the prestige" of the Nobel in particular hands. That year, the prize went to Óscar Arias, the Costa Rican president. The committee told him, privately, that they were giving him a weapon against President Reagan. Lech Walesa— a man who, unlike Arias, valued Reagan greatly—had won the prize four years before. He told me that it meant everything to him: that is, to the cause of Solidarity and the defeat of Communism in Poland.

Some prizes look a little silly now, or a lot silly. The prize for 1929 went to Frank Kellogg, who had been Coolidge's secretary of state. (The Nobel Committee was kind to that president's men.) The former secretary of state's name was on the Kellogg-Briand Pact: which "outlawed war." Aristide Briand, the French foreign minister, had won the award before, for the Locarno Treaties— which were supposed to tidy up after the Versailles Treaty and prevent a second world war. The point to make is, every award was given in earnest, at the time. In 2007, the committee gave the award to the Intergovernmental Panel on Climate Change, and to Al Gore, the world's leading global-warming crusader. How will this award look in the future? I suspect silly. I may be wrong.

The title of this book proclaims that the Nobel Peace Prize is not just the world's most famous award, but the world's most controversial one, too. The world's most "problematic," might be a better way to put that. Either way, the point should attract little argument. The idea of peacemaking can be awfully subjective. Some people have given up on the Nobel Peace Prize. They think it's a joke, a farce, a crock—a scandal. I myself have thought that from time to time. Elena Bonner was the wife—then, for 20-some years, the widow—of Andrei Sakharov, the great Russian dissident and physicist who won the peace prize in 1975. Speaking in 2009, Bonner said,

> At one time, the Nobel Peace Prize was the highest moral
> award of our civilization. But after December 1994, when Yas-
> ser Arafat became one of the three new laureates, its ethical
> value was undermined. I haven't always greeted each selection
> of the Nobel Committee . . . with joy, but that one shocked me.
> And to this day, I cannot understand and accept the fact that
> Andrei Sakharov and Yasser Arafat . . . share membership in
> the club of Nobel laureates.

We can well understand that, or I certainly can. Some, however, think that the award to Menachem Begin (who won with Anwar Sadat) was worse than the award to Arafat (who won with Yitzhak Rabin and Shimon Peres). While at work on this book, I mentioned in an e-mail to my friend Lou Cannon—the journalist, biographer, and historian—what I was doing: writing about the peace prize. He e-mailed back, "Most writing about the Nobel prize tells us more about the writer than about the prize or the recipients. If the winner is someone we don't like, we scorn the prize. If it's a favorite, we praise it." True, true. Like you, probably, I have strong views, and these will leak out—or be forthrightly stated—in the course of this book. It is both a history and a view of history: a view of the history covered. But there should be enough information, and a wide enough perspective, to let readers know what *they* think, regardless of what I think.

I found a study of the Nobel Peace Prize very nourishing, historically—even philosophically. I hope others find the same. By the way, you will find a list of laureates, from 1901 on, at the back of this book. But do you know who's just about as interesting— as talented, as impressive—as any of these laureates? As anyone who has ever won the peace prize? The man who established the Nobel prizes, in his will. And we will begin with him, the testator, the father of this all. In fact, we will accord him more than a few brushstrokes.

THE TESTATOR

A SKETCH

His name was Alfred Nobel, and he was a Swede: born in Stockholm on October 21, 1833. The family name came from something longer and Latin: Nobelius. And how do we say Nobel? With the accent on the second syllable: "No-BEL." Alfred was one of eight children, only three of whom would live past 20. He himself was a frail, sickly child. At 18, he wrote something extraordinary, in a long autobiographical poem called *A Riddle*. That poem itself is extraordinary—composed in English, one of Nobel's several languages. The young man wrote,

> My cradle looked a death-bed, and for years
> a mother watched with ever anxious care,
> so little chance, to save the flickering light.

That mother was Andriette Nobel, née Ahlsell, and, by all accounts, she was a dear, warm, devoted, and possibly saintly woman. She had come from wealth, but would suffer many vicissitudes—financial and otherwise—with her husband, Immanuel.

He was a piece of work, a man who merits a biographical sketch, and perhaps a biography, of his own. As Erik Bergengren writes in his superb *Alfred Nobel* (published in 1960), Immanuel was "a natural genius and a noteworthy pioneer in several spheres." He was an engineer, an artist, an inventor, a quester. Frankly, Alfred was much the same, though on a higher plane.

Immanuel did a great deal of construction in Sweden, conceiving and building bridges and the like. He also experimented with blasting techniques, trying to move through the rock that was always in constructors' way. Entrepreneurial and barely containable, he had a hand in almost everything. Yet there were those vicissitudes. About the time Alfred was born, Immanuel went bankrupt. He went east, to Finland and Russia, eventually settling in the imperial capital of St. Petersburg.

There, he met with big success, at least for a time. He was responsible for Russia's first central-heating pipes—indeed, the first central heating was in his own home. But mainly he excelled in another area. The historian Oscar J. Falnes puts it well, in another superb book, *Norway and the Nobel Peace Prize* (1938):

> That the family name of Nobel should have become closely
> identified with the ideal of world peace is a circumstance not
> without its element of irony. The family's reputation was first
> associated not with the arts of peace but with the arts of war . . . .
> A number of the inventions and appliances which play a part in
> modern preparedness and war owe their inception to informa-
> tion and procedures originally made available by the Nobels.

Immanuel's main contribution was naval mines, or sea mines, which aided Russia in the Crimean War. It was Immanuel's mines that kept the British Royal Navy from getting a shot at St. Petersburg. Admiral Napier complained that "the Gulf of Finland is full of infernal machines."

In 1853, a grateful czar gave Immanuel the imperial gold medal "for diligence and artistic skill," an honor not accorded many foreigners. But Immanuel's star soon fell. After the war, he again went bankrupt, and returned to Sweden. Two of his sons, Robert and Ludvig, stayed on. They built their own fortunes, becoming kings of oil down in the Caucasus. In particular, they developed naphtha, a petroleum distillate.

What about the relationship between Immanuel and Alfred? Again, they had much in common, but they could also be contentious. It seems that Immanuel became jealous of his son's prowess, even accusing him one time of stealing an idea that originated with him, the father. The son had to set the father straight in a letter. It began, "My Dear Father," but it laid out the facts in no uncertain terms. Immanuel backed off.

An interesting event occurred in 1868—when Alfred was 35 and Immanuel 67. (The latter would die four years later.) They were jointly awarded the Letterstedt Prize of the Royal Swedish Academy of Sciences. This was a gold medal, and it was for "outstanding original work in the realm of art, literature, or science," and for "important discoveries of practical value to mankind." The Letterstedt Prize would find an echo in the prizes that Alfred would establish almost 30 years later.

But we are getting too far ahead in the story. When Immanuel went bankrupt in Sweden and left for the east, the family did not go with him—not at first. He summoned them in 1842, when Alfred was nine. Alfred was to spend the key years of his youth in St. Petersburg. It was really the city of his formation. He and his brothers had the best of everything, particularly of education. They were tutored at home, by some of the finest teachers the capital had to offer. At the core of their education were sciences, languages, history, and literature. Alfred was especially drawn to English authors, and his favorite was Shelley. That poet was an early, ardent, and lasting love.

As a teenager, Alfred may well have been too poetic for his father's taste, and Immanuel sent him abroad for two years, primarily to study chemical engineering. Alfred was 17 when he went away—west, to Sweden, Germany, and France, and also to America. During these years of study, he mainly lived and trained in Paris, becoming a protégé of Professor Jules Pelouze, a noted chemist. Nobel never attended a university, and he did not obtain a university degree. But a more broadly—even deeply—educated person is hard to imagine. His weirdly huge correspondence bears this out.

Chez Pelouze, he met Ascanio Sobrero, the Italian chemist who, a few years before, discovered nitroglycerine—a liquid far too hot to handle. Of what practical use could such a wild and dangerous substance be? That was to be Alfred's reverberant contribution to science, industry, and the world (unless you wish to count the prizes): He tamed nitroglycerine, making it safe and usable.

It was in 1857—when he was 24—that Nobel obtained his first patent. It was for a gas-measuring apparatus. More than 350 patents would follow, an astounding number: Nobel was a torrent of ideas, a perpetual inventor. The invention for which we know him best is dynamite: the tube in which he controllably placed nitroglycerine. He also gave this stick its name, borrowing from the Greek *dynamis,* for "power." Nobel's assorted inventions helped move the earth, literally. As Immanuel had wanted to do, Alfred and his tools blasted through rock, creating what we might think of as "infrastructure." The St. Gotthard Tunnel through the Swiss Alps, the Corinth Canal in Greece, the Central Pacific Railroad in the United States—these and other wonders were possible because of what Nobel had wrought.

Working with explosives was risky (as it still is). And there were accidents. Among them was a terrible accident in 1864 at the Nobel family's facility in Sweden. It killed five people, including Alfred's younger brother, Emil, who was 20. The accident crippled Immanuel, emotionally. Alfred soldiered stoically on, believing in his projects and their utility to mankind. He was in some respects sentimental, but he was also a tough customer, Alfred Nobel.

If he had had his way, he might have remained a pure scientist and inventor—a lab man. In his writings, he often seems a typical, natural-born scientist. For example, he once said, "If I have a thousand ideas a year, and only one turns out to be good, I'm satisfied." And here he is when he was feeling especially grouchy about another aspect of his life: "I wish absolutely to retire from business—and all kinds of business . . . . To me it is a torture to act as a pacifier in a nest of vultures . . . . There is not the slightest reason why I, who have not been trained to commerce, and cordially hate it, should be plagued with all these commercial matters about which I know little more than the man in the moon."

You are not necessarily to believe him. Nobel was an extraordinary businessman, we might even say a genius businessman. He not only came up with the products, he arranged for their manufacture and pushed them brilliantly. He was as natural an entrepreneur as he was a scientist. He wrote to someone, early in his career, "I am the first to have brought these subjects"—nitroglycerine, etc.—"from the area of science to that of industry." Over time, he established factories and labs in something like 90 different places in more than 20 countries. He had facilities in or around Stockholm, Prague, Hamburg, Turin, Glasgow, Bilbao, San Francisco—all over. And he traveled to these places, constantly, in an age when travel was far more burdensome than it is today. In both his activities and his interests, Nobel practically defined the worldly man. Victor Hugo once dubbed him "Europe's wealthiest vagabond."

As he was in a perpetual state of inventing, promoting, and supervising, he was in a perpetual state of writing. He wrote many thousands of letters, on all sorts of subjects, and always in his own hand. Of the letters he received, a great many were begging letters—letters asking for money. He once said, "The post brings at least two dozen applications and begging letters *per day*, asking for a total of at least 20,000 kronor, which makes at least 7 million kronor a year. I must therefore state that it would be much better to be ill-famed than to have the name of being helpful."

But Nobel was very helpful indeed, and very generous. He gave constantly, and a lot, to people of every kind, but especially to young inventor-entrepreneurs who needed some seed money to get going. Also, he treated his throngs of employees with great generosity. A newspaper noted that Nobel's "companies have free factory doctors and free medicine and there is in fact a systematic social care which aims to prevent retired Nobel workers from having to die in the workhouse or the street."

The letters aside, Nobel was often at some draft: of a poem, play, or novel, usually having some social or pedagogical impetus. He was an assiduous keeper of journals. And he liked to translate writers—e.g., Voltaire—into Swedish.

To visit Nobel's writings—in particular his correspondence— is to visit a rare and multifaceted personality. Nobel could often be biting and ironic. And sometimes he got into real moods—dark ones, which he would describe as "visits from the spirits of Niflheim." He once referred to the doctors treating him as "wretched faculty asses." He also declared that "lice are a sheer blessing in comparison with journalists, these two-legged plague microbes." (Spoken like a scientist.) He makes tart and funny observations about peoples, including this: "In England, conservatism is too flourishing for counsel to accept anything which has no antediluvian sanction." That was after some legal unpleasantness he endured in that country. He also wrote, "All Frenchmen are under the blissful impression that the brain is a *French* organ."

But we see throughout his writings a modesty—almost a puritan modesty. He once wrote, "I have two advantages over competitors: both money-making and praise leave me utterly unmoved." That was evidently true. Another time, he wrote, "It seems contemptible to want to be something or somebody in the motley collection of 1,400 million two-legged, tail-less apes who run about on our circulating earthly projectile." There is also a persistent concern for morality—for honesty and fair-dealing. He described a business partner as "an able fellow and an excellent executive, but with a conscience that stretches like India rubber, which is a pity, for so much intelligence is seldom found in one place."

Clear too, in Nobel's life and letters, is a universality. All those begging letters, those charity-seekers? About them, Nobel said, "I do not enquire where their fathers were born or what Lilliput god they worship; Charity—of the right kind—knows nothing of national frontiers and is confessionless." He said, "My homeland is where I am working and I work everywhere." Yet he was not immune to Swedish patriotism: It flashed from time to time.

We should know something about Nobel's politics: He knew a lot about politics, and always kept abreast of the news, but he had a low opinion of politics, and of politicians: all that double-dealing and power-seeking. Nobel steered clear of politics insofar as possible. His own politics are somewhat hard to discern, but they appear to have been a curious mixture. He was skeptical of democracy, and of the mob. He once wrote, "Formerly, governments were even more short-sighted, narrow, and quarrelsome than their subjects. In our day, it looks as if the governments were at all events making an effort to quell such idiotic popular outbursts as are incited by a malicious press." At the same time, he was an advocate of equal opportunity, individualism, and liberty. He could contradict himself, in a number of areas.

And what of religion? Officially, he was a Lutheran, like most Swedes. But he was far from a conventional believer—or a conventional unbeliever. An early biographer, Henrik Schück, writes in a sketch, "A religion was of value to him only if it expressed itself in love for mankind. By reason of certain hastily spoken remarks he is considered by many to be an out and out atheist, an enemy of all religious belief." But that is untrue. What he was, certainly, was a jouster with God, and with religious belief. In Paris, he supported the work of a clergyman named Nathan Söderblom, who later became the leader of the Church of Sweden. He also became a Nobel peace laureate (1930).

We should know something, just a little, about Nobel and women. For all his 63 years, he remained a bachelor, though not by choice. The inability to find a suitable wife was an ache in his life. He fell in love early—when he was a student in Paris—and she loved him back. But she died suddenly. Nobel writes about this, with extreme poignancy, in that teenage poem of his, *A Riddle*. Flash well forward: In the spring of 1876, he is 42 years old, ensconced in his mansion on the Avenue Malakoff in Paris. In a sense, he advertises for a wife. He places an ad in a Viennese newspaper saying, "Wealthy, highly educated elderly gentleman seeks lady of mature age, versed in languages, as secretary and supervisor of household." ("Elderly" in his early forties.)

Who came to him was an Austrian countess, in reduced circumstances. She was Bertha Kinsky (von Chinic und Tettau), and she was 32. Nobel, enamored of her, asked whether her heart was free. It was not. She was engaged, to the Austrian baron Arthur von Suttner, and she shortly left Paris to marry him. Nobel and Bertha—Baroness von Suttner—would remain friends, and she would be an influence in his life: for she would become an energetic "peace worker," or "peace professional," as she dubbed herself. And he, of course, would establish a certain prize—which she would win (in 1905).

In 1891, when he was 58, Nobel left Paris for San Remo, on the Italian Riviera. There he occupied a villa called "Mio Nido," or "My Nest." When a friend teased that a nest typically had two birds, not one, the bachelor changed the name to "Villa Nobel"— which is how it is known even now. He fell very ill, subject to crippling pains, and wrote to an assistant, "It sounds like the irony of fate that I should be ordered to take nitroglycerin internally. They call it Trinitrin so as not to scare pharmacists and public." That sentence is pure Nobel.

He died in his villa on December 10, 1896. The Nobel prizes are given out that day—on December 10, every year. Nobel's body was taken to Sweden and cremated, its remains interred in the family grave.

WRESTLING WITH WAR AND PEACE

Grant that men, almost all of them, hate war—Nobel probably hated it more than most. He called war "the horror of horrors, the greatest of all crimes," and did so in many languages on many occasions. He hated conflict of any kind, whether between nations or merely between individuals. He wrote once, "I avoid disputes like the plague, even with people who give me every reason" to dispute. He thought that war was well-nigh inexcusable.

Yet he was no babe in the woods. He often cast a jaundiced eye toward peace associations, peace congresses, and peace-makery in general. His friend the baroness, in her efforts to enlist Nobel and his fortune in the peace cause, once asked for a contribution toward a congress in Bern. He supplied a modest sum, and wrote to her,

> I don't think it is money that is lacking, but a real program.
> Good wishes alone will not ensure peace. The same can be
> said about banquets and long speeches. One must be able to

give favorably disposed governments an acceptable plan. To demand disarmament is really only to make oneself ridiculous without doing anyone any good.

In another letter, to someone else, he marveled at "the absurd and futile efforts of windbags who are capable of thwarting the best of aims."

You often hear that Nobel established his peace prize, among his other prizes, out of guilt over his work: in explosives. In condemnatory versions, he is the death-merchant who, late in life, repented, or tried to. In friendlier versions, he is something like, Alfred Nobel, the pyro with a heart.

Strindberg was unfriendly. "Nobel money—some say dynamite money," he once sneered. A greater figure, Einstein, fell for and perpetuated the myth about Nobel and the peace prize. (He won the physics prize for 1921, incidentally.) Giving a speech in 1945, after the atomic bombs had been dropped on Japan, he said, "Alfred Nobel invented an explosive more powerful than any then known—an exceedingly effective means of destruction. To atone for this 'accomplishment' and to relieve his conscience, he instituted his award for the promotion of peace."

We can be sure that Nobel was not insensitive to "the anomaly in his personal position," as the historian Falnes puts it: the position of being an explosives maestro turned to the peace cause. But guilt he apparently did not feel, and atonement he apparently did not seek. He was proud of his inventions, believing that they were of great use to people and their societies, and he said that "there is nothing in the world which cannot be misunderstood or abused." Moreover, he was a very strong believer in deterrence: in the power of overwhelming force, or terrible weapons, to deter war.

In a much-quoted statement, he wrote to Suttner, "My factories may well put an end to war before your congresses. For in the day that two armies are capable of destroying each other in a second, all civilized nations will surely recoil before a war and dismiss their troops." Such was the innocence of the day, even among those so realistic and intelligent as Nobel. A colleague reported him as saying,

> A mere intensification of the deadly precision of war weapons
> will not secure peace for us. The limited effect of explosives
> is a big obstacle to this. To remedy this defect, war must be
> made as death-dealing to the civil population at home as to the
> troops at the front. Let the sword of Damocles hang over every
> head, gentlemen, and you will witness a miracle—all war will
> stop short instantly, if the weapon is bacteriology.

Again, innocence, words that may well make us wince as we read them today. A hundred years after Nobel, Saddam Hussein, for example, was gassing his own, recalcitrant citizens with chemical weapons, as well as gassing other people.

Nobel applied his fertile mind to a great many subjects, including phonographs and aeroplanes. In the same way, he applied his mind to the peace problem, or, if you like, the war problem: how to solve it. He wrote, "I ask myself why there are not the same laws for duels between nations as for duels between individuals. Witnesses are appointed to see if the causes of a duel are weighty enough." Before he decided on his peace prize, he thought of several other ways to benefit the cause: the support of a bureau for peace propaganda in Paris, for example; the subsidizing of a newspaper. But a peace prize it was to be. In 1893, he wrote,

> I should like to leave part of my fortune to a fund for the
> creation of prizes to be awarded every five years (let us say
> six times, for if within thirty years one has not succeeded in
> reforming society such as it is today, we shall inevitably relapse

into barbarism) to the man or woman who has contributed in
the most effective way to the realization of peace in Europe.

Thirty years after Nobel wrote those words, people had recently
finished with their first "world war," and were enjoying a brief
respite before their second, and worse.

Nobel wrote so much, and with such variety, that you can
pluck almost anything from his writings to show him to have
been almost anything: a ridiculous idealist, a steely, dark realist. In 1947, the American Friends Service Committee was a
co-recipient of the Nobel Peace Prize. (Institutions and organizations, as well as individuals, had long been winning the award.)
The AFSC's chairman, Henry Joel Cadbury, gave a Nobel lecture,
in which he said, "In the last two or three weeks, I have been
reading all I could about the views of Mr. Alfred Nobel on the
subject of war and peace. His ideas were not completely consistent and unchanging. He seems to have had several views on this
subject."

So true. Like many of us, I suppose, Nobel was given to bursts
of hope and bursts of despair. He was a strange—and wonderful,
really—mixture of child-like hopefulness and brute tough-mind-
edness. Here is a despairing remark, reported to have escaped
his lips: "I greatly fear that the perpetual peace of which Kant has
spoken will be preceded by the peace of the cemetery." Yet he went
ahead and provided for his peace prize, along with his four other
prizes.

Several people influenced him to include peace—probably
the most startling of the prizes, sitting there along with physics,
chemistry, "physiology or medicine," and literature. Suttner was
the most persistent of the influencers, occasionally reaching the
point of pestering. Some people say that she, through her campaigning and pestering, is responsible for the peace prize. But
Alfred Nobel largely did what he liked. And it was he who wanted

to strike a blow for the cause of peace and to leave a portion of his wealth to this end.

THE WILL

Books about Nobel or the Nobel prizes often have a section entitled "The Will." Here is ours. He thought long and hard about how to dispense his fortune: He had no family, certainly no immediate family. He did not take the task of his will lightly. He wrote three different ones—in 1889, 1893, and 1895. He wrote that final will on November 27 at the Swedish-Norwegian Club in Paris. He used no lawyer, which was to prove a problem in years to come: The will was open to hot dispute. He wrote the document in his own hand, and he wrote it in Swedish. The will is quite short: four pages long, and fewer than 1,000 words. Nobel gives a general outline—a statement of intent—rather than a detailed, meticulous will. He ran his businesses much the same way, with enormous success. He told people basically what he wanted—and expected them to carry out those wishes.

The will left more than 33 million Swedish crowns, which is about $240 million in our terms: in early-21st-century (and American) terms. Nobel's will attracted a great deal of attention across the world, because not many fortunes in those days were dedicated to scientific or charitable purposes.

The will begins with various bequests to different persons: nephews, nieces, friends, servants, former servants. Then the testator says that "the whole of my remaining realizable estate shall be dealt with in the following way"—whereupon we hear for the first time about the fabled prizes. "The capital, invested in safe securities by my executors, shall constitute a fund, the interest on which shall be annually distributed in the form of prizes to those who, during the preceding year, shall have conferred the greatest benefit on mankind." This interest "shall be divided into five equal parts," apportioned as follows:

> one part to the person who shall have made the most important discovery or invention within the field of physics; one part to the person who shall have made the most important chemical discovery or improvement; one part to the person who shall have made the most important discovery within the domain of physiology or medicine; one part to the person who shall have produced in the field of literature the most outstanding work in an ideal direction; and one part to the person who shall have done the most or the best work for fraternity between nations, for the abolition or reduction of standing armies, and for the holding and promotion of peace congresses.

We see how these prizes have grown out of Nobel's interests, his longtime concerns. And you may have noticed two surprising, curious things about the will.

This is a sparse document, with ample leeway, for better or worse. One can interpret liberally. But there is one thing about which Nobel is quite specific, right? He says that his prizes shall go to "those who, during the preceding year, shall have conferred the greatest benefit on mankind." *The preceding year*: not the preceding five, or ten, or fifty, but the preceding one. The Nobel prizes are not meant to be lifetime-achievement awards, or so it would seem. Even the prize for literature? Oh, yes. According to a strict interpretation of the will, the question ought to be, Which of the past year's books should be honored? And if that book is a first novel by a 20-year-old, rather than a thirtieth by a wizened sage—so be it.

Also, did you notice the phrase "in an ideal direction"? The literature prize is to go to the author of "the most outstanding work in an ideal direction." Nobel is speaking of literature that edifies or uplifts—the kind that he himself dearly appreciated, and wrote. It may well be that the best book of the preceding year is a work of nihilism: a masterpiece of nihilism. Fine. But, if we are to read the will strictly, it should not win the Nobel prize—other literary prizes, of course, but not the Nobel.

Nobel, in his sunnier moments, at least, was a passionate believer in the improvement of mankind. And he wanted his prizes to honor those who sped this improvement: material and moral. He wrote,

> To spread enlightenment is to spread prosperity—I mean
> general prosperity, not individual riches—and with prosperity
> most of the evil which is a legacy from the dark ages will disap-
> pear. The conquests of scientific research and its ever-expand-
> ing field wake in us the hope that microbes, the soul's as well
> as the body's, will gradually be exterminated, and that the only
> war humanity will wage in the future will be war against these
> microbes.

That was the spirit of the age, at least in many, including Nobel.

You may have noticed something else about the will—a dog not barking: Where is the prize for economics? It is not there. Nobel did not will it. This Nobel prize, or sort-of Nobel prize, came about more than 70 years after the will was written, in 1968. It was established by the Sveriges Riksbank—the central bank of Sweden—on its 300th anniversary. The prize is known formally as "The Sveriges Riksbank Prize in Economic Sciences in Memory of Alfred Nobel." And it is funded by the bank itself. What other Nobel prizes, or "Nobel prizes," can be tacked on to the original five? The list would seem endless, or at least long.

There was some grumbling, by the original Nobel commit-tees, when the bank came up with its award. To some, it seemed an affront to Nobel's will, as well as a piggybacking onto it. Geir

Lundestad, who is presently the director of the Norwegian Nobel Institute, and the secretary to the peace committee, told me, "Many felt that the economics prize was a mistake. But the general feeling now is, 'What's done is done. They're family now. But let that be the last of the Nobel prizes.'"

We will return to our reading of the will—to discover who was asked to give these awards. The testator writes, "The prizes for physics and chemistry shall be awarded by the Swedish Academy of Sciences"—the outfit from which Nobel, and his father, received the Letterstedt Prize in 1868. The prize for "physiological or medical work" shall be awarded "by the Caroline Institute in Stockholm." The one for literature shall be awarded "by the Academy in Stockholm"—in other words, the Swedish Academy, plain and simple. Finally, the prize for "champions of peace" shall be awarded "by a committee of five persons to be elected by the Norwegian Storting." That is to say, the Norwegian parliament. This was rather out of left field: Why should four of the prizes be given in Sweden—the testator's native land—and the fifth in Norway? We will take up the question in a moment.

You may ask whether Nobel consulted the various institutions, as to whether they would be willing to administer these prizes. He did not. He must have assumed that the institutions would be willing—which, in fact, they turned out to be.

Also in the will, we have a touching statement of Nobel's universality. He writes, "It is my express wish that in awarding the prizes no consideration whatever shall be given to the nationality of the candidates, but that the most worthy shall receive the prize, whether he be a Scandinavian or not." *Whether he be a Scandinavian or not.* This statement may bring snickers today, but the world looks much broader now, and the vision of very few was broader than Nobel's in that day. Besides, he was probably warning the Swedish academies and the Norwegians against provincialism, or regionalism.

PEACE, THEY SAY

Anyway, the course of this will did not run smooth in the first few years after its unveiling. (That was just after New Year's Day 1897. You recall that Nobel died on December 10.) There was an unholy wrangle, as Nobel relatives and others with dollar signs in their eyes—or crown signs in their eyes—contested the will, trying to get more, trying to upset Nobel's grand vision. They did not succeed. In addition, the institutions that were to award the prizes had to figure out how to do so; there were mechanics to set in place. It was all figured out by 1901: when the first prizes were conferred.

WHY NORWAY?

That is a question that people often ask, and that Nobel books take care to address: Why Norway? We can only guess why Nobel turned to the Norwegian parliament for his peace prize, when the other prizes were left in the hands of Swedes. Nobel did not share his reasons with anyone, as far as we know.

Be aware that, in the 1890s, Sweden and Norway were in union. They had been in union since 1814, and would remain so until 1905. Sweden was the dominant partner, or bigger brother; Norway was the junior partner, and littler brother. It could be that Nobel wanted to include Norway in his prizes so as to recognize, even honor, the union. Many Swedes and Norwegians felt a secondary loyalty: Swedes to Norway, Norwegians to Sweden. Nobel could not very well give Norway any of the science prizes, because Sweden was far better equipped in these areas. Norwegian literature was substantial, even renowned—yet Norway had no institution such as the Swedish Academy. That left peace.

Besides which, Norway was building a reputation as a peace nation. The Storting had shown itself exceptionally interested in the European peace movement. Norway was the first country to go on record as favoring the arbitration of international disputes. The Storting was a friend of the Inter-Parliamentary Union, a forerunner to the League of Nations (and therefore to the League's successor, the United Nations).

We should be aware of this, too: At the time of Nobel's will, Norway, the littler brother, was chafing—itching to break free of the union with Sweden. The bigger brother, naturally, was reluctant to let go. In this struggle, Norway was the more peaceable brother—more inclined to turn the other cheek, readier to ease tensions (and weaker, to be sure). This may well have made an impression on Nobel.

Other factors? Again, we are guessing. Nobel was known to admire Bjørnstjerne Bjørnson, the Norwegian writer and patriot who championed peace. Indeed, a few months before Nobel wrote his will, Bjørnson proposed arbitration between Sweden and Norway. Also—this may be too long a reach—Ragnar Sohlman, Nobel's aide and chief executor, and a Swede, had a Norwegian wife.

Consider, too—this is not a long reach—the different places of Sweden and Norway in the world. Not geographical places, of course, but places of influence, status, rank. Øyvind Tønnesson, a historian and expert on the peace prize, writes in an essay,

> Nobel may . . . have feared that the highly political nature of the peace prize would make it a tool in power politics and thereby reduce its significance as an instrument for peace. A prize committee selected by a rather progressive parliament from a small nation on the periphery of Europe, without its own foreign policy and with only a very distant past as an autonomous military power, may perhaps have been expected to be more innocent in matters of power politics than would a committee from the most powerful of the Scandinavian countries, Sweden.

Ah, yes: Norway the pure. A recurring theme.

Whatever Nobel's reasons, whatever his thinking, his choice of Norway for the peace prize caused a hue and cry in Sweden. Many in that country, from Oscar II on down, were not happy with their native son, believing him to have insulted Sweden. They also believed that Norway might use its responsibility, or gift, for mischief: to disadvantage the bigger brother in some way. Norwegians, for their part, were delighted—delighted and flattered. There were exceptions among them, but few. Only four months after the reading of the will, the Storting accepted Nobel's charge: Yes, they would administer the peace prize, gladly.

This prize has always rested with Norway, and that is something to bear strongly in mind: From 1901 onward, the Nobel Peace Prize, this monumental world honor, has been awarded by five Norwegians, sitting on a committee. These five are chosen by Norway's parliament. You could say that, as Norwegian politics go, so goes the Nobel Peace Prize. It pays us to consider Norway and what some call "Norwegianness" in understanding the prize.

# 'NORWAY THE PEACEFUL'

Norway—formally, the Kingdom of Norway—is a small country that has made a fairly large mark on the world. It is not so small physically, this long, narrow strip on the western side of the Scandinavian peninsula. That is a wondrously beautiful strip, too. Rather, Norway is small in population. Today, the country has just under 5 million people, about the same as Alabama or Colorado. The capital city, Oslo, has about 600,000—like Boston or Milwaukee.

Norway has given the world Henrik Ibsen (1828–1906), who wrote the play *Peer Gynt* and other famous works. Edvard Grieg (1843–1907), the beloved Norwegian composer, wrote incidental music for *Peer Gynt*. He also wrote a *Holberg Suite*, in celebration of Ludvig Holberg (1684–1754), a writer and thinker of considerable breadth. Three Norwegian writers have won the Nobel Prize in Literature: Bjørnson (1832–1910), Knut Hamsun (1859–1952), and Sigrid Undset (1882–1949). Like most other winners of this prize, they are today mainly unread. That is not to say that such neglect is merited.

On the façade of the National Theater in Oslo, three names are inscribed: those of Ibsen, Holberg, and Bjørnson. Statues of the men surround the theater.

Kirsten Flagstad (1895–1962), the dramatic soprano, stands as one of the most admired singers of all time. On today's scene, Leif Ove Andsnes (b. 1970) is a top pianist, and Truls Mørk (b. 1961) a top cellist. Edvard Munch (1863–1944) created one of the most recognized paintings in the world: *The Scream.* In his book *Art: A New History*, Paul Johnson calls it "the most often-reproduced and influential single image of the twentieth century." The actress Liv Ullmann (b. 1938) fashioned an international career. There have been many Olympians, which is to say Winter Olympians, for Norwegians have excelled in the snow-and-ice sports. Everyone knew Sonja Henie (1912–1969), the figure skater. In warmer seasons, Grete Waitz (1953–2011) achieved fame as a marathon runner. Magnus Carlsen (b. 1990) rose to the top of the chess world.

Norway's best-known politician, sad to say, is probably Vidkun Quisling (1887–1945). His name became a byword for treasonous collaboration. (Incidentally, the Nobel laureate Hamsun was an ardent Nazi, or ardently pro-Nazi—in the middle of the war, he made a gift of his Nobel medal to Goebbels.) More pleasant associations belong to Trygve Lie (1896–1968), who was the first secretary-general of the United Nations. Gro Harlem Brundtland (b. 1939) is another Norwegian politician who has been prominent in international organizations. Norway is a little country whose players often strut on a big, world stage.

Consider a little incident that occurred in August 2009. Norway's ambassador to the U.N., Mona Juul, sent a letter to her foreign ministry. It complained that the U.N.'s secretary-general, Ban Ki-moon, was a weak leader. The letter was leaked—and made news around the world. Ordinarily, a letter from the U.N. ambassador of a small country to her foreign ministry would barely make a ripple in her country itself. By the way, Juul is married to Terje Rød-Larsen, who gained renown as the U.N. envoy to the Middle East.

The Norwegians, along with the Scandinavians at large, are thought to be a kind of conscience for the world, an example of civilization, and a prod to it. Winston Churchill wrote a nice foreword to the English translation of Erik Bergengren's biography of Nobel, published in 1962. He spoke of "the prominent place the Scandinavian peoples hold in the struggle of civilized humanity for the betterment of the world."

Nobel peace laureates have always bowed to the Norwegians, and their reputation. A 1907 co-laureate, the aforementioned Ernesto Teodoro Moneta, gave his Nobel lecture in 1909. Here is a slice: "I say to you, in all sincerity, that your civic life today is as worthy of admiration in our time as was that of the bold Vikings in the days of war and armed conquest." It was no surprise, he went on to say, that "your country is today in the vanguard of the world peace movement." The laureate for 1933, Norman Angell, noted that a "small state" can make "as great a contribution" as a "vast empire." He mentioned Greece and Palestine, of antiquity. And he said,

> It is the little states, like this one of Norway, which have today
> evolved the highest civilization and the greatest social stability,
> have developed, more than others, the art of free and peaceful
> life together. They, more than others, may show the way by
> which the world may be led to security and peace.

Kim Dae-jung, the 2000 laureate, began his Nobel lecture with this simple and flat claim: "Human rights and peace have a sacred ground in Norway."

Let's have an ounce or two of Norwegian history. In 1015, Olaf Haraldsson became Olaf II, effectively the first king of all Norway.

He presided over the Christianization of Norway, and after his death became Saint Olaf. For more than four centuries—1380 to 1814—Norway was ruled by Danish kings. Then it entered into that union with Sweden, which lasted until 1905, when Norway shook loose. Please note that the name of the capital has undergone some changes: It was originally Oslo; then, following a great fire in 1624, it became Christiania, after King Christian IV; from 1877, the name was spelled "Kristiania"; and in 1925 the capital became Oslo again.

Bjørnson is a figure to reckon with, certainly when we think about the Nobel Peace Prize and the "Scandinavianism," or, more particularly, Norwegianness, that animates it. Bjørnson was a writer, yes: a poet, novelist, and playwright. But he was also a nationalist and—perhaps paradoxically—internationalist. Indeed, he was one of the first of the modern internationalists. I will again turn to Oscar J. Falnes: "Bjørnson chose to make himself a champion of the oppressed and persecuted everywhere, whether they were individuals or nationalities, and by the close of the century he had become the ever-alert conscience of Europe." He supported Zola in the Dreyfus case, argued for the Slovaks against Magyar repression, etc.

And ever before him was the cause of peace. He was one of the great pacifists of his time, and it is to be remembered that pacifism was a more approved stance in his day than it would be later on (particularly after World War II). Bjørnson was one of those who thought that Norway and other small countries could lead the way to peace. Grieg, you may be interested to know, once requested an oratorio from Bjørnson—an oratorio called *Fred*, or *Peace*. Bjørnson duly supplied the text, but Grieg did not persevere in his composing, for reasons not entirely clear. You certainly ought to know that Bjørnson was a member of the original Nobel peace committee. The Storting's election of him was almost foreordained.

Nobel's peace prize—his placing it in Norwegian hands—gave the peace movement in Norway a significant boost. Peace societies in towns and hamlets proliferated. The Storting was more determined than ever to put money into the peace cause. And the motivation was not entirely idealistic or altruistic, of course: Some Norwegian officials were quite open about the national benefits of backing peace. This was a way for a little and powerless country to be somebody. Norwegians would go abroad to attend meetings of the Inter-Parliamentary Union, and they would come back reporting that the mere mention of Norway's name had provoked great applause.

The cause of peace was bound up with other great progressive causes of the time—the late 19th and early 20th centuries. These causes included women's suffrage and the toleration of religious dissent, as you might expect. But they also included temperance, free trade, and gun rights. The Norwegian Quakers, someone once said, sought to destroy "Negro slavery, military slavery, and the slavery of drink." Free trade and pacifism went together naturally, in the thinking of many: Nations that traded with each other did not war on each other. As for gun rights, these were an essential characteristic of a democracy: A society that allowed its citizens, not just its government, to be armed was a democratic and humanistic one indeed. It was dangerous for power, including firepower, to rest solely with the state.

Anyway, such was the progressive thinking of a long time ago.

When World War I came, Norway stayed neutral—and that is a prized and traditional position of the Norwegians, and of the Scandinavians: neutrality. Parties at war are morally equivalent. War is the evil. Victory is perilous, for victors and vanquished alike. A stalemate may well be the best outcome of all. Now, you have just heard a generalization, no more than that: but, as a generalization, it will do. In World War II, Norway tried to stay neutral, as before. But Germany, of course, had other ideas.

They invaded on April 9, 1940. Norway held out for two months before succumbing. King Haakon VII refused to cooperate with the invaders, and escaped to London, where he formed a government-in-exile. He became a symbol of resistance. Vidkun Quisling was a Norwegian of another sort. Foremost of the collaborators, he gave his name to infamy. Norwegians fought the Nazis in multiple ways, compiling an honorable—even a stirring—war record. They fought with the Allies on the ground, at sea, and in the air. Norwegian saboteurs destroyed heavy-water operations in their country, thereby frustrating the Germans in their effort to develop an A-bomb.

The relationship between Britain and Norway in the war is remembered today at Christmas; so is the relationship between America and Norway. Each year, the Norwegians send trees to London and Washington, in gratitude for assistance. The tree in London goes up in Trafalgar Square; the tree in Washington goes up in Union Station. As it happens, the tree in Washington is fake: The Norwegians say that it is impractical to ship a live tree. Yet it is the thought, surely, that counts.

A final word about the war—and not a light one—and the holocaust that was concurrent with it. At the time of the German invasion, there were approximately 1,700 Jews in Norway. About 900 of them managed to escape to Sweden (which had been able to stay neutral), and some others went into hiding. About 760 Jews were deported by a combination of Germans and Norwegians, and almost all of them were murdered at Auschwitz.

Have a glance, now, at Norway today. It is a constitutional monarchy, as it has long been: featuring a king, a prime minister, and the usual accouterments. After World War II, Norway did some rethinking of neutrality and joined NATO. In fact, it is a founding member. It has had troops in both the Afghan and Iraq wars. Norway belongs to the European Economic Area, but it has declined to join the European Union. Not that the country is devoid of EU enthusiasts. This is an old concept, by the way—a United States of Europe. Ferdinand Buisson, a Nobel peace laureate in 1927, advocated it at the Geneva peace conference in 1867.

Norway is a rich country, one of the richest in the world. Or, perhaps more accurately, the Norwegian state is one of the richest in the world. And that is because of oil, which was discovered in the North Sea in the late 1960s. Before then, Norway was modestly off at best, essentially a place of farming and fishing. Today, Norway is the largest producer of oil in Europe, and one of the largest exporters of oil in the world—right up there with the Gulf states and Russia. The Norwegian welfare state is vast and generous: For instance, maternity leave is a year, at 80 percent of salary. (Paternity leave is five weeks.) Leisure time for all Norwegians is ample: If you want to find an official at his desk during the summer, you may have trouble.

A 2007 article in the *Chicago Tribune* began entertainingly and plausibly: "If you wanted to design a small, 21st-century nation from scratch, combining outrageous good fortune with virtue, you'd probably come up with something like Norway." In 2009, the United Nations ranked Norway the most desirable place to live in all the world. (Finishing runner-up was faraway Australia.)

Rich or not, fortunate or not, Norwegians are very keen on self-effacement—self-effacement of a certain kind. You can't be too big for your britches. Lurking in consciousness is a code known as *Janteloven*, a code that is found throughout Scandinavia. It might be rendered as follows: *Don't think you're better than anyone else, don't try to stand out, keep your head down, blend in, think of the collective.* The Norwegians have long been committed egalitarians and collectivists. They have what some call a "consensus society." And the idea of solidarity—social solidarity—is very strong. Some believe it oppressively so: and plenty of Norwegians are chafing, wanting a more individualistic way of life.

In Norway, everyone's tax return is published on the Internet. Everyone can see what everyone else makes. This is a recipe for some social turmoil, or at least stewing. A friend in Oslo explained to me, "You resent everyone who makes one crown more than you, and you feel superior to anyone who makes one crown less than you." Many Norwegians go to considerable lengths to hide what they have.

People tend to pride themselves on peacefulness and peace-mindedness—the idea of Norway the Peaceful. A staffer at the Nobel Institute pointed out to me that, in Norway, the police are unarmed. One year, I was in Bergen just before Constitution Day (May 17). A man was telling me how much he enjoyed the playing of military bands on that day. But then, worried I might get the wrong impression, he said, "There's nothing violent or militarist about these bands, you know—it's just music." In 2007, Norway ranked No. 1 on something called the Global Peace Index. And the words of a Norwegian educational organization are instructive: "Our privileged situation, coupled with the egalitarian values on which Norwegian politics are based, has often given Norwegian politicians a moral imperative to engage in peace processes and advocate human rights and humanitarian aid." The occasional talks between Israelis and Palestinians are known as the "Oslo process," or simply "Oslo," because these talks stem from the Oslo Accords, negotiated in that city in 1993. Norway enjoys the role of facilitator, "setting the table," as they say, for parties in a conflict.

Seeing as I have mentioned the Middle East: For many years, Norway was quite supportive of Israel. Israel was seen by most of the West as a gutsy little outpost of civilization and democracy in a most hostile region. But Norway has become strongly pro-Palestinian in recent decades, as what some have termed "Palestinianism" has taken hold: a devotion to the Palestinian cause, an accompanying dislike of Israel. Of course, this is a Europe-wide phenomenon, not merely a Norwegian one. Furthermore, we all like to make the distinction between an anti-Israel feeling and an anti-Semitic one. But in Norway, as elsewhere, the distinction is sometimes blurred—and the issue of Israel and the Jews has sparked a sometimes anguished debate among Norwegians.

Periodically, there are proposals to boycott Israel. These proposals are for economic boycotts and academic boycotts. The Norwegian state divested from an Israeli company because that company was involved in the West Bank "separation barrier": the barrier meant to stop the murder of Israeli civilians through suicide bombing. (It worked, too.) Norway was the first country in the West to recognize Hamas. Probably the most famous Norwegian writer today is Jostein Gaarder, author of the philosophical novel *Sophie's World*. He is also one of the harshest foes of Israel in the European literary set (which is saying a lot).

Not unrelated to this discussion is Norway's changing population. Like other countries on the continent, Norway has a growing Muslim community: with all the attendant problems of integration, alienation, intimidation, and so on. This is by now a familiar story, unfolding practically everywhere.

In the introduction to this book, I quoted Elena Bonner, Sakharov's widow, speaking in 2009. It was in fact at the Oslo Freedom Forum, a human-rights conference. Here is another quotation from Bonner: "Thirty-four years have passed since the day when I came to this city to represent my husband . . . . I was in love with Norway then. The reception I received filled me with joy." But now things were different, she said: because of the mounting hostility to Israel and, more broadly, to Jews. I will relate one small incident that stands for something larger, in the culture: In 2011, there were news reports in America that President Obama was losing support among Jewish voters, who had been some of the strongest for him. They were concerned about his moves on Israel, perceived by many as unfriendly. Some of these voters were saying that they might withhold campaign contributions from him in the next election cycle. Taking note of this, *Aftenposten*, the leading newspaper in Norway, ran a story: headline, "Rich Jews Threaten Obama."

Two months after that, in July 2011, Norway had probably its worst day since the war. A right-wing or Unabomber-style extremist went on a rampage of bombing and shooting. He killed almost 80 people, most of whom were teenagers enjoying a Labor-party youth camp. The murderer's claim was that Norway was becoming Islamized and that the Labor party was culpable in this process. His atrocities shook not just Norway, but the entire world.

What should we say of Norway and America? In Norway, as in other countries—including America itself—there are pro-Americans, anti-Americans, and those who aren't quite sure. The Socialist Left party seems pretty sure. They are one of the parties now in government, in the coalition led by Labor. Their platform declares that the United States is the number-one threat to world peace. As Norway has divested from Israeli companies, it has divested from American companies, too: from Boeing and Lockheed Martin, for example. Those are defense contractors (among other things). Norway has also divested from Wal-Mart, the retail giant. Why? The claim is that the company exploits the poor abroad, while resisting unionization at home. Describing the general atmosphere, a U.S. diplomat said to me, with a smile, "It's not so much that Norwegian elites are anti-American. It's just that they like America better when it's governed by Democrats," rather than by Republicans.

Norwegian political life is tilted sharply to the left. There is a Conservative party—whose leader attended the 2008 Democratic convention in Denver, the one nominating Barack Obama. That was a display of solidarity and affinity. Norway has a classical-liberal party—a Reaganite or Thatcherite party. It's called the

Progress party, and its leader attended the 2008 Republican convention.

Where world affairs are concerned, is there a general Norwegian view, a consensus view? There is. I have done a fair amount of generalizing in this sketch of Norway (along with some pop anthropology). Have some more: Norwegians greatly value what they're apt to call "bridge-building." And they greatly value dialogue. Critics, even friendly ones, say that Norway is liable to concentrate on form—mere process—at the expense of substantive achievement. Also, this is a country totally devoted to international institutions, and especially to the U.N. Such devotion is not uncharacteristic of small countries, to be sure. But Norway is more devoted than most. In a speech abroad, that Progress-party leader, Siv Jensen, said, "In Norway, you can get away with criticism of the EU, the World Bank, the WTO, NATO, etc. But do not dare raise any critical question about the U.N. In the Norwegian debate, the U.N. is something sacred."

Then there is the question of moral arrogance, vanity: Are Norwegian officials and intellectuals prone to it? Sure. Even their admirers, some of them, will concede that. Norwegians sometimes lecture, preach, and scold, in addition to guide. They relish their role—usually self-appointed, and in one case Nobel-appointed—of arbiter: of judge of the world. The before-quoted U.S. diplomat said, "The Norwegian attitude toward world affairs is very much the Western European one, only more so." It is that attitude distilled. "Norway is the cherry on top of the European attitude." At the same time, the diplomat allowed, "the Norwegians are basically sincere and well-meaning."

Norwegianness can be glimpsed in the person of Thorbjørn Jagland, a Labor politician who has been prime minister, foreign minister, president of the Storting, a vice president of the Socialist International—and who, in 2009, was elected to two different posts: secretary-general of the Council of Europe and chairman of the Norwegian Nobel Committee. A profile of him in the *Wall Street Journal* offered the following: "Asked about his political values, Mr. Jagland cited a respect for human rights, plus the Scandinavian belief in fair distribution of incomes and the right to free health care that every Norwegian enjoys. He classifies himself in the social-democratic tradition of European leaders whose outlook combines faith in international cooperation and diplomacy with trust in social welfare at home."

His predecessor as Nobel Committee chairman, Ole Danbolt Mjøs, said something charming in a *Guardian* profile. He said, "It is hard to believe that the world cares about what five unknown Norwegians think. It is the one day in the year when Norway is on the world stage. When we change prime ministers, there is not much international interest, but there is for the peace prize. We get flooded with reactions from around the world."

How should we describe these "five unknown Norwegians," politically? How should we characterize the committee, in a general, shorthand way? Committee members themselves might call themselves "progressives." They might also say "social democratic," as Jagland has. Some are socialist and left-wing. Some view themselves as conservative, which, in the Norwegian context, might mean rooting for Obama (who, after all, won the 2009 prize). The word "liberal," we should avoid: It means starkly different things in different parts of the world. For instance, it means McGovernite in America, and Reaganite in Australia.

Allow me to approach the matter this way: Think of the editors of *Le Monde*, *Der Spiegel*, the *Guardian*. Think of those who work for the U.N. Secretariat. The faculty of the University of California at Berkeley. These ladies and gentlemen are seldom disappointed by the Nobel Committee's decision, in any given year, and they are in broad ideological agreement with the committeemen. You hear about "world opinion" and the "world community." I might go this far: World opinion is expressed by those "five unknown Norwegians," and the world community is embodied by them. At least, it sometimes appears that way.

We will now take a look at the committee, this fearsome, formidable fivesome: to learn who they are, how they gained their positions, what they do. And we will address the general question, "How does it all work?"

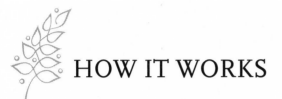

HOW IT WORKS

The committee is elected by the Storting, just as Nobel asked. The Storting is a unicameral legislature, composed of 169 members. As I write these words, there are seven parties with members in the Storting. And, always, the Nobel Committee reflects the Storting as a whole. It reflects the parties in their varying strengths. What does that mean? Say that Labor is flush in seats (as it traditionally is). They might get two picks on the committee—two elections, so to speak—or maybe even three.

In brief, the Norwegian people elect the Storting, and the Storting elects the committee. Therefore, we can say that the committee is a reflection of the Norwegian people and its political culture. Some Norwegians balk at this suggestion, and this is particularly true of those who are often dismayed at the committee. But it is a legitimate claim.

Each committee member is elected to a six-year term, and the members can be reelected indefinitely. In the history of the prize, two members have served 30 years, practically lifers. Members elect their own chairman and deputy chairman. And the committee, though elected by the Storting, is independent of that body, as well as of everything else.

From the very beginning, committee members have been Norwegian, and only Norwegian. There is no requirement that this be so; it is merely custom. This was the subject of considerable debate at the time the peace prize began. Some Norwegians said that responsibility for the prize was too great for Norwegians to bear alone: An international prize should have an international jury. Others said, in effect, Nonsense: We must not shrink from the duty Nobel gave us, and we are perfectly capable of carrying it out. Shall we cast a vote of no confidence in ourselves? Bjørnson said that he would not serve if the committee went international.

There was also, in those early days, debate over how to honor Nobel's request—actually, his stipulation—that the prizes, all of them, reward work done "during the preceding year." The result of the debate was more or less to cough politely when the stipulation came up and move on. Some people, in the beginning, were furious that Nobel's stipulation was being ignored. The prizes were meant to boost and encourage people in their careers, they said; the prizes were not supposed to crown masters in twilight. In practice, the prizes have done both.

The Nobel Foundation was established in Stockholm in 1900, for the administration of the prizes. The foundation has statutes, the relevant one of which reads,

> The provision in the will that the annual award of prizes shall be intended for works "during the preceding year" should be understood in the sense that the awards shall be made for the most recent achievements in the fields of culture referred to in the will and for older works only if their significance has not become apparent until recently.

That is a fudge, maybe, but a fudge that most people can happily live with.

The peace committee has always been double-minded about this "preceding year" business. They cite the will when it suits them, and ignore or dismiss it when it doesn't. In 2008, the committee gave the prize to a Finnish diplomat, Martti Ahtisaari, in acknowledgement of his long career. Chairman Mjøs said— almost quipped—"It is not easy to take every sentence in Nobel's will absolutely literally." The very next year, the committee gave the prize to President Obama, who had barely taken office. A different chairman, Jagland, defending this controversial, and to some mystifying, choice, emphasized a particular term in Nobel's will: "the preceding year." Who else, the chairman asked, had done more for peace during the preceding year than Obama?

Another debate, in earliest days, concerned whether the peace prize should go to just one person in a year—or two. Or more. In his will, Nobel said—says—"person," not "persons." In the first two years of the peace prize, that prize was split, or "divided," as the Nobel people say. And it has been divided many times since. Some people contended that if you split the prize, you diminished its prestige. At any rate, the statutes declare that a prize can go to as many as three people, no more. The peace prize has been awarded to three people only twice: in 1994, when it went to those Oslo peace processors, Arafat, Peres, and Rabin; and in 2011, when it went to three champions of women's rights—Ellen Johnson Sirleaf and Leymah Gbowee of Liberia, and Tawakkul Karman of Yemen.

In the case of 1994, I have used alphabetical order, just as the Nobel Committee did, and does. In the case of 2011, I have used a different order, also as the committee does. The secretary, Geir Lundestad, explained to me that the committee was mainly showing deference to Johnson Sirleaf, a president. (The others had their own involvement in politics, but not at that level.) Where the many pairs in Nobel history are concerned, the order is sometimes alphabetical and sometimes not. Take 1993: Nelson Mandela, the anti-apartheid hero, comes first, and F. W. de Klerk, the South African president in that day, comes second. Here the committee is telling us that Mandela is the more important and deserving figure. The matter of order, as Lundestad and others can confirm, is sometimes delicate.

There is one aspect about a divided prize that is perfectly even: the money. If you share the prize with someone else, you get 50 percent of the pot. Win by yourself, of course, and you get 100 percent.

Here is something else to know about co-laureates: For many decades, co-laureates—two winners of the same year's prize—often had nothing to do with each other. The committee would simply decide that it wanted the prize to go to two different people, working for peace in their own ways. So, for 1931, two Americans won the prize: Jane Addams and Nicholas Murray Butler. But they were not partners. In 1974, Seán MacBride, an Irishman associated with human rights, and Eisaku Sato, a former prime minister of Japan, shared the prize. They had nothing to do with each other. Since then, however, co-laureates have almost always been partners, or at least closely linked: Mandela and de Klerk, for example, and the Oslo-ers.

According to the statutes, the prize has to be given at least every five years; there is no requirement to give it every year. If the committee thinks that no particular person or organization is worthy of the award, the committee can skip the award for that year. The last time a year was skipped, it was 1972. Who knows when we will next see a year without an award? Maybe never. The world expects the Nobel Peace Prize to come every year, like Christmas. Also, the committee can "reserve" an award, which is to say, it can refrain from giving the award for a particular year until a year later. The last time this happened was in 1976—that is, the award for '76 was determined and announced in '77. Two champions of reconciliation in Northern Ireland, Betty Williams and Máiread Corrigan (that is the order in which the Nobel people list them, by the way), were the winners for 1976. But their award was announced, and given, in 1977. It was announced and given simultaneously with the award for 1977 (which went to Amnesty International).

Can the award be given posthumously? No—or, for the most part, no. The peace prize has been given posthumously only once—in 1961, when it went to Dag Hammarskjöld, the U.N. secretary-general from Sweden who was killed in a plane crash in September of that year. After this award, the rules were changed: no posthumous winners. If a person is announced as the winner, however, and dies before he is able to collect the award, the award still goes to him.

Ideally, the committee would like its choice of prizewinner to be unanimous, but a majority vote will do. There does not need to be a consensus; it is not like the election of a pope. Some votes are 3 to 2. But most of the time, the committee is in broad agreement on the choice. If the winner is not a member's first choice, the winner may well be the member's second or third choice—a choice he can easily live with.

On three different occasions, committee members have resigned: in 1936, just before the award (for '35) was given to Carl von Ossietzky, the aforementioned political prisoner of the Nazis; in 1973, after it was given to Henry Kissinger and Le Duc Tho; and in 1994, after it was given to Arafat-Peres-Rabin. Each case involves a different set of circumstances. As the announcement for Ossietzky approached, two members of the committee resigned: Halvdan Koht, who was Norway's foreign minister, and Johan Ludwig Mowinckel, who had been prime minister three times and was an opposition leader. They resigned in order to put distance between the committee and the Norwegian government, which after all had to deal with the German government. In 1973, another two members of the committee withdrew, in the wake of this most controversial of all peace choices. (We will have more on 1973, and the other years, in due course.) In 1994, a committee-man withdrew because he could not stand for Arafat to have the Nobel Peace Prize, even a third of one.

A natural amount of intrigue goes on in the committee. We know about some of this intrigue, because records are unsealed 50 years after the fact. In other words, we will have some inside information about the 1973 award in 2023. Here is a tidbit from 1946: In that year, the prize was divided between Emily Greene Balch, an American peace activist, and John R. Mott, another American, who was a leader of the YMCA. The chairman of the committee, Gunnar Jahn, refused to give the presentation speech for Mott, but said nothing in public about his disagreement. Indeed, committee members are to keep a dignified silence if they disagree with a choice. If they feel strongly enough, they can resign.

After the award to Ossietzky, the Storting made a change: Henceforward, no member of the government could serve on the committee; the potential for conflict was too great. And, in the mid-1970s, the Storting made another change: No member of the Storting itself could serve on the committee—or rather, should serve on the committee. This change is not a formal rule; it is more like a custom, or all-but-rule. Parliament changed the name of the committee from the Nobel Committee of the Norwegian Storting to the Norwegian Nobel Committee. Committee members are often former parliamentarians, or former government ministers, or both. Norwegian officialdom is a pretty small pond.

In 1981, giving his presentation speech (the winner that year was the U.N. refugee office), the chairman, John Sanness, made a strong statement. He said, "In making its awards, the Norwegian Nobel Committee is never swayed by the hope of maximum popularity and general approval. It must never act under pressure from public opinion or from any form of political pressure. It is independent of all authorities, and its duty is to arrive at its decision in accordance with its best judgment and conviction."

The committee is assisted by the Norwegian Nobel Institute, established in 1904. The institute occupies a beautiful building, at 51 Henrik Ibsen Street, just behind the royal palace. It is a gold-yellow mansion, with a bust of Nobel outside, sitting on a fairly high pedestal. The director of the institute also serves as secretary to the committee (the incumbent being Lundestad). And the role of the institute, broadly speaking, is to help the committee in selecting worthy prizewinners, and to organize the various annual Nobel events. The committee has four "permanent advisers," and they tend to be professors in either history or political science at the University of Oslo. The committee may call on others, from around the world, as it wishes.

Where do candidates for the Nobel prize come from? They are nominated. And nominated by whom? Those eligible to nominate are a great many. Indeed, there are seven categories of nominator. These include "present and past members of the Norwegian Nobel Committee"; "members of national assemblies and governments"—which is a huge number of people; and "university chancellors" and "university professors of social science, history, philosophy, law and theology"—probably a huger number of people. You may find that you are eligible to nominate Nobel Peace Prize winners and never knew it. If people in general knew of their eligibility, the Nobel Committee would get many, many more nominations than it does. The openness of the process is rather a secret.

In 2009, Obama's year, there were 205 nominations in all. That was a record number. There were many more nominators than 205. But, of course, quite a few nominate the same person or organization. Nominations can be expected to grow as the years wear on. Interest in this prize is waxing, not waning.

The Nobel Committee sends out invitations to nominate, which is to say, it solicits nominations. These are both invitations and reminders: reminders of the right to nominate. As it does this, the committee works primarily through the different embassies in Oslo. Incidentally, a person may not nominate himself, though this happens—and can lead to awkward situations. Can a person campaign for himself? He certainly can: but this usually—not always, but usually—backfires. The wise Nobel-seeker gets others to campaign for him (and their campaign should be discreet).

The deadline for submission of nominations is February 1. And the deadline is strict. In 1978, Anwar Sadat and Menachem Begin won for the Camp David Accords—accords that were signed in September of that year. We can assume that they were nominated before February 1. The committee wanted to give the prize—a third of it—to Jimmy Carter, along with the Middle Easterners. But he had not been nominated. And the lawyers told the committee that the rule was the rule. (As you can see, we know some things before the passage of 50 years: Sometimes people associated with the committee or the institute simply make disclosures.)

By the way, what is a "year"? What does "the preceding year" mean? Say you win the Nobel prize in 2015. (Congratulations.) In theory, have you won it for work done in 2015 or for work done in 2014 or for work done before February 1, 2015? When Obama was announced as the winner in October 2009, some people guffawed: He had to have been nominated before February 1, and he was sworn in as president on January 20. Did he win the peace prize on the basis of twelve days' performance? The answer is this: In the committee's mind, the "year" is December 10 to December 10—Presentation Day to Presentation Day (which is, for all intents and purposes, the calendar year). Obama won for the year between December 10, 2008, and December 10, 2009.

A person must be nominated before February 1, yes: but the work he does can be evaluated right up until the winner is announced in October. The Camp David Accords were signed on September 17; the committee announced for Sadat and Begin on October 27.

The committee first meets in late February or early March. They conduct their deliberations in a room decked out with pictures of all the peace laureates. At the first meeting, they come up with an initial shortlist—say, 35 names. They meet again in April, when they whittle down that list to a still shorter one: say, five, six, seven names. They then study these nominations, or cases, until October. And on the second Friday of that month, traditionally, their decision is announced. They give the reason for this decision in a statement, or press release. Many people call this document the "Nobel citation": "According to the citation . . ."; "The citation reads . . ." But the committee and the institute do not call it a citation: They call it an announcement or press release. The press release does not figure in the prize ceremony on December 10.

The committee, as you will discover—or know already—gives the peace prize for a variety of reasons: to alter the course of a conflict; to promote a cause; to rebuke a disfavored leader or nation; to make a moral statement; to congratulate a peacemaker of recent success; to crown a master, after a lifetime's labor. The committee has a wonderful bauble to give, and it is a bauble with power, often. We will explore all this, and we will learn more about the Nobel calendar, or Nobel season, later—after meeting some laureates.

PRELUDE TO A PARADE

From 1901, when the inaugural prize was given, to 2011, the latest year we will touch on, the prize was given 92 times. In 19 years, the prize was not given, for various reasons. (To take the most dramatic: During World War II, the committee members were scattered.) On 62 occasions, the award was given to one person or organization; on 28 occasions, it was given to two persons, two organizations, or a person and an organization; and on two occasions, as we have seen, it was given to three persons. A hundred and one individuals received the prize, and 20 organizations. The International Committee of the Red Cross has won it three times, the Office of the U.N. High Commissioner for Refugees twice.

One individual has won the peace prize plus another Nobel prize: That was Linus Pauling, the American scientist and activist who won the prize for chemistry in 1954 and the prize for peace in 1962. (To be most accurate, he won the peace prize for 1962 in 1963. He won it primarily for his advocacy of a nuclear test ban.) You know about the one posthumous award, to Hammarskjöld. Also, one winner refused the prize: Le Duc Tho, the North Vietnamese official who won with Kissinger in 1973. The Nobel

Committee still lists Le Duc Tho as a laureate. You can refuse the committee, but that does not mean that the committee will refuse you.

More laureates have come from the United States than from any other country: 21. The next most laureate-rich nations are Great Britain and France, with eight each. (Most of the British and French wins occurred early in the prize's history.) Five laureates have come from Northern Ireland, that troubled land. (One of these laureates—MacBride—won for reasons not having to do with Northern Ireland.) The American laureates include three sitting presidents (Theodore Roosevelt, Wilson, and Obama), one former president (Carter), two former vice presidents (Charles G. Dawes, who served under Coolidge, and Al Gore, who served under Clinton), five sitting or former secretaries of state, and at least two heroes: Martin Luther King and Norman Borlaug (the agronomist who fed so many). Two laureates have come from Russia: Sakharov, the physicist-dissident, and Mikhail S. Gorbachev, the last boss of the USSR. One laureate has come from China: the 2010 recipient, Liu Xiaobo, a dissident and political prisoner.

The Norwegian Nobel Committee can hardly be accused of favoring its own. Only two Norwegians have won, and, curiously enough, they won in successive years. In 1921, Christian Lange was a co-laureate with Hjalmar Branting (the father of Swedish socialism). In 1922, Fridtjof Nansen, the superhero, won on his own. How about Scandinavia more broadly? You remember what Nobel said in his will: "It is my express wish that in awarding the prizes no consideration whatever shall be given to the nationality of the candidates, but that the most worthy shall receive the prize, whether he be a Scandinavian or not." The Norwegian committee has given the peace prize to eight Scandinavians. Besides the two Norwegians, there have been five Swedes and one Dane. Some count Finland and Iceland as parts of Scandinavia, and there has been one winner from Finland: Ahtisaari in 2008.

These days, the Norwegian Nobel Institute seems eager to say how "globalized" the prize has become. Here is a taste of the official literature: "Up to 1960, the Nobel Peace Prize was almost exclusively the preserve of highly educated white men from Europe and the USA. . . . Only once did the Prize go to a candidate from a country outside Europe and the USA, when it was awarded to the Argentine Foreign Minister Carlos Saavedra Lamas (1936)." The institute also keeps track of women: 15 of whom have won. The first was Nobel's friend Bertha von Suttner in 1905; the most recent three came in one year, 2011.

The youngest person to receive the prize? That distinction belongs to 2011's Tawakkul Karman, barely. She was 32, and so was Máiread Corrigan in 1976, when she did her prizewinning work—but Karman was the younger by a week and a half. The oldest winner is Joseph Rotblat, the physicist and anti-nuclear activist (a man in the Pauling mold) who won in 1995 at 87.

Who has been nominated more than any other person? It's hard to say, without the unsealing of records, but the answer is possibly Jane Addams, who was nominated 91 times, starting in 1916, before she became a co-laureate in 1931. Frank N. D. Buchman may not be a name familiar to you, but he was familiar to many. He was an American evangelist who lived from 1878 to 1961, and he led a group and movement called Moral Re-Armament. Buchman was nominated almost as often as Addams: 85 times. But did not win. As our book unfolds, we will meet quite a few others who were nominated without winning. These include a slew of statesmen. From Great Britain alone, there were MacDonald, Chamberlain, Churchill, Atlee, and Eden. (Chamberlain very nearly won, and Churchill won the Nobel Prize in Literature for 1953.) Nominees from other countries include Hitler, Stalin, and Mussolini. Yes, the committee begged off.

And now we will have a parade . . .

A PARADE OF LAUREATES, 1901 *to* 1913

The first Nobel Peace Prize was awarded at 10 A.M. in the Storting on December 10, 1901. The date was exactly five years after Alfred Nobel's death. The parliamentary president, Carl Christian Berner, gave some introductory remarks, saying this about Nobel:

> Today, when this peace prize is to be awarded for the first time,
> our thoughts turn back in respectful recognition to the man of
> noble sentiments who, perceiving things to come, knew how
> to give priority to the great problems of civilization, putting in
> first place among them work for peace and fraternity among
> nations. We hope that what he has done in the interest of this
> great cause will achieve results which will live up to his noble
> intentions.

"Noble sentiments" and "noble intentions." In English—which, to be sure, was not Berner's language—people have long played with the similarity between "Nobel" and "noble." If a writer or publication approves of a committee choice, the headline might be "A Noble Nobel." People have also played with the word "ignoble"—and a headline might be "An Ignoble Nobel," or "An Ignoble Prize."

There were several interesting things about this first-ever peace prize; these things were precedent-setting, too. First, the prize was divided. Each of the other Nobel committees—the four in Stockholm—gave its 1901 prize to one person. Those committees, too, would soon divide their prizes. Second, the 1901 peace prize was given to two men quite advanced in age: graybeards, and literal ones. (Actually, to be most precise, they had white beards.) There was no contention that they had done anything special in the "preceding year." And we have already mentioned the controversy over "lifetime-achievement awards," as over a split prize. A third precedent? One of the winners was not, strictly speaking, a peaceworker. This was highly controversial, especially among peace professionals such as Baroness von Suttner.

The winners in 1901 were Henry Dunant and Frédéric Passy. The latter was the non-controversial winner. He was one of the grand men of peace in all of Europe, the very epitome of a peace champion. Indeed, he was known as "the apostle of peace." Virtually everyone associated with the peace cause wanted him to win the Nobel prize, and expected him to do so. A Frenchman, he was the leader of his country's peace movement. He was also a co-founder of the Inter-Parliamentary Union. He had been the chief organizer of the first Universal Peace Congress, in 1889. How could the Nobel Committee resist?

Passy was 79 when he won the prize, having been born in 1822. He was a lawyer, an economist, a politician, a writer. In philosophy, he was a classical liberal, a follower of Bastiat and Cobden. Passy was one of those who believed that free trade and peace went hand in hand. He also thought that economic freedom in general was peace-tending. He died in 1912, at 90, and just before the end, he wrote an agonizing letter to Suttner. Irwin Abrams quotes it in his 1988 book, *The Nobel Peace Prize and the*

Laureates. Passy sensed that the world was unraveling, and he was all too right: A world war was merely two years off. He wondered whether the work of the pacifists was all in vain. Was the world destined to be "a mêlée of cupidity and violence"? "I am trying to get a hold of myself," he wrote to his comrade Suttner. "I would not want to finish in discouragement and weakness."

As for Henry Dunant, he is a famous and fascinating story. He was born in Geneva in 1828. From the beginning, he had a humane and religious spirit. He was an early leader of the Young Men's Christian Association—indeed, a founder of the worldwide movement. Subsequently, he went into business, going abroad to North Africa. He wrote a book about his experiences in Tunis, and this book included a chapter that was later published separately: *Slavery among the Muslims and in the United States*. The U.S.? Yes. His interest was sparked by a meeting, in Geneva, with none other than Harriet Beecher Stowe (author of *Uncle Tom's Cabin*).

It was in June 1859 that the pivotal event occurred. For a North African business venture, Dunant needed water rights, and he needed them from the emperor of France, Napoleon III, himself. The emperor happened to be in the field at the time, in Lombardy, near the town of Solferino. So Dunant went to him. He never gained an audience with the emperor, but he saw one of the most horrific battles of the entire 19th century.

This was the Battle of Solferino, an event of the Second Italian War of Independence. It pitted an alliance of Napoleon's army and the Sardinian army against the Austrian Empire. The Franco-Sardinian alliance proved victorious, and the casualties proved high: over 30,000 dead, thousands more wounded or missing. Dunant was traumatized—but not so traumatized as to fail to do anything. He organized relief efforts, calling on the women and girls of the area. They tended to the wounded, heedless of which side they were on. The soldiers, said the women, were "tutti fratelli," all brothers.

Three years later, Dunant wrote a book, *A Memory of Solferino*, which he published at his own expense. It caused a sensation, going around the world in its many translations. The book described the battle and the relief efforts. It also had a plea and a plan. "Could not the means be found in time of peace to organize relief societies," wrote Dunant, "whose aim would be to provide care for the wounded in time of war by volunteers of zeal and devotion properly qualified for such work?" Dunant was pleading for something like the International Red Cross—which shortly came into being. Then there was the first Geneva Convention, which allowed this new organization, or network, to operate unimpeded. Dunant was spreading and institutionalizing the *Tutti fratelli* spirit.

But later, something curious and tragic happened: Immersed in his humanitarian efforts, Dunant forgot his business responsibilities, and went bankrupt. He took others down with him—friends and associates in Geneva who had invested in him. He left his hometown in disgrace, and never went back. He became a vagabond and a wretch, reduced to begging. He sometimes slept outdoors. It was he who needed humanitarian help. Eventually, he entered a hospice in a Swiss village called Heiden, in the northeast corner of the country. He lived there ever after, in Room 12.

In 1895, a journalist discovered him, and Dunant was, in effect, rediscovered by the world. Attention and prizes came his way. He promoted his various causes, including the establishment of a Jewish homeland. A campaign was mounted to get him the first Nobel prize, which, of course, succeeded. Dunant died in 1910, age 82. He did not want an elaborate funeral. He said he wanted to be carried to his grave "like a dog," which he was.

As I've suggested, the award to Dunant caused much consternation among the peace professionals. Why was that? Dunant was a humanitarian, and the Red Cross was humanitarian, and the Geneva Convention was humanitarian. What did that have to do with peacework? What the humanitarians were doing, said the peace-movement critics, was "humanizing war," putting a bandage over it. They were making war more palatable and less horrible to the public. And would that not make war likelier? You were not supposed to improve the laws of war; you were supposed to abolish or prevent war. Suttner said that making war better was like lowering the temperature when you were boiling a man in oil. It was like agreeing to whip a slave less. In a flourish, she wrote, "Saint George rode forth to kill the dragon, not merely to trim its claws." But the Nobel Committee had its own ideas, and has been "expanding" the concept of peace ever since.

Neither Passy nor Dunant traveled to Oslo—to Kristiania, we should say—for the prize ceremony. It was not a grand affair, just a 15-minute meeting. Neither laureate would give a Nobel lecture, then or later.

∽

The winners in 1902 gave lectures, however (though a considerable time after their winning was announced). The peace prize in its second year was divided between two Swiss. And the chairman of the committee, Jørgen Løvland, noted that three of the first four prizewinners were Swiss. This was fitting, he said—"quite natural"—because Switzerland was a home for the ideals and principles that the prize sought to honor. He also said, "The Swiss were the people who founded the Red Cross, and it is two Swiss who now lead two important branches of the peace movement, the parliamentary branch and the popular branch."

He meant that Charles Albert Gobat was secretary-general of the Inter-Parliamentary Union and that Elie Ducommun filled the equivalent role for the Permanent International Peace Bureau (a central and coordinating office for myriad peace societies). Thus, they were responsible for the two institutions most prominent in the peace movement. They were exemplars of professional peace-making—and they were the co-laureates for 1902.

Both men were versatile, formidable, impressive. They were dynamos, as so many Nobelists are. Gobat gave his lecture quite late, in 1906. And he devoted it to a discussion of developments since the Hague peace convention of 1899. He said he wanted to talk about the "preservation of general peace" and "international arbitration." "To keep the peace!" he cried. "What a noble and magnificent idea!" He continued,

> How many hopes are stirred by the thought that this greatest
> of all ideals—the maintenance of peace—should be the objec-
> tive of an international convention bearing the signatures of
> most of the nations of the world! How sad to relate, then, that
> it is precisely this part of the Hague Convention of July 29,
> 1899, which to date has been applied least. For it has averted
> neither the Boer War nor the Russo–Japanese War, not to
> speak of colonial wars.

Ducommun gave his lecture earlier, in 1904—and what a lecture it was. Titled "The Futility of War Demonstrated by History," it was an elegantly rip-roaring refutation of the notion that war ever did any good: that it ever contributed an iota to civilization. The lecture was a survey and dissection of war from ancient times up to the lecturer's own day. It is a minor masterpiece of learning, sarcasm, invective, and argument. I will provide just a sampling.

Why is a certain Alexander known as "the Great"? "No doubt because of his large-scale massacres." The Crusades were an "absurd epic," benefiting and crediting no one. "It is certain that the peoples of Europe who had taken part in the Crusades were even more ignorant at the end of these distant expeditions than when they had first heard the cry of Peter the Hermit: 'God wills it! God wills it!'" France, in the early 19th century, dedicated herself to war and domination. Then she had to "begin the toilsome climb from the depth of the abyss into which militarism had hurled her." And "the other countries in Europe, mutilated and devastated" by those years of French war, "did not, in the midst of their ruins, seem to appreciate very much the lessons in civilization which were supposedly imparted to them along with the grapeshot."

All through his lecture, Ducommun slashed the "apologists for war" and the "militarists." And he found hope in the new way of international organizations, arbitration, and the signing of treaties—such activity was "a true sign of the times and, for once, the militaristic mind will be hard put to plunge mankind again into the follies of the past."

Ducommun was born in 1833 and died in 1906—spared the sight of the world war, and of the rest of the 20th century, for that matter. Gobat, born in 1843, died in 1914, about five months before it all began.

～

It was in 1903 that a winner first had the prize all to himself: That was William Randal Cremer, the Englishman who had co-founded the Inter-Parliamentary Union, with Passy. If you gave the award to Passy, you might as well give it to Cremer. And Cremer had been feeling passed over. The 1903 prize, undivided, was worth about £8,000: £457,000, or $734,000, in early-21st-century terms. Cremer gave almost all of this money to the International Arbitration League, which he had organized in 1870. (It was first called the Workmen's Peace Committee; the IAL was an outgrowth.)

He was born in 1828, to a poor and fractured family—the father abandoned them. When a teenager, Cremer was apprenticed to an uncle in the building trades. He became a carpenter, and eventually a labor leader. He served as secretary of the International Workingmen's Association, but resigned when Karl Marx and his crew took over. Cremer observed that these were "men who cared more for their isms than for the cause of real progress." This shows us something of the man: a liberal reformer—indeed, a Liberal reformer—and a loyal subject of the Crown. He was elected to Parliament in 1885. Ten years later, he was defeated, but he was returned in 1900, and remained in office until his death in 1908. The year before, he was knighted, becoming Sir Randal. He had long done without his first name, William.

Cremer got to Kristiania in January 1905, to give his Nobel lecture. He was a grand old man of 76. Chairman Løvland welcomed him by saying, "That you have come here, despite your age and despite the long journey in an inclement season of the year, is proof to us of the untiring energy you have for so many years devoted to the great cause which you have served with such enthusiasm and with such success." Cremer's lecture was on the subject he loved so well, "The Progress and Advantages of International Arbitration." And he spoke with the eloquence and dash typical of British parliamentarians as a class. The cause of arbitration, he said, had risen in the world. "Scoffers" had "pooh-poohed" the idea, but "those who ridiculed" were now "put to shame." "The advocates of peace," said Cremer, "are no longer regarded as idle dreamers." Oh, no. They were men of concrete action, who delivered results. Cremer ended his address stirringly:

> The world has passed through a long night of tribulation and suffering, millions of our fellow creatures have been sacrificed to the demon of war; their blood has saturated every plain and dyed every ocean. But courage, friends, courage! The darkness is ending, a new day is dawning, and the future is ours. Hurrah! Hurrah!

Cremer's lecture had included two terms that catch attention. As Gobat would do, he spoke of the Boer War and the Russo–

Japanese War. The first war, he said, saw "the untimely deaths of 15,378 children in the concentration camps." And the second— taking place even as Cremer spoke—had already seen an "unparalleled holocaust."

~

It was in 1904 that the Nobel Peace Prize first went to an institution. It was the Institut de droit international, or the Institute of International Law, in Ghent. This body had been established in 1873—and it had a motto of undoubted appeal to the Nobel Committee: *Justitia et pace*, "Justice and Peace." Speeches concerning the 1904 prize took place a long time after the fact: in 1912. Speaking for the institute was its president, who was Norwegian: Georg Francis Hagerup, a former justice minister and a former prime minister. Moreover, he was a member of the committee, having gone on in 1907. He ended his lecture by quoting Mirabeau, to wit, "Law will one day become the sovereign of the world."

Also giving a speech was Johannes Irgens, Norway's foreign minister. He noted that one of the institute's aims was "to make the laws of war more humane." If she heard it, that must have made Bertha von Suttner's blood boil.

~

It was she who won the 1905 Nobel prize—and high time. For four years, she had been passed over, in favor of six others. And one of those "others" was an institution, to add insult to injury. Many people were dismayed that Suttner had not been given the prize, and regarded the prize as her due: because of her friendship with the testator; because of her role in his creation of the prize; and because of her leading position in the general peace movement. Among those dismayed was the baroness herself. (Peace, one learns, is not a field for small egos.) She was sure that she was exactly the kind of person for whom Nobel had intended his peace prize. And she was doubtless correct.

Baroness Bertha Sophie Felicita von Suttner, originally Countess Kinsky von Chinic und Tettau, was born in 1843, a daughter of the Austrian court. More specifically, she was the daughter of a field marshal, who died before she saw the light of day. She was brought up to respect military life and culture—but she was to have a great mid-life change. The peace cause and arguments seized her attention, and, already the author of many novels, she wrote an anti-war one: *Die Waffen nieder!*, given in English as *Lay Down Your Arms!* The book appeared in 1889—the same year the first Universal Peace Congress took place—and it was a huge success. It gave the peace movement a significant boost. Tolstoy compared *Lay Down Your Arms!*, in its impact, to *Uncle Tom's Cabin.* (An exaggeration, but a point.) Suttner then threw herself into the movement tirelessly. She was the "commander-in-chief," as even so important a figure as Passy said. She was also called the "generalissimo."

As you know, she was the first woman to be awarded the peace prize—but not the first woman to be awarded a Nobel prize. That distinction lies with "Madame Curie," Marie Skłodowska Curie, who won a quarter of the physics prize in 1903: She and her husband Pierre shared half the prize; the other half went to Antoine Henri Becquerel. Marie Curie went on to win the chemistry prize by herself in 1911. There was a woman winner between Suttner's peace prize and Curie's chemistry prize: Selma Lagerlöf, a Swede who won for literature in 1909.

Paying tribute to Suttner, Chairman Løvland said that "history constantly demonstrates the great influence of women." He further said, "Many are the individual women who have set an example in sacrifice and work, who have followed the armies as angels of consolation and healing, tending the sick and suffering. How much more effective it is to do one's utmost to prevent misfortune!" Those words must have rung very agreeably in the baroness's ears. It may have been all right to be a Florence Nightingale or a Clara Barton, but how much better it was to be a Bertha von Suttner!

Her lecture—given in April 1906—was titled "The Evolution of the Peace Movement." That word "evolution" is meaningful. Like so many of her contemporaries, Suttner was fired by Darwin's theory and its application to the affairs of humanity. In her lecture, she said, "That the future will always be one degree better than what is past and discarded is the conviction of those who understand the laws of evolution and try to assist their action." Right now, she said, "there is taking place in the world a process of internationalization and unification."

The baroness had recently gone on a speaking tour of America, and she said, "I wish to dwell for a moment on the subject of America." She continued,

> This land of limitless opportunities is marked by its ability to carry out new and daring plans of enormous imagination and scope, while often using the simplest methods. In other words, it is a nation idealistic in its concepts and practical in its execution of them. We feel that the modern peace movement has every chance in America of attracting strong support and of finding a clear formula for the implementation of its aims.

President Theodore Roosevelt had embraced the cause of arbitration, she said, and had just told Congress, "It remains our clear duty to strive in every practicable way to bring nearer the time when the sword shall not be the arbiter among nations." He and Suttner met during the latter's tour. As she told the audience in Kristiania, the two met at the White House on October 17, 1904—and he said to her, "World peace is coming, it certainly is coming, but only step by step" (i.e., in an evolutionary way). But

Suttner knew the difficulty of confronting and overthrowing "the old order," as she said in her lecture. By this she meant the order of aggression and war. "Thus pacifism faces no easy struggle."

She died on June 21, 1914, exactly a week before Princip took his gun, assassinated the archduke (and his wife), and triggered the world war.

～

In 1906, Roosevelt won: won the Nobel Peace Prize. And this caused an uproar. Indeed, the committee's 1906 decision remains one of the most controversial in the entire history of the prize—practically up there with the award to Kissinger. (No one was much exercised about Le Duc Tho's half of that prize.) There are still people, devotees of the peace prize, who are grousing about the 1906 award. TR, a man of peace, and not a man of war? This Roosevelt of the Spanish–American War, this Rough Rider, this imperialist and colonizer, this shouter of "Bully!"? In the same company as Passy and Cremer? His image was one of bellicosity, or at least exceptional robustness—not one of peace.

Some criticism of the award came from America itself. A Philadelphia newspaper said that the national press at large was perplexed: perplexed that "the preacher of the strenuous life, the disseminater of the doctrine that there are dangers to the moral fiber of a nation from the cankers of a long peace, the militant champion of a large army and navy and the wielder of the 'big stick' should be crowned as America's great pacificator." The *New York Times* thought "a broad smile illuminated the face of the globe when the prize was awarded . . . to the most warlike citizen of these United States."

Critics thought darkly about the motivation of the Nobel Committee, and think this way even now. The dark thinking goes like this: Norway had just gained its independence, splitting from Sweden. The Norwegians were eager to fortify their new status.

The committee chairman, Løvland, was now foreign minister. And wouldn't he, and Norway, like to have a friend and ally in the president of this fast-emerging country—this America that was beginning to stride, and sail, around the world?

Whatever the committee's underlying motivation, there was a stated motivation—and that motivation can be credited. Roosevelt had championed arbitration (just as Suttner said). He was a crucial supporter of the new international court at The Hague. In fact, he was the first to submit a matter for arbitration there: a lingering dispute between the United States and Mexico. That gave the court something to do; and it set an example for others to follow. But more important than arbitration, for the Nobel Committee, was Roosevelt's mediation in the Russo–Japanese War. The war had lasted from February 1904 to September 1905. And something like 200,000 people had died in the "unparalleled holocaust," to use Cremer's (hyperbolic) words. Roosevelt offered his good offices to settle the war, and this resulted in the Portsmouth Treaty of September 5, 1905. The "Portsmouth" in question was Portsmouth, New Hampshire, where Roosevelt had taken the parties: It offered a pleasanter late summer than Washington, D.C. (in this age before air conditioning).

We see that, for the first time, a particular and troublesome term of Nobel's will was fulfilled: The 1906 laureate won for work performed "during the preceding year," at least as one might conceive of "preceding." It was what I call a "neat win": Clear peacework was done in a particular year, and the next year came the Nobel prize. Also, this was the first award given to a statesman. People questioned whether the testator would approve. Was his peace prize for people in grand positions, or for people challenging those in grand positions? For more than 100 years, it has been for both.

A presentation ceremony duly took place on December 10, 1906, but Roosevelt was not present. The American ambassador in Norway, Herbert H. D. Peirce, accepted the award in his stead. By sheer coincidence—one presumes—this same Peirce had been a key diplomat in the Portsmouth negotiations. In Kristiania, he read a telegram from Roosevelt—who appeared in the capital himself three and a half years later, in May 1910, after his presidency, and at the end of an international speaking tour.

The ex-president delivered his lecture in the National Theater to an audience of 2,000. It is one of his most striking statements, a tough-minded and thoughtful discussion of war and peace. He said,

> Peace is generally good in itself, but it is never the highest good unless it comes as the handmaid of righteousness; and it becomes a very evil thing if it serves merely as a mask for cowardice and sloth, or as an instrument to further the ends of despotism or anarchy. We despise and abhor the bully, the brawler, the oppressor, whether in private or public life, but we despise no less the coward and the voluptuary. No man is worth calling a man who will not fight rather than submit to infamy or see those that are dear to him suffer wrong. No nation deserves to exist if it permits itself to lose the stern and virile virtues; and this without regard to whether the loss is due to the growth of a heartless and all-absorbing commercialism, to prolonged indulgence in luxury and soft, effortless ease, or to the deification of a warped and twisted sentimentality.

Very, very seldom has a Nobel peace lecture sounded this way—indeed, pretty much never. Here is another swatch that is very unusual—for a Nobel lecture, but not for TR:

> Moreover, and above all, let us remember that words count only when they give expression to deeds, or are to be translated

into them. The leaders of the Red Terror prattled of peace while they steeped their hands in the blood of the innocent; and many a tyrant has called it peace when he has scourged honest protest into silence. Our words must be judged by our deeds; and in striving for a lofty ideal we must use practical methods; and if we cannot attain all at one leap, we must advance towards it step by step, reasonably content so long as we do actually make some progress in the right direction.

Roosevelt proceeded to suggest some of those steps, ending with something especially juicy:

[I]t would be a masterstroke if those great powers honestly bent on peace would form a League of Peace, not only to keep the peace among themselves, but to prevent, by force if necessary, its being broken by others. The supreme difficulty in connection with developing the peace work of The Hague arises from the lack of any executive power, of any police power to enforce the decrees of the court.

This sort of talk is still heard, from many quarters, where international institutions and their powers, or lack of powers, are concerned.

Obviously, Roosevelt had a very strong sense of what kept the peace, and what invited aggression. He wrote in his autobiography, "In my own judgment the most important service that I rendered to peace was the voyage of the battle fleet around the world." This statement has stuck in the craws of many peace-prize devotees; it has had the clear ring of truth and sense to others. Christian Lange took a swipe at Roosevelt. He did it in 1936, when he, as a committee member, was presenting the peace prize to Carlos Saavedra Lamas. He said that the 1906 laureate was "the most pronounced representative" of "North American imperialism."

Before moving on to the 1907 award, let's have a word about money: Roosevelt felt he could not accept his prize money, personally. He telegrammed,

> There is no gift I could appreciate more and I wish it were in my power fully to express my gratitude. I thank you for it, and I thank you on behalf of the United States; for what I did, I was able to accomplish only as the representative of the nation of which, for the time being, I am president. After much thought, I have concluded that the best and most fitting way to apply the amount of the prize is by using it as a foundation to establish at Washington a permanent industrial peace committee.

This committee, or institution, never came about. The prize money was held in trust—gaining interest—until 1917, when Roosevelt used it to give to charities that were helping the wounded in the world war.

Years before, he explained to his son Kermit that he could not accept for himself what had come his way because of his position as president. "But I hated to come to the decision, because I very much wisht for the extra money to leave to all you children." We can presume they got something, however—for in his Nobel lecture, Roosevelt said, "The gold medal which formed part of the prize I shall always keep, and I shall hand it on to my children as a precious heirloom." In 1982, that precious heirloom went to the Roosevelt Room in the West Wing of the White House. There it sits, the first Nobel medal, in any of the five categories, won by an American.

~

The 1907 award was shared by two men: Ernesto Teodoro Moneta, the leader of the pacifist cause in Italy, and Louis Renault, a professor of international law in France, and a prime participant in the Hague peace conferences. Thus did the committee return to awarding figures of the organized peace movement in Europe. The 1907 award caused no hue and cry, unlike the previous one.

Moneta was a pacifist with a difference. He was what you might call a vigorous pacifist, a pacifist with some of the TR spirit and swagger. A Milanese, he was born in 1833, the same year as Alfred Nobel and Elie Ducommun. He fought in the Italian wars of independence—those same wars one of whose battles changed the life of Henry Dunant. Moneta was an eager partisan, a fighter alongside Garibaldi. But the reality of war sickened him, as it tends to do men. In his Nobel lecture, Moneta recounted an event from 1848, during the "Five Days" uprising of Milanese against Austrian rule:

> One day when my father and brothers were absent, I watched, from the windows of my home, three Austrian soldiers fall amid a hail of bullets. Apparently dead, they were carried away to a neighboring square. I saw them again two hours later: One of them was still in the throes of dying. This sight froze the blood in my veins and I was overcome by a great compassion. In these three soldiers I no longer saw enemies but men like myself, and with remorse as keenly suffered as if I had killed them with my own hands, I thought of their families who were perhaps at that very moment preparing for their return.
>
> In that instant I felt all the cruelty and inhumanity of war which sets peoples against one another to their mutual detriment, peoples who should have every interest in understanding and being friends with each other. I was to feel this way many times as I looked at the dead and the wounded in all the wars for our independence in which I took part.

Moneta became an army officer. But then he turned to journalism, in which he distinguished himself throughout Italy. And peace became his cause. But, to say it once more, he was a pacifist with a difference. For one thing, he had a strongly national bent, an intense patriotism. He was a liberal internationalist, like the other pacifists: but also a super-Italian. He, for one, saw no contradiction.

He gave his Nobel lecture in August 1909 (in French, by the way). He said that all his fellow Italians rejoiced in the honor conferred on him, including King Victor Emmanuel, who had telegrammed him to reaffirm his "ardent desire that the great cause of peace should triumph." (The words are apparently the king's, reported by the laureate.) Moneta's peculiar and pointed kind of pacifism can be glimpsed in the following passages:

> Today, unfortunately, what many facts indicate only too well is that universal peace, as we conceive of it, still lies far in the distant future, and in view of the growing greed for the lands of others, the weaker countries can no longer trust the stronger ones.
>
> "Keep your powder dry and always be ready to defend yourself"; this is for Italy, as well as for others, a hard necessity at the present time.

Four years after Moneta's Nobel victory, his country, using its powder, went to war against the Ottoman Empire. This was the conflict over Tripoli and Libya. (It was also the first conflict, anywhere, in which air power was used.) Moneta supported the Italian effort, to the consternation of some of his fellow peaceworkers. He also supported his country's actions when the world war came. He died in the last year of that war, 1918. In Milan, there is a monument to him, the base of which gives a good summation of the man: It calls him a "Garibaldino," which is to say, a partisan with Garibaldi; a "thinker" and "journalist"; and an "apostle of peace." But this last term has a qualification, or at least an addition: "fra libere genti," i.e., "between free peoples."

Louis Renault, Moneta's co-laureate, lived one decade less than he, dying in the same year: His dates are 1843 to 1918. Løvland called him "the guiding genius in the teaching of international law in France." Renault gave his Nobel lecture in May 1908, saying how pleased he was to thank and address the Norwegians in person. Then he said, "I should like also to keep a promise made to my distinguished colleague Mr. Frédéric Passy when I saw him on the eve of my departure, by conveying to you his regrets that age has prohibited him from discharging the same duty." Renault went on to say, "It is not only on my own behalf that I thank you; I thank you also on behalf of all the jurists who have devoted their efforts to the study of international law . . . ." It will come as no surprise that Renault was a member of the Institute of International Law, the 1904 laureate. And "from this pacifist army of internationalists," he said, "you have now singled out one soldier . . . ."

This Louis Renault, incidentally, is not to be confused with the Louis Renault who, with his brothers, founded the automobile company. The latter Louis Renault lived from 1877 to 1944, and still has his name stamped on cars; our Louis Renault is forgotten, except in the context of this most glorious—and most contentious—of prizes.

Two P-Words

Before continuing to 1908—and more pacifists—it might be desirable to comment on the very word "pacifist." In the course of events, it acquired an odor. Relatively few people today would like to be called a pacifist. The charge or imputation of pacifism is likely to bring an offended denial. But it was not always so (as we have clearly seen). In earlier decades—certainly before World War II—if you had said to someone, "Hey, you're a pacifist," he might well have replied, "Of course I am. What are you, a militarist?"

The word "propaganda" acquired an odor too—an odor that says, "The claims being presented are false." But the word used to be perfectly neutral. In 1919, the *Times* (of London) published a history of the war that included a section on "British Propaganda in Enemy Countries." No one thought that was dishonest or dishonorable. In the early years, members of the peace movement would speak freely and unblushingly of "peace propaganda" or "pacifist propaganda." Here is Ludwig Quidde, a 1927 co-laureate, in his Nobel lecture: "It was of immense significance to our propaganda that governments themselves now accepted our postulates"; and, "Pacifist propaganda and the resolutions of the parliamentarians encouraged such treaties . . . ."

The pacifists were not a monolithic bunch, as I have indicated. There were varying types. You had the pure, or absolute, pacifists—opposed to war and war-making no matter what. And you had pacifists who supported wars of defense or wars of liberation. There were pacifists who supported an "armed peace," which is to say, a peace during which nations are armed, even to the teeth. Indeed, some pacifists maintained that the arms kept the peace. (This is deterrence, in short.) Other people said that an armed peace was no kind of peace at all, but rather a war waiting to happen. Peace could not truly be safe unless nations were disarmed, or armed extremely lightly.

Some pacifists were what you might call pure internationalists, scorning any national thought as primitive and dangerous. Other pacifists were like Moneta: perfectly nationalist, or nation-minded, and patriotic, as well as internationalist and global-minded. Some pacifists, like Moneta, backed their countries in World War I. Others said that such people could not be real pacifists, and they declared a pox on all warring houses.

∼

The year 1908 was an all-Scandinavian affair, as the committee divided the prize between Klas Pontus Arnoldson, a Swede, and

Fredrik Bajer, a Dane. Each man was a prince of the peace move-
ment. Each man was also a parliamentarian and liberal idealist.
Bajer (1837–1922) had been a soldier as a young man. He was a
lieutenant in the Dragoons. He fought in the 1864 war between
Denmark, on the one side, and Prussia and Austria on the other.
Then he joined up with an army of pacifists, fighting against war.

Arnoldson (1844–1916) was a quasi-religious figure, a conscientious Christian. And his Nobel lecture was a beautiful thing,
almost a sermon. It ranged on peace and freedom, individualism
and nationalism, and other central questions. In Arnoldson's
view, "every normal human being must be as susceptible to the
light of knowledge as he is to the light of the sun. It is in his
nature to want peace rather than war. Education is the only certain
road to the final goal of peace. And there is no higher goal." He
further said, "Warlike adventures do not suit the peaceful nature
of the Chinese. The 'Yellow Peril' is probably not all that perilous!
The Sultanate of Turkey is developing into a great civilized state, a
powerful center of peace for all of the Moslem world."

Arnoldson said that even "those in power" were coming to
realize that war was folly and peace the only way. He mentioned
the czar of Russia; "the aged ruler of Austria-Hungary" ("often
called the 'Emperor of Peace'"); "the British head of state"; and so
on. Here is what he had to say about the German leader, just six
years before the war: "Kaiser Wilhelm, in a telegram to the Inter-
parliamentary Conference in Berlin, said that he took the blessings of peace very much to heart, and the Crown Prince echoed
these words, stating on behalf of his father that the latter's greatest concern was the maintenance of peace, 'which is, and shall
ever be, the foundation of all true cultural progress.'"

In due course, Arnoldson proposed a pledge, or declaration,
something for every person of good will to endorse. It went as
follows:

> I, the undersigned, desire peace on earth. I want all armed
> forces to be abolished. I want a joint police force to be created,
> to which each nation should contribute according to the size
> of its population. I want that force to be subject to an Interna-
> tional Supreme Court. I want all states to be in duty bound to
> refer any kind of international controversy to this court, and
> subject themselves to the judgments of the court.

That is an expression of purest, most true-believing internationalist idealism.

∾

For the third year in a row, the Nobel Committee divided its prize,
again crowning two princes of the peace movement. They were
not Scandinavian. The 1909 laureates were Auguste Beernaert,
a Belgian, and a French baron named d'Estournelles. Beernaert
(1829–1912) was a lawyer and politician—indeed, for ten years
the Belgian prime minister (1884–1894). He was a man of strong
conscience, opposing the slave trade and his country's misdeeds
in the Congo. As for the baron (1852–1924), he boasted a name to
rival or surpass Bertha von Suttner's: Paul Henri Benjamin Bal-
luet d'Estournelles, baron de Constant de Rebecque. His life can
be judged as full and glorious as his name. Scion of a very old aristocratic family, he became a diplomat, a scholar, a writer, a sports-
man-adventurer, a politician—sitting in the French senate as a
Radical-Socialist. (Such is the way of aristocrats, often.) He was
one of those who envisioned, and advocated, a European union.
And he was one of those pacifists who supported their national
colors in the world war. Also, he helped wounded soldiers, con-
verting his château on the Loire into a hospital.

Both of these men—both the '09 laureates—have a connection to the '06 laureate, Roosevelt. Like Suttner, d'Estournelles
went on a speaking tour of the U.S. This was in 1902. His wife

was an American, Daisy Sedgwick-Berend. He met the president, and, as the story is told, he said to him, "You are a danger or hope for the world. It is believed you are inclined to the side of violence. Prove the contrary." "How?" asked Roosevelt. By giving the court at The Hague something to do, replied d'Estournelles. It had been sitting there for three years with nothing to work on, nothing to arbitrate. Roosevelt obliged by providing the dispute with Mexico (which had to do with funds and California). Representing Mexico, in The Hague's first case, was the lawyer Beernaert.

∼

In 1910, it was institution time again: with the prize going to the Permanent International Peace Bureau. This was the organization—that coordinating office for peace societies—that Ducommun, a 1902 laureate, headed. When Ducommun died in 1906, the other '02 laureate, Albert Gobat, took responsibility for the PIPB, while keeping his position at the Inter-Parliamentary Union. By 1910, the PIPB was in serious need of funds, and pacifists had been agitating for it to win the Nobel prize: to win it as an institution. Chairman Løvland, giving his presentation speech for 1910, explicitly acknowledged the bureau's need of money—and said that the testator had intended to meet just such a need.

∼

Another year, two more princes of the peace movement. The laureates for 1911 were Tobias Asser (1838–1913) and Alfred Hermann Fried (1864–1921). Asser, a Dutchman, was like Louis Renault, a big figure in international law. He was a mover behind that winner of the '04 prize, the Institute of International Law. And he was a judge in that first case at The Hague: the one that TR provided. (The judgment ultimately went to the United States.) Fried was born in Vienna, but had much of his career in Germany. He was a journalist, publisher, and organizer: a full-time, full-out peace campaigner. Presenting the prize, Løvland said of Fried, "He has probably been the most industrious literary pacifist in the past 20 years." In 1891, Fried pitched an idea to Suttner: a peace journal, which she would edit and he would publish. She agreed. And the journal assumed the same name as her famous anti-war novel, *Die Waffen nieder!* Later, Fried himself took over the editing, and the journal became *Die Friedenswarte,* or *The Peace Watch.*

Here is a detail from Fried's life (which came to a bad end after the war, when the laureate was reduced to poverty and bitterness): He was prominent in the movement for Esperanto. This, as you know, is the proposed international second language, or "auxiliary" language. Advocacy of Esperanto has always been for strong, somewhat quixotic internationalists.

~

The committee did not give an award in 1912—we see it now in a "reserving" mood. They held, or reserved, the award until 1913, when they declared the winner for '12 to be Elihu Root. He was another American, the second American to win this prize, and, in fact, he had been Roosevelt's secretary of state.

Born in Clinton, New York, in 1845, he became one of the country's leading lawyers, eventually serving as president of the American Bar Association. In 1899, President McKinley asked him to take the post of secretary of war. Agreeing, Root said that he was honored to represent "the greatest of all our clients, the government of our country." In 1905, when secretary of state John Hay died, Roosevelt asked Root to replace him. He would also serve in the Senate—going there in 1909, and staying one (six-year) term. He was, of course, sitting there when the Nobel Committee gave him its crown.

Why did the committee give it to him, several years after his governmental service, or, better put, his executive-branch service? Furthermore, it is of some interest that a former secretary of war won the peace prize. Speaking for the committee was its secretary, Ragnvald Moe. And he said that, while in the McKinley and Roosevelt administrations, Root "had to settle a number of particularly difficult problems." For instance, "it was he who was chiefly responsible for organizing affairs in Cuba and in the Philippines after the Spanish–American War." And "even more important was his work in bringing about better understanding between the countries of North and South America." Root was a proponent and shaper of what, under a future President Roosevelt, would be known as a "good-neighbor policy."

Also, said Moe, Root had given himself "heart and soul to the cause of peace." He was a firm advocate of arbitration and of international courts. And he was president—the first president— of the Carnegie Endowment for International Peace, established in 1910. Andrew Carnegie announced this institute on his 75th birthday, November 25, 1910. He plunked down $10 million for it. What he said was that he wanted his trustees to "hasten the abolition of international war, the foulest blot upon our civilization."

Root was already a senior statesman when he won the peace prize, almost 70. But he had many active years thereafter, going to Russia as President Wilson's envoy in 1917, and helping to found the Council on Foreign Relations: He was its first chairman. Root died in 1937, a week before his 92nd birthday.

He was a Republican, a conservative, a scholar, a problem-solver. He was a realist with a healthy dose of idealism. And his manifold qualities come out in his Nobel lecture. He was scheduled to give it in September 1914, but the outbreak of war in August changed his plans, along with everybody else's. His lecture was later published among his addresses.

Here is an observation typical of the man: "There is no international controversy so serious that it cannot be settled if both parties really wish to settle it. There are few controversies so trifling that they cannot be made the occasion for war if the parties really wish to fight." That is in the final pages of his lecture. Root's practicality can be seen in its very opening sentence: "The humanitarian purpose of Alfred Nobel in establishing the peace prize which bears his name was doubtless not merely to reward those who should promote peace among nations, but to stimulate thought upon the means and methods best adapted, under the changing conditions of future years, to approach and ultimately attain the end he so much desired."

Again in the final pages, he quoted what he called "a homely English saying": "Leg over leg, the dog went to Dover." This proverb, he said, "states the method of our true progress. We cannot arrive at our goal *per saltum*," that is, by leaps. A study of Root's life and thought shows that he is one of the most sensible and useful men ever to win Nobel's peace prize.

～

When Elihu Root was announced as a laureate, so was Henri La Fontaine. He was the laureate for 1913. As such, he is the last laureate before the war. And, perhaps fittingly, he was a pure representative of the European peace movement: what would become known as the "old, pre-war" peace movement. La Fontaine was a Belgian, and, in the style of Nobel laureates, a dynamo. He was a professor of international law (another one of those). A member of the Belgian senate (a Socialist). A theorist and planner of world government. An advocate of women's rights. An Alpinist (and writer about Alpinism). A translator of Wagner's librettos—etc. When the war broke out, La Fontaine fled to England, then to the United States. At war's end, he was an adviser to the Belgian delegation to the Paris Peace Conference, and later he was a delegate to the First Assembly of the League of Nations. He lived from 1854 to 1943. You might think of it this way: He was born during the Crimean War and died while a second world war was raging.

A Mockery

What did Sir Edward Grey, the British foreign secretary, say? "The lights are going out all over Europe." The war lasted from August 1914 to November 1918. It laughed in the face of the peace campaigners: so many of their words, so many of their efforts. Ten million were killed, with millions more wounded and wrecked. The great concern after the war was to prevent another one— another world war. Which came so quickly, didn't it? Just about a generation later. Slightly more than 20 years after Armistice Day.

 INTERLUDES

NOBEL SEASON

We have had a taste of the Nobel calendar already—for instance, you know that the deadline for nominations is February 1. Down the decades, the calendar and procedures have varied somewhat. We have seen that sometimes there were no lectures in the early years, or that lectures were given well after prizes were announced, or formally conferred. It was not so easy to get to Norway during the winter in those days. From the end of World War II to 1990, the laureate gave two speeches, as a rule. The first was on Presentation Day, December 10. That was the "acceptance speech": a short address, often poetic, often personal, and usually expressing heartfelt thanks. The next day, the laureate gave his Nobel lecture: a longer and more formal address. Since 1990, however, the laureate has given one speech, only: the lecture, which takes place during the December 10 ceremony. (When there were two speeches—the acceptance speech and the lecture—sometimes very few—embarrassingly few—showed up for the lecture.)

Here is how the Nobel season unfolds. On the second Friday in October, the Nobel Committee announces the winner or winners. At least, the second Friday is the usual day—it is not set in stone. At 11 A.M., the committee chairman emerges from a seminar room into Nobel Hall, on the third floor of the Nobel Institute. This is a beautiful little hall—stunning—with four chandeliers and, on the ceiling, a bevy of plaster doves. (Peace, you know.) Once upon a time, Nobel ceremonies themselves took place there. In any case, the chairman reads the announcement in front of assembled press, then takes questions.

When the laureate comes in December, he traditionally stays at the Grand Hotel, a venerable institution, a haunt of Ibsen's. The hotel is on Oslo's main thoroughfare, Karl Johans gate, or Karl Johan Street. Naturally, the laureate stays in the Nobel Suite. On December 9, he usually holds a press conference at the Nobel Institute. Afterward, there is a rehearsal at City Hall for the prize ceremony. The ceremony itself will take place there—has done so since 1990. City Hall is brown and stark, far from the most beautiful building in Oslo. But it is not quite an eyesore. And the large space inside that hosts the ceremony is suitably majestic. On the evening of the 9th, there is what's known as the "little dinner," at the Grand. Attending are the laureate (plus spouse), the committee members, and the committee secretary.

When the 10th comes, the laureate usually has an audience with the king at the palace. That's in the morning. The prize ceremony begins at 1. A thousand guests are in their places. On the steps outside, a red carpet sits. Inside, trumpeters sound a fanfare, and the laureate comes in, accompanied by four members of the committee. Shortly after, the trumpeters sound a different fanfare. And the royal family comes in, accompanied by the committee chairman and secretary. The laureate is seated on a stage, along with the five committee members and the secretary.

The chairman gives the presentation speech, in which he hails the laureate and explains why the prize has been given to him (or to them or to it, in the case of an institution). The speech is in Norwegian, although in 2009 the chairman made an exception, giving it in English: That was Obama's year. After the presentation speech, the chairman presents the laureate with two items: the Nobel medal and the Nobel diploma. (More about these souvenirs in a moment.) Then the laureate gives the lecture.

Throughout the ceremony, there is music, of varying sorts. You can expect Norwegian musicians to perform. But the laureate is allowed to pick one musician to take part in the ceremony. Obama chose a jazz musician named Esperanza Spalding, from Portland, Oregon. In 2002, Jimmy Carter had chosen a great soprano from his home state, Georgia: Jessye Norman. Often there is a national flavor in the ceremony's music: In 2008, when the Finnish diplomat Ahtisaari was the laureate, Sibelius was played.

At night, starting about 6, there is a torchlight parade, in honor of the laureate. It winds up in front of the Grand about 7. The laureate and his party observe from the balcony of the Nobel Suite. Then there is another meal at the hotel: not a "little dinner" but a very big one, the Nobel banquet, a five-course affair. The laureate's table is in the middle of the room. He is seated with a roster of luminaries, consisting of the committee members and their secretary (with whom he has already spent a lot of time), the president of the Storting, the prime minister, and, not least, the king and queen. Traditionally, speeches during the evening are three. First, the deputy chairman of the committee says a few words about the laureate, and these words should have a "humorous slant," as a piece of Nobel literature puts it. Then the laureate speaks. And, after dinner, the room hears from the president of the Storting.

If ever you are invited to these affairs, you may wish to know how to dress. For the prize ceremony, men should have a dark suit and tie, and ladies a dress. For the banquet, men wear black tie, and ladies the complementary evening gowns. The Nobel people inform us that "wearing your national costume is a perfectly acceptable alternative to black tie/evening gown."

Does anything happen the next day, December 11? Yes. The laureate meets with Norwegian politicians, beginning with the prime minister (one of his dinner partners from the evening before). And, that night, there is a concert, the Nobel concert, which takes place at the Oslo Spektrum and is televised to various countries. The concert has a pair of "hosts," usually a well-known actor and actress: for example Meryl Streep and Liam Neeson, or Jessica Lange and Anthony Hopkins, or Kevin Spacey and Uma Thurman. The concert is essentially a pop concert, with such performers as Bon Jovi, Cindy Lauper, Annie Lennox, and Earth, Wind & Fire, although there are some classical performers included, such as the Welsh bass-baritone Bryn Terfel.

Now, about those souvenirs, the medal and the diploma—they are decidedly handsome objects. The peace-prize medal was designed by Gustav Vigeland, a Norwegian sculptor who lived from 1869 to 1943. (The Vigeland Sculpture Park is one of the most impressive and popular sights in Oslo.) It was the only medal he ever designed. He had the assistance of Erik Lindberg, a Swedish sculptor and engraver (1873–1966). They had their medal ready for the second ceremony, in 1902. And Lindberg, and Lindberg alone, created the medals for the other Nobel prizes: the Swedish Nobels. The peace-prize medal used to be 23-carat gold, weighing 192 grams; after 1980, it was 18-carat gold, weighing 196 grams. The diameter has always been 6.6 centimeters.

On the front of the medal is a portrait in relief of Alfred Nobel. His name and dates are engraved along the perimeter. On the reverse are three men, embracing. They are naked, in classical style. And the inscription reads, *Pro pace et fraternitate gentium,* or "For peace and fraternity among peoples." The edge of the medal is 5 millimeters thick, and on it are engraved the words "Prix Nobel de la Paix," the particular year, and the name of the laureate.

The diploma? More than the medal, it has undergone some changes in the century-plus history of the prize. From 1901 to 1969, the diploma was that conceived and executed by Gerhard Munthe, a Norwegian painter (1849–1929). For the next 20 years, the diploma had a woodcut by another Norwegian artist, Ørnulf Ranheimsæter (1919–2007). From 1991, the diploma has been different in appearance each year, bearing an artwork commissioned for the occasion. The artists are all Norwegian. And, whereas the diploma once had machine-printed letters, it now has multicolor printing and calligraphy. The diploma reads, "The Norwegian Nobel Committee, in accordance with Alfred Nobel's will of 27 November 1895, has decided to award [name of laureate] the Nobel Peace Prize for [year]."

Finally, a word about moolah: The laureate does not receive the money—at this writing, about $1.5 million—at the ceremony. A check is not presented along with the medal and diploma. In fact, it never was. The laureate always received that before or after the ceremony. These days, the money is likely to be wired into a laureate's account.

'PEACE' (AN ESSAY)

"What is this thing called love?" goes the old Cole Porter song. In the same spirit, we might ask, "What is this thing called peace?" Everyone wants it, everyone talks about it, everyone lauds it. But what is it, exactly? The Nobel Committee must determine what peace is, and who has furthered it—furthered it enough to merit the grand prize.

There is probably no subject about which it is easier to be glib than that of peace. In 2010, *The National Interest*, an American magazine, had a cover bearing a photo of Neville Chamberlain and the word "Appeaser!" The cover then described this as "the Most Abused Word in History." I would say that "peace" is by far the more abused. ("Love," of course, is the most abused word in world history.) In 1988, the U.N. Peacekeeping Forces won the peace prize, and the secretary-general, Javier Pérez de Cuéllar, gave the Nobel lecture on their behalf. He said something wise:

> Peace is an easy word to say in any language. As secretary-general of the United Nations, I hear it so frequently from so many different mouths and different sources that it sometimes seems to me to be a general incantation more or less deprived of practical meaning.

We can confidently say what peace is not: It is not the mere absence of war, as President Kennedy noted, and as countless others have noted. And yet, peace is not war either. "I hate war," said FDR, in that incomparable voice of his. Well, who doesn't? Who doesn't hate war, except for psychopaths, some of whom rise to power? And the man who said "I hate war" waged it, in Europe, in the Pacific, and wherever else he found it necessary.

When people debate whether their country should go to war, they are divided into "pro-war" and "anti-war" camps (and we speak here of democratic countries, because, in non-democratic countries, there is no real debate). Those labels are more than a little unfair; they are at the least bothersome. Are those who conclude that war is necessary, or just, or the lesser of two evils, really pro-war, and not anti-war?

Here is a story from early Nobel days. Fredrik Bajer and Wollert Konow were talking. Bajer was the Dane who was a laureate in 1908, as you know; Konow was an important Norwegian politician (prime minister from 1910 to 1912, and later a member of the Nobel Committee). Bajer asked why it had taken so long, as he saw it, for Norwegian peace societies to get going. Konow answered that everyone was in favor of peace—so why form societies over it?

There are those who think that nothing is worse than war, that war is the worst thing in all the world. In a letter to Bertha von Suttner, Alfred Nobel said, "Let us grant that anything is better than war." It can be doubted, from other things he said and wrote, that Nobel strictly meant that. But maybe he did. Erasmus said, "The most disadvantageous peace is better than the most just war." Benjamin Franklin added, "There was never a good war or a bad peace." In 1938, Clive Bell, the British art critic and Bloomsbury member, wrote, "A Nazi Europe would be, to my mind, heaven on earth compared with Europe at war." Have just one more quotation, less dramatic, from 1984. It comes from Mario Cuomo, in his famous keynote address to the Democratic national convention. Cuomo was then governor of New York, and one of the leading politicians in America—thought of as a thinker-politician. He said, ". . . we proclaim as loudly as we can the utter insanity of nuclear proliferation and the need for a nuclear freeze, if only to affirm the simple truth that peace is better than war because life is better than death."

Yes, peace is better than war—but it can get tricky. Which is worse: genocide in Sudan (or elsewhere) or some war whose purpose is to put an end to it? But then you might say, a condition of genocide is not a condition of peace in the first place.

You are familiar with the slogan, or bumper sticker, "War is not the answer." But it is the answer to some questions, of course—as when it put paid to Nazi Germany and Imperial Japan. Emerson insisted, "Peace cannot be achieved through violence, it can only be attained through understanding." This is a fine sentiment, but it has the disadvantage of being untrue—or not strictly true. Again, World War II is instructive. And you might say that understanding can lead a person, or a nation, to see that violence is the only way to put down a threat, and thereby keep or attain peace.

In Salzburg one summer, I encountered a graffito. It said (in English), "Fighting for peace is like f***ing for virginity." (There were no asterisks.) I later learned that this is a well-known line, in some circles—but I first encountered it scrawled under a bridge. And the concept of fighting for peace can be difficult; it can even seem perverse. But it gets less difficult, and less perverse, when you think of the neighborhood bully, and the necessity of dealing with him, so that the neighborhood can be at peace.

Allow me a walk a long way down Memory Lane. I was a child during the Vietnam War, growing up in Michigan. And there was a poster in my parents' kitchen. It was an immensely popular poster at the time, the product of a group called Another Mother for Peace. The poster said, "War is not healthy for children and other living things." That is unquestionably true as a generality. But later I got to thinking: What about Anne Frank and the other children in the camps? What was "not healthy" to them—war or tyranny? War or the fact that liberating armies were not reaching so many of them in time? And this, of course, relates to my comment on Sudan, above.

Years after those Vietnam days, when I was in graduate school, I heard General Vernon Walters speak. He was the longtime soldier, diplomat, and CIA man who ended his career as ambassador to Germany—the first American ambassador to a reunited Germany. This particular night, he said something arresting about war and peace. He said (and I paraphrase), "For over ten years, bombs rained down on every village and hamlet in South Vietnam, and no one budged. It took the coming of a Communist 'peace' to send hundreds of thousands of people out into the South China Sea, on anything that could float, or might float, to risk dehydration, piracy, drowning . . . "

The churchman Beilby Porteus said, "War its thousands slays, peace its ten thousands." Then there is the classic, "They made a desert and called it peace." And, of course, it always pays to beware the talker about peace—the mere talker about peace.

Bob Dylan has a song called "Man of Peace"—a rather tart and cynical, but not unreasonable, song. "He got a sweet gift of gab, he got a harmonious tongue, / He knows every song of love that ever has been sung. . . . He's a great humanitarian, he's a great philanthropist . . . . You know that sometimes Satan comes as a man of peace." That is the song's refrain: "You know that sometimes Satan comes as a man of peace." And if Dylan's not your bag, you might consider a line from Psalms—the 28th Psalm—which talks of "the workers of iniquity, which speak peace to their neighbours, but mischief is in their hearts."

Move now to America in 1917. President Wilson is standing before Congress, giving his historic war address—asking the country to cross the ocean and enter the world war. He says,

It is a fearful thing to lead this great peaceful people into war, into the most terrible and disastrous of all wars, civilization itself seeming to be in the balance. But the right is more precious than peace, and we shall fight for the things which we

93

have always carried nearest our hearts—for democracy, for the
right of those who submit to authority to have a voice in their
own governments, for the rights and liberties of small nations,
for a universal dominion of right by such a concert of free
peoples as shall bring peace and safety to all nations and make
the world itself at last free.

The right is more precious than peace. This is one of the most
famous and important things ever said about peace. But is it true?
It is sometimes true, is the inevitable answer. How do you define
"right"? How do you define "peace"? It can all be very slippery,
very tricky—very hard.

No one enjoys a greater reputation than peacemakers—
"Blessed are the peacemakers." There are "peace concerts" everywhere, and no "war concerts" (although there have been events in
support of general "war drives"). Has there ever been a "freedom
concert"? If so, it has been an anomaly. There is a peace sign,
and it is ubiquitous—one of the most recognized symbols in the
world: on posters, on bumper stickers, on flags, on various articles
of clothing, on everything. There is no freedom sign, although the
Statue of Liberty is a potent symbol. And then there is the peace
sign you make with your hand: a gesture that came about during
anti–Vietnam War protests. Earlier, that same gesture, made by
Churchill most illustriously, meant "V" for "Victory."

You are familiar with the great, clichéd line in beauty pag-
eants. The contestant is asked what she most wants. She answers,
"World peace." Has a contestant ever said, "World freedom"? That
would shake up the judges.

Every now and then, there is a tension between peace and
freedom—and people confront a choice. New Hampshire has a
blazing motto, "Live free or die." Yet how many people would live,
or die, by these words? William F. Buckley, Jr., once observed that
big moral questions can sometimes be boiled down into bumper-

sticker language: "Better red than dead"; "Better dead than red." This is terribly simple, even crude and embarrassing, language, of course—but it can concentrate the mind. And here is Eisenhower, on those concepts of peace and freedom: "We seek peace, knowing that peace is the climate of freedom."

Stephen Suleyman Schwartz wrote an essay called "Peace vs. Freedom," which puts it starkly: that preposition "vs." He noted "a dissonance between Europe, which historically favored peace over freedom, and America, which has supported freedom over peace." The European view, he said, was embodied in the League of Nations, and later in its successor, the U.N. Both were created to "secure peace, rather than freedom." Decade after decade, in case after case, there has been appeasement ("Most Abused Word"!) of dictators and aggressors: a "habitual surrender," said Schwartz, "in the name of peace." This is the instinct that causes a person, or an organization, to make nice with the People's Republic of China, rather than peep for Tibet—or for the Chinese, for that matter.

Most of the time, the Nobel Committee is an embodiment of the "European" view: a smaller, all-Norwegian version of the League or the U.N. But it peeped for Tibet, didn't it? The committee gave the peace prize to the Dalai Lama in 1989. And they peeped for the Chinese when they gave it to Liu Xiaobo in 2010. The committee has also given the prize to Sakharov, Walesa, Aung San Suu Kyi, Mandela—all symbols of freedom in their nations. Should figures such as these have received an award called a "peace prize"—or would some "freedom prize" have been more appropriate? Midge Decter, the American intellectual who headed the Committee for the Free World, said something scalding after Gorbachev won the Nobel Peace Prize in 1990: "Peace prizes are a kind of abomination, as if peace were a primary value when evil is stalking the world."

The Cold War provided many lessons in freedom and peace, and those words were used a lot—more than usual—during those years. Soviet officials were big, very big, on the word "peace." If Western countries called themselves "freedom-loving nations," the Soviets referred to themselves and their bloc as "peace-loving nations." Touché! The World Peace Council was one of the most prominent Communist fronts. The Soviets named their space station "Mir," meaning Peace (and also World). What the Americans had was Space Station Freedom—which after the collapse of the Soviet Union evolved into the International Space Station, in which Russia collaborated.

In 1949, Stalin or the Soviet government—was there a difference?—created the Stalin Peace Prize, more formally the International Stalin Prize for Strengthening Peace among Peoples. This was the Kremlin's answer to the Nobel prize. Among the early winners of the Stalin Peace Prize was Howard Fast, the American novelist. He received his award from the hand of an even more celebrated American, W. E. B. Du Bois. In his acceptance speech, Fast lamented that neither this peace prize nor "the name it bears"—Stalin's—was "greatly honored by the men who govern my country." But "peace is honored and beloved of millions of the American people, indeed, of almost all of them." Fast also said, "If I had no other cause for honoring the Soviet Union, I would honor it greatly and profoundly for giving prizes for peace." (A quick reminder: The Soviet state killed about 20 million people.)

As the Cold War progressed, few wanted to be seen as a disturber of the peace. If you brought up human rights behind the Iron Curtain, you might have been met with, "Do you want to spoil the chances for peace? Do you wish to precipitate war? Won't you give peace a chance?" That was a great slogan of the time: "Give peace a chance." In the 1970s and '80s, if you peeped about human rights, you might have been met with another slogan, or very common phrase: "poisoning the atmosphere of détente." You were "poisoning the atmosphere of détente." President Reagan was the poisoner-in-chief: an enemy of peace, many thought, or at least an obstacle to it. He talked of human rights and freedom—even calling the Soviet Union and its satellites an "evil empire." As many of us see it, the firmness of his first term in office led to historic dealmaking in his second.

At the end of that first term, the First Lady, Nancy Reagan, had a tête-à-tête with the Soviet foreign minister, Andrei Gromyko. He said to her, "Does your husband believe in peace or war?" (Note the choice—very narrow.) Mrs. Reagan answered, "Peace." "You're sure?" he said. Mrs. Reagan said she was. Later on, Gromyko said to her, "Whisper 'peace' in his ear every night." She rejoined, "I will. I'll also whisper it in your ear."

It was broadly thought that Mrs. Reagan wanted her husband to win the Nobel Peace Prize, in the worst way. And this had some Cold Warriors alarmed—worried that the president would make harmful concessions, in order to curry favor with "world opinion." Indeed, "trying for the Nobel Peace Prize" became an expression of scorn and concern in hawkish circles. For some, a "Nobel" kind of peace meant, and still means, a paper or superficial peace, not a real one. As he commenced his diplomacy in the Arab–Israeli conflict, Tony Blair said to George W. Bush, "If I win the Nobel Peace Prize, you will know I have failed." That is one of the most stinging criticisms of the committee I have ever heard (and I have heard many—and made a few).

One of Blair's predecessors, a Cold War leader, was most impatient with cries of peace. Margaret Thatcher said, "We speak of peace, yes, but whose peace? Poland's? Bulgaria's? The peace of the grave?" And I give you a leader from a much earlier period, Hungary's Kossuth: "I am a man of peace—God knows how I love peace. But I hope I shall never be such a coward as to mistake oppression for peace."

Consider, now, the question of deterrence—a doctrine dismissed and detested by some, viewed as inarguable by others.

The classic expression is, *Si vis pacem, para bellum*—"If you want peace, prepare for war." Peace people—or "peace" people—like to turn this on its head. They say, *Si vis pacem, para pacem*, or, "If you want peace, prepare for peace." We will see this as our Nobel history continues. Peace people also like to quote Einstein, who said, "Peace cannot be kept by force. It can only be achieved by understanding." That sounds more like something that ought to be true than like something that actually is. The 1929 laureate, Frank Kellogg, had caustic words for deterrence at his Nobel banquet:

> I know that military alliances and armament have been the reliance for peace for centuries, but they do not produce peace; and when war comes, as it inevitably does under such conditions, these armaments and alliances but intensify and broaden the conflict. Adequate defense has been the catchword of every militarist for centuries.

George Washington was not of Kellogg's mind. He said, "To be prepared for war is one of the most effectual means of preserving peace." A much later president, Kennedy, said, "We prepare for war in order to deter war." Reagan once put it more simply yet: "No one ever picked a fight with Jack Dempsey" (heavyweight boxing champion in the 1920s). A Reagan conservative, Jack Kemp, liked to say he was a dove—but "a heavily armed dove."

In the Reagan years, there was a missile called the "Peacekeeper"—and this was a name that caused many to gag. A missile? "Peacekeeper"? In 1984, Reagan campaigned for reelection on the slogan "Peace through Strength." This, too, caused many to gag. And return to what Cuomo said, in that same year, 1984: ". . . we proclaim as loudly as we can the utter insanity of nuclear proliferation and the need for a nuclear freeze . . . ." Which approach seems better, more peace-tending, in retrospect—Reagan's or Cuomo's? Who would have been more likely to win the Nobel Peace Prize?

(Hint: Not Reagan.) And have one more slogan, this one of the U.S. Strategic Air Command: "Peace is our profession." There could hardly be a balder proclamation of the deterrence doctrine.

Bald, too, was what Teddy Roosevelt said: ". . . the most important service that I rendered to peace was the voyage of the battle fleet around the world." Once, the magazine that Bill Buckley founded, *National Review*—to which Ronald Reagan was a charter subscriber—quipped editorially that, every year, the Nobel Peace Prize should go to the U.S. military. Why? Because it was the world's foremost guarantor of peace.

Earlier, I quoted Ben Franklin on how there was never a good war or a bad peace. But he is also quoted as saying that "even peace may be purchased at too high a price." George Herbert had a neat formulation: "One sword keeps another in the sheath." And speaking of swords, there is a lovely passage in Kipling's *Kim.* An old soldier is guiding the old lama to a particular destination. The soldier has a sword. And the lama, a man of peace, says, "What profit to kill men?" The soldier answers, "Very little—as I know; but if evil men were not now and then slain it would not be a good world for weaponless dreamers." Less beautiful, but making more or less the same point, is the bumper sticker that goes, "Pacifism is a luxury paid for by warriors."

How about the place of justice with peace? Thatcher liked a slogan: "Peace—with freedom and justice." Engraved on Ludwig Quidde's tombstone is, "I have loved justice." He did not say, "I have loved peace" (which he did). "No justice, no peace!" That is a slogan that can be heard in American streets, from black militants and others. It is a slogan, yes—but also a threat: *Unless you meet our demands, there will be no peace.* In a sense, you put a gun to society's head. The International Labour Organization—winner of the Nobel Peace Prize for 1969—has a motto: *Si vis pacem, cole justitiam,* or, "If you desire peace, cultivate justice." The ILO's constitution begins with the assertion that "universal and lasting peace can be established only if it is based on social justice." Sure, but what is social justice—besides one of the slipperiest terms in our language? And people will always have grievances, legitimate or not—when is peacebreaking justified?

These are questions to wrestle with, and we may also recall the closing sentence of Lincoln's Second Inaugural Address, which speaks of a "just and lasting peace." Could anything be more desirable? "A just and lasting peace."

Lincoln liked the Bible, and it pervaded his speech (and thought). That is a highly interesting book, on peace as on other subjects. The Bible contains some 400 references to "peace." I have already quoted Psalms, and will continue in it: "Depart from evil, and do good; seek peace, and pursue it." That is from Psalm 34. A later Psalm, 120, ends with a bitter complaint: "My soul hath long dwelt with him that hateth peace. I am for peace: but when I speak, they are for war." How many nations and persons, throughout time, have shared this complaint? In Proverbs, there is that lovely passage about wisdom: "Her ways are ways of pleasantness, and all her paths are peace." In Jeremiah, we find the famous cry against a false peace: ". . . they have healed the hurt of the daughter of my people slightly, saying, Peace, peace; when there is no peace." Those words have been quoted more than a few times by people unhappy with a Nobel Committee choice. And in Isaiah, the coming Messiah is heralded as, among other things, "The Prince of Peace."

Jesus was terribly interesting—and perhaps surprising—on the subject of peace. He said, "Think not that I am come to send peace on earth: I came not to send peace, but a sword. For I am come to set a man at variance against his father, and the daughter against her mother, and the daughter in law against her mother in law. And a man's foes shall be they of his own household." Those words are recorded in Matthew—and they speak of a great convulsion. In Luke, we find similar words: "Suppose ye that I am come to give peace on earth? I tell you, Nay; but rather division." And yet Jesus spoke that Beatitude, "Blessed are the peacemakers: for they shall be called the children of God." And, shortly before his departure, he said, "Peace I leave with you, my peace I give unto you: not as the world giveth, give I unto you." Also, "These things I have spoken unto you, that in me ye might have peace."

Later in the New Testament, we hear about "them that preach the gospel of peace," and we are invited to contemplate "the peace of God, which passeth all understanding." Returning to the Old Testament—Isaiah—we have a remarkable, hard-to-forget statement: "And the work of righteousness shall be peace; and the effect of righteousness quietness and assurance for ever."

The Nobel Committee has been mulling the question of peace since the inception of that little band. There are many "paths to peace," the committee likes to say: That's why Mother Teresa and Yasser Arafat can win the prize. In his presentation speech of 1930, Johan Ludwig Mowinckel—who was prime minister at the time—waxed eloquent: ". . . just as it is said that all roads lead to the Eternal City, so it can also truthfully be claimed that many are the roads which must be followed and many the means which must be explored if the human race is to attain the great and sacred goal which is eternal peace among nations." He also said, "Alfred Nobel himself had no illusions as to the difficulties and the complexity of work for peace. For this reason he placed no strict limitations on his peace prize; any serious and noble effort to advance the cause of peace could qualify."

The committee, we have seen, stirred things up when it gave half the inaugural prize to the humanitarian Dunant. Many more humanitarians would follow, including Mother Teresa. In 1947, the committee gave the prize to the two main Quaker relief organizations, one in England, the other in the United States. The Quakers had done splendid work during the war—humanitarian work—and now they were helping to rebuild Europe. Chairman

Gunnar Jahn quoted a Norwegian poet, Arnulf Øverland: "Only the unarmed can draw on sources eternal. / To the Spirit alone will be the victory." Fine, fine, who can argue? But we might ask, cheekily, Who will defeat the Nazis? Anyone? Who will put the barbarians down? General Patton would never have won a peace prize. But whose contribution to the peace of Europe was greater: his or the Quakers'?

Over the years, as we have discussed, heroes of freedom have won the peace prize. In giving such awards, the committee likes to stress the link between peace and freedom. Then there is the question of material well-being—food, clothing, housing. In Trygve Lie Plaza, at the United Nations in New York, you will find a plaque honoring Ralph Bunche, the American U.N. diplomat who won the peace prize for 1950. The plaque quotes from his Nobel lecture: "Peace, to have meaning for many who have known only suffering in both peace and war, must be translated into bread or rice, shelter, health, and education, as well as freedom and human dignity." In 1970, the award went to Norman Borlaug, that feeder of multitudes.

Then we move on to environmentalism—and the award in 2004 to Wangari Maathai, the Kenyan woman who founded an organization devoted to planting trees and generally "greening" the land. Two years later came Muhammad Yunus and the bank he set up: the Grameen Bank. They make "microloans," which is to say, they lend small but critical amounts of money to the poor. The next year came the Intergovernmental Panel on Climate Change and Al Gore. Said Chairman Mjøs, ". . . there are those who doubt that there is any connection between the environment and the climate on the one hand and war and conflict on the other. Why have the IPCC and Al Gore been awarded a Nobel prize for *peace*?" A good question. Mjøs said that "a goal in our modern world must be to maintain 'human security' in the broadest sense." And "environmental problems certainly affect human security in this broad sense"—for example, when floods threaten a population.

Many have worried, or despaired, that the committee has made the definition of peace far too elastic. They will stretch it, some fear, to fit basically anything. Sometimes the committee seems to say, "We admire you, we support you, you are our flavor of the month. Therefore, we will reward you. And we'll call it peace." How might the committee expand its definition of peace in the future? What will the next frontiers be? It would not be shocking to see the committee award animal-rights activists, or campaigners for gay marriage. Whatever they are, there will be new frontiers.

Peace, peace, peace—if you hear about it enough, and hear the word abused enough, you might think that peace is meaningless, and, worse, a scandal. "Peace" can even be a fighting word! Spend enough time immersed in the world of peace and peaceniks—"peace cranks," General MacArthur called them—and the very mention of "peace" might cause you to roll your eyes, or simply to tune out. Yet peace—real peace—is meaningful. Real peace is worth a prize, of at least $1.5 million. On General Grant's monumental tomb in New York, it says, "Let us have peace." So many died in that war, the American Civil War: over 600,000. George Orwell had a line in his novel *Coming Up for Air*. His narrator says, "Before the war," meaning World War I, "and especially before the Boer War, it was summer all the year round." The very next line is, "I'm quite aware that that's a delusion." But still: Peace as permanent summer. How perfect.

A PARADE OF LAUREATES,
1914 *to* 1948

The Nobel Committee in Kristiania did not award the prize in most of the World War I years. The peace cause simply seemed lost in this period—lost and defeated. An award for peace would have struck many people as preposterous, if not insulting. There was no Nobel in 1914, 1915, 1916, or 1918. But in 1917, the committee did award the prize: to the organization that Dunant had fathered, the International Committee of the Red Cross. Amid the mass and monstrous killing, the Red Cross was demonstrating the *Tutti fratelli* spirit, the idea that all men are brothers, no matter what. Red Cross societies were helping those in uniform in any way they could. They were treating the wounded, of course, and they were relaying messages between prisoners of war and their families. Not everyone was content about the 1917 award. As Ivar Libæk writes in an essay called "The Red Cross: Three-Time Recipient of the Peace Prize," there were "references to the paradox that the Red Cross nursed wounded soldiers back to health so that they could be sent to their death once more." But not many begrudged the ICRC its 1917 Nobel, as not many would begrudge it its next two.

~

The committee withheld its prize in 1919; it was not ready to give an award for that year. The world was in tremendous flux. The Versailles Treaty had been signed only in June, and its ramifications were far from clear. In 1920, the committee was ready: and gave the prize for 1919 to Woodrow Wilson, the American president—the very man who had taken his country across the sea into the war, declaring "the right" to be "more precious than peace."

Recall that Wilson was elected in 1912. When the war broke out, he kept the United States neutral, and even offered to mediate between the belligerents. Here is a typical statement from him: "It would look as if Europe had finally determined to commit suicide, as Carlyle thought it had at the time of the French Revolution—and the only way we can help is by changing the current of its thought." Some Americans were furious at Wilson for not jumping into the war on the side of the Allies. Those Americans were represented by a former president, Roosevelt, who compared Wilson to the priest and the Levite in the story of the Good Samaritan: indifferent souls who passed by the desperately needy man on the Jericho road. In 1916, Wilson ran for reelection on the slogan "He kept us out of war." But Germany seemed determined to bring America into the war, sinking its ships at sea. On April 2, 1917, less than a month after he was sworn in for his second term, Wilson went before Congress to ask for a war declaration, and got it.

In January 1918, he addressed Congress again, laying out his famous Fourteen Points—a statement of war aims, a vision for post-war Europe, a declaration of ideals. After the war, Wilson went abroad—the first American president to travel to Europe—to attend the peace conference in Paris. His main goal was to secure his fourteenth point, which read, "A general association of nations must be formed under specific covenants for the purpose of affording mutual guarantees of political independence and territorial integrity to great and small states alike." This meant the League of Nations—an association that Wilson's own country, of course, was never to join.

The Nobel Committee gave Wilson its prize for the formation of that league; without his pushing, it would never have been included in the Versailles Treaty. And peace campaigners had long hoped and striven for a body such as this. But there was great dissension on the committee, and the vote was close: 3 to 2. (We know this from the unsealed records.) There was great dissension in the general peace movement, too. Some were pleased with the award, finding in Wilson a statesman who embodied their principles, and acted on them to the extent possible. Others were disgusted: A peace medal for Wilson? Better to give him a war medal, for he had involved his country in the war at almost the earliest opportunity. Also, he had spoken grandly of a "peace without victory," and the Allies, with the Versailles Treaty, had imposed a traditional victor's peace. German pacifists were especially outspoken against the award for 1919.

In any case, Wilson had his three votes on the committee. But he was in no shape to come to Norway to accept the award, even if his presidential duties had permitted. In September 1919, barnstorming America in support of the League, and U.S. participation in it, Wilson collapsed. Shortly after, he suffered a stroke, which left him incapacitated, physically. He sent to the Norwegians a telegram of thanks and appreciation, read by the U.S. ambassador, Albert G. Schmedeman—who later became governor of Wisconsin.

In that 1930 presentation speech, already quoted, Prime Minister Mowinckel called the League of Nations "that gigantic world monument which President Wilson erected in 1918 . . . to the glory of his own country and for the happiness and salvation of the world!" The League, Mowinckel said, was "the greatest, the most powerful, the most remarkable institution acting for peace that the world has ever known." A later presentation speaker, Gunnar Jahn, said in 1959—a full two decades after the second war began—"Those who never knew the years after the First World War will find it hard to realize how many hopes were pinned to the League of Nations."

~

When Wilson's prize, for 1919, was announced, the prize for 1920 was announced as well: and it went to Léon Bourgeois, another father of the League. He was a Frenchman, and a veteran peace campaigner—also a veteran politician. He held just about every office in the Third Republic except president, a post he could have had but eschewed. Bourgeois (1851–1925) was another of those dynamos who win the Nobel prize: a scholar and statesman, a thinker and doer, a man not just of France and Europe, but of the world at large. Among his subjects were Hinduism and Sanskrit.

As Wilson did not travel to Kristiania, neither did Bourgeois, who, like the American president, was ill. In 1922, he sent what he called a "communication"—in fact his Nobel lecture. It examined the relationship between patriotism and internationalism, a matter much debated, especially in the peace movement:

> The concept of patriotism is not incompatible with that of
> humanity; on the contrary, let me state emphatically that he
> who best serves pacifism, serves patriotism best. The nation
> is . . . the vital basic unit of any international league. Just as the
> formation of the family is basic to the formation of the state,
> so the states themselves are the only units that can form the
> basic constitution of a viable international organization.

Bourgeois further said that nations should "understand that mutual consent to certain principles of law and to certain agreements, acknowledged to be equally profitable to the contracting parties, no more implies a surrender of sovereignty than a contract in private business implies a renunciation of personal liberty."

The 1919 and 1920 laureates shared a worldview, and they had worked together: on the League of Nations Commission. But they had not worked harmoniously. They repeatedly clashed, for instance on the weighty matter of French security: Bourgeois wanted greater American guarantees. August Heckscher, in his 1991 biography of Wilson, writes that the president's "pleasure" on winning the Nobel prize was "diminished" by the fact that Bourgeois was winning too.

～

The year 1921, like the year 1908, was an all-Scandinavian affair. The winners were Hjalmar Branting—whom we have already met as "the father of Swedish socialism"—and Norway's own, Christian Lange. Somewhat poetically—although Nobel had warned against Scandinavian provincialism or partiality—their ceremony took place on the 25th anniversary of the testator's death.

Branting (1860–1925) began his career as a scientist, but then turned to journalism and politics. Part of the politics was peace campaigning. He was a strong advocate for the peaceful separation between his country and Norway, when it came time to break up that union, and the Norwegians appreciated him for it. Three times he was prime minister of Sweden—and was, indeed, in that office on the day of the prize ceremony. He was also prominent in the League of Nations, serving as chairman of the Assembly's disarmament committee, for example.

In his lecture, he spoke, naturally, of the world war (during which Sweden, like Norway, had been neutral). He began by talking about Nobel's "great goal": fraternity between nations. And he would not hear of defeatism:

> No matter how far off this high goal may appear to be, no matter how violently shattered may be the illusion entertained at times by many of us that any future war between highly civilized nations is as inconceivable as one between the Scandinavian brothers, we may be certain of one thing: that for those who cherish humanity, even after its relapse into barbarism these past years, the only road to follow is that of the imperishable ideal of the fraternity of nations.

The League, said Branting, was a "great benefit" that had "resulted from the past years of darkness."

When it came to internationalism, he was in solid agreement with Bourgeois: "The sort of internationalism which rejects the sovereignty of a nation within its own borders and which aims ultimately at its complete obliteration in favor of a cosmopolitan unity, has never been other than a caricature of the true international spirit." A "deeply rooted feeling for the importance of the nation," Branting went on, is "the basis and starting point for true internationalism, for a humanity built not of stateless atoms but of sovereign nations in a free union."

Lange (1869–1938) devoted virtually his entire lecture to this question of internationalism: what it is, or should be, and what it is not, or should not be. Above, I described him as Norway's own. He was also the Nobel Committee's own, because he had been its first-ever secretary. He left the Nobel Institute in 1909, to become the secretary-general of the Inter-Parliamentary Union, succeeding Albert Gobat, one of the 1902 laureates. Lange could be a scold, but he was unquestionably a brilliant scholar, diplomat, and writer. In the last five years of his life, he served the Nobel Committee as a member. Thus did he achieve a trifecta: secretary, member, and laureate (though not in that order). As an official of the Nobel Institute remarked to me, Lange was everything but committee chairman. Almost certainly, there will never again be a secretary-member-laureate.

Lecturing in his capital, Lange said, "I shall discuss *Internationalism*, and not 'Pacifism.' The latter word has never appealed to me—it is a linguistic hybrid, directing one-sided attention to the negative aspect of the peace movement, the struggle against war; 'antimilitarism' is a better word for this aspect of our efforts." He spoke of internationalism versus nationalism—also of the harmony between the two. "Internationalism . . . recognizes, by its very name, that nations do exist. It simply limits their scope more than one-sided nationalism does." In Lange's rendering, the foe of both nationalism and internationalism, properly understood, was cosmopolitanism.

What was needed now, he said, was a dramatically improved internationalism. "It is a matter of nothing less than our civilization's 'to be or not to be.' Europe cannot survive another world war." Many, many people felt that way in those years. It is something you hear over and over, in the Nobel lectures and presentation speeches: Europe cannot survive another war.

～

In 1922, it was hero time—with the award going to a second Norwegian, Fridtjof Nansen. How to describe him? In thumbnail fashion, as follows: scientist, explorer, athlete, professor, diplomat, executive, humanitarian. He was famous all the world over, a living legend. (Every now and then, that cliché is apt.) Nansen resembled a future movie hero, Indiana Jones, although Nansen was perhaps more wide-ranging, in addition to real.

Here are a few brushstrokes from this life (1861–1930): At 17, Nansen won Norway's distance-skating championship. The next year, he broke a world speed-skating record. There were skiing exploits, too. He became a zoologist, an oceanographer, an anthropologist. He explored and charted the Arctic regions, enduring many hardships and braving many dangers. He wrote *The First Crossing of Greenland* and *Eskimo Life*. He curated at the Bergen Museum. He was Norway's first ambassador to Great Britain. (During the Swedish-Norwegian union, Stockholm had controlled foreign affairs.)

But why did he win the Nobel prize? After the war, the world, particularly in the form of the League of Nations, asked him to do several important things. The League asked him to take charge of the repatriation of those prisoners of war whose cases were still unresolved. There were hundreds of thousands of them. Then the League asked him to take care of refugees—who were all too numerous, too—making him its first high commissioner. In this capacity, he created the famous "Nansen passports," which gave the homeless and storm-tossed something to hang on to, and present. Among the holders of these passports were Rachmaninoff, Stravinsky, Chagall, and Pavlova. Later, the Red Cross asked Nansen to relieve mass famine in Russia. (By the way, his assistant there was Quisling—who was not worthless his entire life.) Then the League asked him to deal with the population exchanges and resettlement following the Greco–Turkish War. When his fellow Norwegians—five of them—gave him the Nobel prize, he was the second humanitarian to win, after Dunant. Although, it is true, Dunant's organization, the Red Cross, won too.

Giving the 1922 presentation speech was a new chairman, Fredrik Stang. He had been Norway's justice minister, and he was the grandson of another national hero: Frederik Stang, who was Norway's first prime minister in the union with Sweden. (You may have noticed that grandfather and grandson spelled their first names slightly differently.) Chairman Stang's speech for Nansen was long, emotional, and eloquent. He gave a picture of the whirlwind that was the man:

We see him incessantly on the move: One day we read in a cable that he is having talks with Lloyd George in London; then we suddenly learn that he has gone to Rome for a conference with the pope. Next he is in Russia to study the famine at first hand and to negotiate with the Soviet government; typhus claims some of his closest collaborators, but he himself, as so often before, emerges safe and sound from the danger. Another day he is to be found in the League of Nations Assembly in Geneva, pleading the cause of humanity in the face of all political prejudices. Then he is off once more on his travels, most recently to Constantinople and Greece, until he now stands for a moment among us, in his homeland, to receive the peace prize awarded to him without his even having been aware of his candidacy.

Here is another flight from Stang, and you can forgive him, for it is not an unjustified one:

What burdens he has borne upon his shoulders! What organizing ability his work has demanded, what energy and initiative, what self-sacrificing patience, what talent for coming straight to the heart of any problem! What he has lived through, this man who has seen Europe's misery at first hand and who has felt a sense of responsibility for it!

And it was natural to express some national pride, or at least some national feeling, for Nansen had been part of the Norwegian consciousness for more than 40 years. "Seeing him in our midst today," said Stang, "awakens many memories. Behind him is a life which we have all, in our thoughts, lived with him." For example, "we remember a young boy—for he was but little more than that—crossing Greenland on skis."

In addition to everything else he was, Nansen was a writer—as attested by his Nobel lecture. It is a gripping read. He spoke mainly of people's suffering: "the suffering people of Europe, bleeding to death on deserted battlefields after conflicts which to a great extent were not their own." This horrible fate, he said, was "the outcome of the lust for power, the imperialism, the milita- rism, that have run amok across the earth. . . . People bow their heads in silent despair. The shrill battle cries still clamor around them, but they hardly hear them anymore."

Nansen wondered where the remedy could be found. "At the hands of politicians? They may mean well enough, many of them at any rate, but politics and new political programs are no longer of service to the world—the world has had only too many of them. In the final analysis, the struggle of the politician amounts to lit- tle more than a struggle for power." Well, how about diplomats? "Their intentions may also be good enough, but they are once and for all a sterile race which has brought mankind more harm than good over the years. Call to mind the settlements arranged after the great wars—the Treaty of Westphalia, the Congress in Vienna with the Holy Alliance, and others. Has a single one of these diplomatic congresses contributed to any great extent to the progress of the world?" Nansen looked to the League of Nations: and "if this fails to introduce a new era, then I see no salvation, at any rate at present."

Nansen had some reservations about being awarded the peace prize. A Norwegian, Lange, had just won. And the committee was again turning to a Norwegian. This did not look good. But Nan- sen need not have worried, because close to a century has passed, and still no other Norwegian has won. He himself said that two men were more deserving than he—both British, both men of the League: Robert Cecil and Philip Noel-Baker. Each would win in time.

～

As you know, the prize ceremony for Nansen was held in Decem- ber 1922. There would not be another such ceremony until four

Decembers later. The Nobel Committee did not award a prize for 1923 or 1924. It reserved the prize for 1925, awarding it in 1926. These were years of further flux, further uncertainty. Europe was still trying to recover from the war and work out a new order. On December 10, 1926, four laureates were announced: two for the previous year, two for the current one. The winners for 1925 were Charles G. Dawes, vice president of the United States, and Sir Austen Chamberlain, the British foreign secretary. The winners for 1926 were two other foreign secretaries: Aristide Briand of France and Gustav Stresemann of Germany. The vice president won for the "Dawes Plan," which gave Germany a new schedule and new terms for reparations; and the three foreign ministers won for crafting the Locarno Treaties, which were supposed to secure exactly the new order that so many longed for and depended on.

The main speaker at the 1926 ceremony was the man who had been the main speaker at the previous ceremony: Nansen. He was not on the committee, and this was not, strictly speaking, a presentation speech: but it served as a presentation speech, and discoursed with typical verve on recent events. Europe, said Nansen, had been pulled from the abyss and given new hope and life, particularly by the Dawes Plan and the Locarno Treaties.

Dawes was not vice president when the plan was formulated. He took office in 1925, following his election with Coolidge. The committee on reparations of which he was chairman did its work in 1924. Nansen said that the Dawes Plan "marked the beginning of the policy of reconciliation and peace which led to the Locarno agreements."

He was a Westerner, Dawes was, or a Midwesterner, we would say today: born in Marietta, Ohio, in 1865. He came from an old American family—as old as the Pilgrims. One ancestor, William Dawes, rode with Paul Revere, when the British were coming. Our Dawes became a businessman, banker, and financier, known for his acumen and reliability—also for a pointed wit. In the McKin-ley administration, he was comptroller of the currency. Years later, when the war came, he went to Europe with General Pershing, an old friend. He was purchasing agent for the American forces and was made a brigadier general. After the war, some hearings were held in Congress to investigate charges of waste and abuse "over there." One member wanted to know whether the Americans had paid too much for French mules. Dawes exploded, "Helen Maria, I'd have paid horse prices for sheep if the sheep could have pulled artillery to the front!" He explained, in no uncertain terms, that the Americans were trying to win a world war, not "haggle over pennies." Ever after, Dawes had the nickname "Hell and Maria," or "Hell 'n' Maria"—the papers printed it up in those ways. Dawes himself insisted that, where he came from, it was "Helen Maria."

In the Harding administration, Dawes became budget direc-tor—the first director of the new Bureau of the Budget. In his years as vice president, he did not compile much of a record, because he was not given much to do: Dawes and President Coolidge didn't get along. Under the next president, Hoover, Dawes served as ambassador to Great Britain, until 1932, when the president called him home to lead the Reconstruction Finance Corporation. This was one of those bodies meant to ease the Great Depression.

Dawes may not have been a superman like Nansen, but he was a man of parts. For instance, he was a musician: a pianist, a flutist, and a composer. In 1912, he wrote something called *Melody in A*. Just a little ditty for his friends and family to enjoy in their drawing rooms? Not exactly. It was published, then played by people all over America, on the piano and other instruments. Fritz Kreisler, one of the great violinists, took up the piece, mak-ing it a signature encore. He also recorded it. And, when Dawes died in 1951, his piece assumed another life. That year, Carl Sig-mund put words to it, making a song called "It's All in the Game."

It became a big hit for the singer Tommy Edwards, after which it was covered by any number of musicians—including Louis Armstrong, Dinah Shore, Nat King Cole, Engelbert Humperdinck, Van Morrison, Barry Manilow, and Elton John. Dawes's tune may be better known than the fact that he won the Nobel Peace Prize, or that he was vice president of the United States. Indeed, in this melody may lie the man's immortality.

"The outstanding work of the Dawes Committee," said Sir Austen Chamberlain, "greatly facilitated our task." He meant the task of making the Locarno Treaties. And what were those? They are judged folly now, but they were thought magnificent, even salvific, at the time. They were a series of agreements—seven—hammered out at Locarno, the little town in Italian Switzerland at the northern tip of Lake Maggiore. The Locarno Treaties were meant to tie up some loose and wretched ends from the Versailles Treaty. Participating at Locarno were France, Germany, Britain, Italy, Belgium, Poland, and Czechoslovakia. (Incidentally, Italy was represented by Mussolini.) The Locarno Treaties did a number of things, but the upshot was this: Germany's western borders were fixed; Germany's eastern borders were left open to revision (ominously, of course); international disputes were to be resolved by arbitration, not by arms; the Rhineland would be demilitarized; Germany would join the League of Nations.

The Locarno Treaties were greeted with jubilation around the world. The *New York Times* trumpeted, "France and Germany Ban War Forever," and the *Times* of London said, "Peace at Last." The great feeling of relief, of further catastrophe averted, was expressed by the French foreign minister at the League of Nations, when Germany entered. Briand said, "No more war! . . . From now on it will be for the judge to decide what is right. Just as individual citizens settle their disagreements before a judge, so shall we also resolve ours by peaceful means. Away with rifles, machine guns, cannons. Make way for conciliation, arbitration, peace!"

The three principal "men of Locarno," as all the participants were known, shared in Nobels—those three foreign ministers from Britain, France, and Germany. Chamberlain (1863–1937) was a statesman of considerable experience and ability, having been secretary of state for India, chancellor of the Exchequer, and other things. He was the son of Joseph Chamberlain, the statesman known as "the empire-builder," and the half-brother of Neville Chamberlain, who became prime minister in 1937. Briand (1862–1932) was a statesman with a particular gift for talking—you could even say a genius for talking. His audiences large and small were amazed. Gustav Stresemann (1878–1929) was a highly skilled diplomat, a German known as a European, and a self-conscious European, but one with an iron devotion to national interest. He was the only one of the 1925 or 1926 laureates to give a lecture—and it was on the "New Germany," as contrasted with the Old. Here is a section of particular interest:

> A people that has experienced all that the Germans have been through, naturally offers fertile soil for the extremists. The ballast in the center of the German ship which saved it from heavy rolling in the past, that valuable and steady middle-class group, no longer exists. The uprooted saw their hope in a complete reversal of affairs. It was at this time that the great tide of Bolshevism broke over Germany, appearing on the left as Communism and on the right as National Socialism. That a nation, whose currency had collapsed, whose social and economic reorganization had been as ruthless as ours—that this nation, which had to learn to live in an entirely new situation, has been able to master Bolshevism of the Right and of the Left, shows the healthiness of its spirit, the zeal of its industriousness, and the victory of *Realpolitik* over the imaginary and illusory.

Another passage of interest:

> It was a turning point in European history when the Germans
> initiated the policy which led by way of Locarno to Geneva [site
> of the League of Nations]. . . . I do not think of Locarno only in
> terms of its consequences for Germany. Locarno means much
> more to me. It is the achievement of lasting peace on the
> Rhine, guaranteed by the formal renunciation of force by the
> two great neighboring nations and also by the commitment of
> other states to come to the aid of the victim of an act of aggres-
> sion in violation of this treaty. *Treuga Dei*, the peace of God,
> shall reign where for centuries bloody wars have raged.

Allied troops left the Rhineland in 1930, five years ahead of
schedule. In March 1936, Hitler sent troops into the Rhineland, in
violation of Locarno. The other countries stood by impotently. And
that was that. Now, you can say that the Locarno Nobels look pretty
foolish. But we can see why the committee conferred those prizes.
They were honest prizes, given in the spirit of Alfred Nobel's will.
Who was doing more for "fraternity between nations"? The men
of Locarno were the best and, really, the only peace game in town.
Still, it's true: It all blew up so quickly.

~

In 1927, the committee turned away from statesmen and turned
back to the peace movement, whose leaders and organizations
won so many of the first Nobels—so many of the peace prizes
from 1901 to World War II. Also, the committee wished to keep
emphasizing Franco-German reconciliation. Almost nothing was
more critical to the peace of Europe, went the thinking of the time.
Therefore, the committee divided the 1927 prize between a peace
stalwart in France and a peace stalwart in Germany: Ferdinand

Buisson and Ludwig Quidde. In his presentation speech, Chairman Stang said, "It is in the task of reorienting public opinion that Buisson and Quidde have played such prominent roles." Moreover, "they have guided this work in two countries where it has been particularly difficult to accomplish, but where the need for it has been commensurately great."

Buisson (1841–1932) was known as "the world's most persistent pacifist." He had been at it a very long time: You remember that he attended the peace conference at Geneva in 1867, his first. In 1927, he may well have been seen as a link to Frédéric Passy and the origins of this movement. In addition to a pacifist, Buisson was an education theorist and official, a professor at the Sorbonne, a Dreyfusard (which is to say, a defender of Captain Dreyfus, who was falsely accused of treason, in the classic case of French anti-Semitism). He was a politician as well, elected to the Chamber of Deputies as a Radical-Socialist—the party also of his countryman and fellow Nobelist d'Estournelles. A sense of Buisson's thinking can be found in the titles of two of his writings: *The Abolition of War through Education* and *Liberal Christianity*.

Not a pure pacifist, Buisson supported his country when the world war came. He thought France had been wrongly attacked, and that the war needed to be won to put an end to wars in general. He was appalled by the Versailles Treaty, however, thinking it merely victor's justice and dangerous. In the mid-Twenties, when he was well into his eighties, he went on a speaking tour of Germany, promoting peace. This greatly impressed the Nobel Committee, which was honoring him for the recent work, in addition, we can presume, to his longtime service. He was 85 when he won the peace prize—the oldest ever to have won it. He was not passed in this respect until 1995, when Joseph Rotblat won. He was 87.

In lieu of a Nobel lecture, Buisson wrote an essay, which he submitted to Oslo. In it, he echoed a theme from the testator, who thought that war would stop when civilian populations became targets. Do you recall? "War must be made as death-dealing to the civil population at home as to the troops at the front. Let the sword of Damocles hang over every head, gentlemen, and you will witness a miracle—all war will stop short instantly, if the weapon is bacteriology." In his essay, Buisson said that "professional soldiers" once "took upon themselves the job of defending national interests, and it was understood that the war affected only them; the country itself went on living and working." But "those happy days are over."

War was now entirely different, he said. "From the day war conquered the skies, nothing could check its progress. It is now possible to drop from unmeasurable heights which defy any defense tons of chemical products, some capable of destroying the largest cities in the world in a matter of hours, others of spreading terrible diseases over vast areas, making resistance totally impossible." Therefore, "war has put an end to itself. It has put itself in the position of executioner of the whole earth."

Ludwig Quidde, born in 1858, was a writer, politician, and ardent pacifist, a liberal not afraid to speak his mind in forbidding circumstances. He often paid for his views, including with imprisonment. In 1905, he had something of a historic handshake with Passy at the World Peace Congress in Lucerne: The possibility of Franco-German friendship was seen in a clasp. In 1914, he became head of the German Peace Society, and after the war the head of the German Peace Cartel (rather jarringly named). It was an umbrella group for some 20 societies.

Stang, speaking at the Nobel ceremony, said, "Two qualities stand out in Quidde's writing and in his work as a whole: moderation and courage." That is a just assessment. Quidde gave a lecture, analyzing the relationship between security and disarmament, which is not a simple relationship. He said, "Lightly armed nations can move toward war just as easily as those which are armed to the teeth, and they will do so if the usual causes of war are not removed." And he quoted his countryman and fellow Nobelist Alfred Fried, who said, "Disarmament will be the result of secure peace rather than the means of obtaining it."

Have just one more quotation from Quidde himself—one in which we can see some of his sobriety about the affairs of men and nations: "Since Locarno, the security of western and central Europe is provided for, to the extent that treaties are ever capable of guaranteeing security."

When Hitler came to power, Quidde had to flee, and he fled to Geneva. He stayed there until his death in 1941. In addition to his Nobel prize money, he had funds from the Nobel Institute to write about German pacifism during World War I. The Nobel money meant a great deal to him, for he had lost his fortune— which had once been large—to the post-war economic wreckage. In this, he was far from alone, of course. The Nobel money kept him together, and kept him working for the cause, which we can presume is what Nobel wanted his estate to do.

∽

The committee gave no prize for 1928. And they reserved the next year's award until 1930—when they gave it to Frank B. Kellogg, who had been secretary of state under Coolidge, from 1925 to 1929. As I mentioned in our introduction, the Nobel Committee was particularly good to Coolidge's men. Kellogg was the author—or co-author—of the Kellogg-Briand Pact, which "outlawed war" (to use the common shorthand). And the Nobel Committee gave the prize to him for this curious treaty. The rules did not prevent the committee from giving half the '29 prize to the other author, Briand—nothing prevents a person from winning more than once. But Briand had just received a half-prize, for the Locarno Treaties.

Dopey as the Kellogg-Briand Pact seems, particularly in light of World War II, which followed shortly after it, Kellogg was not really a dope: He was an able and serious man. Born in 1856, he grew up on a Minnesota farm. He had to leave school early to work. But he taught himself in many subjects, including law, and he became a major corporate lawyer—friend and counselor to such men as Rockefeller and Carnegie. In an interesting twist, he became a major trustbuster, doing the work that President Roosevelt loved so well. In 1916, Minnesotans elected him to the Senate. When Coolidge assumed the presidency, following the death of Harding in 1923, he made Kellogg ambassador to Great Britain. When he was elected in his own right—with Dawes—he made him secretary of state. After those four years, Kellogg was not done with his international work: He served as a judge in the Permanent Court of International Justice at The Hague. He died in 1937.

The Kellogg-Briand Pact came about in this way: On April 6, 1927, Foreign Minister Briand made a proposal. The date was not accidental: It was the tenth anniversary of America's entry into the war. Briand proposed a treaty between his country and the United States guaranteeing "perpetual friendship" and prohibiting war. The Americans, represented by Kellogg, did not jump at this strange offer. What prospect of war could there be between France and America? Obviously, the French were looking for a way to bind the Americans to them, which was understandable (given all they had endured). Kellogg took his sweet time responding to Briand, and when he did—at the very end of 1927—he countered with a larger treaty: one for all nations to sign, really. They would renounce war as an instrument of national policy, and arbitration would rule. The treaty—also known as the Pact of Paris—was signed in the French capital on August 27, 1928.

This treaty was the ripened fruit of the "outlawry of war movement," a movement led by an American named Salmon O. Levinson. He was a Chicago lawyer who lobbied throughout the world for this outlawry. He was reacting, as so many were, to the world war. Maybe illegalization would not stop war. But it would make it . . . well, illegal. And you could shame the war-makers and law-breakers with this fact.

The countries that signed the Kellogg-Briand Pact left themselves outs: caveats, exemptions, loopholes. The United States was one such country: It would not forsake the Monroe Doctrine, for example. And no country would forsake the right of self-defense, or the right to determine what their self-defense was. The upshot was, no country was truly bound by the pact. A common sentiment was expressed by the U.S. senator who said that the treaty was "worthless but perfectly harmless."

When Kellogg traveled to France to sign the treaty, the people of Le Havre gave him a gold pen in a box that had an inscription: *Si vis pacem, para pacem*—"If you want peace, prepare for peace," an upending of the traditional *Si vis pacem, para bellum.* In Paris, 15 countries signed the pact, and some 40 others joined later. Germany, Italy, Japan—they were all onboard.

It is a fact that famously sensible people said foolish—or foolish-seeming—things about Kellogg-Briand. There was Coolidge himself, who told Congress that the pact "promises more for the peace of the world than any other agreement ever negotiated among the nations." (If that was true, it did not say much for agreements negotiated "among the nations.") Kellogg's successor as secretary of state, Henry L. Stimson, noted that the pact provided "no sanctions of force"—that was a common, and obvious, criticism. Instead, the pact rested on "the sanction of public opinion, which can be made one of the most potent sanctions of the world. . . . Those critics who scoff at it have not accurately appraised the evolution in world opinion since the Great War." That was a very common defense of the pact.

At prize time, Kellogg traveled to Oslo, and spoke of many things. He talked about the "terrible carnage" of "the greatest war of all time"; the "millions of men who gave their lives, who made the supreme sacrifice, and who today, beneath the soil of France and Belgium, sleep the eternal sleep." Said Kellogg, "Their supreme sacrifice should inspire a pledge never again to inflict humanity with such a crime. I have said before and I wish to repeat today, with all the solemn emphasis which I can place upon my words, that Western civilization would not survive another such conflict, but would disappear in the universal chaos."

Perhaps surprisingly, the Kellogg-Briand Pact took a full three years to break. That happened when the Japanese invaded Manchuria. But the pact lived on, technically, and was one of the bases on which the Nazis at Nuremberg were prosecuted. If we wish to speak very technically, the Kellogg-Briand Pact lives on today. Back when the pact was signed, Josef Stalin, who knew something about world affairs, and the mind of the West, said, "They talk about pacifism; they speak about peace among European states. . . . All this is nonsense."

~

You will recall that the testator knew a young clergyman in Paris, whose work he supported, and with whom he argued, about God and truth. That was Nathan Söderblom. When the time came, Söderblom conducted Nobel's memorial service in San Remo. Seventeen years later, in 1914, he became archbishop of Uppsala and primate of Sweden. He also became a leader of the ecumenical movement in Europe. In 1925, he organized a large ecumenical conference in Stockholm. He preached unity among the churches, unity among the nations. And in 1930 he won the peace prize established by his old friend. Söderblom has the distinction in Nobel history of being the first churchman to win.

Mowinckel, giving the presentation speech, said that the laureate's "great achievement is that he has thrown the power of the spirit into the fight for peace." He further said, "The Christian church has sinned grievously and often against the teaching of him whose first commandment to men was that they should love one another. This church surely has a unique opportunity now of creating that new attitude of mind which is necessary if peace between nations is to become reality." He then quoted Robert de Traz, a French-Swiss essayist and novelist. The words are even more hard-hitting than Mowinckel's own: "If a new war threatens, the churches will not, this time, bless the guns. They will halt the nations in the name of him who called himself the Prince of Peace. At least they say this and they commit themselves to it. And because in 1914 they denied their Master more than twice, they now beg mankind for forgiveness." (De Traz can be forgiven a minor error: Jesus never called himself the "Prince of Peace," that designation being found only in Isaiah, with reference to the coming Messiah. Also, did the writer mean to say "thrice" rather than "twice"?)

Söderblom's Nobel lecture, unsurprisingly, had aspects of a sermon. It was on "The Role of the Church in Promoting Peace." He said that "peace can be reached only through fighting against the ancient Adam in ourselves and in others," and that "reckless nationalism" had to be "replaced by Christian brotherhood." Söderblom, born in 1866, died in 1931, the year after he got Nobel's peace prize.

∾

First nominated in 1916, nominated 90 times thereafter, and six times shortlisted, Jane Addams finally won her Nobel in 1931. She had to share it, however, which did not make her fans and boosters very happy. She shared it with another American, Nicholas Murray Butler, the president of Columbia University. At the prize ceremony, Halvdan Koht did some tallying:

> In awarding the peace prize to two Americans, the Nobel Committee today brings the United States into first place among those nations whose representatives have received the prize

during the past 30 years. Previously, France had the highest number of prizewinners, a total of six, while other nations had no more than two or three. As of today, seven peace prizes will have gone to America, four of them during the last five years.

Koht said it was "only natural that so many peace prizes should have gone to the United States in recent years." America was "a world in itself, as large as the whole of Europe," and "this world is a great land of peace where war between states, either economic or military, is unthinkable." (The unpleasantness of 1861–1865 was long over.) He said that, at this juncture, America "wields greater power over war and peace than any other country on earth," meaning that "all who yearn for a lasting peace must . . . look to America for help."

Koht was a committee member and Labor politician who would soon become foreign minister. And he had much more to say about America, that upstart nation across the Atlantic, in this presentation speech. For instance,

> It must be said . . . that the United States is not the power for peace in the world that we should have wished her to be. She has sometimes let herself drift into the imperialism which is the natural outcome of industrial capitalism in our age. In many ways she is typical of the wildest form of capitalist society . . . .

There is a true voice of Norway. But Koht allowed that, even while being wildly capitalistic, "America has . . . fostered some of the most spirited idealism on earth." And "to the American mind," he said, "nothing is impossible. This attitude applies not only to science and technology but to social forms and conditions as well. To an American, an ideal is not just a beautiful mirage but a practical reality, the implementation of which is every man's duty."

In Koht's estimation, the 1931 laureates were "two of the finest representatives" of an "American idealism," particularly a "social idealism." We can certainly say that they were dynamos and whirl-winds: thinking and talking and doing their entire lives.

Addams was born in 1860, in Cedarville, Illinois. Her father was a businessman, banker, and politician—a founder of the Republican party. And he knew Lincoln. Indeed, Lincoln would address letters to him "My Dear Double D-ed Addams." Lincoln enjoyed noticing and commenting on such things. Do you remember the famous quip he made about his future in-laws? "One 'd' was good enough for God, but not for the Todds." In 1889, Jane Addams, with a friend, founded Hull House in Chicago: the first settlement house in America, a haven for the poor, and an educational boost to them. She was instrumental in women's suffrage, the field of sociology, the founding of the American Civil Liberties Union, and on and on. In his speech, Koht called her "the leading woman" in America, and "one might almost say its leading citizen." Those were grand claims, but not implausible. This leading citizen died in 1935.

Among her many activities was, of course, peace campaigning. She gave a series of lectures in 1906, resulting in the book *Newer Ideals of Peace*. Shortly after the war began, she co-founded and led the Woman's Peace party. In April 1915, she sailed to the Netherlands for a women's international peace congress. (Roosevelt wrote a harsh note to one of her co-passengers: "Pacifists are cowards, and your scheme is silly and base.") From this congress came the Women's International League for Peace and Freedom, which Addams, naturally, led. When the United States entered the war, she remained firmly opposed: opposed to U.S. participation and to the war altogether. This harmed her popularity in America, whose people were generally foursquare behind the war effort. But she would rise again in public affections.

And her co-laureate, Nicholas Murray Butler? He was "Nicholas Miraculous," as his friend TR dubbed him. He was president of Columbia University for virtually the entire first half of the 20th century: 1901 to 1945. (Butler was born in 1862 and died in 1947.) Amazingly, he traveled to Europe more than a hundred times—this in an age of sailing, not flying. He always had a hand in Republican politics, and he sought the presidential nomination, more than once. His longstanding and perpetual concern was the development of what he called "the international mind." Sometimes that was capitalized: "the International Mind." By this, he meant an ability and willingness to think in broad, global terms.

Ungenerously, he has been called a gadfly. More generously, he has been called a citizen extraordinaire: a public intellectual and a public conscience. Koht said in his speech, "If there be a man who can truly be called American, then Butler is that man: a greathearted worker and a splendid organizer."

The laureate's peacework began in the first decade of the century: He teamed with Baron d'Estournelles in an organization—more like a movement—called International Conciliation. He encouraged Andrew Carnegie to set up the Carnegie Endowment. He always had a role in that endowment, and succeeded Elihu Root—another great friend—as its president. When Briand proposed his anti-war pact, the State Department, as we know, had reservations: grave reservations about this French maneuver. Butler did not. He promoted the pact energetically (which is how he did everything). Spying a new age, he said,

> Gone is the fear of national security; gone is the argument
> for compulsory military service and huge standing armies;
> gone is the plea for the protection of sea-borne commerce and
> a navy as powerful as any in the world; gone is the haste to
> build bombing planes and to store up vast supplies of poison

gas; gone is the whole gospel of preparedness for a war which is promised never to be fought—gone are all these unless all men and all governments are liars.

Were they liars? And are they? Indeed. At any rate, Briand wrote to his friend Butler on the day the Pact of Paris was signed: to thank him for all he had done.

Earlier, I said something about tallying—and here is a little more: Addams was the second woman to win the peace prize, after Suttner. Koht took note of this, saying, "In honoring Jane Addams, we also pay tribute to the work which women can do for peace and fraternity among nations." At times, though, "women have not altogether fulfilled the hopes we have placed in them." How so? "They have allowed too much scope to the old morality of men, the morality of war. In practical politics we have seen too little of that love, that warm maternal feeling which renders murder and war so hateful to every woman."

Obviously, the oft-nominated Addams had many who wanted her to win the peace prize. Butler had backers too: including Butler. He campaigned for the prize, as people sometimes do. He was very keen on prizes and honors, as people sometimes are. In his 2006 biography (*Nicholas Miraculous: The Amazing Career of the Redoubtable Nicholas Murray Butler*), Michael Rosenthal tells us that Butler appointed something of a campaign manager—James B. Scott, who, like Butler, was a stalwart in peace organizations. Scott attended to every detail of Butler's Nobel nomination. When the good news came from Oslo, Butler telegraphed his campaign manager: "Prussia once had a Great Elector. America now has a Great Nominator. Accept my grateful congratulations upon the success of his enterprise."

～

There was a time when everyone knew who Sir Norman Angell was: certainly everyone interested in the affairs of the world. He was an economist and, more than that, a peace propagandist—perhaps the leading such propagandist there was. (Allow me to remind you that "propagandist," particularly "peace propagandist," was no putdown, generations ago.) Angell wrote over 40 books, constantly agitating for rationality in international affairs, for cooperation among nations (including free trade), and for the prevention of war. And he won the Nobel prize for 1933. The committee declined to award a prize for 1932. And it reserved the prize for 1933, giving it to Angell in 1934.

As the "Sir" before his name tells you, the laureate was a Briton, and he lived a long, as well as a productive, life: from 1872 to 1967. He served briefly in Parliament, representing the Labour party: That was from 1929 to 1931. Otherwise, he was writing, lecturing, and agitating, working right into his nineties.

His big book was *The Great Illusion*, published in 1910. The author's contention, in sum, was that war doesn't pay; that it is of no advantage to the victor, particularly economically. The idea that war could benefit a victor was "the great illusion," "a gross and desperately dangerous misconception." Angell explained that prosperity was not at all dependent on military might or even political power, as witness such countries as Holland. And with the world locked in economic interdependence, militarism would, or should, have no chance. Christian Lange, in his Nobel lecture, said, "Some years before the war, Norman Angell coined the word 'interdependence' to denote the situation that stamps the economic and spiritual culture of our time . . . ."

The Great Illusion was translated into some 25 languages and sold more than 2 million copies. This was one of those books that sweep into consciousness—or many consciousnesses—such as Suttner's *Lay Down Your Arms!* People even spoke of "Norman

Angellism," in reference to the author's theories. He twice updated *The Great Illusion*, once in 1933 and once in 1938. The famous 1937 film by Jean Renoir, *La Grande Illusion*, borrows his title.

Angell gave his Nobel lecture the summer following the announcement of his prize: in June 1935. And this was the first Nobel lecture to be given after the National Socialists had won power in Germany. He referred to that victory in his lecture, saying that the Nazis had been able to get at "the public mind." "The politician does not become dictator by the strength of his own muscles," he said. "He must persuade others, millions of others, to use their muscles in a certain way." He continued, "The German National Socialists began as a party of ten persons. And it would have remained a party of ten persons had not its promoters been able to *persuade*—not force—others. Ten persons had no force as against the power of the German nation." Without popular appeal, the Nazi party would never have gotten anywhere. "And if, and when, it loses that popular appeal, it will cease to be."

Sir Norman was that relatively rare Nobelist who campaigned for the peace prize—and campaigned hard—and won. He was more energetic, or at least more overt, than Nicholas Murray Butler. Angell enlisted Jane Addams and many others in his cause. It may well be, as Norman Angellism has it, that war doesn't pay. But the author's unblushing efforts to win the prize certainly did.

❧

You remember the laureate for 1903: Sir Randal Cremer, who grew up very poor, and fatherless, and became a labor leader and parliamentarian—in addition to a Nobel Peace Prize winner. Arthur Henderson, the laureate for 1934, had a similar trajectory. We will glance at his beginnings in a moment. In 1934, he was serving as president of the Disarmament Conference, a project of the League of Nations. The conference was going very badly: For one thing, the Germans had pulled out of it, as they had from the

League as a whole. But Henderson was doing his utmost to keep the conference alive. He was the human symbol of disarmament efforts.

He was born in 1863, in Glasgow. When his father died nine years later, the boy had to go to work. He had no formal schooling at all past the age of twelve. Henderson was a strongly religious and utopian man—a Methodist lay preacher. When the war came, his Labour party was divided: Ramsay MacDonald led the pacifist wing; Henderson led the "fight" wing, which was larger. During the war, he was a minister in Lloyd George's cabinet, but he resigned when the prime minister and his cabinet refused to authorize a British delegation to the socialist peace conference proposed for Stockholm—a conference to be presided over by Hjalmar Branting. (In the end, the gathering did not take place.)

With Sidney Webb, the celebrated Fabian, Henderson wrote the Labour constitution. And he rose to the post of foreign secretary in 1929, when MacDonald was prime minister. Henderson served until 1931. And in that year, while he was still foreign secretary, he was named president of the Disarmament Conference. In July 1933, he met Hitler in Munich, to talk and plead disarmament.

At the 1934 prize ceremony in Oslo, Prime Minister Mowinckel gave the speech for Henderson. In these ominous times, he said, with war rumbles growing louder, the League of Nations was "our only consolation, our best hope." And Henderson was a faithful servant of that league. Aristide Briand had died two years before, and Mowinckel said,

> On Briand's coffin, as a tribute from the heart and as a token
> of gratitude to him who died in the struggle for international
> peace and understanding, a woman laid a small bunch of
> spring violets, with a slip of paper on which were written these

touching words: "From a mother who has lost much, but who still has a son aged 18."

Lest our world, our community, our civilization, our future, our children perish in a new Armageddon, every one of us must today remember the violets of this mother.

Mowinckel noted that people were saying, "Germany is arming." "Well!" replied the prime minister. "In the divine comedy by our immortal Ludvig Holberg about the unhappy Jeppe, we find this sentence: 'Everybody says that Jeppe drinks, but nobody asks *why* Jeppe drinks.'" Mowinckel was citing Holberg's *Jeppe på Bjerget*, or *Jeppe of the Hill* (a work from the early 1720s). The prime minister said, "Let us all who now complain that Germany also is arming look into our own consciences and ask *why* Germany is arming." And that, Mowinckel was saying, was because other nations were arming, or rearming: acting warlike.

In his lecture, the laureate, Henderson, claimed much the same thing. Nations were "preparing for war, although pledged to peace." And "perhaps the grimmest aspect of this great paradox is that the very nations that are chiefly responsible for starting and for maintaining the Disarmament Conference are also the nations that have begun a new arms race." Henderson went on to attack "the international anarchy of nationalism and the economic anarchy of competitive enterprise." He said, "I think we must get the better of both those forces and subordinate them to the common good through world union on the basis of social justice. I believe that the League of Nations and the International Labour Organization are the instruments to our hand for conceiving and executing such a policy."

And he had a question, followed by an answer:

Is it possible to stay halfway on the road that leads to total disarmament and the setting up of a League police force? If we contemplate as our ultimate end a League which controls the world's economic life and the world's armed forces, then we must say frankly that our ultimate ideal is the creation of nothing less than a World Commonwealth. I think we must make this admission. The establishment of a World Commonwealth is, in the long run, the only alternative to a relapse into a world war.

He added a few words about the Soviet Union, saying that, "in its international policy," it had "shown that it is devoted to peace, abhors war, and sincerely believes in the ideal of world union and world cooperation . . . ."

As these words indicate, Henderson was a warm supporter of the Soviet Union. Lenin, no less, had found him quite useful. During the Genoa Conference of 1922, which had to do with economic relations between West and East, Lenin wrote to his foreign-affairs commissar, Chicherin. He said, "Henderson is as stupid as Kerensky"—the Russian prime minister before Lenin's takeover—"and for this reason he is helping us." Lenin was looking for a way to wreck Genoa without being blamed for this eventuality. As the historian Richard Pipes writes in *The Unknown Lenin*, the Soviet boss wanted to prevent a rapprochement between the Allies and Germany at all costs, the better for Communism to penetrate Europe. He said, "The fool Henderson and Co. will help us a lot if we cleverly prod them."

Henderson died in 1935, the year after he won the peace prize. He represents the cast of mind that has often won the peace prize—right through to the present day. Disarmament has often been thought the key to peace. Armies have often been thought a goad to war, rather than a deterrent to it. It is true that, in his will, Alfred Nobel specified "the abolition or reduction of standing armies." Butler, a pillar of the Republican establishment in America, outlined a peace program after he won a share of the

1931 prize. It included the shrinking of armies to "police forces and skeletons of an emergency organization."

~

The committee reserved the prize for 1935—then, in 1936, made an important, nearly explosive announcement: The prize for '35 would go to Carl von Ossietzky. He was a German pacifist, and, as you have heard, a prisoner of the Nazis. His main work had been in journalism, but he had also been active in his country's peace movement: He was secretary of the German Peace Society, whose president was Ludwig Quidde. The slogan of the movement was *Nie wieder Krieg,* or "Never again war." During the Weimar period, Ossietzky warned in his writings that Germany was secretly rearming, in violation of the Versailles Treaty and Germany's own laws. He was arrested and imprisoned even before the Nazis came to power: He spent most of 1932 in jail. When the Nazis were ensconced, he was arrested again almost immediately: on February 28, 1933, the day after the Reichstag fire. He was sent first to prison and then to concentration camps.

He had had opportunities to flee the country, but, unlike others, he had declined those opportunities. He thought his dissent would be more effective within the country than outside it. Besides, he was a German, and he wanted a role in his country's national life. The authorities repeatedly asked him to sign a statement renouncing his principles. He refused. And he was tortured: A Red Cross official found him in a wretched, pulverized state—the state of a person who "had reached the uttermost limits of what can be borne."

His friends—German refugees—decided that he should have the Nobel Peace Prize, and they launched a campaign to this end. In his presentation speech, Chairman Stang said that no fewer than six previous winners had spoken for Ossietzky. Laureates in other fields did too, notably Einstein (who won the physics prize for 1921, you remember) and Thomas Mann (who won the literature prize for 1929). In Oslo, the young German émigré Willy Brandt—who would be West German chancellor and the peace laureate for 1971—pressed Ossietzky's case. The idea was threefold: to save the man's life; to embarrass the Nazis; and to honor "the other Germany"—the Germany that was neither Nazi nor belligerent.

Was the German government concerned that Ossietzky would win the peace prize? Oh, yes. The Germans warned the Norwegian government that, if Ossietzky got the prize, this development would be very bad for German-Norwegian relations. You have learned that, in the run-up to the Nobel announcement, two committee members resigned. They were Koht, the foreign minister, and Mowinckel, who had been prime minister three times, and was now an opposition leader. These resignations were meant to put distance between the Norwegian government and the Nobel Committee. It has been remarked that Mowinckel had no real need to resign, as he was no longer in government. But we can assume that he still would have been identified—by Berlin, for example—with the Norwegian state.

When the committee did indeed announce for Ossietzky, Goering tried to get the prisoner to refuse the prize. The prisoner did not. He refused to refuse. The Nazis did not allow him to go to Oslo.

For the first time ever, the Norwegian king did not attend the prize ceremony—to emphasize the distance between the government and the committee. Stang's speech touched on several subjects—including the role of journalists and journalism—and it was strikingly beautiful. He said,

> . . . many people ask, Has Ossietzky really contributed so
> much to peace? Has he not become a symbol of the struggle
> for peace rather than its champion?

In my opinion, this is not so. But even if it were, how great is the significance of the symbol in our life! In religion, in politics, in public affairs, in peace and war, we rally round symbols. We understand the power they hold over us. . . . The symbol certainly has its value. But Ossietzky is not just a symbol. He is something quite different and something much more. He is a deed; and he is a man.

Also, Stang made clear that Ossietzky was receiving the prize for his career-long pacifism, and not specifically for his stance against the present German government. Stang, too, emphasized distance:

If we look back upon all the men and women who have received the peace prize over the years, we find that they are of widely divergent personalities and views and that the lives of many of them were marked by passion, grief, and struggle. It is quite obvious that the Nobel Committee, in awarding the prize to these different personalities, has neither shared all the opinions which they held nor declared its solidarity with all of their work. The wish of the Nobel Committee has always been to fulfill its task and its obligation, namely, to reward work for peace—that and nothing else. And the Nobel Committee has been able to do so because it is totally independent. It is not answerable to anyone, nor do its decisions commit anyone other than itself.

In awarding this year's Nobel Peace Prize to Carl von Ossietzky, we are therefore recognizing his valuable contribution to the cause of peace—nothing more, and certainly nothing less.

The granting of the prize to Ossietzky did not turn the trick of freeing him. But the Germans made two concessions: During the campaign for Ossietzky, they transferred him from a camp to a prison hospital; after the prize was given to him, they transferred him to a private sanatorium. Even in this place, he was kept under 24-hour guard. Sick with tuberculosis, and suffering from the effects of torture and hard labor, he died in May 1938, at age 48.

I will remind you of two things that followed the award to Ossietzky. One of these happened in Germany, and the other in Norway. In Germany, the government forbade citizens to accept any Nobel prize, in any of the five fields. By way of compensation, the Nazis set up a national prize for "art and science." Two Nobel committees—the ones for chemistry and physiology or medicine—went ahead and gave prizes to Germans anyway. And in Norway, the Storting changed the rules so that never again would a person belong to both the government and the Nobel Committee. The potential for conflict of interest, went the thinking, was too great.

The committee in 1936 showed guts in honoring Ossietzky. They knew they would incur the wrath of the government in Berlin, a government growing ever more powerful and menacing. Norway had remained neutral in one world war, and was anxious to remain neutral in a second, if one were to come. After the committee made the decision for Ossietzky, other nations were cross with Norway, for rocking the boat, for provoking Germany. Wasn't the peace prize supposed to promote harmony instead of strife? The Swedes, in particular, were upset, because now Berlin was growling at them, too, not just at the Norwegians. As the peace prize was taboo for Germans, so were the "Swedish Nobels." Members of Alfred Nobel's own family spoke against the award to Ossietzky, claiming (unsustainably) that the testator would have disapproved.

Supreme guts, of course, were shown by Ossietzky, one of the most heroic and defiant spirits ever to get Nobel's peace prize.

When the committee announced the award for 1935, it announced the award for 1936 as well—an award that was overshadowed by the Ossietzky controversy. The award for 1936 went to Carlos Saavedra Lamas, the Argentinean foreign minister. I referred to Theodore Roosevelt's award as a "neat win": He settled a war one year, and won the prize the next. Saavedra Lamas's award was on the same line.

Born in 1878, he became the very image of the Latin American intellectual and diplomat. He was suave, aristocratic, well-rounded, urbane, effortlessly capable. He looked like a dashing film star. And he married a daughter of the president of the Republic. Saavedra Lamas was a law professor, and he became foreign minister in 1932. In that capacity, he fashioned or promoted several nonaggression treaties, and in 1936 he was elected president of the League of Nations Assembly. He was the first person outside Europe or the United States to win the Nobel Peace Prize. But he was hardly unknown in European or American circles.

He played the leading role in the mediation that led to an armistice in the Chaco War—a war that lasted from 1932 to 1935. The Chaco War pitted Bolivia and Paraguay over the Gran Chaco region, which was thought to contain oil. Today, few know about this war, at least beyond South America. And it can be presented as a kind of comic-opera affair. But 100,000 men lost their lives (even if the main killers were malaria and the lack of water). Saavedra Lamas angled for his Nobel prize, by the way: He asked the U.S. secretary of state, Cordell Hull, to nominate him, which he did.

Saavedra Lamas died in 1959. And to the Chaco War, there is a coda. In April 2009, Bolivia's president, Evo Morales, and Paraguay's president, Fernando Lugo, signed an accord resolving once and for all—or so it would seem—the countries' dispute over the Gran Chaco. As they celebrated the accord, they and other South American leaders said that the war had been the fault of foreign interests, namely oil companies, which had pushed the locals into war. That makes a good and comforting story anyway.

~

The 1937 winner? Formally speaking, he was Edgar Algernon Robert Gascoyne-Cecil, 1st Viscount Cecil of Chelwood. Less formally speaking, he was Robert Cecil. You will recall that he was one of those whom Nansen said deserved the award more than he. Cecil was almost synonymous with the League of Nations: with its workings, with its promotion. A jury that liked to honor the League, such as the one in Oslo, would surely get around to honoring Cecil.

He was born in 1864, a son of the 3rd marquess of Salisbury, who was a foreign secretary under Disraeli and then prime minister three times. Young Robert went to Eton and Oxford, thereafter to the law bar and Parliament. By the time the world war came, he was 50, and ineligible for military action. He joined the Red Cross, serving in an administrative role. Then he went into the British government.

The war, which made a deep impression on everyone, made a very deep impression on him. He thought it imperative to win. To fall short of total victory, he wrote during the war, would leave the world "at the mercy of the most arrogant and bloodiest tyranny that has ever been organized." He felt that Europe's civilization had been "murderously assaulted" and that there was no choice except to vanquish the "desperate enemy" of this civilization or *"perish in the effort."* But he hated what the war did. For two years, he was minister of blockade, and to inflict want on innocent civilians, no matter what the greater cause, is hard on conscience.

Once the war was over, he threw himself into an international system: a new system that would prevent the catastrophe of widespread war from ever occurring again. He was the principal author of the League's covenant. When the Assembly first met, in November 1920, he gave a maiden speech. He said, "Do not let us be afraid of our power"—the power to constrain individual nations. "Let us go on from strength to strength. It is not by doing too much that the League is in any danger." From then on, Cecil would serve the League, whether in an official capacity or by arguing for it to peoples across the world.

At the 1937 prize ceremony, Christian Lange gave the presentation speech. Cecil did not give his lecture until the following summer. He gave it in an English scarcely heard today: majestic and queerly accented, with boldly rolled r's. This is the English of a marquess's son born in the 1860s (you can hear it on a recording). Cecil began his lecture by offering a reply to his old friend Lange—who, in the presentation speech, had discussed the fact that Cecil had come from a privileged background, only to undergo a "conversion" that immersed him in the peace cause. Lange was quite snotty about this, actually. His tone was, *How remarkable that this pampered, imperial child should abandon his class to do something noble for humanity!* Here is Cecil:

> [Lange] was good enough to emphasize that at the time I began working for the League and for peace, I belonged to what he called an "old aristocratic and Conservative family," and he intimated [more than intimated] that he thought it added to my merit that, coming from such surroundings, I should have taken up the cause of peace. May I just say this: I was brought up from my earliest youth to believe in the enormous importance of peace. I have often heard my father, the late Lord Salisbury, say that, though he did not see how it was possible under the then existing circumstances to avoid wars altogether, yet he had never been able to satisfy himself that they were in principle morally defensible.

The laureate proceeded to quote his father at some length, and most interestingly. It added up to a rebuke of Lange's notions and presumptions.

Cecil's lecture was "The Future of Civilization," an audacious subject, but not unfitting for June 1938. He first wanted to look back, saying this about the League: "Almost all those engaged in the work at Geneva had personal knowledge of the vast slaughter and destruction which the war had produced." Militarism, he said, "had been stunned by the disasters which had been brought upon the world in the Great War. One saw not only the terrible suffering the war had caused, but also the fact that even the victors had gained little or no advantage." Is that not Norman Angellism? Inevitably, memories of the war faded: "That tremendous argument for peace, the horror of war, was a diminishing asset." And now militarism was again on the march.

"Do not let us underrate the danger," Cecil said. "It threatens everything we care for. For if it does succeed, it will not only bring us back to 1914—in itself bad enough—but to something far worse even than that." And a prime example of that "something far worse," said the laureate, was "the wholesale destruction of unfortified cities and their inhabitants." Civilian populations would be involved—would be hit—as never before. It was not too late to prevent a war, Cecil insisted. "In my view, it is quite certain that we can prevent it." He concluded his lecture with the prayer that statesmen work through "that great institution for the maintenance of peace on which the future of civilization so largely depends. I mean, of course, the League of Nations."

The League ceased to be in April 1946—and Cecil gave one of the last speeches there. That speech ended, "The League is dead. Long live the United Nations." Cecil lived on until 1958, dying at 94. He had been honorary president for life of the United Nations Association. Did Cecil and his fellow League men make a difference for peace—any positive difference at all? Lange, in that presentation speech, quoted a Danish poet (unnamed) who wrote of Sisyphus: "Not the deed fulfilled, but tireless exertion / Shall hear you, o Man, into the ranks of the Heroes." That Cecil and his like gave tireless exertion, there is no doubt.

~

Before the war came, the committee in Oslo gave a final award: a blast of appreciation to the League, to humanitarianism, and to the national and international hero, Nansen. When he died in 1930, the work of looking after refugees was not yet finished—it would never be finished. The League set up the Nansen International Office for Refugees. It was this institution that won the 1938 Nobel prize. The League gave the Nansen Office a mandate of eight years—it would expire on December 31, 1938 (a few weeks after the prize ceremony). The League would then have another and larger agency.

Making the presentation speech, Fredrik Stang said, "It is not only the Nansen Office that we should remember on this, its day of tribute. It was created by the League of Nations and supported by it, and at this time when many appear to be losing faith in the League, it is right and fitting to recall this fact." There was a Nobel lecture, given by the president of the expiring office, Michael Hansson—a Norwegian, despite his Swedish name. His was a beautiful, wise, and startling lecture, also a moving one. It has much to say to us today.

Like Nansen before him, Hansson described the lot of the stateless and homeless. "The refugee problem has, all in all, become the greatest social problem of our time," he said. Human beings "are driven out of one country like infested animals only to be thrown back again from another in which they had perforce to seek refuge." There was the problem of acceptance of refugees by states, and also of assimilation. The nature of America, he noted, "transforms most immigrants into 'Americans' within a relatively short period of time." Other countries had quite different natures.

Hansson spoke at length about a specific, present darkness: "Animosity toward the Jews is spreading like a plague over many countries, especially in southern and eastern Europe." Jews would eventually need a homeland of their own. Where it might be "does not really matter as long as they can be together on their own." He continued,

> How the Jews have suffered! What persecution and humiliation they have been forced to endure for so many centuries, as the result of the most sinister religious fanaticism! If they have acquired some faults and if they often seem uncongenial, it is not surprising. But it is nothing less than revolting nowadays to hear people, and especially those whose own records would not bear close examination, assert that the Jews are now paying for their wrongdoings of the past. One is tempted to ask: When will the Christians have to pay for theirs?

This prize ceremony took place on December 10, 1938. The next one, in the normal course of things, might well have taken place a year from that date. But the war came.

'Peace for Our Time,' for a Moment

I have quoted much apocalyptic talk from the years leading to World War II. Have just a little more such talk. Speaking at the 1926 prize ceremony—the one that honored Dawes and the Locarno ministers—Nansen said, "Even if the next war is no worse than the last, I believe it will destroy our European civilization. But of course the next war will not be like the last. It will be incomparably worse." It was. The second war was fought over several continents and left some 70 million dead. But Nansen and the others were wrong about one thing: The war did not destroy

European civilization, right? Between 1918 and 1939, people said constantly that Europe would not survive another war. But that was blessedly wrong, right? Yes, sure. But it was perhaps not entirely wrong. Half the continent would be ruled, for decades, by Moscow-dominated Communism. The other half would lose its place in the world, and, some argue, lose its confidence: its very civilizational confidence.

The Nobel Committee gave no award for 1939. There were nominations, however. For example, the British prime minister, Neville Chamberlain, was nominated by many people, including twelve members of the Swedish parliament, for the Munich Agreement. That was true, prize-worthy peacemaking, from a particular point of view. Chamberlain returned home from Germany and, standing outside No. 10 Downing Street, said, "I believe it is peace for our time"—"it" being the Munich Agreement. "And now I recommend you to go home and sleep quietly in your beds." Chamberlain's statement concerning "peace for our time" has led many to be skeptical upon hearing about "peace." The very assertion of "peace" makes some sleep less quietly in their beds.

Chamberlain was not the only signer of the Munich Agreement to be nominated for the peace prize. Hitler was nominated too, by a member of the Swedish parliament. That nomination was withdrawn.

Receiving several nominations for 1939 was Edvard Beneš, the Czechoslovakian president who had been forced into exile. One of those nominations came from a British parliamentarian, soon to be prime minister, Winston Churchill. The nomination was typical of the man—typical of Churchill. A Nobel Peace Prize to Beneš would have been a neat black eye to the Nazis and other enemies of the peace and freedom of the continent; it also might have served as a rebuke to misguided appeasers.

As you know, the Nazis invaded Norway in April 1940, and the members of the Nobel Committee were scattered. The Nobel

Institute itself was unmolested—because of its connection to the Nobel people in Sweden, a neutral country. In the years of the war, there were almost no peace nominations at all. And there were no awards for 1940, 1941, 1942, or 1943, as well as for 1939. In 1945, the committee—reassembled—was ready to present prizes again. That year, they presented one for 1944 and another for 1945.

∼

The prize for 1944 went to the International Committee of the Red Cross—just as the prize for 1917 went to it. For the penultimate year of each war, the Nobel Committee honored the ICRC. There were the usual grumbles after the 1944 award was announced—the grumbles that had accompanied the other Red Cross awards. (I am thinking of Dunant, as well as the organization.) Some asked, "Maybe an award for medicine, rather than peace?" In an acceptance speech, the ICRC's honorary president, Max Huber, addressed the critics:

> Although there seems to be a big difference between construc-
> tive peace and aid to war victims—indeed, in the eyes of some,
> an antagonism—there is this implicit and fundamental bond:
> Helping the victims of war is not the only objective set by the
> Red Cross; in giving aid, it serves another purpose no less
> important, that of rescuing in the dark storm of war the idea
> of human solidarity and respect for the dignity of every human
> being—precisely at a time when the real or alleged necessities
> of war push moral values into the background.

∼

The prize for 1945? Halvdan Koht nominated several wartime lead-ers, including Churchill and his foreign secretary Eden, Franklin Roosevelt and his secretary of state Hull, and Stalin and one of his diplomats, Litvinov. The winner was Cordell Hull—taking the prize primarily for his role in the creation of the United Nations. His president, FDR, called him no less than the "father" of the U.N. We might think of it this way: The 1944 prize was basically a repeat of the 1917 prize, and the 1945 prize was rather a repeat of the 1919 prize. After the first war, the committee honored Wilson, for the League of Nations; after the second war, the committee honored the American secretary of state, for the new League.

Hull was born in a log cabin in Tennessee, in 1871. He rose to be a congressman, a senator—and then secretary of state. Roosevelt asked him to serve right at the beginning of his presidency, which is to say, in 1933. He served almost to the end of that presidency, resigning in November 1944 because of illness. (FDR died in office in April 1945.) No one has ever served longer than Hull as secretary of state. He lived for more than a decade after his resignation—until 1955. It was in 1943, with the war still raging, that Hull drafted the U.N. Charter. He did so with his staff in the State Department. Once more would men set up an international body designed to prevent another world war. And this time, the United States would join.

Giving the presentation speeches in 1945 was a new committee chairman, Gunnar Jahn—an economist of the Liberal party, a Resistance leader during the war. In his speech for Hull, he cited and praised the laureate's fathering of the U.N., of course. But he spoke about much more than that. Hull had evidently not received the Nobel prize for the U.N. alone. Jahn spent some time on Hull's career-long devotion to lower tariffs and free trade, hailing him as "representative of all that is best in liberalism, a liberalism with a strong social implication." He also made a point of Hull's opposition to isolationism in foreign policy.

Then there was Hull's leading role in the Roosevelt administration's "good neighbor" policy: the policy aimed at bringing international harmony to the Americas. Such a policy played a role in another peace prize—the one to another secretary of state, in another Roosevelt administration: TR's Elihu Root. Hull had actually been nominated many times for the good-neighbor policy. FDR himself was one of those who had pressed his candidacy, although he did so behind the scenes, not even telling Hull himself. He thought it would be unseemly for a president to be an open lobbyist for his own secretary of state. But he made his feelings known to his ambassador in Oslo, instructing him to convey those feelings to the committee. The president said that Hull had been the "guiding spirit of the Inter-American contribution to world peace."

Hull was too ill to travel to Oslo in 1945. But he sent a message, read by the ambassador. Hull said, "There is no greater responsibility resting upon peoples and governments everywhere than to make sure that enduring peace will this time—at long last—be established *and maintained.*" He further said,

> I fully realize that the new organization is a human rather
> than a perfect instrumentality for the attainment of its great
> objective. As time goes on it will, I am sure, be improved.
> The Charter is sufficiently flexible to provide for growth and
> development, in the light of experience and performance, but I
> am firmly convinced that with all its imperfections the United
> Nations Organization offers the peace-loving nations of the
> world, now, a fully workable mechanism which will give them
> peace, if they want peace.

The "crucial test," he observed, was whether men had "suffered enough" and "learned enough" to put aside their differences and unite in the common interest of peace. As it had awarded the League—and the Inter-Parliamentary Union before that—the Nobel Committee in Norway would continually award the U.N.

~

The 1946 award was like the 1931 award: divided between two Americans. They were not U.N. people, but they had labored long in international vineyards. The 1946 laureates were Emily Greene Balch, a colleague of one of the '31 laureates, Jane Addams, and John R. Mott, the leader of the YMCA—a movement and network that Henry Dunant helped to launch.

Balch was much like Addams: a social reformer, an intellectual, a pacifist, a whirlwind. She was born in 1867 into an old New England family. She was a member of the first graduating class at Bryn Mawr College: They received their diplomas in 1889. She became a professor herself, teaching economics and sociology at Wellesley College. But peacework claimed much of her attention. She converted to Quakerism, and pacifism was a calling. With Addams, she was involved in the Woman's Peace party and, shortly after, the Women's International League for Peace and Freedom. When Addams was president of that organization, Balch was secretary-treasurer. She later became honorary president of the WILPF, after Addams died.

Like Addams, she opposed American participation in World War I. On this basis, Wellesley declined to renew her contract. She then joined the staff of *The Nation* magazine in New York. Twenty or so years later, when the second war came, she changed her mind, breaking with the "pure," or "absolute," pacifists: and backing the fight against Hitler and his like. As Chairman Jahn put it in his presentation speech, "She had to ask herself the question which faced all those who had worked for peace: Shall we submit meekly and allow ourselves to be devoured?"

Balch, who received the Nobel prize at 79, lived to 94. Jahn quoted a remark she had made on the occasion of her 75th birthday: "My grandfather used to say, an old woman is as tough as a boiled owl."

She was a brilliant woman, Balch, and her Nobel lecture shows it. It is a sweeping assessment of the world situation entitled "Toward Human Unity, or Beyond Nationalism." She gave a staunch defense of conscientious objectors, though she herself, of course, had supported the war against fascism. And she issued a blast against conscription. Also, she pitched for perhaps the ultimate cause, "actual world government," to use her words. About Soviet Communism, she was not so much brilliant as absurd. She said in her lecture that both Lincoln and Lenin were democrats, committed to reducing "inequities and inequalities," though in different ways. And she was pleased to note something about this mid-Forties period:

> . . . men are everywhere becoming less "private-minded."
> There is a growing community sense. . . . In the political field
> this consciousness of the common interest and of the rich
> possibilities of common action has embodied itself in part in
> the great movements toward economic democracy, coopera-
> tion, democratic socialism, and communism. I am sure we
> make a great mistake if we underrate the element of unselfish
> idealism in these historic movements which are today writing
> history at such a rate.

John R. Mott was a different sort, and certainly no less impressive. He was the second religious figure to win the Nobel prize, after Archbishop Söderblom. Unlike that distinguished Swede, however, he was not a cleric, but a layman. Mott wore a number of hats: evangelist, executive, humanitarian. He was also an advocate of ecumenism (as was Söderblom). Moreover, he did all he could to bring black and white together in America. Speaking for the Nobel Committee, Herman Smitt Ingebretsen said of Mott,

"He has never been a politician, he has never taken an active part in organized peace work. But he has always been a living force, a tireless fighter in the service of Christ, opening young minds to the light which he thinks can lead the world to peace and bring men together in understanding and goodwill."

The laureate was born in Livingston Manor, New York, in 1865. He spent his entire career with the YMCA. President Wilson asked him to be ambassador to China, but he demurred, believing that his place was with the YMCA. Later in the Wilson administration, he took part in a delegation to Mexico, and also to Russia. This latter was the delegation led by the 1912 laureate, Root. The former secretary of state said of Mott, "His powerful personality and completely self-sacrificing devotion to the cause of peace have, I believe, never been equaled." In the two world wars, Mott and the YMCA did much humanitarian work, particularly for prisoners of war.

He wrote 16 books and traveled incessantly. As Nicholas Murray Butler crossed the Atlantic more than 100 times, so did Mott. He also crossed the Pacific 14 times. For a half-century, he averaged 34 days a year on the ocean. He was 81 when he received the peace prize, and would live to 89. A sense of the man can be had in the titles of two books about him: *Layman Extraordinary* and *World Citizen*.

As the 1946 prize was divided, so was the committee: It was a fractious year. There was a campaign to get the prize for Alexandra Kollontay, who had been the Soviet ambassador to Sweden from 1930 through the war. Prior to that, she had been the Soviets' ambassador to Norway. She was appointed to that position in 1923—and is commonly called the world's first female ambassador. The United States did not have a female ambassador until 1933, when FDR sent Ruth Bryan Rhodes to another Scandinavian state (as it happens), Denmark. More generally, Kollontay was a kind of moll of the Bolshevik Revolution: a Soviet It girl, a glamour puss, an advocate of "free love" and the smashing of bourgeois conventions.

In any case, she was nominated for the '46 prize by many people, especially in the parliaments of Sweden, Norway, and Finland. Her backers credited her with forging a peace between the Soviet Union and Finland.

She had a champion on the committee: Martin Tranmæl, of the Labor party. He had been friendly toward Moscow from the beginning, i.e., since 1917. Tranmæl and Jahn opposed Mott, but were agreeable on Balch. Jahn, who was chairman, remember, refused to give the presentation speech for Mott, which was why Smitt Ingebretsen did so. Tranmæl edited *Arbeiderbladet*, the Labor newspaper. (The name literally means that.) In an editorial, the paper lamented that Mott had won and that Kollontay had not. In all likelihood, Kollontay came closer than any other Soviet official ever did to winning the Nobel Peace Prize—until 1990, when the general secretary himself, Gorbachev, won it. In later years, incidentally, Martin Tranmæl became firmly anti-Communist.

∼

In 1947 came the turn of the Quakers—of the relief organization in London, the Friends Service Council, and the relief organization in Philadelphia, the American Friends Service Committee. They were joint winners of the prize. As I mentioned in the earlier discussion of peace and its meaning, these groups had performed humanitarian work during the war and were now helping to rebuild Europe. This, according to the Nobel Committee, was a great blow for peace.

Speaking in Oslo for the London group was its chairman, Margaret A. Backhouse. And speaking for the Philadelphia group was its own chairman, Henry Joel Cadbury. He was a divinity professor at Harvard. Along with some fellow Quakers, he set up the American Friends Service Committee when the United States entered World War I. These founders wanted young Quaker men, and others who would not carry arms, to have "a service of love in wartime."

Cadbury began his lecture by noting that Quakers were once persecuted in Norway, leading them to seek refuge in America. "Today," he told the assemblage, "you have atoned for that persecution of the Quakers." He then lectured in a thoughtful, searching way about some big questions: having to do with war, peace, and pacifism. Emily Greene Balch may have been for the second war, but Cadbury was evidently a pacifist of a different kind—a more absolute, less yielding kind. Quakers "have been met with the argument that war is the lesser of two evils," he said. "I will not admit the validity of that argument. We have heard time and time again for over 300 years that 'this war is different,' that this time it really is for a purpose which was not successful in the last war. In thinking this over, we have mostly learned that war could have been prevented." Cleverly, almost mischievously, he quoted a statement made by President Roosevelt in 1936 (three years before the war, and five years before America's entry into it): "We can keep out of war if those who watch and decide . . . make certain that the small decisions of each day do not lead toward war and if at the same time they possess the courage to say no to those who selfishly or unwisely would let us go to war."

We see that the Nobel Committee has given its prize to a diversity of people—even in a short span, such as the three years from 1945 to 1947. The prize went to former secretary of state Hull, who was hardly against fighting the war; to Balch, a pacifist who drew the line at refusing to fight the Nazis; and to Quakers who were committed to pacifism come what may.

In his acceptance speech—given two days before his Nobel lecture—Cadbury spoke of a new war that was developing, a "cold war":

All Europe is rightly anxious about the relations between the United States and the Soviet Union. Here is a place where you can help. Norway, your well-loved country, and the other nations of Europe must be the bridge of understanding. You must not take sides with either of us, you must help both of us cooperate.

That must have rung very sweetly in Norwegian ears, because that accorded with Norway's sense of itself: a bridge, a neutral, an arbiter, a peacemaker. But this little northern country found it prudent to take sides after the second war: In April 1949, it would join the new North Atlantic Treaty Organization. If you're going to be the moral arbiter of the world, better—far safer—to be that under American military protection.

In 1948, the Nobel Committee declined to give an award. And thereby hangs a tale, maybe two . . .

 INTERLUDES

THE COMMITTEE AND THE KREMLIN, A DOLLOP OF HISTORY

Why was there no Nobel Peace Prize for 1948? Chairman Jahn announced, late in the year, that "there was no suitable living candidate." That did not please Josef Stalin. You remember that he was nominated in 1945, by Halvdan Koht. He was also nominated in 1948—by a professor in Prague. Stalin's foreign minister, Molotov, was nominated too—by professors in Bucharest. "No suitable living candidate"?

Even before 1948, the Kremlin had been growing cross at the Nobel Committee of the Norwegian Storting. Olav Njølstad, the research director of the Norwegian Nobel Institute, has observed that the term "peace prize" started to appear in quotation marks in Soviet communications. (This observation comes in Njølstad's essay "The Nobel Peace Prize: Revelations from the Soviet Past.") For years, probably from the beginning, people unhappy with the committee's choices have put "peace prize" in quotation marks— "sneer quotes," they're called. The sneerers have included critics left, right, and center. (They have even included me.)

The Kremlin was unhappy when Alexandra Kollontay failed to win in 1946. The Kremlin was unhappier, of course, when the boss failed to win in 1948. Stalin was not used to failing. He was not used to being denied. And he was in a position to do something about this insult. Just as Hitler had created his own prize after Oslo's award to his prisoner Ossietzky, Stalin created his own prize after being snubbed by Oslo, or allowed it to be created. We have discussed this prize before: the Stalin Peace Prize, or, formally, the International Stalin Prize for Strengthening Peace among Peoples. The award was born in 1949, part of the dictator's 70th-birthday celebrations. (Never mind that Stalin's actual 70th birthday was in 1948.) In later years, when the Kremlin was erasing the name "Stalin," the prize was rechristened the Lenin Peace Prize, or the International Lenin Prize for Strengthening Peace among Peoples.

Lenin's name on a peace prize is no less obnoxious than Stalin's name on a peace prize. But we can say this: Both men stood for a certain kind of peace—the kind of peace, or "peace," that comes from an individual's absolute submission to the party and state.

Until the end of the Soviet Union, the Stalin or Lenin Peace Prize was given to a host of international glitterati, either Communists or pro-Communists, in any case loyal friends of the Soviet Union. One of the earliest winners was Paul Robeson, the famous American singer, actor, and activist. Accepting the award, he said, "We must join with the tens of millions all over the world who see in peace our most sacred responsibility." He extolled the "heroic efforts of the friendly peoples in Poland, Czechoslovakia, Hungary, Albania, Romania, Bulgaria, great, new China, and North Korea" (this was before the Sino–Soviet split). He vowed to answer "the endless falsehoods of the warmongering press," which was blackening the Soviet Union's good name. And he said,

... we can make clear what co-existence means. It means living in peace and friendship with another kind of society—
a fully integrated society where the people control their desti-
nies, where poverty and illiteracy have been eliminated, and
where new kinds of human beings develop in the framework
of a new level of social living.

That was how the most fervent and most deluded admirers of
the Soviet Union talked. And you recall what the novelist Howard
Fast said, on receiving the Stalin Peace Prize: "If I had no other
cause for honoring the Soviet Union, I would honor it greatly and
profoundly for giving prizes for peace." Allow me to mention
once more that the Soviet state killed some 20 million people, in
addition to stunting and wrecking the lives of countless millions
more.

Other winners of the Stalin or Lenin Peace Prize included
Pablo Neruda, Bertolt Brecht, Khrushchev (who may well have had
friends on the jury), Castro, Picasso, Brezhnev (again, friends),
Angela Davis, and Miguel d'Escoto. Davis was the renowned
American Communist and campus darling; d'Escoto was the Sandinista foreign minister in Nicaragua, and years later the president of the U.N. General Assembly.

Were there Nobel peace laureates who were also Stalin-Lenin
laureates? There were: three of them. Linus Pauling won the
Nobel Peace Prize for 1962; he accepted the Lenin Peace Prize at
the Soviet embassy in Washington in 1970. Seán MacBride won
half the Nobel prize in 1974; he received the Lenin Peace Prize
three years later. Nelson Mandela was the very last winner of the
Lenin Peace Prize—it was conferred on him in 1990. He shared
the Nobel prize in 1993. It was not until 2002, twelve years after
the Soviet government honored him, that he gave a speech accepting the Lenin Peace Prize. He did so at the Russian embassy in

Pretoria. And, reflecting on his days in the anti-apartheid struggle, he said,

> The world has changed since then, and the Soviet Union and
> the other then-existing socialist states of Eastern Europe have
> disappeared. It is not for us to lament developments that the
> people of those countries wished for and welcomed. Neither is
> it for us, however, to deny the value of the support we received
> from those countries or to mask the immense appreciation we
> had for those countries.

He concluded, "I thank you for the honor of awarding me a prize
in the name of a revolutionary that history will never be able to forget." It is undoubtedly true that history will never forget the name
of Lenin—or the name of Stalin. I might add that Cyrus Eaton
won the Soviets' peace prize. He was the Canadian-American steel
magnate (1883–1979) who established the Pugwash Conferences,
the anti-nuclear meetings that were honored by the Norwegian
Nobel Committee in 1995. We will find out more about all of these
laureates, of course, later in this book.

Back in the late 1940s, the Kremlin began to snub the Nobel
Committee, just as the committee had snubbed Stalin et al., from
the Soviets' point of view. Every year, the committee invited the
Kremlin to submit nominations; every year, the Kremlin ignored
this invitation. But in the first month of 1960, something funny
happened: Khrushchev got it into his head that he should win the
Nobel Peace Prize. He took steps toward this end. He further got
it into his head that he and President Eisenhower should win the
prize jointly—and took steps toward this end, too. He never won
the prize, by himself or with Ike.

The first citizen of the Soviet Union to win the Nobel Peace
Prize was Sakharov, the physicist, dissident, and hero. That was
in 1975. The Kremlin did everything it could to block this award.

And, in the ensuing years, the Kremlin was in an anti-Nobel mood, understandably. But its mood lightened in 1985, when the Nobel Committee gave the prize to a group called International Physicians for the Prevention of Nuclear War. Its co-founder and co-chairman was Evgeny Chazov, the "Kremlin doctor," as he was known, and a member of the Central Committee of the Soviet Communist Party. (The Central Committee was never well known as a peace organization.) Chazov and his American counterpart, Dr. Bernard Lown, gave Nobel lectures. Chazov held—holds—the distinction of signing the document that launched the official campaign of persecution against Sakharov. The relation of the Nobel Committee to the Soviet Union—its officials and victims—was strange. The last Soviet to receive the Nobel Peace Prize was the last general secretary, Gorbachev. That was in 1990, a year before the Soviet Union was no more.

GANDHI AND OTHER MISSING LAUREATES

Chairman Jahn's statement at the end of 1948, that "there was no suitable living candidate," was rather peculiar. What did he mean? He may well have been making a specific allusion, to a man who had died—been killed, actually—at the beginning of the year. Certainly his statement was interpreted as alluding to a particular man. And his name was mentioned, as it happened, by both 1946 laureates, in their Nobel lectures. John R. Mott of the YMCA said,

> The most trustworthy leader is one who adopts and applies
> guiding principles. He trusts them like the North Star. He
> follows his principles no matter how many oppose him and
> no matter how few go with him. This has been the real secret
> of the wonderful leadership of Mahatma Gandhi. In the midst
> of most bewildering conditions he has followed, cost what it
> might, the guiding principles of non-violence, religious unity,
> removal of untouchability, and economic independence.

Emily Greene Balch delivered her lecture late, on April 7, 1948, a little more than two months after Gandhi was murdered. She said, "The most dramatic exponent of [a] refusal of violence is the great-souled Indian Gandhi." (The literal meaning of "mahatma" is "great-souled.") "He gave his life trying to find ways to oppose domination and coercion without resort to hate or violence."

Gandhi is almost surely the outstanding peace figure of the 20th century—that is, the person most identified with peace and peaceableness and peaceful change. Øyvind Tønnesson, a previously cited expert on the Nobel Peace Prize, penned an essay entitled "Mahatma Gandhi, the Missing Laureate." A committee chairman giving the presentation speech in 2000 said, simply, that Gandhi "did not receive the prize" but "deserved it." People often want to know why Gandhi did not receive this most famous of all peace prizes. And there is an answer, in several parts.

He was nominated many times: in 1937, 1938, 1939, 1947, and 1948. (He was killed on January 30, two days before nominations were due.) Three times, he made the shortlist: in 1937, 1947, and 1948. (In that final year, the committee mulled whether to give him the award posthumously.) So, why did the committee shrink from awarding Gandhi? It is well to remember that, in life, he was not necessarily the universally admired and beloved figure he is now. Some people had doubts about him, and that included people in what we might broadly term the peace movement. Did his campaigns and demonstrations not sometimes lead to violence, no matter what the Mahatma's intentions? Was he not, first and foremost, an Indian nationalist?

In the summer of 1947, British India was being partitioned, and brutally, bloodily so. The committee faced a dilemma: If they gave the prize to Gandhi, they could be seen as favoring India and Hindus over Pakistan and Muslims. They could be seen as taking sides. The Subcontinent was a battleground in the latter part of that year. We know from Gunnar Jahn's diary that two committeemen wanted to give the prize to Gandhi. They were a Conservative and a Liberal, both conscientious Christians: Herman Smitt Ingebretsen and Christian Oftedal. The year before, these two had argued for Mott, and won. This time, however, they were unsuccessful: None of the other members could be persuaded about Gandhi. And the 1947 prize, as you know, went to the Quaker relief groups.

Jahn recorded in his diary what he had said to his colleagues: "While it is true that [Gandhi] is the greatest personality among the nominees—plenty of good things could be said about him— we should remember that he is not only an apostle for peace; he is first and foremost a patriot.... Moreover, we have to bear in mind that Gandhi is not naive. He is an excellent jurist and a lawyer."

We might chuckle at the implication that naivety is an asset for a Nobel peace candidate.

In 1948, when Gandhi was murdered, the great question became, Should we give him the award posthumously? No award had ever been given to a deceased person. And the committee concluded that it should not break precedent now. Jahn wrote in his diary, "To me it seems beyond doubt that a posthumous award would be contrary to the intentions of the testator." Nobel wanted his prizes to go to people who would use the money to continue their good works. So, the committee, through Jahn, announced to the world that "there was no suitable living candidate." Some hold that the 1948 prize, never given, is truly Gandhi's prize: a sort of unofficial, understood, silent prize. (The committee would give a posthumous prize just once, you remember: to Dag Hammarskjöld, in 1961.)

Over the years, some people have speculated that the Nobel Committee withheld the prize from Gandhi because it did not want to offend the British, Gandhi's opponent and Norway's great helper during the war. There is no evidence that this was the case. It seems likely that the committee did not feel comfortable giving Gandhi the award before 1948—and then, of course, in the committee's view, it was too late.

In 1989, the Dalai Lama, Tibet's spiritual and political leader, won the peace prize. And the committee chairman said, "It would be natural to compare him with Mahatma Gandhi, one of this century's greatest protagonists of peace, and the Dalai Lama likes to consider himself one of Gandhi's successors. People have occasionally wondered why Gandhi himself was never awarded the Nobel Peace Prize, and the present Nobel Committee can with impunity share this surprise, while regarding this year's award of the prize as in part a tribute to the memory of Mahatma Gandhi."

Nobel people tend to be a little embarrassed that Gandhi never won the prize, and critics of the whole Nobel enterprise like to hold Gandhi's non-win against it. "If the Nobel Peace Prize is so great or important," they say, "how come Gandhi never won it?" We might bear in mind, however, that Gandhi did not exactly need the prize. His fame and legacy are large without it. He is bigger than the prize, unlike some of the winners, whose status comes from having won.

There have been other "missing laureates," though maybe none so glaring as Gandhi. Shall we run through a few? Everyone can make his own list, detailing his own favorites (and airing his own grievances). In the first decade of the prize, Tolstoy was nominated several times. He had become a peace visionary. Also nominated and not winning was Andrew Carnegie, the money behind so many peace endeavors. Some of his associates won— Root, Butler—but not Carnegie himself. Herbert Hoover was nominated many times, for his relief efforts during World War I and after. "He fed Europe," people used to say, and there was truth to the statement. In his Nobel lecture of 1922, Nansen praised Hoover and his countrymen to the skies:

> I must . . . mention the gigantic task performed by the Americans under the remarkable leadership of Hoover. It was begun during the war with the Belgian Relief . . . . After the war, it was extended to Central Europe, where hundreds of thousands of children were given new hope by the invaluable aid from the Americans, and finally, but not least, to Russia. When the whole story of this work is written, it will take pride of place as a glorious page in the annals of mankind, and its charity will shine like a brilliant star in a long and dark night.

After World War II, President Truman sent the former president, Hoover, to Germany, to assess the food situation there. (It was very grim.) Former secretary of state Cordell Hull, the year after he won the peace prize, which is to say, in 1946, nominated

Hoover for the prize. That was an example of "reaching across the aisle," so to speak, for Hull was a Democrat and Hoover a Republican. Incidentally, Hoover wrote a book about another former president—and a Nobel peace laureate: Wilson. That was *The Ordeal of Woodrow Wilson*, written in 1958, when Hoover was 84.

Many times nominated was Lord Baden-Powell, the founder of the Boy Scouts. Another frequent nominee was Baron de Coubertin, the founder of the modern Olympic Games. Raoul Wallenberg was heavily nominated in 1948 (the "Gandhi year"). He was the Swedish businessman and diplomat who rescued thousands of Hungarian Jews during the war. When the Soviets reached Hungary, they captured Wallenberg, and that was the end of him. He died at their hands, in what year we don't quite know for sure. Jean Monnet, the French political economist and diplomat, was a possible peace laureate for his role in the rebuilding of Europe. Eleanor Roosevelt won many a prize—including the first Nansen Medal (more about that later)—but not the Nobel. And I previously mentioned Frank N. D. Buchman, the American evangelist who led the Moral Re-Armament movement. Very few must have been nominated so many times without winning.

There are more missing laureates, of course—and we will list some of them later in this book, in another interlude. But now, back to our parading.

A PARADE OF LAUREATES,
1949 *to* 1969

In 1949, the Nobel Committee found, to borrow a phrase, a
"suitable living candidate," and he was an offbeat choice—
offbeat for a laureate at that point in Nobel history. Later, such
a peace laureate would be seen as conventional. The committee
choice in 1949 was John Boyd Orr, the first director-general of the
Food and Agriculture Organization, a branch of the new United
Nations. Presenting the prize, Gunnar Jahn cited the Atlantic
Charter, that 1941 document worked out between Churchill and
FDR. The charter called for, among other things, "freedom from
want."

Boyd Orr was a scientist—a specialist in agriculture, diet, and
nutrition. He was born a Scottish farm boy in 1880. In 1935, he
became Sir John. In 1949, the year of his Nobel prize, he became
Baron Boyd Orr of Brechin Mearns. He was a public man as well
as a scientist: a parliamentarian; head of the FAO, of course; the
president of the World Union of Peace Organizations; the president of the World Movement for World Federal Government. I
have called him an offbeat laureate, which he was; but he was
also, as you can see, a natural and typical one.

Lecturing in Oslo, he said that "most" wars had had "an economic basis: the conquest of foreign territory in the interest of trade, or of land with rich agricultural or other resources." He further said that "the control of oil-bearing land" had become "an important factor in the foreign policy of some governments." This was only in 1949, remember. Oil would loom much larger in future years. Boyd Orr summed up his general view rather pithily, in a sentence: "World peace must be based on world plenty."

He was a man who spoke and wrote with considerable flair. We have a recording of his lecture, given in a sonorous, burry English. Have a paragraph that provides a flavor—a further flavor—of the laureate:

> Mr. Henry Wallace, the former vice president of the United
> States, was caricatured as saying that the job of the United
> Nations was to give every Hottentot mother a pint of milk
> a day. That indeed would be in accordance with the highest
> ideal of a World Government. When the time comes that so-
> called Christian nations are prepared to recognize the com-
> mon brotherhood of man and follow the example of the great
> Prince of Peace in feeding the hungry, relieving misery and
> disease, there will be such a new spirit in the world that the
> very thought of war would be abhorrent.

Boyd Orr, in common with other laureates, thought that the world was in a "great transition phase," moving from the old order of nation-states, with its competition and wars, to world government, which would rein in the bad tribal and national passions of men. "As we have seen," he said, "the wireless and the airplane have made the world so small and nations so dependent on each other that the only alternative to war is the United States of the World."

In this lecture, he stood on a middle ground between the Free West and the Soviet Union—the ground that so many peace laureates, during the Cold War years, were proud to occupy. Boyd Orr said that both sides had much to learn. "Let our communist friends admit that the worst evils of a ruthless capitalism, which Karl Marx saw in England and rightly hated, have disappeared." And the West should "give full credit to what the U.S.S.R. has done against appalling difficulties, including the hostility of capitalist countries, in its great expansion of technical education, in its public-health work in some aspects of which it seems to be in advance of almost any country, and in its astonishing agricultural and industrial development." Who knew that the Soviet Union was such a success? Certainly not those living in it. Boyd Orr pleaded for a "new generous sympathetic approach" to Stalin's Russia.

Despite some foolish views, Boyd Orr was a seriously accomplished and able man. He died in his native Scotland in 1971, age 90. The year before, there was another award like his in '49: to the great agronomist Borlaug. By the way, Nobel laureates have the right to nominate others, and Boyd Orr exercised his in an unusual fashion: Twice, he nominated for the Nobel Peace Prize the Edinburgh Festival Society, for its furtherance of "international understanding through music festivals."

$\sim$

As in 1949, the 1950 award went to a U.N. man, but this time the issue wasn't food: It was the Middle East. The laureate was Ralph Bunche, the American who served the U.N. as an envoy. He had negotiated a series of armistice agreements between Arab states and Israel. And he was one of the most talented and remarkable men we will encounter.

He was born in Detroit, in either 1903 or 1904—the year is uncertain. His parents, both of them, died when he was about

13. He was raised principally by his grandmother, and he spent his teenage years in Los Angeles. In high school, he was a sports star and the class valedictorian. Afterward, he went to UCLA—the University of California at Los Angeles—on a basketball scholarship. There too, he was a sports star and the class valedictorian. This is so unusual, it flirts with the unique. And to make these accomplishments even more unusual: We are talking about a young black man in the 1910s and '20s. From UCLA, Bunche proceeded across the country to Harvard, where he would earn two graduate degrees. He was the first black person in America to earn a Ph.D. in political science.

At the beginning of his career, Bunche tended to the radical in his views. He was a founder of the National Negro Congress, a Popular Front organization. He was not a Communist, however, and did not want to belong to a group controlled by Communists, which the NNC was. So he left. He worked with Gunnar Myrdal, the Swedish scholar who, under the auspices of the Carnegie Corporation—another of that benefactor's many projects—studied race relations in America. This studying resulted in the 1944 classic *An American Dilemma*. Myrdal's wife, Alva, would become a Nobel peace laureate in 1982.

When the U.S. entered World War II, Bunche joined American intelligence, and eventually the State Department. After the war, Trygve Lie asked him to work for the U.N.—and he found himself in the Middle East, a tinderbox then, a tinderbox for decades to come. Recall the central events: In November 1947, the U.N. offered a partition of Palestine: one state for the Jews, one state for the Arabs. The Jews accepted, the Arabs did not. When the Jews declared their state in May 1948, a cluster of Arab states declared war. The U.N. appointed a chief mediator, Count Folke Bernadotte of Sweden; Bunche was his top lieutenant. Jahn, in his 1950 presentation speech, said that the two men "could hardly have been more unlike. On the one hand, Folke Bernadotte, grandson of King Oscar II of Sweden and nephew of Sweden's reigning monarch, steeped in all the traditions of a royal family; on the other, Bunche, whose grandmother had been born in slavery . . . ." On September 17, 1948, Bernadotte was murdered—murdered by the extremists of Israel's Stern Gang. (The country immediately banned that organization.) Bunche bravely took over as chief mediator.

On the isle of Rhodes, a suitable distance from the theater of war, he conducted negotiations between Israel and four Arab states, separately: Egypt, Lebanon, Jordan, and Syria. By late July 1949, armistice agreements had been concluded with all. Asked to explain his success (however temporary), Bunche said,

> Like every Negro in America, I've been buffeted about a great deal. I've suffered many disillusioning experiences. Inevitably, I've become allergic to prejudice. On the other hand, from my earliest years I was taught the virtues of tolerance; militancy in fighting for rights—but not bitterness. And as a social scientist I've always cultivated a coolness of temper, an attitude of objectivity when dealing with human sensitivities and irrationalities, which has always proved invaluable—never more so than in the Palestine negotiations. Success there was dependent upon maintaining complete objectivity.

On his return to New York, Bunche was given a ticker-tape parade. Los Angeles did its part too, declaring "Ralph Bunche Day."

And the following year, he won the Nobel Peace Prize. This was another of those neat wins: Clear peacework in one year was honored the next, just as the testator envisioned (and instructed, really). Bunche was nominated by two Norwegians, two members of the Storting, who had close ties to the U.N. They thought a prize to Bunche would "express trust and faith in the ability of the United Nations to solve international disputes by way of mediation between the parties." (I am quoting the Norwegians themselves.) They also thought that "giving the Nobel Peace Prize to a member of the colored race" would be "a boost to peace in itself." Bunche was the first black person to win the prize; he was, indeed, the first non-white person.

In his acceptance speech, he said, "I am but one of many cogs in the United Nations, the greatest peace organization ever dedicated to the salvation of mankind's future on earth." In his subsequent lecture, he said that the U.N. "is but a cross section of the world's peoples." Some years later, Aleksandr Solzhenitsyn, the Russian writer, would make a contradictory point. The U.N. is not really the united nations or peoples, he said. It is the assembled governments or regimes. Some of these governments exist by popular consent, some are dictatorships—boots stomping on the peoples' faces. The U.N. itself is only as good as the governments or regimes that compose it.

In his Nobel lecture, Bunche also said something I have mentioned before—and that Jimmy Carter would mention in his own Nobel lecture, in 2002:

> There are some in the world who are prematurely resigned
> to the inevitability of war. Among them are the advocates of
> the so-called "preventive war," who, in their resignation to
> war, wish merely to select their own time for initiating it. To
> suggest that war can prevent war is a base play on words and a
> despicable form of warmongering.

The issue of preventive or preemptive war is less simple than Bunche said. A later American foreign-policy figure, George Shultz, secretary of state under Reagan, would make an analogy to a rattlesnake in your backyard: Do you kill it before it has its jaws around your child, or do you hope it will slink off harmlessly? And how long do you wait before making a decision? In any case, few would have contradicted Bunche that day at the University of Oslo.

He was one of the youngest people ever to win the peace prize: 46 or 47. In fact, he was the first laureate to have been born in the 20th century. He lived until 1971 (same as Boyd Orr, who had been born almost a quarter-century before Bunche). As I write now, in the second decade of the 21st century, the issue of negotiations between Arabs and Israelis is prominent in the headlines. The armistices of 1949 were supposed to be the basis "for a permanent peace" (to use Bunche's words). They were anything but. They were rocked, blown up, in later wars. But in 1978, Sadat and Begin signed the Camp David Accords, leading to peace between Egypt and Israel. They signed the accords on September 17, which, for those interested in historical coincidences, was 30 years to the day after Bernadotte's assassination. In 1994, Jordan, in the person of King Hussein, became the second Arab state to make peace with Israel. So far, there have been no others. And Israel's right to exist is contested throughout the Middle East.

In 1949, Bunche said, "I have a bias in favor of both Arabs and Jews in the sense that I believe that both are good, honorable, and essentially peace-loving peoples, and are therefore as capable of making peace as of waging war."

～

The 1951 award was like a couple of previous awards: the one in 1903 to Randal Cremer and the one in 1934 to Arthur Henderson. It went to a labor leader and peace warrior. The 1951 laureate was not British, however, like his predecessors: He was French, the dean of the French labor movement, Léon Jouhaux. This man was always in and around events. He took part in the Paris Peace Conference. He joined with the American Samuel Gompers to set up the International Labour Organization. He was active in the League, naturally, and later in the U.N. One of his great passions, along with trade unionism, was disarmament. In his Nobel lecture, he recalled that the League's disarmament efforts failed miserably. "All the same," he said, "I cannot forget the first sessions of the Conference for the Limitation and Reduction of Armaments. Those early days of February 1932 were days of hope for humanity. Millions confidently awaited the results of the proceedings of this conference, which was presided over by that veteran militant Labourite Henderson . . . ."

Jouhaux was a man of the Left—a veteran militant himself—but he was not a Communist. Through his decades as a labor leader, he sometimes worked with Communists, sometimes not: most often not. He split off from the World Federation of Trade Unions when Communist control was absolute. An internal Soviet memorandum on the Nobel Peace Prize dismissed him as "a well-known traitor to the workers' interests"—a high compliment, considering the source.

Jouhaux was 72 when he received the peace prize. He had lived a dramatic life, from worker days in a match factory, through one world war, through another. During the second, he was in the Resistance, and fell into Nazi hands. He was imprisoned in Buchenwald, among other places. He lectured in Oslo in a grand, gravelly voice—a voice obviously long accustomed to public speaking, exhortation, and reflection. (I think of him as kind of a trade-union de Gaulle.) At the beginning of his speech, he confided that, the night he learned of his Nobel victory, he couldn't sleep. *Le grand Léon* died three years after winning the prize, in 1954.

∿

The committee reserved the 1952 award until 1953—then gave it to Albert Schweitzer, no less. He was one of the golden men of the 20th century. Was he German or French? Neither, and both. He was Alsatian. And he was one of the ultimate universal men. Churchill, perfect as ever with a phrase, called him "a genius of humanity." By vocation and avocation, he was . . . what? A theologian, a philosopher, an organist, a musicologist, a medical doctor, a missionary, a humanitarian. Indeed, his name is virtually synonymous with humanitarianism, and with the philosophy or outlook that he summed up as "reverence for life."

People had been nominating him for the Nobel Peace Prize since 1930. And when the committee decided to honor him, they were departing from practice, setting a bit of a precedent: Schweitzer was not an organization man or a statesman; he was barely even a public man, except as author (and musical performer, you could say); he was an individual carrying out his work of mercy in the Central African Rainforest. He was setting an example, if you will, living a philosophy. There would be other awards like his—Mother Teresa's, for one.

When the Nobel Committee made its announcement, Schweitzer was where he usually was, at his medical compound in Lambaréné, in present-day Gabon. Irwin Abrams, the historian, tells a charming story:

> One day late in 1953 . . . Schweitzer's nephew, Dr. Guy
> Schweitzer, burst into his room to congratulate his uncle. "For
> what?" Albert Schweitzer asked. "Has my black cat finally had
> her kittens?" Dr. Guy told him that the radio station in Brazzaville had just announced that Schweitzer had been awarded
> the Nobel Peace Prize.

Schweitzer informed the committee that he would not be able to travel to Oslo for the December ceremony, but that he would come in 1954, during a European trip that he was already planning. He also expressed gratitude for the prize money: the equivalent of $33,000, which he would use for his lepers' hospital.

He cut quite a figure in Oslo, as elsewhere, when he gave his Nobel lecture on November 4, 1954: bushy mustache, unkempt mane. A film of the occasion tells us that he spoke in a high-pitched, rather undistinguished voice—a little surprising, given how distinguished the owner of that voice was. His lecture was titled "The Problem of Peace in the World of Today," and it circulated throughout the world. One of the most quoted passages from it was this: "Man has become superman. He is a superman because he not only has at his disposal innate physical forces, but also commands, thanks to scientific and technological advances, the latent forces of nature which he can now put to his own use." Unfortunately, said the laureate, "we are becoming inhuman to the extent that we become supermen. We have learned to tolerate the facts of war . . . ." The great need was "to attain, through a change in spirit, that superior reason which will dissuade us from misusing the power at our disposal."

There is a coda to Schweitzer and the Nobel Peace Prize. In 1957, he was persuaded to issue a statement concerning atomic testing. The chief persuader was Norman Cousins, the American journalist who would do much writing about Schweitzer. On April 24, 1957, Schweitzer's "Declaration of Conscience" was read out over Radio Oslo, under the sponsorship of the Nobel Committee. He said, "My age [82] and the generous understanding so many people have shown of my work permit me to hope that my appeal may contribute to the preparing of the way for the insights so urgently needed." He went on to explain the dangers of atomic testing in a patient, thorough way: simple but uncondescending. He concluded, "The end of further experiments with atom bombs would be like the early sunrays of hope which suffering humanity is longing for."

I said that Baron Boyd Orr made an unusual nomination for the peace prize: the Edinburgh Festival Society. Schweitzer too exercised his right of nomination imaginatively. At least once, he nominated his fellow musician Pablo Casals, one of those artists given to public pronouncements.

~

December 10, 1953, was an interesting day in Oslo. Schweitzer was honored as the 1952 laureate, and the 1953 laureate was honored as well. The second one was present in the hall, and he was George C. Marshall, who had been America's secretary of state and secretary of defense—and before that, during World War II, the Army chief of staff. What was Churchill's designation of him? "The organizer of victory." Marshall was the only career military man to have received the Nobel Peace Prize, and he remains that still. He received the prize, not for his service during the war—although the subduing of genocidal aggressors was surely a contribution to peace—but for his achievements after the war: primarily the Marshall Plan.

This was the program to aid Europe, to put a continent back on its feet—or to "reconstruct" it, as people often said at the time. The Soviet Union and its associated Communist parties were making many inroads even into Western Europe, and the material needs of the people were helping the Communist cause. Democracy did not seem, to some, a winning proposition. A chief purpose of the Marshall Plan was to see to it that democracy did, in fact, win. Secretary Marshall, a modest man, did not call the program "the Marshall Plan"—he referred to it by its formal name, the European Recovery Program. But most everyone else called it the Marshall Plan, as we do today.

Chairman Jahn made the presentation speech for Schweitzer. Then another committee member, C. J. Hambro, made the presentation speech for Marshall. Hambro, a Conservative politician, is a significant and stirring figure in Norwegian history: It was he who arranged for the escape of the royal family and of many members of the government and the Storting, just as the Nazis were closing in. Speaking at the 1953 ceremony, he went over the long, amazing career of George Catlett Marshall. And he did a lot of referring to, and quoting of, Alfred Nobel. Presentation speakers reliably did this in the first decades of the prize; they do it to a degree today as well. But Hambro did more than the usual amount.

Here he is on American readiness, or unreadiness, as World War II loomed: "The United States had no military strength that could prevent war or even an attack on America. And Marshall, who saw the total war approaching and his own country powerless, clearly realized the truth of Alfred Nobel's words: 'Good intentions alone can never secure peace.'" Hambro also said that "the organs which have grown from the Marshall Aid have, more than anything else in these difficult years, contributed to what Nobel termed 'the idea of a general peace in Europe'. . . ." Perhaps the committee was signaling, through Hambro, that an award to the old general was perfectly in line with the thought and desires of the testator. Hambro put the committee's position in a nutshell: "Nobel's peace prize is not given to Marshall for what he accomplished during the war. Nevertheless, what he has done, after the war, for peace is a corollary to this achievement . . . ."

Following the presentation speech, Chairman Jahn handed Marshall the customary trinkets: the Nobel medal and diploma. As he was doing so, something strange occurred: Three young Communist journalists in the balcony shouted a protest and dropped leaflets on the audience below. They shouted about Hiroshima and Nagasaki and said that Marshall was no peacemaker. There is a film of this event. We can see Marshall, calm and courtly, looking on matter-of-factly. Jahn says to him, "Communists," and Marshall smiles knowingly. The story goes that, sometime later, Marshall told Hambro that he was used to being jeered at by anti-Communists, not Communists: because some on the right at home were incensed at Truman's policy of containment (versus a policy of "rollback"). Marshall's cabinet service was under this president.

After the disruption in the balcony, Marshall gave brief remarks of acceptance, in his laconic, Middle American style—he sort of talked out the side of his mouth (but not both sides). He said that he was accepting the award on behalf of the American people, who had made the Marshall Plan—or, as he put it, the European Recovery Program—possible with their understanding and tax dollars. The next evening, December 11, he gave his Nobel lecture proper. And he began in an unusual way—unusual for a peace laureate.

He said that, "in my country, my military associates frequently tell me that we Americans have learned our lesson." Their lesson about what? About military preparedness, about letting one's guard down and keeping it up. Marshall went on,

> I completely disagree with this contention and point to the rapid disintegration between 1945 and 1950 of our once vast power for maintaining the peace. As a direct consequence, in my opinion, there resulted the brutal invasion of South Korea, which for a time threatened the complete defeat of our hastily arranged forces in that field. I speak of this with deep feeling because in 1939 and again in the early fall of 1950 it suddenly became my duty, my responsibility, to rebuild our national military strength in the very face of the gravest emergencies.

Not very often does a Nobel laureate decry the effects of demilitarization. (In his will, Nobel, remember, had spoken of "the abolition or reduction of standing armies.") Not very often is a mighty military called a "vast power for maintaining the peace."

Marshall then said, "These opening remarks may lead you to assume that my suggestions for the advancement of world peace will rest largely on military strength." But that was not the case. He would discuss other means of keeping and extending the peace—for instance, the promotion of democracy, and "spiritual regeneration." Marshall also addressed a concern—a concern of the hour—in a memorable way:

> There has been considerable comment over the awarding of the Nobel Peace Prize to a soldier. I am afraid this does not seem as remarkable to me as it quite evidently appears to others. I know a great deal of the horrors and tragedies of war. Today, as chairman of the American Battle Monuments Commission, it is my duty to supervise the construction and maintenance of military cemeteries in many countries overseas, particularly in Western Europe. The cost of war in human lives is constantly spread before me, written neatly in many ledgers whose columns are gravestones. I am deeply moved to find some means or method of avoiding another calamity of war. Almost daily I hear from the wives, or mothers, or families of the fallen. The tragedy of the aftermath is almost constantly before me.

Very often a peace advocate will believe that he hates war more than a soldier does, or than a general or defense planner does. It is not necessarily so.

At the beginning of his lecture, Marshall issued a little apology: He did not have "the magic and artistry of that great orator whom the Nobel committee in Stockholm so appropriately honored yesterday." Who was that? It was Churchill, who had been given the Nobel Prize in Literature. The presentation speaker, Sigfrid Siwertz of the Swedish Academy, said something exceptionally graceful and gracious that day. He said, "A literary prize is intended to cast luster over the author, but here it is the author who gives luster to the prize." The Nobel Committee in Oslo might well have felt a similar satisfaction over its own 1953 prize.

It's not easy to convey, at this remove, how esteemed Marshall was on the Continent, and in Britain. Maybe this anecdote will help. In June 1953—six months before he received the Nobel prize—he attended the coronation of Queen Elizabeth II, as the American representative. When he entered Westminster Abbey, unannounced and, as usual, unassuming, the entire congregation rose. Marshall, aware that people were standing, looked around to see who had entered. It was he.

~

In a reserving mood, the committee held the 1954 award until 1955, then gave it to a U.N. agency: the Office of the United Nations High Commissioner for Refugees. Accepting the prize was the current high commissioner, a Dutch journalist and politician named Dr. Gerrit Jan van Heuven Goedhart. In his lecture, he spoke about Alfred Nobel and, of course, Fridtjof Nansen. The latter had been the first high commissioner, and he was still, 25 years after his death, the towering Norwegian hero. The end of the Dutchman's lecture was rather beautiful:

> Many years ago I participated in a discussion on the problem
> of international education. After many experts had presented
> their complicated theories, an old headmaster of a certain
> school got up and quietly said: "There is only one system of
> education, through love and one's own example." He was
> right. What is true for education is true also for the refugee
> problem of today. With love and our own example—example
> in the sense of sacrifice—it can be solved. And if in the cynical
> times in which we live someone might be inclined to laugh at
> "love" and "example" as factors in politics, he would do well to

be reminded of Nansen's hard-hitting, direct, and courageous words, based on a life full of sacrifice and devotion: "Love of man is practical policy."

In 1954, Van Heuven Goedhart established an award of his own, or rather, of his agency's—the UNHCR's—own: This was the Nansen Medal, designed to reward an individual or organization for "extraordinary and dedicated service to refugees." On the medal was an inscription: "Nestekjærlighet er realpolitikk"— "Love of man is practical policy," in Nansen's native tongue. The honor is now called the Nansen Refugee Award and comes with $100,000, donated by the governments of Norway and Switzerland. A diverse group of people have won the Nansen prize, beginning with the first recipient, Mrs. Roosevelt, and continuing with such figures as Norway's King Olav V, the tenor Luciano Pavarotti, and Senator Edward Kennedy.

∼

The committee sat out two years in the mid-Fifties, not giving an award for either 1955 or 1956. In 1957, it conferred one—on Lester Bowles Pearson of Canada. He was one of those classic international men, one of those classic U.N. men. The Canadians and the Norwegians, when you think about it, have had much in common, since the war: They are small-state actors who play an important role on the world stage, and are inclined to tutor and temper the big states. In 1956, Pearson essentially created the United Nations Emergency Force, which brought an end to the Suez crisis. It was this act that was chiefly responsible for winning him the Nobel prize. So, the 1957 award was a neat award, much like the one in 1950, given to Ralph Bunche: A diplomat won for problem-solving in the Middle East during the preceding year.

Pearson was born outside Toronto in 1897. Like Bunche, he was an excellent athlete: a standout in baseball, basketball, hockey, rugby, and still other sports. While training to be a fighter pilot in World War I, he acquired a nickname. His instructor decided that "Lester" was much too mild a name for a fighter pilot—so the instructor dubbed him "Mike." The name stuck. Pearson would always be "Mike," except in formal situations (such as a Nobel prize ceremony).

He was Canada's foreign minister from 1948 to 1957. He headed his country's delegation to the U.N., and he was president of the General Assembly in 1952 and 1953. He had a role in the proposed partition of Palestine, and in the founding of NATO. On July 26, 1956, Nasser, the Egyptian leader, nationalized the Suez Canal. On October 29, Israel went into Egypt, and Britain and France followed on November 5. Pearson proposed and organized the emergency force—UNEF—so that the invading parties could withdraw with some face. He is sometimes thought of as the father of U.N. "peacekeeping."

Jahn presented the 1957 prize, saying,

> Never, since the end of the last war, has the world situation been darker than during the Suez crisis, and never has the United Nations had a more difficult case to deal with. However, what actually happened has shown that moral force can be a bulwark against aggression and that it is possible to make aggressive forces yield without resorting to power. Therefore, it may well be said that the Suez crisis was a victory for the United Nations and for the man who contributed more than anyone else to save the world at that time. That man was Lester Pearson.

"Save the world"? That was strong language—a flamboyant piece of Nobel-ceremony rhetoric—but Pearson had indeed performed imaginatively and quickly. Jahn further noted that the U.N. had been able to do nothing about another situation that arose during that same period. On November 4, 1956, Soviet tanks rolled into Hungary, crushing the revolt for freedom there. In the General Assembly, Pearson asked a plaintive question: "Why should we not now establish a suitable United Nations mission for Hungary when it has been agreed to form a United Nations authority in the Middle East?" In his Nobel lecture, he acknowledged that "the idea of an international police force effective against a big disturber of the peace seems today unrealizable to the point of absurdity."

That lecture was wise, realistic, idealistic, graceful, and witty. It was also modest, particularly in its claims about UNEF. Pearson said, "I do not exaggerate the significance of what has been done. There is no peace in the area," no peace in the Middle East. But UNEF, he said, "may have prevented a brush fire becoming an all-consuming blaze," and "it could do so again in similar circumstances in the future." In 1967, Nasser thought he could at last take Israel out, and ordered UNEF to leave, which it did. As for Pearson, he became leader of the Liberal party, and found himself prime minister in 1963. He served until 1968. He died in 1972 while writing his memoirs, *Mike.*

~

In 1958, the committee crowned a great humanitarian, Father Dominique Pire. As with other laureates, individual and institutional, he dedicated himself to relieving the plight of refugees. He was a Belgian, born with the name Georges Pire in 1910. During World War I, he and his family fled to France; four years later, they returned to what was left of their home, which was not much. It was unsurprising that, when the second war came, he felt a kinship with refugees.

In his early twenties, he became a Dominican friar, adopting the name of the order's founder. During that second war, he was chaplain to the Belgian resistance, and performed a variety of underground heroics. Interestingly for a famous man of gentleness and peace, he won a chestful of war medals from his country. For the rest of his life, he gave his all for refugees: initially World War II refugees, then any other refugees who needed help, such as the Hungarians fleeing in 1956. Like so many of our laureates, he had prodigious energy and imagination. Organizations and projects simply flowed from him. At Huy, in Belgium, he established an institution first known as the Mahatma Gandhi International Peace Center. Later it was renamed the University of Peace. There were development programs abroad—beginning with the Subcontinent—which Pire called "Islands of Peace."

And he set up villages for refugees—seven of them, in Belgium, Austria, and West Germany. These were places where cruelly displaced and dazed people could try to begin life anew. One of the villages was named for Nansen. Another was named for Schweitzer. A third was named for a German-Dutch girl who died in the Holocaust and whose diary was subsequently published: Anne Frank.

Father Pire was a striking sight in Oslo, wearing his white friar's robe. In the hall for the ceremony, along with the usual royal and other luminaries, were nuns, looking on with particular interest and perhaps pride. The friar's lecture was called "Brotherly Love: Foundation for Peace." In truth, he referred to his lecture as, not a lecture, but a "lesson." Father Pire was little known before he won the prize, and the prize made him famous. (The Nobel Committee has often done that.) As with so many saints, this one was not devoid of ego. A good deal of his "lesson" consisted of other people's praise of him—that is, he quoted that praise. And he had angled to win the prize. But his purpose was to win funds for his projects, which bloomed with the testator's largesse. This Nobel-worthy Nobelist died in 1969.

∼

You remember what Nansen said when the Nobel Committee crowned him in 1922—that someone else should win the prize. Robert Cecil, for instance, or Philip Noel-Baker. Cecil, as you know, got the Nobel 15 years later, in 1937; Noel-Baker got his 37 years later, in 1959. It is a curious fact—hardly important to us, but maybe interesting—that Cecil and Noel-Baker lived in the same house in London, at different times. You will find two blue plaques at 16 South Eaton Place in Belgravia, recording this fact. In any event, Noel-Baker's was truly a "lifetime achievement" award, a Nobel for decades in peacework and international-organization work. Noel-Baker was above all an advocate of disarmament. And, in his various endeavors, he worked side by side with a string of Nobel peace laureates: Nansen, Cecil, Henderson, Lange. He was also a close friend of Norman Angell. And he mentioned all these people in his Nobel lecture. Noel-Baker might be called a member of the Nobel family, in the first half-century of the award.

He was a British parliamentarian and intellectual, born in 1889 (year of the first Universal Peace Congress, organized by Passy; year of the publication of *Lay Down Your Arms!*). His family was Quaker and quite wealthy. His father was Joseph Allen Baker, a noted pacifist and parliamentarian, as Philip too would become. Like some other laureates, Noel-Baker excelled as an athlete—really excelled. He ran track for Britain at the Olympic Games of 1912, 1920, and 1924. In those middle Games—1920, in Antwerp—he won the silver medal in the 1500 meters.

In World War I, Noel-Baker did not take up arms. Instead, he organized a Quaker ambulance service, and he witnessed ghastly combat. He recalled some of this in his Nobel lecture: "In the First War, we had poison gas—I was at Ypres when the chlorine cloud was first released—a gas wall a hundred feet high and two miles long; I saw the French Colonial Troops flying in terror and throwing away their weapons as they ran; I saw the Canadian soldiers choking to death, with an evil yellow froth oozing from their mouths . . . ." To a reporter after his Nobel was announced, he said, "War is a damnable, filthy thing and has destroyed civilization after civilization—that is the essence of my belief."

Noel-Baker wrote many books, carrying such titles as "Hawkers of Death: The Private Manufacture and Trade in Arms." His most important book was *Disarmament*, published in 1926. In 1958, the year before his Nobel prize, he came out with *The Arms Race: A Programme for World Disarmament*. He did not believe in an armed peace, or in the worth of armaments at all: He believed that they were inherently evil, no matter who possessed them. And he thought that deterrence was a chimera.

His Nobel lecture, "Peace and the Arms Race," was at a minimum a brilliant piece of speechwriting. At one point in it, he addressed himself to a particular madness of the age. He said that when the Nazis were exterminating millions of Jews, "we had millions of German prisoners in our hands; we did not kill them; we took no reprisals of any kind." But "now governments are constantly asserting that if they or their allies are attacked, they will instantly reply with weapons that will wipe out tens of millions of men and women and little children, who may bear no shadow of personal responsibility for what their government has done." As it happens, that is *exactly* the kind of thing Ronald Reagan said, when, as president, he explained that he could not abide by Mutual Assured Destruction and was determined to build antimissile defenses. He said it would be immoral to retaliate against innocents after a strike on one's own country. A leader needed an alternative to blunt carnage.

Noel-Baker, who had little use for the likes of Reagan and Margaret Thatcher, died when they held office, in 1982. His 92-year life spanned a convulsive stretch of history. The year before his death, he wrote and recorded a song about world disarmament.

Charles G. Dawes was not the only peace laureate with a musical bent.

◡

The committee reserved its prize for 1960, conferring it in 1961. And, with this award, they departed from traditions and set a precedent: The 1960 prize went to a man who was engaged in a human-rights struggle, or freedom struggle, plain and simple. The laureate was Albert John Lutuli, leader of the anti-apartheid struggle in South Africa as the president of the African National Congress. (His name is sometimes spelled Luthuli, though the laureate himself preferred Lutuli.) In making this award, the committee was positing a connection between freedom and peace. Jahn said, "Lutuli's fight has been waged within the borders of his own country; but the issues raised go far beyond them. He brings a message to all who work and strive to establish respect for human rights both within nations and between nations."

Those who knew Lutuli, or who know much about him, speak of him with awe, and understandably so. He was one of those exemplary men: meek and bold, practical and principled, common and uncommon. Born in 1898, he became a teacher, a Zulu chief, and an ANC president. He was not the kind to seek political or social leadership, but the kind who is asked by others to assume it. The government demanded that he choose between being a Zulu chief and the ANC. He resisted, making the famous statement, "The road to freedom is via the cross." After the Sharpeville Massacre of March 1960, the government banned the ANC. As you know, Lutuli received the call to Oslo at the end of the following year.

The government had him under severe restriction, confining him to his home village, Groutville. But they let him out of the country for ten days. Presenting the Nobel prize, Jahn hailed Lutuli for his dedication to nonviolence, despite dreadful provocation and injustice. Near the conclusion of his speech, the chairman said,

> If the nonwhite people of South Africa ever lift themselves
> from their humiliation without resorting to violence and
> terror, then it will be above all because of the work of Lutuli,
> their fearless and incorruptible leader who, thanks to his own
> high ethical standards, has rallied his people in support of this
> policy, and who throughout his adult life has staked everything
> and suffered everything without bitterness and without allow-
> ing hatred and aggression to replace his abiding love of his
> fellowmen.

In his acceptance speech, Lutuli said one of the funniest and most graceful things ever uttered at a Nobel prize ceremony. He noted that the interior minister in South Africa had said that he, Lutuli, did not deserve the Nobel Peace Prize. "Such is the magic of a peace prize," said Lutuli, "that it has even managed to produce an issue on which I agree with the government of South Africa." He said that no one appreciating the "profound significance" of this prize "can escape a feeling of inadequacy."

His Nobel lecture must have had a profound effect on its audience, and would affect readers today. Imagine him giving it in resplendent tribal dress (leopard-skin cap with monkey tails, necklace of lion's teeth). He explained his participation in public life, saying that, "as a Christian and patriot," he "could not look on while systematic attempts were made, almost in every department of life, to debase the God-factor in man or to set a limit beyond which the human being in his black form might not strive to serve his Creator to the best of his ability." He continued, "To remain neutral in a situation where the laws of the land virtually criticized God for having created men of color was the sort of thing I could not, as a Christian, tolerate." Of apartheid South

Africa, Lutuli said, "It is a museum piece in our time, a hangover from the dark past of mankind, a relic of an age which everywhere else is dead or dying. Here the cult of race superiority and of white supremacy is worshiped like a god."

After his speech, the lecturer-laureate burst into song, and that song was "God Bless Africa," which Lutuli sang in Zulu. Fellow Africans in the hall joined him.

If freedom champions are to have peace prizes, the Nobel prize for 1960 is one of the best the committee has ever bestowed. I say this because of the moral character of the recipient. Because of the justice and urgency of his cause. And because of this: He was a black man on a continent that was, to much of the world, mysterious and unknown. Never before had the committee chosen a laureate from a continent other than Europe or North America—except in 1936, when they chose Carlos Saavedra Lamas, who in any case was a diplomat well known in Europe and throughout the world: the president of the League of Nations Assembly, no less. Lutuli was essentially a man of Groutville—"a rural backwater," as he said in his lecture, a place that "does not even feature on many maps."

Soon after he picked up his award, ANC men and women departed from nonviolence, trying other means to end apartheid. Lutuli died in July 1967. Walking across a bridge near his home, he was hit by a train and killed. The award to him was the first of the Nobel Committee's South African awards: In 1984, Bishop Tutu would receive it, and in 1993 Mandela and de Klerk would receive it, as the nasty story of apartheid closed.

~

The 1961 award was the posthumous award: the one given to Dag Hammarskjöld. The U.N. secretary-general had died in a plane crash on September 18 of that year. He was the committee's fellow Scandinavian, a Swede, born in 1905 and brought up in

Uppsala, where Archbishop Söderblom presided. The Hammar-skjölds and the Söderbloms knew one another well. Dag's father, Hjalmar, was prime minister of Sweden from 1914 to 1917 and later the chairman of the Nobel Foundation. Dag Hammarskjöld succeeded another Scandinavian, Trygve Lie, as U.N. secretary-general in 1953. The Soviets had opposed Lie, thinking him too favorable to the West and the democracies; they figured that Hammarskjöld, from long-neutral Sweden, was a better bet. When his plane crashed, he was in Africa, on a U.N. mission to the Congo, which was being brutalized by war. Fifteen others died in that same crash. On December 10, Gunnar Jahn closed his presentation speech with, "Let us stand in tribute to the memory of Dag Hammarskjöld."

Here is a rude question: Would Hammarskjöld have been given the Nobel Peace Prize if he had not been killed? The answer is not so rude: Quite possibly so, at some point. The Nobel Committee has always been devoted to the U.N. (and its forerunners), and Hammarskjöld's views were in line with those of the committee in general. Hammarskjöld was seen as a bridge between the Free World and the Communist, and he showed deference to the Third World leaders taking power after colonialism. He was a leading example of the new international man then developing.

∾

The award for 1962 was given in 1963—and the winner was a Nobel laureate already. He was Linus Pauling, the great chemist born in Oregon in 1901. He won the chemistry prize in 1954. He is one of just four people who have won more than one Nobel prize. As you will recall, Madame Marie Curie won a piece of the physics prize in 1903 and all of the chemistry prize in 1911. John Bardeen, an American, shared the physics prize in both 1956 and 1972. Frederick Sanger, a Briton, won the chemistry prize by himself in 1958 and won it again with two others in 1980. Pauling is the only person to have won two undivided—two unshared—prizes, and that was in two different fields.

After winning the chemistry prize, Pauling was increasingly visible as an anti-nuclear activist. We have mentioned Schweitzer's "Declaration of Conscience," broadcast from Oslo, which dealt with the question of nuclear testing. Opposition to such testing was Pauling's main cause. He and his wife, Ava Helen, circulated a petition calling for a ban, and they got more than 11,000 scientists to sign it. In 1958, they presented this petition to the U.N.—to Secretary-General Hammarskjöld, in particular. In that same year, Pauling published his anti-nuclear manifesto *No More War!* Is that title reminiscent? We may think of Baroness von Suttner's classic, *Lay Down Your Arms!* Pauling's cause achieved a victory in the summer of 1963 when the United States, Great Britain, and the Soviet Union signed what was known as the Partial Test Ban Treaty, or Limited Test Ban Treaty. (It permitted testing underground.) The treaty went into effect on October 10, 1963, the very day the peace prize for Pauling was announced. That was considered by all concerned poetic.

The Nobel Committee was not exactly eager to reward Pauling. In his essay on the first hundred years of the Nobel Peace Prize, Geir Lundestad writes, ". . . in many American circles Pauling was considered to harbor pro-Communist sympathies. The Western-oriented majority of [the committee] was actually against giving him the prize. What secured him the prize was chairman Jahn's threat to resign from the committee unless Pauling got it. Jahn, too, had become increasingly preoccupied with the danger of nuclear weapons." Jahn, we see, was a chairman with clout, and apparently a majority-thwarting clout.

He used part of his presentation speech to mock and dispute the idea that Pauling was a Communist or anything like a Communist. He noted that the U.S. government had at times made life difficult for him, even denying him a passport. Also, he brought up the opposition of some scientists to a nuclear test ban, specifically mentioning Edward Teller and Willard Libby. The latter had won the Nobel Prize for Chemistry in 1960. As for Teller, Pauling had had a starry television debate with him. One of Teller's contentions (and Libby's contentions) was that testing allowed a more effective deterrent, and therefore made war less likely. Pauling scorned such arguments, and so did Jahn. So, by extension, did the Nobel Committee.

Pauling's lecture in Oslo was both fascinating and bizarre. He said that Alfred Nobel had looked forward to the day when weapons would be so terrible that war would be rendered impossible. That day had come. "War has been made impossible forever," said Pauling. He very much welcomed the A-bomb and its even more destructive companions on the grounds that they took war out of consideration. "The world has now begun its metamorphosis from its primitive period of history, when disputes between nations were settled by war, to its period of maturity, in which war will be abolished and world law will take its place." In Pauling's judgment, the Partial Test Ban Treaty was "the first great stage of this metamorphosis."

He had very warm words for John Kennedy, as might have been expected, for the president had been killed only 19 days before. Yet Pauling had been hard on Kennedy, when the president displeased him. In March 1962, Kennedy announced that the United States would resume nuclear testing, following the Soviets' resumption of the same. Pauling fired off a telegram: "Are you going to give an order that will cause you to go down in history as one of the most immoral men of all time and one of the greatest enemies of the human race?" In October of that year came the Cuban missile crisis, when Kennedy issued an ultimatum to the Soviets. Pauling again sent a telegram—a message of fiery denunciation, using such words as "horrifying," "warlike," and "recklessly militaristic."

Pauling had immense charm, in addition to other qualities, and that was on display in Oslo. In his acceptance speech, he said that there were similarities between the testator's life and his own. Indeed, said Pauling, he had more in common with Nobel than had any other peace laureate to that point. "Alfred Nobel was a chemical engineer and chemist, with a deep antipathy for war. I was educated as a chemical engineer and chemist, and I have striven to eliminate war from the world." Moreover, "most of Nobel's 355 patents dealt with explosives. Two of my four patents are on explosives."

Of Pauling's brilliance as a chemist, there is no doubt. Authorities rank him as a scientist of a very high order, maybe the highest. Some of his allies and admirers were embarrassed when Pauling became a great enthusiast for vitamin C. This started at the end of the 1960s. For the rest of his life, he promoted vitamin C as a cure for most any ill. But this crusade could possibly be written off as a genius's eccentricity or lark. Where serious debate about Pauling takes place is over the wisdom of his politics, his role in the Cold War. In America, many were aghast when Pauling got the Nobel Peace Prize. A much-quoted headline in *Life* read, "A Weird Insult from Norway." The *New York Herald Tribune* editorialized that the award to Pauling, "whatever the committee's reasons, inevitably associates this semisacrosanct honor with the extravagant posturings of a placarding peacenik." Were Pauling's critics merely red-baiters and boobs?

Consider a couple of sentences from an admiring biography by Ted and Ben Goertzel (*Linus Pauling: A Life in Science and Politics*, published in 1995): "Pauling's views on many issues were strongly anti-American. He advocated friendship and reconciliation with the Soviet Union at a time when the Soviets were, in fact, an authoritarian dictatorship and threatening military power. Pauling's political views during this period were those of a New

Left radical, very much in tune with the positions expressed by groups such as Students for a Democratic Society."

For years, people have been writing about Pauling's views and activities, and his public record is extensive. I will confine myself to a few pertinent words. He was a hard-core socialist and fellow traveler, with a résumé like many others': support for Henry Wallace in 1948, attendance at the Communists' World Peace Congresses, and so on. He was not a Communist, not card-carrying. But he would have been of much less use to the Soviets if he had been. Decade after decade, he was one of their darlings. They invited him regularly, to visit, lecture, and vacation. He gave no indication that he was troubled by being in a country with a vast system of slave-labor camps. He did not use his enormous prestige as a scientist to help anyone: either a fellow scientist or an artist or an ordinary person. He said in an interview once that he requested to see Sakharov—but his hosts and minders said no, and that was that. A little fuss from Pauling would have been huge.

The Soviets asked him to celebrate an anniversary of the Bolshevik Revolution with them. They made him a member of the Soviet Academy of Sciences. They gave him their highest scientific award, the Lomonosov Medal. And, of course, they gave him the Lenin Peace Prize. As I mentioned earlier, he accepted that at the Soviet embassy in Washington in 1970. Two years later, the general secretary himself, Brezhnev, won the peace prize. The Soviet government did not give that prize lightly or recklessly; its recipients earned it. In 2001, the journalist Tom Bethell profiled Arthur Robinson, once Pauling's "principal and most valued collaborator" (Pauling's own words). As Robinson recounted, Pauling told him that he was prouder of the award from the Soviets than he was of the award from the Nobel Committee.

In the 1980s, Pauling laughed at Reagan's contention that, with assorted pressures, the Soviet Union could be brought down.

You can see this in a television interview: Pauling's face full of mirth, as he quotes Reagan's hope that Marxism-Leninism could be left "on the ash heap of history." Pauling died in 1994, three years after the Soviet Union. He did not have the last laugh. But he did have those two Nobel prizes. And Robinson told the Goertzels that Pauling asked him to initiate a campaign for a third one: in medicine. That was not to be.

∼

In 1963, for 1963, the Red Cross won its third Nobel Peace Prize. You can call it a fourth award, if you count the 1901 honor for Henry Dunant. We know why the Red Cross won for 1917 and 1944, which were world-war years. But why for 1963? It was an anniversary year, the hundredth anniversary of the founding of the Red Cross. And the Nobel Committee loves an anniversary. You might argue that an anniversary is not a good enough reason to win, or to award, the peace prize. But anniversary awards are a firmly established part of Nobel Peace Prize tradition. Besides, the Red Cross is presumed to perform noble works every year.

The 1963 prize was actually divided, between the International Committee of the Red Cross (the mother ship in Geneva) and the League of Red Cross Societies, founded by the American banker Henry P. Davison in 1919. This was a federation of all the national Red Cross societies. Representing the ICRC in Oslo was its president, Léopold Boissier. He was a grand Swiss long active in peace and humanitarian circles. Have a taste of his lecture, in which he addresses some of the old criticism of the Red Cross— that it tidies up war, rather than stopping it:

> Every institution, like every individual, should contribute to
> the crusade for peace, with the means at its disposal. The
> Red Cross, for its part, struggles against war by making it
> less inhuman; does it not rescue war victims, even on the

battlefield? But, given the present state of the world, it cannot pretend to be able to eliminate the scourge of war; it therefore tries to alleviate its evils.

The alleviation of evils is no trifling thing, we can agree.

〜

In 1964, the Nobel Committee turned to America, and to its civil-rights movement: They gave the prize to Martin Luther King, Jr., the extraordinary, heroic young man (35) at the head of this movement. The year before, he had led the "March on Washington," during which he gave his famous "I Have a Dream" speech. When his Nobel prize was announced in October 1964, the United States was nearing the end of a presidential campaign: between the incumbent, Lyndon Johnson (who had assumed the presidency after the Kennedy assassination), and Senator Barry Goldwater, the Republican nominee. David J. Garrow points out in his celebrated biography of King (*Bearing the Cross*) that Johnson did not congratulate King after the Nobel announcement, an omission that stung Coretta King, the laureate's wife, in particular. King himself explained the omission as Johnson's reluctance to offend white Southerners so close to the November election.

Arriving in Oslo in December, King met with the local press, saying that he and his team viewed their trip as an educational opportunity: "We feel we have much to learn from Scandinavia's democratic socialist tradition . . . ." At the prize ceremony, the Norwegians offered music from Gershwin's *Porgy and Bess* (an opera about blacks in the "sea islands" of South Carolina by a Jewish composer from New York). And Jahn stressed the reason for King's receipt of the prize: nonviolence. The chairman quoted the Sermon on the Mount: ". . . whosoever shall smite thee on thy right cheek, turn to him the other also." And, as he had in the past, he cited "the words of our poet Arnulf Øverland": "Only the unarmed can draw on sources eternal. / To the Spirit alone will be the victory."

The laureate, in his acceptance speech, said that "civilization and violence are antithetical concepts." The "Negroes of the United States," he noted, had followed the people of India in demonstrating that "nonviolence is not sterile passivity but a powerful moral force which makes for social transformation." He also said, "I accept this award today with an abiding faith in America and an audacious faith in the future of mankind." His Nobel lecture, delivered the next day, was one of his greatest orations, which is saying something. Part sermon, part political speech, part philosophical meditation, it is wise and beautiful. Some passages achieve transcendence. But one passage, I regard as beneath him—and beneath the occasion of the address. Johnson had beaten Goldwater the month before, in a landslide. And, in Oslo, King said,

> Another indication that progress is being made was found
> in the recent presidential election in the United States. The
> American people revealed great maturity by overwhelmingly
> rejecting a presidential candidate who had become identi-
> fied with extremism, racism, and retrogression. The voters of
> our nation rendered a telling blow to the radical right. They
> defeated those elements in our society which seek to pit white
> against Negro and lead the nation down a dangerous Fascist
> path.

An older King might well have been ashamed of that rhetoric, or at least regretted it. For one thing, Goldwater's view of government and economics was the opposite of fascist: was the classical-liberal view.

After his stay in Oslo, King traveled to nearby Stockholm, where he went to the home of the Myrdals, Gunnar and Alva. Later, like Ralph Bunche after his Middle East negotiations, he arrived in New York to a hero's welcome. He was fired with the idea of social democracy, saying that, in Scandinavia, they had "no unemployment and no slums." He wanted a "broad alliance," encompassing black and white alike, in the pursuit of "economic justice." The election won, Johnson invited King to the White House, to which the laureate flew from New York on Governor Nelson Rockefeller's private jet. Finally, he went home to Atlanta, where young people in his church, the Ebenezer Baptist Church, greeted him with Christmas carols.

As David Garrow tells us, Mrs. King had wanted some of the Nobel prize money—$54,000—to be spent on transport to Scandinavia for family and friends. She also thought that some of the money should be set aside for the King children's college education. King thought otherwise, believing that the funds in their entirety should be poured into the cause, the civil-rights movement: which they were. At this point in history, King was the youngest person ever to win the peace prize. He did not live much longer, being assassinated in April 1968 at 39.

∽

In 1965, the committee made a U.N. award—the prize went to the U.N.'s child-aid agency, UNICEF. Over the years, many people have known UNICEF for its celebrity ambassadors. The most memorable of them was probably Audrey Hepburn, the late actress. Giving the acceptance speech for UNICEF was Henry R. Labouisse, Jr., an American diplomat who was the agency's new executive director. Giving the Nobel lecture was Zena Harman, an Israeli who was chairman of the executive board. Both speakers dwelt on the testator. Labouisse, for his part, said,

> We know from Alfred Nobel's own childhood what care and
> tireless effort can mean in enabling a fragile, sickly boy to
> attain great heights in later life. Nobel's parents succeeded in

overcoming the ill fortune which beset their son; everything that could be done for him was done. He lived, and his name today is associated with mankind's highest achievements. Had Alfred Nobel been born not in 1833 but even in 1965, in a steamy, isolated village of Asia, Africa, Latin America, what would be his chances of survival and of success?

Years later, in 2001, Carol Bellamy was UNICEF's executive director. And she spoke during the Nobel Institute's centennial symposium. She said that when she arrived at UNICEF, they had their Nobel prize—we can assume she meant the medal or diploma or both—"hanging on a very dark wall." When she asked why, they told her, "We don't want anyone to steal it." She replied, "Don't worry, no one knows we even have it." And she moved the evidence of UNICEF's victory to a more prominent spot.

∽

Not until 1968 was the Nobel Peace Prize given again. The committee has not since skipped two years, and not since 1972 has it skipped even one. The 1968 prize was a U.N. prize, in a way: It went to Réné Cassin, the venerable French jurist, humanitarian, and internationalist who was the principal drafter of the Universal Declaration of Human Rights. Or rather, he was held to be, in 1968. Since then, authorship of the document has been in dispute. In any case, Cassin made a contribution to it.

The Universal Declaration was adopted by the United Nations on December 10, 1948. Cassin's prize ceremony took place exactly 20 years from that day. The U.N. was calling 1968 the International Human Rights Year, in recognition of the twentieth anniversary. Every year, December 10 is Human Rights Day (in the eyes of the U.N.). It is sheer coincidence that this day is also Nobel Presentation Day.

Alfred Nobel, an extraordinary mind and spirit, author of an extraordinary will. *Library of Congress, Bain Collection, LC-DIG-ggbain-17492*

Henry Dunant, the father of the Red Cross, co-recipient of the first Nobel Peace Prize, in 1901. *Library of Congress, Farm Security Administration/ Office of War Information Black-and-White Negatives, LC-USW33-042485*

Theodore Roosevelt, the 1906 laureate, a man whose win excites controversy even today. *Library of Congress, Harris & Ewing Collection, LC-DIG-hec-15043*

Fridtjof Nansen, a real-life Indiana Jones, and the 1922 laureate. *Library of Congress, Bain Collection, LC-DIG-ggbain-25031*

Ralph Bunche, the American U.N. diplomat who won in 1950. *Library of Congress, Prints & Photographs Division, Carl Van Vechten Collection, LC-USZ62-109113*

Seán MacBride, a Nobel peace laureate for 1974 (and soon thereafter a Lenin peace laureate). *UN Photo/Saw Lwin*

Mother Teresa, the 1979 winner, and almost surely the saintliest of them all. *Wikimedia-Commons User Túrelio, Creative Commons BY-SA 2.0-de*

Rigoberta Menchú Tum, the Guatemalan peasant-memoirist who won in the "Columbus year" of 1992. © *Micheline Pelletier/Sygma/Corbis*

Yasser Arafat, chairman of the Palestine Liberation Organization, who won in 1994 with two Israeli statesmen. © *World Economic Forum (www.weforum.org) www.swiss-image.ch/ Photo by Remy Steinegger*

Wangari Maathai, the 2004 laureate, with King Harald and Queen Sonja (of Norway). *Ricardo Medina*

Mohamed ElBaradei, co-winner in 2005 with the outfit he directed, the International Atomic Energy Agency. *D. Calma/IAEA*

Cassin lived from 1887 to 1976, and all of these years were eventful: for him and for the world. Seriously wounded in World War I, he was taken to a field hospital where his mother happened to be working as a nurse. The story goes that she pleaded with a doctor to perform an operation that saved her son's life. In his Nobel lecture, Cassin said, "That war put its indelible stamp on me, as it did on many of my contemporaries." After the war, Cassin became a leader—a pioneer—in veterans affairs. And he took up any number of professional responsibilities. As he observed in his lecture, he had a "capacity for involvement." So have many, probably most, winners of the Nobel Peace Prize. Indeed, a "capacity for involvement" is one of the most common traits among them.

It was for the Universal Declaration, primarily, that Cassin won the peace prize, at 81. (Informed of his selection, he said, "Already?") Making the presentation speech was a new chairman, Aase Lionæs, a Labor politician. Jahn had gone off the committee in 1966, having gone on in 1938. He died in 1971. In her speech, Lionæs said that the Universal Declaration of Human Rights "moved the stakes farther ahead than had either the American Declaration of Independence in 1776 or the French Declaration of the Rights of Man in 1789." What did she mean? The U.N. declaration "dealt with economic and social rights, being influenced by the Russian Declaration of Rights of 1918." She was referring to the Soviet constitution. Lionæs further said that Cassin "played a positive role as a mediator between the Western European way of thought, which emphasized civil and political rights, and the Eastern European viewpoint, which laid more weight on economic, social, and cultural rights." That is an interesting phrase, "the Eastern European viewpoint." Were the Eastern Europeans consulted about what they thought of as human rights? Certainly those who ruled without consent were.

In his lecture, Cassin was in harmony with Lionæs. He referred to "political," "religious," "judicial," and other such rights as "the old liberties," making "economic," "social," and "cultural" rights the new. He said that the Universal Declaration had "established a careful balance" between these two sets of rights. What he did not say was that experience had shown that unfree countries—such as the Soviet satellites he negotiated with—had practically nothing: neither the "old liberties" nor material well-being.

Like others, Cassin made big claims for the Universal Declaration. To his audience in Oslo, he described the declaration's "very existence" as "a historical event of the first magnitude," for "it is the first document of an ethical sort that organized humanity has ever adopted." In a later speech, he said, "From the very day that the Universal Declaration of Human Rights was adopted by the United Nations, on December 10, 1948, the world could not help but compare it to the Ten Commandments. Happily, the relationship between the two has generally been confirmed." In her presentation speech, Lionæs had said that "the moral commandments contained in the declaration, like those written on the tablets of Moses, will in the years to come play a forceful role in reforming the conscience of man and his understanding of what is right and wrong."

The Universal Declaration is a fine document indeed, spelling out rules that all nations should live by. But does it matter? Has the document done any good in the world? Is anyone aware of it, or does anyone feel obligated to live by it? Cassin was once vice-chairman of the U.N. Human Rights Commission, when Eleanor Roosevelt was chairman. Then Cassin rose to the chairmanship. In 2003, Moammar Qaddafi's Libya took over the presidency of the commission. Genocidal Sudan was also a member. In 2010, after U.N. reforms that some hoped would prevent such outrages, Qaddafi's Libya was again elected—joining the Castros' Cuba, Communist China (with its gulag, *laogai*), Saudi Arabia, and other such beauties. For decades, the world's human-rights body has been a gathering-place of the world's worst tyrannies. Their favorite, sometimes sole, pastime is to devise resolutions against Israel. (Cassin, incidentally, was Jewish, and a fervent campaigner for Zionism and other Jewish causes.)

We might say this for Cassin and his confreres: They drew up a document that illustrates the gap between what ought to be and what is, in a great many countries. And they pushed the principle that what governments do with, or to, the people under their control is not merely those governments' business but everyone's business. Governments must not brutalize people under them while telling off the rest of the world with the word "sovereignty." Cassin said, "World progress cannot be built on the ashes of human suffering." Whatever the utility or relevance of the Universal Declaration, Cassin, in a variety of ways, was a great man.

⁓

The 1969 award was another U.N. prize, and another anniversary prize: It went to the International Labour Organization, founded in the Versailles Treaty, 1919. The ILO was an "affiliated agency" of the League. When the second war came, the ILO left its Geneva home to set up temporary headquarters in Montreal. After the war, it moved back to Geneva and became affiliated with the U.N. (which, true, was in North America, which the ILO had just left). The ILO was the only League agency to transfer to the U.N. And you are familiar with its slogan: *Si vis pacem, cole justitiam,* or, "If you desire peace, cultivate justice."

Accepting the Nobel prize, and giving the Nobel lecture, for the ILO was its director-general, David A. Morse, an American. He harked back to a couple of earlier peace laureates: Sir Randal Cremer and *le grand Léon,* Léon Jouhaux. The latter had played a part in the ILO's founding; Morse called him "my good friend." And he ended the lecture by citing one of the inaugural winners, from 1901: "... there are still, to paraphrase the words of Frédéric Passy, dangerous explosives in the hidden depths of the community—the national community and the world community. To the defusing of these explosives, to the building of a truly peaceful world order based on social justice, the ILO, with the immense encouragement it derives from the unique distinction of the Nobel Peace Prize, solemnly dedicates its second half-century of existence."

Six years later, in 1975, the United States gave notice that it intended to withdraw from the ILO. In the American view, the organization had been captured by the Soviet bloc, the radical Arab states, and other such actors. It was no longer a democratic entity: more like an anti-democratic one. In 1977, the U.S. indeed withdrew—but rejoined in 1980, apparently having more confidence in the ILO's ability to be what it was meant to be.

INTERLUDE

A SIGN OF THE TIMES

If the 1960s had a symbol, it was the peace sign. And this sign has, of course, lived on. It was not the first symbol of peace, obviously. In the ancient world, peace was represented by the dove, or an olive branch, or both—the branch in the bird's beak. These things still mean peace. I think of those white plaster doves all over the ceiling of Nobel Hall, in the Norwegian Nobel Institute. Also, when he played at the 2009 ceremony for President Obama, the pianist Lang Lang wore a dove on his tunic. But the modern peace sign—that crow's foot, as it has been called, within a circle—is our concern for this "interlude." It has been spoken of as "the best-known protest symbol in the world." Is it also the best-known symbol, of any kind? Probably not—the Christian cross would be ahead of it. But the peace sign would not be far behind.

It was created in 1958, by an English artist and designer, Gerald Holtom. He had been a conscientious objector in World War II. And he designed this symbol for an anti-nuclear march, organized by a group called the Direct Action Committee against Nuclear War. On Easter Weekend 1958, protesters marched from

Trafalgar Square in London to the Atomic Weapons Research Establishment in Aldermaston (52 miles). The symbol was later adopted and popularized by CND, the Campaign for Nuclear Disarmament.

How did Holtom come up with it? What did he intend? He was using the flag-semaphore alphabet. In this system, you make an N by holding two flags, one in each hand, on a diagonal, downward—at 5 o'clock and 7 o'clock, so to speak. You make a D by holding one flag straight up and the other straight down—at 12 o'clock and 6 o'clock. Holtom merged the two. And he placed them within a circle. "ND" stood for "nuclear disarmament."

This is what you might call the plain idea behind the symbol. But Holtom once wrote the following, to the editor of *Peace News*: "I was in despair. Deep despair. I drew myself: the representative of an individual in despair," with arms outstretched, "in the manner of Goya's peasant before the firing squad." That's putting it more dramatically. And we learn something interesting from Ken Kolsbun, author of *Peace: The Biography of a Symbol*, which appeared in the fiftieth-anniversary year of the peace sign, 2008. Allow me to quote, not from the book, but from a BBC report: "American pacifist Ken Kolsbun, who corresponded with Mr Holtom until his death in 1985, says the designer came to regret the connotation of despair and had wanted the sign inverted. 'He thought peace was something that should be celebrated,' says Mr Kolsbun . . . ."

Holtom indeed liked his alternative idea. The semaphore sign for U is two flags pointing upward: at 11 o'clock and 1 o'clock (roughly). Replace the N in the peace sign with a U—or simply turn the peace sign upside down—and you get something rather exultant. And the initials UD stand for "unilateral disarmament." Kolsbun told the BBC, "Mr. Holtom was all for unilateral disarmament."

The peace sign, in its original form, quickly crossed the Atlantic from England to America, where it became an icon. It became an icon everywhere else, too. Seldom can a design have so quickly become a world symbol. In America, it stood for an anti-nuclear stance and an anti-war stance. It also came to stand for the counterculture generally—"peace, love, and rock 'n' roll." And this symbol could be found on anything and everything: clothing, jewelry, postage stamps, gravestones . . . So far, each generation has discovered it. During the first year of their father's presidency, the Obama girls stepped out a few times in peace-sign garb. Political analysts wondered what they should read into it.

Enthusiasts for Gerald Holtom and the peace sign like to point out that the sign was never copyrighted, making it open to all. People have certainly taken advantage. There have been endless variations on the peace sign, incorporating national flags and practically anything else that can be thought of. Some people have used the symbol negatively, of course. During the Vietnam War, there was a bumper sticker showing the peace sign and declaring, "The Footprint of the American Chicken." There is a fairly well-known variation on the sign using a B-52, made to look like Holtom's merged "ND." The sign is accompanied by the words "Peace the Old-Fashioned Way." At the beginning of 2010, an American named Stephen Reid decided that he was tired of seeing peace, and its symbol, associated with the political Left. He made a peace sign, coloring it red, white, and blue, with the following words underneath: "Through Strength." He was harking back to "Peace through Strength," the Reagan slogan from 1984 (and more than a slogan: an encapsulation of a policy).

But we will leave the last word to a Holtom follower and true-believer, Mr. Kolsbun. This time, I will not quote from a news report, but from his book itself, its epilogue:

> Children of today easily identify [the peace sign]. They may not know its original meaning, but they know it stands for good things—be nice to friends, be kind to animals, no fighting. This is a marvelous achievement for Gerald Holtom's simple design. Peoples around the world have marched with it, worn it, displayed it during combat, held it high on banners, and been arrested in its name. Ask any man, woman or child, "What one thing would everyone in the world want more than anything else?" The answer would surely be world peace.

A PARADE OF LAUREATES,
1970 *to* 1990

Norman Borlaug was an American, but the Nobel Committee would have been within its rights to take a certain national pride in him: He was a Norwegian American, born and raised in a Norwegian-American farm community. When he went to Oslo to collect his prize—he was the 1970 laureate—he spoke of being "in the land of my fathers." He won because he was the agronomist who led the Green Revolution. That term did not refer to environmentalism as it was later understood; it referred to high-yield agriculture, an enormous increase in cereal-grain production. This increase—this revolution—fed millions, and hundreds of millions, who otherwise would have starved to death. There are people who say that Norman Borlaug saved more lives than anyone else in the 20th century. This is not a silly claim.

He was born in 1914, near Cresco, Iowa, where he grew up. By the time he began his career, America was a land of plenty. But, in the Depression, he had seen people starving. This left a burning impression on him. And he had a burning desire to feed the poor. Working in Mexico, he wrote to his wife, "These places I've seen have clubbed my mind—they are so poor and depressing." He made them less so. In the decades of his long life, he traveled to the most desolate and afflicted places, enduring various hardships, in order to meet the needs of the people. He had a missionary spirit, really—a scientific and missionary spirit.

In Oslo, Chairman Lionæs gave the presentation speech, and it captures perfectly the zeitgeist of 1970:

> During the 25 years that have elapsed since the end of the war, those of us who live in the affluent industrialized societies have debated in almost panic-stricken terms the race between the world's population explosion and the world's available food resources. Most experts who have expressed an opinion on the issue of this race have been pessimistic.
>
> The world has been oscillating between fears of two catastrophes—the population explosion and the atom bomb. Both pose a mortal threat.
>
> In this intolerable situation, with the menace of doomsday hanging over us, Dr. Borlaug comes onto the stage and cuts the Gordian knot. He has given us a well-founded hope, an alternative of peace and of life—the Green Revolution.

Giving his lecture, Borlaug quoted what he called the "famous words" of his predecessor, the 1949 laureate, John Boyd Orr: "You can't build peace on empty stomachs."

He lectured again in Oslo in 2000, on the thirtieth anniversary of his award. He made many fascinating points, one of which was this: He had won the Nobel Peace Prize only because there was no Nobel prize for food and agriculture. According to Borlaug, if Alfred Nobel had written his will 50 years earlier, which is to say, in the 1840s rather than the 1890s, he would first have provided a prize for food and agriculture. In that earlier period, Europe was experiencing terrible famine. But those problems were eventually relieved, first by mass emigration to the Americas, and second by improved agricultural techniques. When it came time for Nobel to write his will, Borlaug said, "there was no serious food-production problem haunting Europe." In 1986, Borlaug created what Nobel did not: a World Food Prize. It is given annually in Des Moines, Iowa, and is worth $250,000.

Elsewhere in his 2000 lecture, Borlaug stressed the importance of entrepreneurship in feeding the poor—a point that the testator would have appreciated, keenly. "I agree with the late Nobel economist T. W. Schultz," said Borlaug, "that most working scientists are research entrepreneurs and that centralized control is an anathema to progress."

Borlaug died in 2009, when he was 95. The obituary in the *New York Times* quoted an agriculture expert who calculated that, in the paper's words, "about half the world's population goes to bed every night after consuming grain descended from one of the high-yield varieties developed by Dr. Borlaug and his colleagues of the Green Revolution."

In the last decades of his life, Borlaug was attacked by people in the environmentalist movement, and one of its subsets, the organic-foods movement. They accused him of poisoning soils, being a toady of capitalism—agribusiness—and so on. All through his career, Borlaug had been supported by the Rockefeller Foundation, the Ford Foundation, and the World Bank. But these patrons fell away, under pressure from the new "greens." Borlaug was at the same time understanding and angry—and appalled by the ignorance and smugness of his critics. "Some of the environmental lobbyists of the Western nations are the salt of the earth," he said, "but many of them are elitists. They've never experienced the physical sensation of hunger. They do their lobbying from comfortable office suites in Washington or Brussels. If they lived just one month amid the misery of the developing world, as I have for 50 years . . . "

A question: Could the great Norman Borlaug have won the Nobel Peace Prize at a time when he was under attack from fashionable greens? Would the Nobel Committee, which has so often followed political, cultural, and attitudinal fashion, have honored him when much of the Left was against him? Or would the committee have been like the Rockefeller and Ford foundations, and the World Bank? Personally, I think it was a good thing Borlaug got his Nobel when he did.

∾

The 1971 prize was a real natural, for the Nobel Committee: It went to Willy Brandt, the chancellor of the Federal Republic of Germany, or, to use the more common name, West Germany. He was a statesman after the committee's own heart, and after the Norwegian political culture's own heart: a reacher-out, a "bridge-builder," a seeker of rapprochement between the Free West and the Communist East. He was the champion and practitioner of what was first called the *Neue Ostpolitik*—the new East policy—and then shortened to *Ostpolitik*. Brandt had made treaties with the Soviet Union and Poland; he would soon make one with East Germany. *Ostpolitik* might be described as one country's détente: that of Brandtian West Germany.

In his Nobel lecture, the chancellor himself said he did not much care for "the label *Ostpolitik*, but how can one take back something that has almost become a byword" and that, "like *Gemütlichkeit*," had entered "international terminology"?

Brandt had strong connections to Norway, much stronger than Borlaug's: He spoke Norwegian well, and had been a Norwegian citizen. You remember, from our discussion of the 1935 laureate Ossietzky, that Brandt spent exile years in Norway. He fled there when the Nazis came to power in 1933. He was 19 years old, and a left-wing firebrand. He arrived in the North with almost nothing—a bit of money and a copy of *Das Kapital*. In Oslo, he fell in with the Labor crowd, worked as a journalist, campaigned for Ossietzky's Nobel. When the war came, he fled to Sweden, where he took part in the Myrdals' circle. There is a Willy Brandt Park in Stockholm today. Through the war, while in Sweden, he never stopped pleading the cause of Norway, his adopted and occupied country. Chairman Lionæs said, "Our country is deeply indebted to Willy Brandt for his deeds during these evil years."

A Social Democrat, he was elected mayor of Berlin in 1957. He stayed in that post until 1966—meaning that he was mayor during the fateful year of 1961, when the Communists put up the Wall. In 1964, he became chairman of his party. By the end of 1966, he was foreign minister and vice-chancellor (in a coalition government). By the end of 1969, he was chancellor.

His Nobel lecture? A highly interesting, highly thoughtful address. Brandt spoke of previous German peace laureates, saying, "I realize that in the annals of Nobel-prize history the Germans have been more outstanding for their achievements in the fields of chemistry and physics than for their contribution to peace. Yet in this field, too, we have our representatives." He remembered Quidde, Stresemann, and, of course, Ossietzky. "That award was a moral victory over the ruling powers of barbarism. Today, in the name of free Germany, I wish to express belated thanks to the Nobel Committee for making that choice." He also remembered Bertha von Suttner and *Lay Down Your Arms!* He had read it. "I am still one of those who were deeply impressed by the book, and after all else I gladly identify myself with the naive Humanism of my youth."

Somewhat movingly, and contentiously, he meditated on the peculiar nature of Germany and Germanness: "I say here what I say in Germany: A good German cannot be a nationalist. A good German knows that he cannot refuse a European calling. Through Europe, Germany returns to itself and to the constructive forces of its history." And he interpreted his Nobel prize as a key moment in the German experience. His winning, he said, had "demonstrated to the whole world that Germany has come to terms with itself, just like an exile rediscovering the peaceful and human features of his fatherland."

In 1974, Brandt's chancellorship came to an end, when it was discovered that a top aide, Günter Guillaume, was an East German spy. Brandt remained chairman of the Social Democrats until 1987. He was also the head of the Socialist International, from 1976 until his death in 1992. During the 1980s, he fought very hard against President Reagan and his allies, and everything they stood for. Brandt's big principle was co-existence: co-existence between the democratic and Communist worlds. In his Nobel lecture, he said that "co-existence has become a question of the very existence of man." Co-existence was not merely "one of several acceptable possibilities but the only chance of survival." Reagan et al. thought that man could have it both ways: be free and survive. This view, for many years, was considered not only dangerous, but criminally so.

∽

The Nobel Committee passed over 1972—then created a sensation, with its 1973 award. This was not a sensation of a positive kind. They gave the prize to the lead negotiators of the Paris Agreement: Henry Kissinger, the American secretary of state, and Le Duc Tho, the envoy from North Vietnam. The Paris Agreement was a ceasefire in the Vietnam War, inked in January of that year, 1973. (Kissinger, at the time, was national security adviser. He became secretary of state in September.) The Vietnam War had been long and, of course, bloody. Chairman Lionæs said that "news of the Paris Agreement brought a wave of joy and hope to the entire world." She said that the committee hoped the parties would "feel a moral responsibility" to see the agreement through. They did not, or at least one party did not. And the 1973 award—whether for right or wrong reasons—lives in a degree of infamy.

Kissinger, according to his memoirs, was quite surprised at the award: "I had not even known that I was a candidate." He was, of course, moved to receive the Nobel prize, because there is no "comparable honor." And yet he felt queasy. He knew that the Paris Agreement was a house of cards. "I would have been far happier with recognition for a less precarious achievement. Without false modesty, I am prouder of what I accomplished in the next two years in the Middle East." Here Kissinger is referring to his well-known "shuttle diplomacy."

Furthermore, there was the problem of Nixon, the president under whom he was serving. Kissinger says that Nixon had "set his heart" on the Nobel prize. And to see his secretary of state win it instead must have been "painful." The recognition that Nixon most longed for, according to Kissinger, was recognition as a peacemaker. "Only those who knew Nixon well could perceive beneath the gallant congratulations" something amiss: a "hurt that I was being given all the credit for actions that had cost him so much."

Kissinger's share of the prize—in other words, half—was worth about $65,000, and he used it to set up a scholarship fund for the children of fallen or missing servicemen. He named the fund after his parents.

His co-laureate, Le Duc Tho, turned down the prize, on the strange grounds that the Paris Agreement was not being implemented. Kissinger puts it very well when he says that this was "another insolence" on the part of North Vietnam: Its violations had, in fact, turned the agreement into a "farce." Lionæs let it be known that Le Duc Tho had until October 1974—a year after the announcement—to accept the prize. He never did. And he is the only Nobel peace laureate to refuse the prize.

Around the Western world, reaction to the 1973 award was fierce, scornful, and bitter. Reaction in the Nobel Committee itself was not exactly happy. Two of the five members resigned. They had been against the award to the Paris negotiators, preferring Archbishop Hélder Câmara of Brazil, an apostle of "social justice" and "liberation theology." Câmara was a great favorite of the Left, in Norway and elsewhere. In the home of the Nobel Peace Prize, money was quickly raised to give him a Norwegian People's Peace Prize, which he traveled to Oslo to accept. As for the committee-men who resigned, their reason for doing so is slightly murky. They objected to the award, yes. But what they seem to have objected to most was Chairman Lionæs's handling of the stormy aftermath. In their view, she gave the impression to the press that the vote had been unanimous, when it had not: It was 3–2.

Representing a fair chunk of establishment opinion, the *New York Times* was aghast at the vote, saying it resulted in "the Nobel War Prize." The two Quaker organizations from 1947—the Friends Service Council and the American Friends Service Committee—sent a delegation to Oslo, to remonstrate with the committee. The committee declined to see them. Incidentally, these groups—the 1947 co-laureates—had nominated Archbishop Câmara for the prize.

Kissinger opted against going to Oslo, because mass demonstrations were planned, and he was loath to add fuel to the fire. He seized on a pretext: The life of a secretary of state is so busy. He tells us, in those memoirs, that the Norwegian government "seemed relieved." He sent a message, a kind of acceptance speech, to be read by the American ambassador there, Thomas Byrne. The ambassador ducked into a rear entrance, to avoid snowballs and such. Kissinger's message was, in part, a meditation on peace and its difficulties. He quoted from a Nobel address known to a great many Americans: the one given by a literature laureate, William Faulkner, in 1950. Faulkner said, "I believe that man will not merely endure, he will prevail." Kissinger said, "We live today in a world so complex that even only to endure, man must prevail—over an accelerating technology that threatens to escape his control and over the habits of conflict that have obscured his peaceful nature."

Lionæs, for her part, gave a very carefully written and reasoned presentation speech, in defense of this most controversial of awards. She said that, in making its decision, the committee was "fully aware that a ceasefire and not a peace agreement was involved." They "realized that peace has not yet come to Vietnam, and that the sufferings of the population of Vietnam are not at an end." But they wanted to honor the effort, and strengthen the chances for real peace. Lionæs remembered Ralph Bunche, in 1950. The general armistice he negotiated was shot to hell, in a succession of Arab–Israeli wars—the latest of which had occurred only two months before. (This was the Yom Kippur War.) But the committee felt no shame at honoring the effort.

Everyone says that the 1973 award is the "most unpopular" Nobel award ever, and that is probably true. But the nature of the unpopularity is worth pondering. The critics mainly objected to the half of the prize going to Kissinger, not the half going to Le Duc Tho. They thought it outrageous that the American secretary of state had won the Nobel prize, not so much that the representative of a totalitarian and mass-murdering dictatorship had done so. It is legend that Tom Lehrer, the American musician-satirist, gave up his career after Kissinger won the peace prize. That is not true: He had bowed out before. But he did say that "political satire became obsolete" when Kissinger won.

As the Bunche-mediated armistice was shot to hell, so was the Paris Agreement: North Vietnam conquered the South in April 1975, uniting the peninsula under Communism. Kissinger wrote to Lionæs, returning his gold medal, his diploma, and the money. He said he felt "honor bound" to do this. "I regret, more profoundly than I can ever express, the necessity for this letter. But the anguish and tragedy that have been inflicted upon millions who sought nothing more than the chance to live their own lives leave me no alternative." The committee would not accept Kissinger's gesture (or medal, or diploma, or cash): The Nobel Peace Prize is not returnable. The committee explained that events in Vietnam in no way reduced their "appreciation of Mr. Kissinger's sincere efforts to get a ceasefire agreement put into force in 1973."

War and Peace (or 'Peace')

In 1965, eight Nobel peace laureates banded together to issue what they called an "appeal." The eight were (in order of their awards) Angell, Boyd Orr, Schweitzer, Pire, Noel-Baker, Lutuli, Pauling, and King. Their appeal began,

> The war in Vietnam challenges the conscience of the world. None of us can read day after day the reports of the killing, the maiming, and the burning without calling for this inhumanity to end. Our present object is not to apportion blame among the groups of combatants. The one imperative is that this crime against all that is civilized in the family of man shall cease.

Speaking of crimes against all that is civilized in the family of man: When peace came to Vietnam—or, rather, when the war ended—the rulers killed approximately 1 million of their citizens. (Some say this estimate is too high. Call it 783,694, then.) That is in addition to the "reeducation" camps and similar horrors. Nobel peace laureates were not apt to talk about these things, or issue "appeals" concerning them. The "conscience of the world" was not so "challenged." Then too, you were not apt to "read day after day" about atrocities once the peace had come. The war was over, and that was that. Nothing can be worse than war, right?

∼

The 1974 award was much less controversial than its immediate predecessor, as it could hardly help being—but it still had a con-

troversial aspect. The Nobel was split between a Japanese statesman and a romantic figure who was both an Irish nationalist and
a prince of international organizations. First, the Japanese statesman. He was Eisaku Sato, who had been prime minister from
1964 to 1972. He was not the only prime minister in the family: His brother—who had a different last name, Kishi—had been
prime minister from 1957 to 1960. Under him, Sato served as
finance minister. In her presentation speech, Chairman Lionæs
said that Sato was the first Asian "who has received this prize."
That word "received" has some importance; Le Duc Tho was the
first Asian to be chosen for the prize, no matter his reaction.

And what did Sato win for? Lionæs gave many reasons, and
she gave them at length. First, Japan was rising again in the
world: but it was eschewing nationalism, a nationalism that had
caused horrific damage short decades before. Japan was pursuing
a "good-neighbor policy," Lionæs said, and the "chief exponent" of
this policy was Sato. Also, Japan had eschewed nuclear weapons.
Therefore, this nation—the only one to have been hit with nuclear
bombs—was showing the way for others. Lionæs further talked
about Sato's independence from Japan's most important ally, the
United States. He had reached an agreement with the Americans
returning Okinawa and other islands to Japanese control.

Sato, in his lecture, said that the bombings of Hiroshima
and Nagasaki had made his country "passionately determined
to renounce all wars." And he said that, unusually for a "major
power," Japan had absorbed "the philosophy of the Kellogg-Briand
Pact." (Japan was the first nation to violate that pact—the first, but
not the last.) Since this Nobel lecture in 1974, has the Kellogg-
Briand Pact been mentioned favorably in a big public address? It
would seem unlikely.

The half of the '74 prize to Sato was unpopular with "world
opinion," which is to say, really, with the Left, soft and hard. Okinawa and the other islands aside, Sato had been very close to the

United States, and this closeness included support for the Vietnam War. Also, Sato had withheld recognition from Communist China, keeping Japan's relationship with Taiwan. And how antinuclear was he? Sato and Japan had permitted American ships to moor in Japanese harbors, and some of those ships were nuclear-armed. Listen to one more complaint—this one not ideological but stylistic: Sato and his people had campaigned for the prize! (An activity not unknown to laureates, and would-be laureates, to be sure.)

No doubt because of the Left's unhappiness, Chairman Lionæs was especially specific and forceful in her explanations and defense of the half-prize to Sato. This was the second consecutive year in which she had to be especially forceful. She addressed the cluster of criticisms, in one way or another. Only months after this ceremony, in June 1975, Sato died. He had been born in 1901—the same year as the Nobel prizes, as he noted in his lecture.

The other laureate, that Irish nationalist and prince of international organizations? He was not unpopular on the left, quite the opposite. Seán MacBride was born in Paris, in 1904. His father was Major John MacBride, who had led the Irish Transvaal Brigade against the British in the Second Boer War. At home, the major took part in the Easter Rising, the rebellion of republicans against British rule in 1916. He was thereafter executed. Seán's mother was the famous Maud Gonne, an Irish revolutionary who was one of the founders of Sinn Féin. She was also an actress—and the love interest and muse of Yeats (no less). He proposed to her several times. She always said no. He also proposed to Maud's daughter, Seán's half-sister, when the young woman was 23. The daughter, Iseult, said no too. She had an affair with another poet, Pound.

At twelve, after his father's execution, Seán was taken from France to Ireland. He would become an IRA man, a leading actor in the Irish Republican Army. He rose to chief of staff. He then became a distinguished lawyer, a politician, and the foreign minister of Ireland. In following decades, he engaged in his multiplicity of international doings. For example, he was the chairman of Amnesty International (which won the Nobel prize in 1977). He was chairman, then president, of the International Peace Bureau (the laureate for 1910). He also held many U.N. posts, including high commissioner for Namibia.

In 1973, he played an important role at the World Congress of Peace Forces in Moscow. He was vice-chairman. The event took place in October, exactly a year before his Nobel prize was announced. The main speaker at the congress was, of course, that champion of peace, Brezhnev—winner of the Lenin Peace Prize. Brezhnev told his guests that the congress was "an important stage in the public movement to defend peace."

MacBride died in 1988. Every year, the International Peace Bureau gives a Seán MacBride Peace Prize. A sense of the prize can be had in the following: In 1994, it went to Mordechai Vanunu, the Israeli who spilled secrets about his country's nuclear capabilities. And in 2002, it went to Barbara Lee, the radical California congresswoman who was the only member of Congress to vote against the Afghan War.

We can see in MacBride's Nobel lecture that he was a sharp and commanding man, highly skilled in the art of polemics. He must have been a force in the courtroom, and in his sundry other forums. In his lecture, he outlined what he called "eight imperatives," beginning with "General and Complete Disarmament" and ending with "a world parliament and government." And he was not one to position himself between the Free World and the Communist, as so many Nobel laureates had, and would. He leaned in one direction.

"Peaceful conditions in the world," he said, "are not welcome to the arms industry. General and Complete Disarmament would spell disaster to the industrial-military complexes in the United States, France, Britain and Germany, to mention but a few of the countries that thrive on increased armament." On the other hand,

> the socialist countries [i.e., the Soviet Union and its satellites] do not have a profit-motivated industrial-military complex. They can therefore adjust more readily to disarmament. The military-industrial complex is state-owned and -controlled. To them disarmament means an automatic switch from increased arms production to increase in production for industrial development and for the consumer and export markets. They cannot lose by disarmament, they can only gain. This, no doubt, accounts for the much more sincere and far-reaching approach of the Soviet Union to General and Complete Disarmament than that of the Western powers.

Praising various groups that worked toward disarmament, MacBride said that "special credit should be given to the Soviet Peace Council for its initiative in organizing and hosting the World Congress of Peace Forces." You would never know from this Nobel lecture that the Soviet Peace Council and its congress were shams, completely typical of the CPSU, the Communist Party of the Soviet Union.

Not long after MacBride won his Nobel prize, he won his Lenin prize. As I said when discussing Linus Pauling, the Soviet government did not give this award carelessly or thoughtlessly: Its recipients earned it. Men and women such as MacBride had no problem accepting a peace prize—indeed, were pleased and proud to accept a peace prize—from an unelected government dedicated to controlling human beings by violence. In 1974, complaints about the Nobel Peace Prize were directed at Sato's share in it. As some of us see it, Sato was the more honorable winner that year, by far.

∿

The next year, the Nobel Committee did something remarkable: It gave the peace prize to someone of whom the Soviet government was not so fond, and who was certainly not fond of it. Moreover, this government had long before stopped giving this man prizes. The 1975 laureate was Andrei Sakharov, the hero-scientist-turned-hero-dissident.

Born in 1921, Sakharov became one of the leading scientists in his country. He was the physicist principally responsible for giving the Soviet Union the hydrogen bomb. The government rewarded him handsomely: with the Hero of Socialist Labor award (three times), with the Stalin Prize, and with the Lenin Prize. (These last two are not to be confused with the Soviets' peace prize, first named for Stalin and then for Lenin. The prizes that Sakharov won were the highest honors in the Soviet chest.) Sakharov was made a member of the Soviet Academy of Sciences at the age of 32; he was the youngest member. For the rest of his life, he could have lived as an esteemed and privileged member of the nomen-klatura, as a favorite son of the regime. But, in the late 1960s, he made the fateful decision to become a human-rights champion and dissident. He suffered terribly for it. He also showed himself one of the noblest human beings of his age.

A couple of things happened in 1975, his Nobel year. He published a famous piece of writing, *My Country and the World*—in which he pleaded with people and governments around the globe to oppose the dictatorship in Moscow and force it to liberalize. And the Soviets signed the Helsinki Accords, in which they made some promises concerning human rights.

When the Nobel announcement came in October, the Norwegian ambassador in Moscow sent Sakharov a vase of six pink roses. (Why they didn't spring for a dozen, I cannot say.) Sakharov's immediate response to winning the prize was, "I hope this will help political prisoners." The Soviet government's response was furious displeasure. They called Sakharov an "anti-patriot," an "enemy of détente," a "Judas for whom the Nobel prize was 30 pieces of silver from the West." (Interesting that Soviet authorities should have reached for a Gospel reference.) They had the Academy of Sciences denounce him. And, in an especially charming touch, they forged a telegram from Pinochet, the right-wing dictator of Chile, congratulating him.

When December came, they would not let him out of the country to receive his prize. But his wife, a fellow dissident, Elena Bonner, was already out of the country, in Italy, for medical treatment. Indeed, she had been in Italy when the announcement was made. And she stayed on in Europe, representing Sakharov in Oslo. At the ceremony, Chairman Lionæs said, "In a convincing manner, Sakharov has emphasized that man's inviolable rights provide the only safe foundation for genuine and enduring international cooperation." And she said this: "The Nobel Committee deeply deplores the fact that Andrei Sakharov has been prevented from being present here today in person to receive the peace prize. This is a fate he shares with the man who, 40 years ago in 1935, was awarded the peace prize. His name was Carl von Ossietzky." Never mind the technical detail that Ossietzky got the award, for 1935, in 1936: The chairman had delivered a bull's-eye. The Soviets' behavior was linked to the Nazis'.

Bonner read both an acceptance speech and a Nobel lecture, written by her husband. In the former speech, he thanked his friends living abroad who were in attendance. He had wanted to invite four friends living in the Soviet Union, but they could not be present, for essentially the same reason he himself could not be present. He said, "Still, I beg you to kindly consider all of them my official guests." Rarely has something so touching or poignant been said at a Nobel ceremony.

The lecture was a formidable, penetrating thing. Titled "Peace, Progress, Human Rights," it examined conditions in the Soviet Union and in the world at large. Sakharov even stepped into the realm of agriculture, Norman Borlaug's territory. Speaking as a scientist, he addressed the critics of the Green Revolution, who were multiplying and growing louder:

> It is not so very long since men were unfamiliar with artificial fertilizers, mechanized farming, toxic chemicals, and intensive agricultural methods. There are voices calling for a return to more traditional and possibly less dangerous forms of agriculture. But can this be put into practice in a world in which hundreds of millions of people are suffering the pangs of hunger? On the contrary, there is no doubt that we need increasingly intensive methods of farming, and we need to spread modern methods all over the world, including the developing countries.

Further on in the speech, he said that he considered the United Nations "one of mankind's most important hopes for a better future." But he laid into the resolution the organization had adopted a month before: the infamous Resolution 3379, which said that Zionism equals racism. Sakharov said that, "in my opinion," the resolution had "dealt the prestige of the United Nations a hard blow."

Still further in the speech, as it neared its end, he did something stunning: He named names—names of political prisoners held in his country. What is most encouraging to such prisoners is to be remembered, talked about; what is most discouraging is to be forgotten, to suffer in oblivion. Sakharov, through his wife, said, "Here are some of the names that are known to me." Then he began, "Plyush, Bukovsky, Glusman, Moros, Maria Semyonova, Nadeshda Svetlishnaya . . . ." He named about a hundred names, concluding with, "and many, many others." In a 2010 letter to me, Bonner said that "the listing of names brought joy to the prisoners of conscience, and to their relatives. More important, it somewhat protected them from the camp administration. Besides, listing specific people, and caring about a particular person, as opposed to general arguments about human rights, fulfilled a most important inner need for Sakharov."

The Nobel prize did not afford Sakharov much protection, or much self-evident protection. In her letter, Bonner said that Soviet authorities treated him and his family even worse than before. He had embarrassed them on the world stage. In 1980, five years after the ceremony, the government sent him into internal exile. He was isolated in the closed city of Gorky, and underwent much torment. In 1986, as Gorbachev liberalized, Sakharov was allowed to return to Moscow. In 1989, he was elected to the First Congress of People's Deputies. He died at the end of that year, age 68. Some 100,000 people attended his funeral, as sleet fell. At the time he won the Nobel prize, he said something distinctive and characteristic. He said, "Even if what I am doing will not produce change in my lifetime, it is not useless, because it is a moral act. It is being true to what I believe in and must do."

The struggle against Soviet Communism lasted as long as Soviet Communism itself: some 75 years. In the USSR and captive nations farther afield, there were many heroes, many dissidents, many prisoners of conscience. Only two persons in the general anti-Soviet struggle were honored with the Nobel Peace Prize: Sakharov and, in 1983, Lech Walesa, the Polish trade-union leader, who would become the first president of a free Poland. By contrast, the Nobel Committee honored the anti-apartheid struggle in South Africa three times (the first in 1960, as we have seen, and the next two in 1984 and 1993, as we will see).

Since 1988, the European Parliament has given a Sakharov Prize for Freedom of Thought. It is traditionally awarded on December 10, the U.N.'s Human Rights Day. Sometimes the prize has gone to those who could well win the Nobel prize too, and have: Nelson Mandela, for example. Sometimes it has gone to individuals who would be unlikely to win the Nobel. I have particularly in mind Cuban dissidents, such as Oswaldo Payá and Guillermo Fariñas. In Cuba, the Pro–Human Rights party is very proud of its affiliation with the Andrei Sakharov Foundation. The party uses that affiliation in its very name, calling itself El Partido Pro Derechos Umanos de Cuba, afiliado a la Fundación Andrei Sajarov.

The year after Sakharov's death, 1990, the Nobel Committee gave the peace prize to Gorbachev. Elena Bonner was sickened by this, and sent a letter of protest to the Nobel Committee. By 2010, she was able to say, "I maintain an incomparably more peaceful attitude" toward the prize to Gorbachev. And "I respect Mikhail Sergeyevich personally." The year before, 2009, she made her speech to the Oslo Freedom Forum, which I've previously cited. She decried the anti-Semitism and anti-Zionism sweeping Europe, and other regions. And the Nobel prize had for some time been fairly bitter in her mouth. Arafat was a fellow laureate with her husband, as she pointed out. And she wrote to me, "I'd like to remind you that, in 1973, there came to our house two members of Arafat's Palestine Liberation Organization, who threatened to kill Sakharov and our whole family—and they knew about the recent birth of my first grandson!—if Sakharov did not cease his pro-Israeli statements."

Regardless of what came before, and regardless of what came afterward, 1975, the Sakharov year, was a peak moment in Nobel history.

~

Twice has the Nobel Committee given awards having to do with "the Troubles" in Northern Ireland: the conflict between Protestants and Catholics, loyalists and republicans. The first time was in 1977, when it gave the award for 1976 to two young women from Belfast; the second time—and the last, one presumes?—was in 1998. The half-prize to MacBride in 1974 doesn't count. That award did not relate to the laureate's IRA past but rather to what the committee regarded as his important work in international organizations and human rights.

The co-laureates for 1976 were Betty Williams and Máiread Corrigan—who, in that year, were 33 and 32. Either would have passed Martin Luther King (who had been 35) as the youngest laureate. Corrigan remained the youngest until 2011, when Yemen's Tawakkul Karman was a winner. (Karman, like Corrigan, was 32, but younger by mere days.) When Williams and Corrigan began their peacework, both were office assistants, and Williams also worked as a waitress. People will naturally want to know about religion: Corrigan was Catholic. As for Williams, she had a Catholic mother and a Protestant father—plus a Jewish grandfather— and she went to Catholic schools. Suffice it to say, both women were tolerant where religion was concerned. Otherwise they probably would not have done that prizewinning work.

Their prize comes with a tragic story. On August 10, 1976, Anne Maguire was out walking with four of her children. There had been a shootout between the IRA and the British army. Driving a fleeing car, an IRA man was shot through the head. The car crashed into the Maguire family, killing two of the children instantly and claiming a third later. Their mother was badly injured. Of the dead children, the youngest was six weeks, and the others were two years and eight. A witness to the horrible event was Williams. In the following days, she got together with Corrigan, a sister of Anne Maguire and an aunt of those children. They formed a group called Women for Peace. They then coordinated with a journalist named Ciaran McKeown, and the group was expanded into the Community of the Peace People. This group, or movement, attracted Protestants and Catholics, any and all who wanted an end to the violence. They marched and protested in great numbers.

In 1980, Anne Maguire, unable to live with her torment, killed herself. As Corrigan told it in a speech, Anne left a note saying, "Forgive me. I can't go on. I love you." Corrigan went to care for the remaining Maguire children, and in 1981 married their father, her former brother-in-law. She is known today as Máiread Corrigan Maguire.

Giving the presentation speech for the 1976 laureates was a committeeman named Egil Aarvik. (He would become chairman in 1982.) He said, "Betty Williams and Máiread Corrigan have shown us what ordinary people can do to promote the cause of peace." Indeed, never before had such "ordinary" people won the prize—that is, they were not authors, statesmen, or peace-movement professionals. But they soon became professionals. There is a peace circuit, same as there are circuits in other fields. And Williams and Maguire have ridden the peace circuit for many years, attending conferences, giving lectures, and picking up award after award. They are, you might say, professional Nobel peace laureates. There are others, and this is a relatively recent phenomenon.

In 2006, six female Nobel peace laureates established what they called the Nobel Women's Initiative—and the Northern Irish women were among them. The purpose of this group is a popular one: "peace with justice and equality." Both Williams and Maguire are dynamic speakers, full of charm and personality (being Irish, after all). Not long after their Nobel prize, they had a falling-out, and for 20 years refused to speak to each other. They mended that, however.

Maguire has made a specialty of anti-Israel activism. Her hatred of, certainly her opposition to, that state burns hot. She speaks of the country's "apartheid system" and has accused the Israelis of "carrying out a policy of ethnic cleansing against the Palestinians." She participated in efforts to break the Israeli-Egyptian blockade of Gaza, a blockade intended to keep further war matériel out of that brutal, Hamas-ruled strip. She has repeatedly accused Israel of "war crimes" and "crimes against humanity." She is not one to denounce or criticize Hamas and the PLO for their abuses of citizens under their control; she concentrates her fire on Israel.

She saves some, however, for the United States, which she has also accused of war crimes and crimes against humanity. For her, there is one criminal, one wrongdoer, in Iraq and Afghanistan: the United States. Not for her is criticism of Saddam Hussein, the Taliban, the ayatollahs in Iran, and other such actors. She was greatly upset when President Obama won the Nobel Peace Prize in 2009. She said, "Giving this award to the leader of the most militarized country in the world, which has taken the human family against its will to war, will be rightly seen by many people around the world as a reward for his country's aggression and domination." She also said, "This is not the first time the Nobel peace committee in Oslo has ignored the will of Alfred Nobel and acted against the spirit of what the Nobel Peace Prize is all about." It is very, very rare for a peace laureate to criticize a subsequent decision by the committee—or to claim to know more about Nobel and his intentions than does the committee itself.

The other '76 laureate, Betty Williams, is cut from basically the same cloth. In 2006, she was speaking to schoolchildren in Brisbane, Australia. She said, "I have a very hard time with this word 'nonviolence,' because I don't believe that I am nonviolent. Right now, I would love to kill George Bush. I don't know how I ever got a Nobel Peace Prize, because when I see children die the anger in me is just beyond belief." (In her eyes, Bush was devoted to killing children.) She reprised her performance in 2007, speaking, not to schoolkids, but to the International Women's Peace Conference in Dallas. She said, "Right now, I could kill George Bush, no problem. No, I don't mean that. I mean, how could you nonviolently kill somebody? I would love to be able to do that." She then laughed, as did much of her audience. She later denied, flat-out, that she had made any statement expressing a desire to kill the president. Confronted with tape—both audio and video—she backpedaled and apologized.

Whatever we think of Williams and Maguire in these last decades—whatever we think of the ways they have used their Nobel fame and prestige—they did something noble in that summer of '76, after the death of those three children. And they were very, very brave. Here were two women, going on nothing but nerve, telling the IRA to lay down their arms. The IRA might have killed them for that—they killed for less. And they certainly threatened the women and their followers. Undaunted, the women went to America, to tell the Irish Americans to stop sending money to the IRA. The IRA might have killed them for that, too. Possibly, the Nobel prize, when it came, protected the women, making the gunmen think it unwise to target them—unwise from a PR point of view. The women were called traitors, turncoats, British spies, worse. They persisted, crying against violence and urging peace.

Here is a final detail, from a dramatic, terrible time: On the day those children were buried—her nephews and niece—Máiread Corrigan took roses from their grave and presented them to the mother of Danny Lennon, the IRA driver of that fleeing car.

～

The 1977 winner, as I have mentioned, was Amnesty International, the most famous human-rights organization in the world. It is also one of the most contentious organizations in the world. The story of its founding is an oft-told and stirring one: One day in 1960, Peter Benenson was riding on a train in London. He was a British lawyer who had defended political prisoners in Hungary, South Africa, and elsewhere. On that train, he read in the papers about the imprisonment of two students in Portugal, then ruled by the dictator Salazar. (António de Oliveira Salazar lorded it over Portugal from 1932 to 1968.) The students' offense was to have drunk a toast to freedom. Benenson decided that he should help those students, and that there should be a movement for all such prisoners. In 1961, he launched the Appeal for Amnesty. That British effort quickly grew into the globally sprawling Amnesty International (chaired by MacBride).

The purpose of Amnesty—or "AI," as it is also called—was to work for the release of prisoners of conscience. And that term, in fact—"prisoners of conscience"—was an Amnesty invention. It referred to prisoners who had been jailed for expressing their opinions; they were distinct from prisoners who had employed violence, or advocated violence. Amnesty's technique was to "adopt" prisoners, making them their own: their own concern.

So, why is Amnesty so contentious? It would seem the most unimpeachable, blameless, and praiseworthy of organizations—indeed, a sacrosanct organization. Early on, Amnesty decided that it would be "evenhanded" regarding the countries of the world: liberal democratic, Communist, "developing," whatever they were. This led to some moral screwiness, some screwy equating. For example, in a given year, Amnesty might fault the Soviet Union for the depredations of the Gulag; in equal tones, it would fault the United States for the existence of capital punishment.

In the 2000s, Amnesty took after the U.S. with a vengeance. In 2006, it issued 13 "country reports" on the U.S. (which is to say, against the U.S.). One thing Amnesty objected to was the use of Tasers—stun guns—by the police. No reports were issued against North Korea, one of the most sadistic and depraved states in history. And there was relatively little on other brutal states: one report on the Assads' Syria, for example, and no report on Qaddafi's Libya. Meanwhile, there were seven reports against Israel. Granted, free and open countries—liberal democracies—are easier to report on than absolute dictatorships. But how hard was Amnesty trying? Besides, they seemed to exult in blasting the democracies, particularly their bêtes noires, the U.S. and Israel.

In 2005, Amnesty's secretary-general, Irene Khan, made a pronouncement on the American prison at Guantánamo Bay, where terrorists and terror suspects were held: She called it the "Gulag of our times." That was too much even for standard liberal opinion. The *Washington Post* editorialized, "It's always sad when a solid, trustworthy institution loses its bearings . . . ." The paper noted that, for 40 years, Amnesty had challenged dictators on the right and on the left. "But lately the organization has tended to save its most vitriolic condemnations not for the world's dictators but for the United States." The paper went on to explain, for those who had forgotten, what the Soviet gulag had been; and what Saddam Hussein's gulag (recently smashed) had been; and what the Cuban, North Korean, and Chinese gulags still were.

Three weeks later, the *Post* published an article by Pavel Litvinov, who had been in the Soviet gulag. He is the grandson of Maxim Litvinov, a foreign minister under Stalin, and one of those whom Halvdan Koht nominated for the Nobel Peace Prize after World War II. He began his article,

> Several days ago I received a telephone call from an old friend who is a longtime Amnesty International staffer. He asked me whether I, as a former Soviet "prisoner of conscience" adopted

by Amnesty, would support the statement . . . that the Guantanamo Bay prison in Cuba is the "gulag of our time."

"Don't you think that there's an enormous difference?" I asked him.

"Sure," he said, "but after all, it attracts attention to the problem of Guantanamo detainees."

Further infamy attached to Amnesty in 2010, when the organization allied itself with a group called Cageprisoners, headed by Moazzam Begg—a former Guantánamo prisoner who was one of the leading Islamists in Britain. He had trained in al-Qaeda camps in Afghanistan. His claim was that prisoners such as those at Guantánamo Bay—terror detainees—were really human-rights victims. One of those speaking out against the alliance between Amnesty and Begg was Salman Rushdie. He is the Anglo-Indian novelist against whom the Iranian government issued a *fatwa*, calling for his death. Rushdie wrote, "It looks very much as if Amnesty's leadership is suffering from a kind of moral bankruptcy, and has lost the ability to distinguish right from wrong."

In many eyes, Amnesty has compromised itself beyond repair. It has followed the zeitgeist—Left fashion—over the edge, into a moral swamp. But it still accomplishes some good, speaking up for prisoners alone in their dungeons. Amnesty International is not unlike the Nobel Peace Prize: sometimes vexing, sometimes outrageous and indefensible, sometimes laudable. Just as it's hard to write off the peace prize altogether, it's hard to write off Amnesty altogether. But the temptation to write off either is understandable.

⁓

The 1978 Nobel was as natural a prize as the committee has ever conferred. This is the one that went to Anwar Sadat, the president of Egypt, and Menachem Begin, the prime minister of Israel, for the Camp David Accords. Those accords were signed on September 17, 1978. The award was announced on October 27—and, of course, handed out on December 10.

And what did those accords do? They were preliminary, laying the groundwork for a formal peace treaty between Egypt and Israel. And one of the Nobel Committee's aims was to help ensure that such a treaty was indeed concluded—which it was, on March 26, 1979. Egypt had waged four wars against Israel, starting with the founding of Israel in 1948. But now, under Sadat, it was seeking peace. After the signing of the peace treaty, Israel returned the whole of the Sinai Peninsula—seized in the 1967 war—to Egypt. And Egypt granted Israel full diplomatic recognition—and, more to the point, peace.

In the West, many on the left were dismayed that Sadat had to share his Nobel prize with Begin—who was hated as a right-winger and a hard-liner. And a curious thing happened in Egypt: Radio Cairo announced the prize to Sadat, but did not report that he was sharing it with Begin. Much of the Arab world was incensed at Sadat for his peacemaking. The PLO, led by Arafat, of course, issued a stern statement about Oslo's decision: "As far as the Palestinian people are concerned, the Nobel prize has been shared by two fascists with a black history."

Menachem Begin was completely surprised and delighted when the committee made its announcement. There was a crowd at the Begins' that night, and it included Artur Rubinstein, the great pianist. As Zev Chafets, the writer who was then director of the Israeli Government Press Office, remembers, Begin asked Rubinstein to sit down and play something in celebration: which he did.

In December, Begin went to Oslo, but Sadat did not. The Egyptian president's official reason was that a peace treaty had not been concluded; merely the Camp David Accords had been signed. The more plausible reason was that Sadat was already paying a heavy price in the Arab world for making peace; linking arms with Begin in Oslo would only make that price heavier. Today, some veterans of Begin's camp think that the prime minister was completely unbothered by Sadat's absence; others think that he was just slightly insulted, or miffed.

Another statesman missing in Oslo was Jimmy Carter, the American president who had hosted and shepherded the Camp David negotiations. Everyone said that Carter, with the Middle Easterners, should have had a piece of the prize. Certainly Begin thought so: He told him this outright. And the Nobel Committee itself thought so, as we said earlier in this book. The committee wanted to make Carter a third laureate, but he had not been nominated before February 1, and the rules were the rules. All three speakers at the prize ceremony—Chairman Lionæs, Sadat (through a proxy), and Begin—paid glowing tribute to Carter (who in any case would win his own Nobel 24 years later).

This is what Carter wrote in his diary on October 27, 1978: "I sent Begin and Sadat a congratulatory message after they received the Nobel Peace Prize jointly. Sadat deserved it; Begin did not."

The ceremony in December did not take place at the University of Oslo, as was planned: Threats against Begin were too great, and the Left was preparing a massive demonstration. The ceremony was moved to Akershus Fortress, on a cliff above the Oslo Fjord. Some people commented on the irony of a peace ceremony in a fortress. Begin was choppered from the royal palace to Akershus, even as he had been choppered from the airport to the palace. As the ceremony took place, police and soldiers coped with demonstrators outside.

In her presentation speech, Lionæs spent several paragraphs praising Henry Kissinger, the laureate from five years before. She spoke of that shuttle diplomacy between Egypt and Israel following the 1973 war. This work, she said, "provided the basis" for the Camp David Accords. We have already heard that Kissinger was prouder of this work than he was of the Vietnam talks, and "agreement." It may well be that Lionæs stressed Kissinger's role in the Middle East because of the immense grief she had gotten over the 1973 award.

Representing Sadat was Sayed Marei, his counselor and confidant. (Marei's son was married to Sadat's daughter.) Marei was with the president three years later, on that terrible day. In the storm of bullets and grenades, he was injured, but not killed. Ten others were killed, along with Sadat.

Begin gave a notable Nobel lecture, written by himself but "Shakespeare-ized" by Yehuda Avner. That was a Begin coinage, "Shakespeare-ize." Avner was an aide and speechwriter to Begin, and later ambassador to Great Britain. He had been born an Englishman, and was a beautiful user of his native language (as he remains). On becoming prime minister, Begin said to him, "I need you to polish my Polish English. Please be my Shakespeare—and Shakespeare-ize what I write."

Begin opened his lecture with some words about the lioness of Israel, who had died two days before: "I ask for permission first to pay tribute to Golda Meir, my predecessor, a great leader and prime minister, who strove with all her heart to achieve peace between Israel and her neighbors. Her blessed memory will live forever in the hearts of the Jewish people and of all peace-loving nations." Begin proceeded to speak about the Holocaust, the nature of Israel, the meaning of peace, and other vital matters. He ended by citing Carl Christian Berner, president of the Storting back when the Nobel Peace Prize started. Begin quoted some words that Berner spoke at the first prize ceremony: "The Norwegian people have always demanded that their independence be respected. They have always been ready to defend it. But at the same time they have always had a keen desire and need for peace." Begin said, in effect, So it is with Israel.

In the short years after the peace treaty, Sadat was subject to many, many assassination plots and attempts. His security forces foiled them all—until October 6, 1981. The killers were religious fundamentalists, belonging to or associated with the Muslim Brotherhood. In on the plot were two men who were to gain further infamy later: Omar Abdel-Rahman, the "Blind Sheikh," who was convicted in the 1993 World Trade Center bombing; and Ayman Zawahiri, who became No. 2 to Osama bin Laden in al-Qaeda, and rose to the top spot after U.S. forces killed his boss.

Sadat did a historic and awesomely brave thing when he traveled to Jerusalem in November 1977 to meet with Begin and address the Knesset—all for the purpose of proposing peace. Sadat risked more than Begin, much more—indeed, he ultimately paid with his life. But Begin did not risk nothing. Israelis more hard-line than he had grave reservations about, for example, returning the whole of the Sinai. Would Egypt really refrain from more war? What about all the Israelis who had settled in the Sinai, built towns there? They would have to be removed, right? (Right.) To devotees of the Nobel Peace Prize, the award to Begin is ignominious. They resent and deplore this award as they do the ones to Kissinger (above all) and Theodore Roosevelt. Those are their three least favorite awards. When Begin had Israel go into Lebanon in the summer of 1982, to rout the PLO, which had been attacking Israelis without cease, there was a movement in the Storting to revoke, somehow, the prime minister's Nobel; but it went nowhere.

~

Did the Nobel prize make Mother Teresa famous? She was well known before 1979, the year of her prize. In the late 1960s, Malcolm Muggeridge, the eminent British journalist and intellectual, traveled to Calcutta to make a BBC documentary about her: *Something Beautiful for God.* He later wrote a book about her, using that same title. And, inspired by Mother Teresa's example, he converted from atheism to Catholicism. In December 1975, Mother

Teresa was pictured on the cover of *Time* magazine, for an article on "Living Saints." She won many awards before the Nobel—but this grandest of all prizes catapulted her into a truly colossal fame.

A living saint indeed, she was the "saint of the gutters," ministering to "the poorest of the poor": the starving, the leprous, the dying. On hearing that she had won the Nobel prize, she said, "I am not worthy." But she knew that winning this glittering and lucrative award would help the poor, who were her concern. The chairman presenting her the prize was a new one: John Sanness, a Labor intellectual who had replaced Aase Lionæs. He said that, in selecting Mother Teresa, the committee had borne in mind the Nansen slogan: "Love of man is practical policy." He also mentioned Schweitzer's philosophy of "reverence for life."

Mother Teresa gave a most unusual Nobel lecture. Simply yet profoundly, she talked about Christ and human obligation. She said, "I feel the greatest destroyer of peace today is abortion, because it is a direct war, a direct killing—direct murder by the mother herself." This is not typical Nobel talk, very far from it. And, obviously, it did not sit well with many. Also, she told stories, about the people she encountered in her daily walk and work. There was a man immobilized, flat on his back—but he had the use of his right hand. He used it to smoke, his one pleasure in life. But he gave up smoking for a week, and sent the money he saved to Mother Teresa—who used it to buy bread for the poor.

The night of the prize ceremony, there was no banquet, as there traditionally is: Mother Teresa had requested that the organizers cancel it, and give the money to the poor. They did. And, of course, the poor got Mother Teresa's prize money. In 1964, Pope Paul visited India, and gave Mother Teresa the limousine he used. Without ever getting into it, she raffled it off, and applied the money to her leper colony. Mother Teresa had her critics and detractors, because everyone does, it seems. But acquaintance with her life confirms that she was as good as her reputation. She was born in 1910 to an Albanian family in Macedonia; she died in 1997.

∼

Winning the 1980 prize was a human-rights activist from Argentina, Adolfo Pérez Esquivel. He was born in 1931 and became a sculptor and architect. He would also do some painting: The Norwegian Nobel Institute has in its possession a painting by Pérez Esquivel of mothers of the "disappeared." Those mothers have haunting and haunted Picasso eyes.

In the 1970s, Argentina was rife with political violence—terror—from left and right. Pérez Esquivel was a professor at the National School of Fine Arts; he was also occupied with social concerns. In 1974, he left his academic and artistic career to be secretary-general of Servicio Paz y Justicia en América Latina—Service for Peace and Justice in Latin America. This was a religious group, ecumenical; Pérez Esquivel was strongly religious, a Catholic lay leader. In 1976, a military junta took over Argentina, and Pérez Esquivel was soon in its crosshairs. In April 1977, he went to renew his passport. They arrested him, threw him in prison, and tortured him. Amnesty International adopted him as a prisoner of conscience; there was also pressure from the Catholic Church. After 14 months, the junta released him, but kept him under police supervision. Eventually, Pérez Esquivel was free to resume his activism, which he did, fearlessly.

In April 1980, he visited Norway, meeting with all the relevant groups: Amnesty, the foreign ministry, and so on. And that October, the Nobel Committee announced that Pérez Esquivel would receive the peace prize.

He was relatively unknown in the world, but, as with most Nobel laureates, the world quickly got to know him. The committee had started to issue press releases in announcing the prizes. And the press release for 1980 said that Pérez Esquivel was "among those Argentineans who have shone a light in the darkness." In a sense, the committee was shining a light on him. Speaking at the prize ceremony, Chairman Sanness stressed Pérez Esquivel's absolute commitment to nonviolence and his relative freedom from ideology: his opposition to tyranny from any direction, for any purpose. Such opponents, in Latin America as elsewhere, but perhaps especially in Latin America, were not common. Sanness also cited the message that Sakharov, exiled in Gorky, had managed to send to the new laureate. Sakharov said he understood "the gravity and the tragedy of the problems facing your country and other countries in Latin America. Your vigorous struggle for justice and the help you have given to people suffering under oppression are cherished by people who live thousands of miles away, in another world."

Pérez Esquivel gave an acceptance speech, which was almost as religious as Mother Teresa's lecture had been. At the end of it, he said, "Invoking the strength of Christ, our Lord, I would like to share with you, with my people, and with the world what he has taught us in the Sermon on the Mount." Then he recited the Beatitudes, all of them.

His lecture the next day was a gem: beautiful, balanced, pointed, and wise. He decried "violence from both the left and the right, which has resulted in the murdered, the injured, the disappeared, the tortured, the imprisoned, and the exiled." Very, very unusually for a Nobel speaker, he mentioned Cuba: "its prisoners" and the "politicians responsible for clear transgressions against human rights." He saluted Sakharov: "May he soon regain his liberty, together with Mr. Anatoly Shcharansky . . . ." Shcharansky was the "refusenik" who would later write the immortal Gulag memoir *Fear No Evil* and, as Natan Sharansky, become an Israeli politician. Pérez Esquivel's naming of Shcharansky, in such an important talk, with the eyes of the world on the speaker, was yet another of this laureate's gracious and noble acts.

In 1980, in Oslo, Pérez Esquivel stood as a figure of "purity and clarity," to borrow a phrase from Sanness. But Pérez Esquivel seems to have undergone a profound change. Like Máiread Corrigan Maguire, his friend and colleague, he became an activist of the hard Left. (Corrigan and Williams had nominated Pérez Esquivel, by the way, for the peace prize.) His human-rights protests were now selective, ideologically colored. Like Maguire, he is fiercely anti-Israel, anti-American. Most tragically, or most outrageously, he is a Castroite: a friend to Fidel Castro, an apologist for him, an adornment to his court.

He is the type to be invited to Castro's birthday parties. He is the type to sign letters supporting the Cuban regime. Castro has praised Pérez Esquivel in his writings, and the support of this Nobel peace laureate seems to mean a lot to this dictator. Why wouldn't it? Appraising Castro, Pérez Esquivel has said, "He has left a gesture of solidarity to all the peoples of Latin America; a legacy of resistance, autonomy, and sovereignty." Bear in mind that, for over 50 years, Castro has been an absolute dictator, the creator and boss of a totalitarian society, a crusher-out of all rights, the lord of a gulag: in which liberals, reformers, Catholic lay leaders, human-rights activists, and all dissenters are held and tortured, not for 14 months, but for years and decades and forever. What would Pérez Esquivel say to Cuban prisoners of conscience, if he ever faced them?

About the United States, Pérez Esquivel talks the way the most extreme element can be expected to talk. Shortly after the 9/11 attacks, the U.S. went into Afghanistan, to rout al-Qaeda and oust its state sponsor, the Taliban. Two months later, Pérez Esquivel went to Oslo, to speak at the Nobel centennial symposium. He declared that the United States was guilty of "state terrorism." Unsurprisingly, his view did not grow more positive when the U.S. went into Iraq—that was in March 2003. There is a robust debate to be had over the war in Iraq: its wisdom, its advisability, its effects. That debate has been going on for years, and will continue for years more. But of the nature of the regime that the U.S. and its allies toppled, there should be no doubt. Saddam Hussein was a nightmare of nightmares. His regime featured chemical gassings, "rape rooms," the feeding of men into industrial shredders (feet first, the better to hear their screams), the cutting out of tongues for dissent, children's prisons—the worst the mind of man can imagine. You might think that, even if a human-rights activist opposed the war, that activist would at least appreciate the removal of such a regime.

Pérez Esquivel gave no evidence of such appreciation. In April 2003, a month after the invasion, and the removal of Saddam Hussein, he wrote an open letter to President Bush. He said, "Perversion has no boundaries; but you say you pray to God and you believe you are predestined for humanity. Hitler had the same thoughts when he unleashed his madness and wanted to dominate the world." He added, "You talk of God. And you detest God." That is just a flavor of the laureate today.

In 1980, when he won, two other contenders for the peace prize were Lord Carrington, the British foreign secretary, and Robert Mugabe. That was the speculation in the press, which was probably informed. Carrington and Mugabe had been peace partners, if you like, working out the transition from Rhodesia to Zimbabwe. It seems likely that Mugabe came close to being a Nobel laureate. Wouldn't that be something? One of the worst dictators and tyrants of our time—an out-and-out butcher—as a Nobel peace laureate? He would be in a class almost by himself.

∿

The 1981 award was a humanitarian award, a U.N. award, and an anniversary award. It was also a repeat award: to the Office of the U.N. High Commissioner for Refugees, which had won the prize for 1954. The office was established in 1951—so the second Nobel was a present on its thirtieth birthday. For many decades, the refugee cause has been dear to Norwegian hearts. It was widely pointed out in 1981 that Norway gave the largest per capita contribution to UNHCR of any country.

The committee, in its press release, mentioned the recent "mass exodus" from Vietnam: boat people and other wretches. They also mentioned "two million refugees from Afghanistan and an equal number from Ethiopia." The Soviets had invaded Afghanistan in December 1979 and Mengistu had been wreaking his Red Terror, and his terror-famine, on Ethiopia.

Around the world, the choice of UNHCR for the year's Nobel was seen as "conservative" and "safe" (which it was). In remarks to the press, Jakob Sverdrup, secretary to the committee, described the choice as "not being very hard to make, and relatively non-controversial." Some had thought that Lech Walesa, the Solidarity leader in Poland, would win the Nobel. "The 'hottest' name nominated this year," the *Christian Science Monitor* reported, was Walesa's, but "committee members were wary of appearing to be provocative toward the Soviet Union, with which Norway shares a border." The favorite of the Norwegian Left was Alva Myrdal, from another neighbor, Sweden. In the words of the *New York Times*, "Her choice would have been particularly ticklish because her recent writing contends that European countries have become pawns of the superpowers in the international arms race. Mrs. Myrdal has been criticized for lumping the United States and the Soviet Union together without differentiating between the causes of their strategic positions and the character of their military alliances."

Myrdal fans in Norway did something about her failure to win the Nobel prize, or rather, the committee's failure to award it to her: They gave her a Norwegian People's Peace Prize, which included a check for $60,000. The ceremony took place in Oslo

City Hall in February 1982—and later that year, Myrdal would win the Nobel prize itself.

〰

She was then 80, the doyenne of Scandinavian social democracy, which is practically to say, of Scandinavian political culture. She had won many awards before—including the 1981 Nehru Award, with her husband Gunnar. She told Irwin Abrams that the Nobel was the "peak" for her. Yet the People's Peace Prize was "dearer to my heart."

She did not have the Nobel to herself, which irked some of her admirers, in the way split prizes often do. She shared her prize with Alfonso García Robles, a veteran Mexican diplomat. The Nobel Committee rewarded them for their disarmament efforts at the U.N., and for their advocacy of disarmament generally. We can view the 1982 prize as both a disarmament prize and a U.N. prize. Philip Noel-Baker was such a winner: a disarmer and a U.N.-er.

Alva Myrdal, née Reimer, was an impressive woman. She was pretty, well educated, and perpetually achieving. She was born in Uppsala, the city, you remember, of Nathan Söderblom, and of Dag Hammarskjöld. It was in 1924—Alva was 22—that she married Gunnar. And they had a long, productive, and laureled life together. In 1974, Gunnar won the Nobel "memorial prize" in economics—sharing it with someone whose thinking was completely different from his: Friedrich Hayek, the Austrian classical liberal. After 1976, when that same prize was won by another classical liberal, Milton Friedman, Gunnar Myrdal had had enough: He called for the abolition of the prize, if it was going to go to such wayward people; and he said he was sorry he had accepted it.

Mrs. Myrdal had any number of roles in her career: She was Sweden's ambassador to India, for instance; she was a parliamentarian. And she had any number of interests. But she took a particular and sustained interest in disarmament, representing her country at the U.N.'s conference on that subject. She was one of those who stood in the exquisite center between the United States and the Soviet Union, favoring neither, declaring a pox on both their houses. Her thinking and rhetoric are encapsulated in the title of her 1976 book, *The Game of Disarmament: How the United States and Russia Run the Arms Race.*

García Robles, too, was a keen disarmer. Born in 1911, he entered Mexico's foreign service in 1939. He then worked for the U.N. Secretariat. In the 1960s, he was Mexico's ambassador to Brazil, and in the 1970s he was foreign minister. He was an architect of the Nuclear Nonproliferation Treaty, signed in 1968. But his crowning moment had come the year before: when the Treaty of Tlatelolco was signed. This treaty made Latin America a nuclear-free zone; it had been spurred by the Cuban missile crisis of 1962; and García Robles had been the main driver of the treaty.

Presiding over the ceremony in Oslo was the new chairman, Egil Aarvik, a Christian Democratic journalist and politician. In his presentation speech, he said, "Alva Myrdal belongs to the world community: but she is ideologically firmly rooted in Nordic constitutional principles and in our democratic ideals." He also said, "For obvious reasons, Alfonso García Robles is less well known in the Nordic countries. But, as we all know, a considerable part of the world is situated outside the North." Perhaps the chairman spoke this last sentence with a smile in his voice.

He used the bulk of his speech to discourse on the problem of disarmament—and the nuclear Sword of Damocles that hung over the world. He, too, positioned himself at the exquisite center. In his reading, the U.S. and the USSR were two dumb, headstrong actors, engaged in "a power struggle and intense rivalry," unable to "break through the barrier of mutual distrust," and hurtling toward an apocalypse. But he found glimmers of hope. He noted that, in the American congressional elections just held, many advocates of a nuclear "freeze" had triumphed. (He did not report on elections in the Soviet Union, or the expression of popular sentiment there.) His fundamental message was this: Disarmament equals peace; the more you disarm, the more peace you will have. If Aarvik thought that Norway's freedom and independence relied, in part, on the American nuclear deterrent, and on NATO, he gave no hint of it.

Myrdal's lecture, of course, was in the spirit of that presentation speech. Speaking of herself and her co-laureate, she said, "I should in the beginning like to emphasize . . . that I am particularly gratified that on this occasion the award goes to two citizens of nations which are both *denuclearized* and *non-allied.*" Quite true. But after 1945, how long could Sweden have remained non-allied without the military muscle, including nuclear arms, to the west? Would Moscow have been content to let the Swedes live their happy, social-democratic, neutral life? The question was never put to a test. In her lecture, Myrdal described nuclear weapons as "hyper-dangerous"—an incontestable description— and lamented that "there is no defense against them." The next year, President Reagan proposed his Strategic Defense Initiative, his anti-missile scheme (or vision). Myrdal opposed it firmly and dismissively.

In his acceptance speech, García Robles had a most interesting suggestion. He said he felt free to make it because he had already won the Nobel Peace Prize, and could not be judged self-seeking. The prize had gone in recent years to many advocates of human rights, worthy winners, to be sure. But disarmament was clearly the issue of the day, García Robles said. And it was very, very clearly the peace issue of the day. Therefore, should not the Nobel Committee give "highest priority" to those working for disarmament? In the late 1960s, the Bank of Sweden had stepped forward to create an economics prize. (The one that Gunnar Myrdal was now grumbling about abolishing.) "If another

Maecenas were now to be found who might provide the necessary funds, a new prize devoted to human rights could be established and awarded annually by the same Nobel committee of Norway which awards the Nobel Peace Prize." García Robles continued,

> I trust that this suggestion, which I deem constructive, will be interpreted as it is meant: a modest contribution to show my sincere appreciation for the honor which has been conferred on me by the Nobel Committee. Were it to become a reality, the intervals between the Nobel peace prizes awarded for achievements in the field of disarmament would never again be as extended as has unfortunately been the case during the second half of the current century.

It might have taken some cheek to make this suggestion, but the suggestion was certainly not an absurd one. Many have asked over the decades, "What should the Nobel Peace Prize be for?" García Robles died in 1991. We might wonder what he would make of Nobel peace prizes to environmentalists and global-warming activists.

In the 1980s—what turned out to be the last decade of the Cold War—the nuclear question was enormous: almost all-consuming. As Reagan built up the American arsenal, there were massive demonstrations in Western European streets, and in American streets as well. With the demise of the Soviet Union, however, the question of nukes and disarmament died down. It disappeared almost altogether—which suggested that the fundamental matter had never been the weapons themselves, but rather the holders of those weapons. The nuclear question would not return in a big way until the mullahs' regime in Tehran neared its A-bomb.

As the 1980s progressed, Reagan and his partners faced down the nuclear-freeze movement, and indeed the disarmament movement itself: Reagan and the others were "building up to build down," as the saying went. In 1987, Reagan and Gorbachev signed the INF Treaty, the Intermediate-Range Nuclear Forces Treaty. It was the first treaty to abolish an entire class of weapons systems—and the hawks felt vindicated. Who were the more effective disarmers? Reagan and his like, or Alva Myrdal and hers?

Mrs. Myrdal died in 1986, and Mr. Myrdal the following year. An obituary for her noted something charming. Husband and wife spent certain periods apart, with their different work, but they tried to make those periods as short as possible. In all their decades of marriage, said Alva, "we have never found anybody else so interesting to talk to."

~

Lech Walesa had been a candidate for the prize in 1981, and again in 1982. Five days before the 1982 prize was announced, his federation, Solidarity, was formally dissolved by the Polish parliament (a pretend parliament, to be sure, under Communism). Solidarity had been banned when the government imposed martial law, on December 13, 1981; the dissolution by parliament was indeed a formality. In any case, Solidarity had gone underground, and would remain underground until it could walk in the open again, in 1989.

As the 1982 prize was being announced, "five demonstrators stood in a chilly rain outside the Nobel Institute," reported the *New York Times*. They carried banners denouncing the Polish government. The *Times* quoted a Pole in the group, disappointed that the prize had not gone to Walesa: "The Nobel Committee is afraid of provoking the Russians. It's very important for the peace-loving people of the world to support the Polish people right now." Alva Myrdal, in her lecture two months later, nodded to Walesa. "*Oppression* is becoming more and more a part of the systems," she said. "Lech Walesa's sufferings may stand as a symbol for the way in which human rights are being trampled down, in one country after another."

In 1983, Walesa had his turn. When the committee announced for him, he was off in the woods with friends, picking mushrooms. This little group in the woods listened for the news on a portable radio. And they got the news they were hoping to hear. The announcement was a thunderbolt around the world. Reagan said that the award to Walesa was "a triumph of moral force over brute force," and "a victory for those who seek to enlarge the human spirit over those who seek to crush it." The laureate's countryman Pope John Paul II said that the committee's decision spoke with a "special eloquence."

In Poland, the people rejoiced while the government stewed. These rulers expressed their displeasure in several ways—one of which was to ban the playing of Norwegian or American music on the radio. So, for a time, Poles did without Grieg, without Copland.

Walesa was born during the war, 1943. His family was Catholic, and "religion was very important," he explained to me. "I heard how my parents discussed things, and they were of course against the Communist system. That was the way I was brought up. And I was brought up according to some very straightforward principles. For instance, the truth is the truth, and a lie is a lie." We met in 2010, more than 25 years after his Nobel prize. We were in Oslo, in fact, at the Grand Hotel, where the laureates typically stay when they have their moment in the Nobel sun. Walesa became a tradesman—an electrician—and in 1980 rose to head the trade-union federation, Solidarity. He was a natural for the job, really: charismatic, canny, fearless. At the time of his peace prize, the outlook was pretty grim for him. Solidarity was verboten, as we have seen, and the government was waging a vicious propaganda campaign against him. The prize came at a very propitious time. Again, it can be a powerful award.

Walesa did not go to Oslo to pick up his prize in person. There were two reasons for this. First, he was reluctant to go to a rich, vibrant Western capital and "sip champagne" (his words) while other Solidarity men were in jail and hungry. Second, the Polish government might well have prevented him from returning to his homeland. "They could have made me an exile," he said at the Grand Hotel. "The Communists could have said, 'They love you so dearly in the West, they have given you the Nobel Peace Prize, why don't you stay with them there, forever?'" And he wanted to continue to lead the struggle, on native soil.

Five laureates have been prevented—or effectively prevented —from traveling to Oslo by the governments ruling them: Ossietzky in 1936; Sakharov in 1975; Walesa; Aung San Suu Kyi, the Burmese democracy leader, in 1991; and Liu Xiaobo, the Chinese dissident and political prisoner, in 2010. We might note that, even in the depths of apartheid, the South African laureates were able to receive their Nobel prizes in person.

Walesa sent his wife, Danuta, in his stead. She took with her their eldest son, Bogdan. Walesa told me, "What were they [the Communists] going to do about that? It would have been a little bit difficult to act against this mother of so many children"—seven at the time. (An eighth would come later.)

In their announcement, the committeemen had made clear why they were giving the prize to Walesa. He stood for "the universal freedom to organize—a human right as defined by the United Nations." (The U.N. is ever important in the mind of the committee.) Also, Walesa was a practitioner of nonviolence. At the ceremony, Chairman Aarvik said, ". . . this year's prizewinner has raised a burning torch, a shining name, the name of Solidarity. He has lifted the torch unarmed; the word, the spirit, and the thought of freedom and human rights were his weapons." Danuta Walesa read her husband's acceptance speech, in which he remembered

Solidarity members who had been killed, and members who were now in prison: "I think of all those with whom I have traveled the same road and with whom I shared the trials and tribulations of our time."

That evening, Mrs. Walesa and Bogdan stood on a balcony of the Grand to watch the traditional torchlight parade go by—a parade that featured Norwegian trade unions, proud of their comrade in Poland. In our 2010 talk, I asked Walesa how Mrs. Walesa had done, representing him. He shrugged his shoulders with his trademark humor and allowed, "Well, she did all right. She put no shame on me."

His lecture the next day was read, not by Mrs. Walesa, but by a Solidarity comrade, now in exile—another Bogdan, Bogdan Cywinski. The lecture began with a much-quoted, arresting sentence: "Addressing you, as the winner of the 1983 Nobel Peace Prize, is a Polish worker from the Gdansk Shipyard . . . ." It ended—as a great many Nobel lectures do—with something Biblical. Walesa spoke of the monument at the entrance to the shipyard: a monument to demonstrating workers who were gunned down by the government in 1970. On it is inscribed a verse from Psalm 29: "The Lord will give strength unto his people; the Lord will bless his people with peace."

Mrs. Walesa and her son Bogdan returned to Poland, bearing the Nobel gold medal and the diploma. The Walesa family drove to the holiest place in Poland, the Jasna Góra Monastery in Częstochowa, where the "Black Madonna" is. This place has both religious and national importance. And there, the leader of Solidarity offered up his medal and diploma. (They reside in the chapel still.) Seven years later, in 1990, he became president of a free Poland.

Twenty years after that, sitting in the Grand Hotel, I asked him what the Nobel prize had meant—to him, to Solidarity, and to the defeat of Communism in Poland. He answered, in a word, everything. "There was no wind blowing into Poland's sail. It's hard to say what would have happened if I had not won the prize. The Nobel prize blew a strong wind into our sail. Without that prize, it would have been very difficult to continue struggling." From a personal point of view, Walesa added, "it has made me immortal." He said this with a broad smile, and mirthful eyes. "The world could have forgotten a trade-union member," a mere "organizer of strikes." But "a Nobel-prize winner? That is something else."

In his 1983 presentation speech, Aarvik said that "the future will recognize" Walesa as one of those "who contributed to humanity's legacy of freedom." True.

~

Nineteen eighty-four's prize also went to a champion of national freedom and democracy: Desmond Tutu, a bishop of the Anglican Church in South Africa. He was general secretary of the South African Council of Churches, the first black person to hold that position. This was the second anti-apartheid Nobel, the first having been conferred on Chief Lutuli in 1961 (for 1960).

In 1984, the Nobel Committee wanted to encourage the nonviolent path in South Africa, which Tutu represented. Representing an armed struggle was the African National Congress, changed since Lutuli was its president. It was banned, though not idle: It continued to operate unofficially. The ANC's most prominent leader was Nelson Mandela, who sat in prison. In its October announcement, the Nobel Committee said, "The means by which this campaign is conducted is of vital importance for the whole of the continent of Africa and for the cause of peace in the world." By "this campaign," the committee meant, of course, the anti-apartheid campaign.

A Nobel prize for Tutu was not unexpected. He had been in the running in previous years, and he had already visited Oslo in

1984, rallying against apartheid with Scandinavian groups. When the Nobel announcement came, the effect in South Africa was like the effect in Poland, the year before: The people rejoiced— at least black South Africans did, and anti-apartheid whites; the government stewed. "God is saying to us He is on our side." That was one of Tutu's comments. The new laureate also said that the award was not really for him, but for "the little people . . . whose noses are rubbed in the dust every day." Furthermore, he took note of the great tension within the anti-apartheid movement. He said that the South African Council of Churches stood between "this country and catastrophe," and that "more radical" anti-apartheid people were accusing the SACC of "postponing—hindering—the revolution."

With his Nobel lecture, one could certainly differ here and there; not every point is indisputable, far from it. But this lecture is a specimen of eloquence—not for nothing did the speaker rise in the Anglican Church and in anti-apartheid circles. As Lutuli had done, Tutu shamed white South Africa for considering itself Christian. And he catalogued the evils of apartheid. For example, he said, "Many times, in the same family one child has been classified white whilst another, with a slightly darker hue, has been classified colored, with all the horrible consequences for the latter of being shut out from membership of a greatly privileged caste. There have, as a result, been several child suicides. This is too high a price to pay for racial purity . . . ." He also addressed, as before, this question of violence versus nonviolence. "Our people are peace-loving to a fault," he said. *To a fault*: a highly suggestive phrase. He went on, "We in the South African Council of Churches have said we are opposed to all forms of violence . . . . However, we have added that we understand those who say they have had to adopt what is a last resort for them"—namely, the gun, the bomb.

Did Tutu justify or excuse the armed struggle? He can be interpreted, in this lecture and in other statements, one way or the other. In any case, Bishop Tutu became Archbishop Tutu in 1986. And when apartheid at last gave way in 1994, he led his nation's Truth and Reconciliation Commission: a key panel, on which much rode.

For all these years—since the Nobel prize in 1984—he has been a rock star of a laureate, a media star of the first order. He is a spry senior citizen (born in 1931), hopping from continent to continent, backing a variety of causes, preaching, lecturing, scolding, praising: being a symbol of "social justice," that elusive concept. He has received no end of awards. With Mandela, Maya Angelou, Elie Wiesel, and a few others, he is one of the most lauded and decorated people in the world.

And with Máiread Maguire, Adolfo Pérez Esquivel, and many others, he is a persistent, harsh critic of Israel. You are not likely to find him criticizing other Middle Eastern governments or groups. Tutu has promoted divestment from Israel, and has accused this country of being an apartheid state—no light accusation from a South African such as Tutu. In 2002, he had an explanation for why the United States was strong in its support of Israel: "People are scared in this country, to say wrong is wrong, because the Jewish lobby is powerful—very powerful. Well, so what? For goodness' sake, this is God's world! We live in a moral universe. The apartheid government was very powerful, but today it no longer exists. Hitler, Mussolini, Stalin, Pinochet, Milosevic, and Idi Amin were all powerful, but in the end they bit the dust." This was one of those statements that even some of Tutu's admirers had trouble defending. Did he really link the "Jewish lobby" in America to Hitler and those others?

In 2010, the Cape Town Opera was planning to include Israel on an international tour of *Porgy and Bess*. The company had changed the setting of this American opera to apartheid-era Soweto. (You may remember that music from *Porgy and Bess* was performed at the Nobel ceremony for Martin Luther King.) Tutu demanded that the company boycott Israel. He wanted the Jewish state to have the same stigma as apartheid South Africa. The company told the archbishop no. It went ahead to Israel.

Tutu is also like Maguire, Pérez Esquivel, and other such laureates and activists in his view of the United States: particularly of American actions in the War on Terror. No avoider of the limelight, he even participated in an off-Broadway play dedicated to portraying Guantánamo Bay as a house of horrors—the "Gulag of our times" that Amnesty International's Irene Khan claimed it was. He of course opposed the Iraq War, seeing no good in it whatsoever. He said that it was not only "illegal" but "immoral." And he said, "God is weeping. God is weeping. God is weeping because—one of the incredible things, I mean, is that Saddam Hussein, bin Laden, George Bush are all God's children. And as God says, 'What ever got into Me to create that lot?'" Some of us think that Tutu's moral sense can go badly off the rails; his grouping of George W. Bush with Osama bin Laden and Saddam Hussein is the type of thing that prevents a number of people from taking Tutu seriously as a moral thinker or leader.

Obviously, Tutu is in many ways the very model of a contemporary international peace activist. He is even a prominent campaigner against global warming. Yet, in some ways, he departs from conventional peace activism. He is happy to speak out against the government in Beijing: for its oppression in Tibet and for its oppression in China itself. Tutu is a great supporter of his fellow laureate, the Dalai Lama, and of such Chinese dissidents as Jianli Yang. He is also willing to speak out against the failings—moral and political—of the South African government, post-apartheid or not. And he will speak, too, against the dictator next door, Mugabe (the almost peace laureate). That is no common act.

In 2007, he said, "We Africans should hang our heads in shame. How can what is happening in Zimbabwe elicit hardly a word of concern, let alone condemnation, from us leaders of Africa?"

Finally, Tutu can be credited with a sense of humor—which is often impish or biting. He sometimes says he got the Nobel Peace Prize because the committee figured it was high time to "give it to a black." The committee may also have thought, "And, ah, he has an easy surname: Tutu." Imagine "if I had a surname like Waokaokao." In his Nobel lecture, Tutu told an excellent joke, a joke that can be applied to more than one region, country, or situation: "Once a Zambian and a South African, it is said, were talking. The Zambian then boasted about their minister of naval affairs. The South African asked, 'But you have no navy, no access to the sea. How then can you have a minister of naval affairs?' The Zambian retorted, 'Well, in South Africa you have a minister of justice, don't you?'"

~

In 1985, the committee turned back to the issue of nuclear weapons and nuclear war—bestowing the prize on IPPNW. This was a new organization, International Physicians for the Prevention of Nuclear War, set up in 1980. Its founders were two cardiologists, one an American and one a Russian—or, more appositely, a Soviet. They were Dr. Bernard Lown, of the Harvard School of Public Health, and Dr. Evgeny Chazov, of the USSR Cardiological Institute (and other bodies, as we will see). A U.S.–Soviet summit—between Reagan and the new Soviet premier, Gorbachev—was scheduled for Geneva in mid-November. When the committee announced the 1985 prize, Chairman Aarvik told reporters that it was meant to send this message: The two leaders must achieve results.

The *New York Times* quoted a "source close to the committee" who called the choice of IPPNW "a safe one." He elaborated, "You don't get too much criticism for choosing a group. There is no personality you can argue about."

Oh, but there was. The personality to argue about was not so much Dr. Lown: He was an American, a Westerner, of a well-known type. In 1961, he heard a lecture by Philip Noel-Baker about nuclear war. This was two years after Noel-Baker had won the peace prize. Inspired, Lown set up a group called Physicians for Social Responsibility—a group that is still going. He would set up yet more groups, including IPPNW—which is also still going. Lown is still going himself. Born in 1921, he was a refugee from Soviet Communism. With his father and brother, he fled Lithuania in 1935; his mother and sister followed the next year; the family settled in Maine. Regardless, Lown became a classic anti-anti-Communist, snorting at "religious war against heathen Communism," snorting at Reagan's designation of the Soviet Union and its holdings as "an evil empire," snorting at America's conception of itself as "the land of the free and the home of the brave." He was a perfectly typical specimen of his Harvard habitat.

And Dr. Chazov? He was the "personality to argue about"—a member of the Central Committee of the Communist Party of the Soviet Union. The Central Committee was not well known as a peace organization, as I have already observed. In fact, it was the organizer of some of the worst brutality ever inflicted on man. Chazov was also a health minister and "the Kremlin doctor": attending to Brezhnev, Andropov, Chernenko, others. He was the second Russian to bask in the glory of the Nobel Peace Prize: Andrei Sakharov had won ten years before. And Chazov had a connection to Sakharov. In 1973—two years before Sakharov won the peace prize—Chazov signed a letter with 24 other members of the Soviet Academy of Sciences. The letter denounced Sakharov as "a tool for enemy propaganda against the Soviet Union and other socialist countries." The signers said that they, of course, "wholly and completely approve and support the Soviet Union's foreign policy." Etc. This was the letter judged to have launched the official campaign of persecution against Sakharov. If Sakharov was looking for solidarity from his fellow scientists, he would not find it here.

Not long after the 1985 Nobel announcement, this letter was publicized around the world. Sakharov, as we have said, was in Gorky, in internal exile: confined in miserable circumstances. Evgeny Chazov was breezy: "I'm from Gorky. It's a nice town."

For its part, the Nobel Committee said that it had not known of the 1973 letter before deciding on the prize. Would it have made a difference? Would the committee have withheld the prize from IPPNW if it had known of Chazov's connection to the great and suffering man who was the 1975 laureate? These are good questions, impossible to answer with certainty. But, in the midst of bad publicity concerning Chazov, the committee took a fairly hard line: It said, Look, individual rights are important, sure, but the ultimate human right is to live, and not die in a nuclear conflagration. Some things are more important (went this line) than human rights for individuals, and IPPNW is concerned about the survival of the whole planet.

Between Lown and Chazov, there was a gaping and important difference: Lown was a private citizen of a free country; Chazov was an official in the Soviet apparat. Lown was free to express himself as he pleased; Chazov had to hew to the party line—and certainly did. If he had done otherwise, he would have ended up with Sakharov, or worse. Lown and Chazov were in greatly unequal positions.

The Soviet government, needless to say, was delighted with the 1985 Nobel Peace Prize. It instructed its ambassador in Norway to attend the prize ceremony; this marked an end to the Soviet boycott of these ceremonies, which began with the prize to Sakharov. Many Western leaders were not as delighted as the Soviets. One was Helmut Kohl, chancellor of West Germany, who joined with other Christian Democratic leaders in Europe in sending a letter to the Nobel Committee: This group asked the committee to reconsider. When December 10 came, the West German ambassador did not attend the ceremony; neither did the American or British ambassador. Lower-level diplomats were present in their stead. Outside, hundreds protested in the streets. And leading the protest was none other than Aase Lionæs, former chairman of the Nobel Committee. She carried a portrait of Sakharov. Another protester carried a sign that said, "Find Better Friends, Dr. Lown."

His friend, Dr. Chazov, gave a quite pretty Nobel lecture. He even quoted Ibsen, playing to the home crowd. And he noted that, in the Soviet Union, physicians had an amended Hippocratic Oath, in which they swore to oppose nuclear war. Dr. Lown gave the second lecture of the day. Reflecting on history, he said, "The ovens of Auschwitz and the atomic incineration of Hiroshima and Nagasaki inscribed a still darker chapter in the chronicle of human brutality." There was a contentious pairing: the Holocaust and the atomic bombings. Lown went on to attack the whole idea of deterrence. The adage *Si vis pacem, para bellum* was bunk, he said. It had been nothing but "a prelude to war, not a guarantor of peace."

After the Nobel lectures, a Norwegian doctor and peace activist, Dagmar Sørbøe, led the assembled physicians in reciting the Hippocratic Oath—the amended one, which included such lines as, "I believe that medical preparations for nuclear war increase its likelihood by strengthening the illusions of protection, survival, and recovery. Such measures promote the acceptability of a catastrophe which I will not accept. As a matter of individual conscience, I will refuse to participate in any medical preparations for nuclear war."

Sixteen years later, in 2001, Dr. Lown was a participant in the Nobel Institute's centennial symposium. In that period closely following the 9/11 attacks, he focused on what he evidently regarded as the true threat: the United States. The American media were whipping up war fever, he said, and a nuclear taboo was weakening. He said there was an "apartheid" of weaponry. The weapons of the poor were biological and chemical, while the weapons of the rich were nuclear. And the media were spreading the awful fiction that "the weapons of the poor are dangerous, and the weapons of the rich are inconsequential." Nuclear weapons, inconsequential?

Lown then said that "the era of Christopher Columbus has not stopped": The rich were still taking from the poor, as they had from time immemorial. This is a global phenomenon, said Lown, and "as long as it exists, there will be violence." He said that, in the 9/11 attacks, a mere 3,000 died. And yet "that very day 35,000 children died of hunger"—they had "unprivileged lives" (unlike the dead in the attacks). Said the doctor, "Is it possible for affluent nations to purchase security when the deprived and hungry multitudes are clamoring outside the gates of the big house?" Lown's belief was that 9/11 had been a strike by the poor on the rich. (Never mind bin Laden's immense Saudi wealth.) Günter Grass was another such believer. The winner of the 1999 Nobel Prize for Literature had pronounced 9/11 "the revenge of the poor on the rich."

Winding up, Lown said that "the mere possession" of nuclear weapons "is intolerable to the very morality that is now being appealed to against terrorists who are said to disrupt global civil society." Nuclear weapons are "instruments of genocide," he said. "We rejected the doctrine of Hitler, but we adopted some of his methodology."

Go back to 1985 for a moment—and IPPNW's Nobel prize. Lown and Chazov held a press conference on December 9, the day before the ceremony (and two days before the lectures). A most extraordinary event occurred. A Soviet cameraman collapsed, the victim of cardiac arrest; the IPPNW chairmen attended to him, until an ambulance could arrive. Lown then remarked that all had witnessed a "strange parable," illustrating just what IPPNW was about: "When the crisis comes, Soviet and American cardiologists cooperate. We do not ask what are a patient's or a doctor's politics, nationality, or beliefs." No matter what we may think of the organization or its founders, that was an impressive and memorable moment—something outstanding in the annals of the peace prize.

∼

In 1986, the committee made an unusual choice, a choice hard to categorize. It was a human-rights choice, mainly. The committee gave the prize to Elie Wiesel, a survivor of the Holocaust, a writer about the Holocaust, a universal spokesman for human rights, for peace, for justice—and for memory: the act of remembering persecution and its victims, which might help avoid similar persecution in the present and future. In a volume of his memoirs, *And the Sea Is Never Full* (1999), he reports something that Egil Aarvik told him: "Last August, when the decision was made in your favor, I felt like singing. Then, in the train that took me home that night, it seemed to me the very trees were singing."

When it announced the prize in October, the committee said that Wiesel had "emerged as one of the most important spiritual leaders and guides in an age when violence, repression, and racism continue to characterize the world." The committee called him "a messenger to mankind." And "his message is one of peace, atonement, and human dignity." Wiesel, in New York, immediately said, "I dedicate [the prize] to my fellow survivors and their children." He said that having the prize would enable him to "speak louder" and "reach more people." He wasted no time in speaking, louder or not: As soon as he won the prize, he called on Gorbachev to bring Sakharov from internal exile and to allow the refuseniks to emigrate.

In those memoirs, Wiesel calls the Nobel "the greatest honor mankind can bestow on one of its own." He also says, "With a Nobel Prize come quite a few lessons. For one, you learn who is a friend and who is not. Contrary to popular wisdom, a friend is not one who shares your suffering, but one who knows how to share your joy. I was pleasantly surprised by some and sadly disappointed by others." The winning of this lofty honor can spark huge envy and resentment. Wiesel received a most pleasant message from Henry Kissinger—a message tinged with poignancy: "I was not proud of my Nobel, but I am of yours."

Before he went to Oslo, Wiesel went to the Soviet Union, where he pressed for human rights. He repeatedly asked to see Sakharov—now his fellow laureate—but was repeatedly denied this opportunity. He told the authorities that, unless Sakharov was released, he would certainly speak of him and his plight in his Nobel lecture. He notes in his memoirs (written in the present tense), "Interestingly, the Soviet authorities seem to fear the impact of criticism in that address. A member of the French Communist party's Politburo contacts me to persuade me not to mention Sakharov. What is it about the Nobel Prize that worries them?" Sakharov was not released, and Wiesel spoke of him in both his lecture and his acceptance speech.

Before the ceremony, Wiesel had his audience with the king, Olav V, in the palace. The king told him—"smiling shyly," says Wiesel—"In my position, I don't have the right to suggest candidates to the Nobel Committee; otherwise, I would personally have proposed you." Outside the hall, there was a demonstration against Wiesel: a demonstration by Holocaust deniers. Inside, things were saner and warmer. Chairman Aarvik began his speech by saying, "It is today exactly 50 years since the Nobel Peace Prize was awarded to the German public figure and pacifist Carl von Ossietzky." He then spoke of the parallels between Ossietzky, a victim of the Nazis, and Wiesel, a survivor of the Nazis. Aarvik's was a notably beautiful address.

You may remember what Henry Joel Cadbury of the American Friends Service Committee said in 1947. In his acceptance speech, he implored Norwegians not to "take sides": not to take sides with either the United States or the Soviet Union. Wiesel has always been rather a side-taker. In his own acceptance speech, he said,

> We must always take sides. Neutrality helps the oppressor, never the victim. Silence encourages the tormentor, never the tormented. Sometimes we must interfere. When human lives are endangered, when human dignity is in jeopardy, national borders and sensitivities become irrelevant. Wherever men or women are persecuted because of their race, religion, or political views, that place must—at that moment—become the center of the universe.

The following day, Wiesel gave his Nobel lecture, titled "Hope, Despair, and Memory." It was classically Wieselian, a poetic piece of moral teaching. It was also short: one of the shorter Nobel lectures on record (and one of the best). He talked about his life, the Holocaust, and the Jewish people, of course. But he universalized his talk, in his usual fashion. He said, "We must remember the suffering of my people, as we must remember that of the Ethiopians, the Cambodians, the boat people, Palestinians, the Mesquite Indians, the Argentinian *desaparecidos*—the list seems endless." The Mesquite Indians, more commonly known as the Miskito Indians, live in Nicaragua, and were being abused and chased out by the Sandinista government there.

Wiesel also talked about South Africa, saying, "Without comparing apartheid to Nazism and to its 'final solution'—for that defies all comparison—one cannot help but assign the two systems, in their supposed legality, to the same camp." Two years before, in his own Nobel lecture, Bishop Tutu had said the following: "Blacks are systematically being stripped of their South African citizenship and being turned into aliens in the land of their birth. This is apartheid's final solution, just as Nazism had its final solution for the Jews in Hitler's Aryan madness."

Many times prior to 1986, Wiesel had been nominated for the Nobel Peace Prize. He had come within whiskers of winning it (according to informed speculation). For ten years, a campaign had been mounted in his behalf, by admirers around the world. It was thought that he might well win in 1985, on the fortieth anniversary of the end of the war. But IPPNW got it. Among his supporters were the French president, François Mitterrand, and a very popular French singer, Yves Montand. In 1986, after Wiesel's Nobel was announced, the *New York Times* had a paragraph of considerable interest to us and our story:

> Various well-placed Norwegians said one of the committee's most basic impulses was to seek "balance" in its awards from year to year—and that the choice of Mr. Wiesel would offset that of the International Physicians group in 1985. "Last year's prize probably pleased the Kremlin more than the White House," said an Oslo editor who has followed the prizes for two decades. "This year it will be the other way around."

A peculiar event had occurred in 1985, which may have had a bearing on the Nobel Committee's decision for 1986. Keeping a promise to Chancellor Kohl, President Reagan said that he would visit a German military cemetery, as nations marked the fortieth anniversary of V-E Day. Reagan thought it would be a significant act of reconciliation. The cemetery was to be one near Bitburg: and it transpired that, among the 2,000 graves there, about 50 belonged to SS men. That posed a big problem to the White House and all concerned. America was in an uproar over this planned visit. On April 19, Wiesel visited the White House. He was being honored with the Congressional Gold Medal—which, while a congressional honor, is bestowed by the president. Reagan hailed Wiesel in the most glowing terms. Wiesel very much appreciated all this. But, when it was his turn at the podium, he pleaded with Reagan to stay away from the cemetery: "That place, Mr. President, is not your place. Your place is with the victims of the SS." Reagan listened to Wiesel with a pained, intent expression. But he was incredibly—to some, stupefyingly—stubborn on this issue. And he went with Kohl to the cemetery (also to Bergen-Belsen).

Did Wiesel's stance against Reagan help him with the Nobel Committee? It's hard to say—but it could not have hurt. Reagan was a hated figure among Western European political elites, not least in Scandinavia. And Wiesel was not exactly a darling of the international Left: His staunch anti-Communism, and his general support of the Jewish state, made him suspect. The stance against Reagan may have lent him what we know as "street cred" (credibility in the street).

Almost winning the 1986 Nobel prize was Bob Geldof, an Irish rocker. He had organized concerts in behalf of African famine relief—and had done so in the previous year, meaning that a prize to him would definitely have satisfied that (forlorn) element of Nobel's will. Also under consideration was Simon Wiesenthal, the "famed Nazi-hunter," as he was always known. Like Wiesel, he had survived the Holocaust, and his way of honoring the dead was to hunt down and bring to justice those who had carried out the genocide. Wiesenthal had a strange animus against Wiesel. Wiesel says in his memoirs that Wiesenthal campaigned for the Nobel prize "by denigrating me." Also that Wiesenthal was blinded by jealousy.

According to Tom Segev, in *Simon Wiesenthal: The Life and Legends*, the Nazi-hunter expected to win the prize, perhaps along with Wiesel: That would have been a joint Holocaust-remembrance award. But, as everyone learned on the fateful October morning, the award went to Wiesel alone. Segev writes, "Missing out on the prize was the biggest disappointment of Wiesenthal's life. He brought it up again and again, as if he had been the victim of a great injustice, until his dying day."

~

All through this decade, the 1980s, Central America was a "hotspot," or series of hotspots, never far from the world's headlines. For one thing, it was a battleground of the Cold War. Costa Rica's president, Óscar Arias, came up with a peace plan: known as the Arias Plan, as well as by other monikers. For this, he won the 1987 Nobel prize. He had been elected only in 1986. He was a social democrat, a participant in the Socialist International. Sober, serious, and "technocratic," he was not the model of the Latin American leader. A correspondent for Canada's *Globe and Mail* wrote, "On a public platform, he has the charisma of a toaster-oven." Toaster-ovens create heat, of course.

In 1987, the situation in Central America was roughly this: El Salvador, Honduras, and Guatemala had come through terrible political times. They now had democratic governments, but those governments were being challenged by violent extremists of the Left and Right—mainly of the Left. This was particularly true in El Salvador, whose government was fighting off the "FMLN." Supporting these guerrillas was the Sandinista government in Nicaragua, a Marxist-Leninist dictatorship. (This was a description—"Marxist-Leninist"—they proudly applied to themselves.) The Sandinistas, in turn, were supported by the Soviet Union and Cuba. Resisting and warring against the Sandinistas were the

Nicaraguan "contras," supported by the United States: more specifically, by Reagan and his administration.

Arias, a democrat, did not care for the Sandinistas. During his presidential campaign, he said, "Costa Ricans feel tricked by the Sandinistas, because the Sandinistas offered to build a new Nicaragua and not a second Cuba." But neither did Arias like the American-backed war against the Sandinistas. In August 1987, he got five Central American leaders to sign a peace accord. Those leaders were from Nicaragua, El Salvador, Honduras, Guatemala, and Costa Rica (Arias himself). They signed their accord in Guatemala City—which is why it was sometimes known as the "Guatemalan Accord," in addition to the "Arias Plan." (It was also known as "Esquipulas II," in acknowledgement of an earlier summit meeting.) In a nutshell, the accord called for a cessation of war and the democratization of the region.

The Sandinistas' chief, Daniel Ortega, was quite open about his motivations for signing—quite open among his comrades, that is. He said he wished to stop American support for the contras, force the disbandment of the contras themselves, and ensure the longevity of his regime. He had no intention of abiding by the accord, and did not, despite some gestures and feints. The Reagan administration viewed the accord basically the way the Sandinistas did: as a means by which the Sandinistas would try to prevent their military defeat, and proceed as a Central American Cuba.

In America, a harsh, nearly all-consuming debate had been raging between the contra-supporting Republicans and the contra-opposing Democrats. At the very moment the Central American leaders signed the Guatemalan Accord, the Reagan administration was trying to persuade Congress to send more aid to the contras. After the signing, the Democratic speaker of the House, Jim Wright, said that Reagan must not "renew the fangs of war when we have the dove of peace." Wright's majority whip, Tony Coelho, was a little less poetic. He said, "This kills it," meaning contra aid. "It's dead."

When the Nobel Committee handed down its decision in October, that decision was everywhere interpreted as anti-Reagan. The *Globe and Mail*'s correspondent referred to an "implicit rebuff." The newspaper's editorialists were blunter: "a slap in the face." *Newsweek* magazine said "a chop at the knees." You know who else was blunt? The Nobel Committee, at least in conversation with the laureate himself. Robert Kagan interviewed Arias for his book *A Twilight Struggle: American Power and Nicaragua, 1977–1990*. Arias told him that the Nobel Committee made clear that it meant to hand him a weapon against Reagan. Said Arias, "Reagan was responsible for my prize." It would certainly not be the last time a conservative American president was responsible for a Nobel peace prize.

You will be interested to know how Arias came to be nominated. The deadline is February 1. And Arias had not really made a splash in the world until the summer of 1987. Every year, a Swedish parliamentarian named Björn Molin nominated the president of Costa Rica—no matter who he was. Why? Because Costa Rica was known as a peaceable, unarmed, anti-militarist country, and Molin wanted to honor that. When decision time came in October, the Nobel Committee was in luck: The members wanted to honor Arias, and, lo, someone—and just one person—had nominated him.

At the prize ceremony, Aarvik said, "Even though the country has armed guards at its borders, it is still without military forces in the usual sense of the word. It has been said that Costa Rica has more schoolteachers than soldiers. Some have even claimed that the country's artillery wouldn't even be able to fire a 21-gun salute in the event of a state visit . . . ." The prizewinner played up this angle, too: "Mine is an unarmed people, whose children have never seen a fighter or a tank or a warship." He later said, "We believe in dialogue, in agreement, in reaching a consensus. We reject violence. Because my country is a country of teachers, we believe in convincing our opponents, not defeating them." And so on.

What country does this sound like? Norway itself. Costa Rica, with its 2.7 million inhabitants, was a little Scandinavian realm on a Latin American isthmus. Committee members must have seen a country in their own image. The two countries certainly shared similar conceits. What Arias did not say, and what Aarvik did not say, was that Costa Rica was able to enjoy its kind of life in large part because the United States gave it massive aid and protected it militarily. More than a few countries have enjoyed this kind of deal: You get to kick Uncle Sam, secure in the knowledge that this bad old uncle will provide for you anyway.

In 1990, the Soviet Union was winding down, and this meant trouble for its far-flung protectorates. The Sandinistas decided on a great gamble—one that turned out disastrously for them. They permitted an election. And Nicaraguans voted in such large numbers for the democratic opposition, it was difficult for the Sandinistas to steal that election. Former U.S. president and future Nobel peace laureate Jimmy Carter, there to monitor the voting, tried to get the winner, Violeta Chamorro, to share power with the Sandinistas. She said, politely but firmly, No, the people have spoken. Carter was conspicuously churlish about the result. The American political scientist and diplomat Jeane Kirkpatrick would comment, "You'd have thought a democrat would be happy."

Did the Arias Plan have anything to do with the democratization of Nicaragua and of the region as a whole? The laureate and his backers certainly think so. In his Oslo acceptance speech, he had said, "Send our people ploughshares instead of swords, pruning hooks instead of spears." If the great powers, "for their own purposes, cannot refrain from amassing the weapons of war, then, in the name of God, at least they should leave us in peace." Beautiful words, as at all Nobel ceremonies. But American swords and spears, wielded by the contras, put tremendous pressure on the Sandinistas. They wanted to be a Cuba, not a Costa Rica. They did not give way to democracy willingly; they had not undergone a philosophical conversion. And American swords and spears, in the hands of the democratic governments in El Salvador, Honduras, and Guatemala, enabled those governments to hold off extremists. Then, too, the American military had relieved Panama of the dictator Noriega. And, when speaking of the democratization of Nicaragua and the region, I should mention once more the evanescence of the Soviet Union under Gorbachev: a critically important development, in Central America as elsewhere.

Arias made one golden contribution: He reinforced the idea of democracy as the key to peace. On this, he and his bête noire, Reagan, were in agreement. Egil Aarvik, in his 1987 presentation speech, had hailed Arias for advancing "the principle of the intimate relationship between peace and democracy." In his lecture, Arias said, "Liberty performs miracles. To free men, everything is possible. A free and democratic America"—i.e., Latin America—"can meet the challenges confronting it."

Flash forward to 2006. Thanks to electoral machinations and a bizarre set of circumstances, the Sandinistas regained power. They won an election with a 38 percent plurality. Then they set about rigging the game—with what success, for how long, we don't yet know. And the Sandinistas were not the only ones to come back. In that presentation speech, Aarvik had said, "Óscar Arias is, at the age of 46, a relatively young peace-prize laureate. It is probable that the bulk of his life's work is still to be done." With his prize money, Arias established the Arias Foundation for Peace and Human Progress. In 2006, he again ran for the presidency, having left the office in 1990. He won.

∾

In 1988, the Nobel Committee turned back to the cherished body, and cherished idea: the United Nations. It presented the prize to the U.N. Peacekeeping Forces, those "blue helmets" whose job it is to patrol areas where "an armistice has been negotiated but a peace treaty has yet to be established." Those words are from the Nobel Committee's announcement. The award recalled the 1957 Nobel to Canada's man at the U.N., Lester Pearson. It was he who organized the U.N. Emergency Force on the Sinai, during the Suez crisis. UNEF was the original U.N. peacekeeping operation. Nasser, as you know, flicked them out in 1967, as he prepared war.

The Peacekeeping Forces were the Norwegian Nobel Committee's kind of military. In his presentation speech, Aarvik cited the title of a book by Michael Harbottle, a retired British officer and a peace campaigner: *The Impartial Soldier.* In his Nobel lecture, the U.N.'s secretary-general, Javier Pérez de Cuéllar, said, "These are soldiers without enemies. Their duty is to remain above the conflict. They may only use their weapons in the last resort for self-defense. Their strength is that, representing the will of the international community, they provide an honorable alternative to war and a useful pretext for peace." Over the years, the peace-keepers' impartiality has been called into question. For example, they have in recent times looked like partners of Hezbollah in southern Lebanon. At a minimum, they have turned two blind eyes. But impartiality is no doubt a stated principle of the Peacekeeping Forces.

At the ceremony, Aarvik noted that, in the history of U.N. peacekeeping, 733 soldiers—blue helmets—had been killed. He asked for a moment of silence for these dead. Then he made a quite interesting point: "For the first time in its history, the peace prize is to be awarded today to an organization which, at least in part, consists of military forces. It might be reasonable to ask whether this is, in fact, in direct contradiction to the whole idea of the peace prize. The fact that this question has not been raised is an indication that it is universally accepted that the United Nations Peacekeeping Forces are in the spirit of the peace prize." The chairman may not have known it, but there had been some objection. A columnist for the *Washington Post*, Colman McCarthy, who styled himself a peace advocate, or peace guru, was scandalized. He wrote, "How can a peace prize go to a group that is military in nature? How can peace be created by the same methods of organized violence—fighting with military weapons—that destroyed it?" Voices like that were few, however.

Aarvik said that the 1988 prize "gives expression to the hope we all place in the United Nations." He virtually sang a hymn:

> This year's peace prize is a recognition of and homage to one organ of the United Nations. But it ought to be understood as a serious comment on the fact that we must, united and with our whole hearts, invest in the United Nations. It becomes clearer and clearer that what has to be done to secure the future for new generations has to be done together. Our determination has to be channeled into the United Nations. This is the best hope for the future of the world—indeed its only hope!

Seldom has the traditional, unshakable Norwegian faith in the U.N. been more strongly expressed.

Accepting the award, Pérez de Cuéllar mentioned a colonel of the U.S. Marines, William R. Higgins, seconded to the U.N. force in Lebanon. He was "still in the hands of his kidnappers," Pérez de Cuéllar said, and "I take this opportunity to appeal once again for his immediate release." He did not name the kidnappers: They were Hezbollah. They tortured Higgins and eventually hanged him. They circulated a film of this event, one of the first of many snuff films of the jihad.

The 1988 Nobel Peace Prize was the kind that most people applaud, unquestioningly and automatically. The *Washington Post*'s editors—departing sharply from their columnist McCarthy—said, "The award of a Nobel Peace Prize to the United Nations' far-flung peace-keeping forces is almost everyone's idea of the way these things ought to be done." Later on, however, the blue helmets became, to many, a sick joke. U.N. peacekeepers were repeatedly guilty of sex crimes, particularly against children. They committed their crimes all over the world, almost wherever they were stationed: in Kosovo, in Congo, in Sudan, in Haiti, in East Timor, in Cambodia. They raped children, ran prostitution rings, demanded sex in return for food: the worst. Defenders of the U.N. said that the Peacekeeping Forces as a whole should not be tarnished by the criminality of a few, or of some. But the criminality was pervasive—it constituted an emergency. The question was asked, "Who will guard the guardians?"

Then there was genocide—no lighter a matter than that. In 1994, Hutus in Rwanda carried out their genocide against the Tutsis: 800,000 dead. The U.N. was there, standing by, watching, doing nothing. The following year, the Srebrenica massacre, in Bosnia, occurred. It occurred in a U.N. "safe area," and yet the blue helmets served up cowering, desperate Muslims to be killed by Serbs. Eight thousand were systematically murdered. People called it the worst massacre in Europe since World War II. In a 1999 accounting, the U.N. secretary-general, Kofi Annan, wrote, "Through error, misjudgment and an inability to recognize the scope of the evil confronting us, we failed to do our part to help save the people of Srebrenica from the Serb campaign of mass murder." In 2010, on the 15th anniversary of the massacre, a memorial was erected in the hills overlooking Srebrenica. It was called the "Pillar of Shame," and was composed of 16,000 shoes: a pair for each of the victims. From far away, you could tell that the shoes formed the letters "U" and "N." The activist behind this finger-pointing memorial, Phillip Ruch, said that he intended a "warning for all future U.N. employees never again just to stand by when genocide unfolds." Those words "never again" echo throughout history, and echo . . .

It took a NATO bombing campaign, led by the United States, to stop the warring and killing in the Balkans. But Nobel prizes are not given to NATO, and certainly not to the American military. Would the prize have been given to the U.N. peacekeepers in the 1990s or 2000s, after the rash of sex crimes, after genocide? Probably not, for embarrassment. But the Norwegian and social-democratic belief in the U.N. runs very deep.

~

In 1989, the Nobel Committee crowned one of the world's most recognized men, the Dalai Lama. He was the spiritual and political leader of the Tibetan people; some 20 years later, he would relinquish his political duties while remaining the spiritual head. In 1950, when he was 15, the Chinese Communists marched into Tibet. In the next several years, they increased their control, a control that was, of course, brutal and destructive. In 1959, Tibetans rebelled—only to be put down decisively by the Chinese. The Dalai Lama, with 100,000 of his followers, escaped over the Himalayas into India. They have been in exile there ever since. For more than a half-century now, the 14th Dalai Lama has pleaded Tibet's cause the world over.

The year 1989 was eventful in China. In June, the Tiananmen Square massacre occurred, with the Communists simply mowing down peaceful democratic protesters. The Nobel Committee was mindful of Tiananmen Square when giving the prize to the Dalai Lama. Aarvik told the press that the decision should be seen as encouragement to China's democracy movement, as well as to Tibet. The Dalai Lama had long been mentioned as a possible Nobel Peace Prize winner. In fact, the Chinese government had taken the step of warning the Norwegian government against a prize to this meddlesome monk. The committee went ahead, independent and heedless. When the Dalai Lama's prize was announced, a Chinese official in Oslo said, "It is interference in China's internal affairs. It has hurt the Chinese people's feelings. Tibet's affairs are wholly and purely China's own business." In Tibet, the people rejoiced, as openly as they could.

On December 10, Aarvik made a most interesting point about the Tibetans abroad: "This is by no means the first community of exiles in the world, but it is assuredly the first and only one that has not set up any militant liberation movement. This policy of nonviolence is all the more remarkable when it is considered in relation to the sufferings inflicted on the Tibetan people during the occupation of their country." Indeed, said Aarvik, "it would be difficult to cite any historical example of a minority's struggle to secure its rights in which a more conciliatory attitude to the adversary has been adopted than in the case of the Dalai Lama." As we saw earlier in this book, the chairman linked the 1989 prize to a non-prize—to the one not given to Gandhi, in 1948 or before. And, in his Nobel lecture, the Dalai Lama referred to Gandhi as "my mentor." Aarvik had another piece of praise for the Dalai Lama: stressing the leader's "willingness to compromise." The Dalai Lama was not insisting on, or working for, Tibet's complete independence. He was advocating "internal autonomy," leaving China with various military and foreign-policy privileges.

Like Father Pire and some others before him, the Dalai Lama was a sight in Oslo, draped in his red and yellow robes, his arms bare. He said, "I feel honored, humbled, and deeply moved that you should give this important prize to a simple monk from Tibet. I am no one special. But I believe the prize is a recognition of the true values of altruism, love, compassion, and nonviolence which I try to practice . . . ."

The Dalai Lama, like Tutu, Wiesel, and a few others, has won nearly every award there is to give or get. I called him, above, one of the world's most recognized men. He is now. But it was not necessarily so in 1989. Chairman Aarvik said, in tones more caustic than a presentation speaker usually permits himself, that Tibet was an ignored cause. The Nobel Peace Prize made that cause much less ignored. Credit must also go, of course, to the "simple monk" who has pleaded the cause.

∾

Those Tiananmen Square protesters were inspired, to a considerable degree, by what was taking place in the Soviet Union: liberalization, under the names *perestroika* and *glasnost*. The Chinese government, as we know, would have none of it, answering with guns. The man who was carrying out the liberalization in the Soviet Union was Gorbachev—and it was he who won the 1990 Nobel Peace Prize. A leader of the USSR—a general secretary of the Communist Party of the Soviet Union—winning the peace prize? What would Stalin think? He was so perturbed at not winning, or not being able to win, that he created his own peace prize (which would be given for the last time in this same year, 1990). When the award for Gorbachev was announced, the *Chicago Tribune* editorialized, "It wasn't long ago that the only imaginable way a Soviet president could win the Nobel Peace Prize was to invade Norway and install a Nobel committee consisting of Politburo members. But on Monday, the heir to one of the most savage regimes in history received one of humanity's highest honors on his own merits."

The Nobel Committee put it this way: They were honoring Gorbachev "for his leading role in the peace process which today characterizes important parts of the international community."

The language was stilted. What did the committee mean? Gorbachev had withdrawn from Afghanistan, let Eastern Europe go, agreed to arms control, and more. (For example, he had told the Sandinista government that it was more or less on its own.)

In Moscow, the new laureate said, "I am touched and I won't hide this fact. Words fail one at such moments. I am moved. Our fate can be linked to the fate of the world. The prize is a sign of support for what we are trying to do." Dr. Lown, with his partner Dr. Chazov, had visited Gorbachev in 1985, after the ceremony for their International Physicians for the Prevention of Nuclear War. And he now told the *Boston Globe* a story: "He asked me, 'What does the medal look like?' I told him, 'I just happen to have it in my pocket.' I showed it to him, and his eyes lit up, like a young-ster eyeing a toy. I told him, 'You're going to have one of your own someday.' He just gave a little laugh."

In Washington, President Bush hailed his Soviet counter-part as "a courageous force for peaceful change in the world." In London, Prime Minister Thatcher praised the committee's choice as "terrific." Ronald Reagan, in retirement, added his con-gratulations to "my friend on this wonderful recognition of his accomplishments." Many of Reagan's supporters groused that he, Reagan, should have won the peace prize along with Gorbachev—if not on his own.

So, the world at large was cheering this prize for the Soviet leader—for "Gorby," as he was known far and wide. In the Soviet Union itself, however, reaction was far more muted, even bitter: The country was going through distressing economic times. In the Supreme Soviet, the chairman of that body, Anatoly Lukya-nov, made the announcement that Gorbachev had won the Nobel prize. A newspaper recorded that there was just seven seconds of applause—and very lukewarm applause. Some members did not applaud at all. In Stalin's day, people were terrified to be seen as the first to stop applauding, which is why ovations for that leader went on and on. Soviet officials were openly, fearlessly scornful of Gorbachev. Georgi Arbatov, the Kremlin's longtime "Americanist," said, "I am sure that he deserves the peace prize. I wouldn't think he has deserved the Nobel Prize for Economics." Gennadi Gerasimov took the same line: "We must remember this certainly was not the Nobel Prize for Economics." And who was Gerasimov? The official spokesman of the Soviet foreign ministry, no less. This was beyond insubordination: Short years earlier, he would have been killed for a similar remark. One Soviet reporter had the nerve to ask Gorbachev how it felt to have won an award that had gone to famous anti-Communists: Sakharov and Walesa. Gorbachev did not quite answer.

As it happened, the Nobel prize ceremony took place the day after Walesa was elected president of Poland. Gorbachev himself did not attend. The laureate evidently thought that, given trouble and opposition at home, it was not wisest to be seen receiving the applause of the West, not to mention its highest honor (arguably). His medal and diploma (and check?) were collected by a deputy foreign minister, Anatoly Kovalev. It was he who read Gorbachev's acceptance speech, too. The laureate said, ". . . the year 1990 represents a turning point. It marks the end of the unnatural division of Europe. Germany has been reunited." He also said, "I would like to assure you that the leadership of the USSR is doing and will continue to do everything in its power to ensure that future developments in Europe and the world as a whole are based on openness, mutual trust, international law, and universal values."

About six months after the ceremony, on June 5, 1991, Gorbachev went ahead and traveled to Oslo, to give his lecture. He asked the central and enduring question, "What is peace?" His was an interesting, candid, wide-ranging speech—worth reading even today, and not merely from historical curiosity. As he lectured, Gorbachev mentioned Rajiv Gandhi, "who died so tragically a few days ago." The former Indian prime minister, campaigning for his Congress party, had been murdered by Tamil terrorists. (His mother, Prime Minister Indira Gandhi, had been murdered seven years before by two of her bodyguards, Sikh.)

About six and a half months after Gorbachev's Nobel lecture, on Christmas Day 1991, the Soviet Union expired—and Gorbachev gave up power along with it. He looked after his foundation: the Gorbachev Foundation, whose Internet address is "gorby. ru." He ran for the office of Russian president in 1996: receiving a shocking 0.5 percent of the vote. He made an ad for Louis Vuitton, the luxury Paris fashion house. The ad—a print ad—showed him being driven in a limo past the remains of the Berlin Wall. In 2008, he announced a new political party, the Independent Democratic Party of Russia. And he had long had an environmental organization: Green Cross International. What Nobel laureate is complete without environmental activism?

A thorny question, for all these years, has been, Should Gorbachev have won the Nobel Peace Prize? Did he deserve it? I put this question to an insightful observer, the 1983 laureate, Walesa. He chuckled. Then he said, "I'm certainly very fond of Gorbachev, and I respect him. But you should ask him the two questions I always ask him." The first is this: "Did you betray Communism? Are you a traitor to Communist ideology?" According to Walesa, Gorbachev scoffs at this, saying, "Of course not." Walesa then will say, "Okay, but you're a bright guy: Did you really believe it was possible to reform Communism?" At this—again, according to Walesa—Gorbachev reddens and sputters, not answering.

Walesa said to me, "Gorbachev tried to reform the Communist system and failed. If he had succeeded, *I'm* the one who would have failed. So we were all very happy that he failed, and if they wanted to give him the Nobel prize for his failure? That was fine with us. He failed, he got the Nobel prize—everyone was happy." Walesa made a further point: Gorbachev "had the instruments of rape, and he did not use them." That is to say, Gorbachev had the brute power to suppress rebellion, just as his predecessors had done: in Budapest, in Prague, and elsewhere. But Gorbachev refrained from using this power. Walesa went on, "Every male has the instrument of rape. Should we all be awarded Nobel prizes for not raping?"

For some people, events in Vilnius in January 1991—a month after the prize ceremony—rendered Gorbachev's prize outrageous. In that city, Soviet troops fired on unarmed protesters; only about 15 people were killed, and some 600 injured. Small potatoes in the annals of suppression—of course, not small to the killed and their families.

In *The Cold War: A New History* (2005), John Lewis Gaddis writes that Gorbachev "wanted to save socialism" but "would not use force to do so." (Historians tend to phrase things less pungently than trade-union leaders.) In the end, says Gaddis, Gorbachev "gave up an ideology, an empire, and his own country, in preference to using force. He chose love over fear, violating Machiavelli's advice for princes and thereby ensuring that he ceased to be one. It made little sense in traditional geopolitical terms. But it did make him the most deserving recipient ever of the Nobel Peace Prize."

The reader may be curious about my own view, which I will give in any case: I am between the Gaddis view and the view that Gorbachev's prize was an abomination. Gorbachev's prize was what Walesa said it was: a prize for not raping. Why should someone be given a prize for that? In the 1925 U.S. Open, Bobby Jones, the immortal golfer, called a penalty stroke on himself. It may well have cost him the tournament, which he wound up losing by a stroke. Praised for his honesty and sportsmanship, Jones bridled, saying, "You may as well praise a man for not robbing a bank." But consider Gorbachev's non-rape: It was a stunning departure from decades-long Soviet practice, and it made the world infinitely brighter. Gorbachev certainly deserved something. The Nobel Peace Prize? Why not? It has been given to many persons less meritorious.

INTERLUDE

MORE MISSING LAUREATES, AND IMPOSSIBLE LAUREATES

Aleksandr Solzhenitsyn was a Nobelist: the winner of the literature prize in 1970 (though he did not collect his prize until 1974, when he was exiled). He was the great witness against Soviet oppression, and a symbol around the world of resistance to tyranny and the indomitability of the human spirit. He might have made a peace laureate, as well as a literature laureate. But he remained only a literature laureate. Another writer and dissident who might have made a peace laureate was Václav Havel, the Czech. He played a key role in Charter 77, the appeal for human rights in Czechoslovakia. And he was the leading figure in the "Velvet Revolution," which culminated in freedom for that country (or those countries). Lech Walesa was the freedom figure in Eastern Europe who won the Nobel.

Speaking of Poles and freedom figures: A pope has never won the Nobel Peace Prize, but John Paul II would have been an interesting and justified choice. How about a Belarusian? In our 2010 conversation, Walesa mentioned Stanislau Shushkevich, a member of "that little group of people who dissolved the Soviet Union." Walesa added that Shushkevich continues to struggle for democracy today, against formidable odds. Here is another suggestion (offered to me by a scholar of Russia): Boris Yeltsin. He had a rocky, even a calamitous, presidency, but he was pivotal in bringing down the Soviet system in which he rose. Was he less deserving than Gorbachev? More so?

You can think of many other "missing laureates," or possible laureates, no doubt. I will bring up just three more, before moving to different terrain. How about the Salvation Army? How about the U.S. Peace Corps? The Peace Corps is a natural for the prize—"fraternity between nations," said Nobel in his will. It is true, though, that the Nobel Committee might balk at honoring an American or other national agency. It is the U.N. agencies that the committee devoutly honors. Then there is the late Corazon Aquino: the woman who led the democratization of the Philippines, and did so with bravery, skill, and grace. Many have pointed out that Mrs. Aquino would have made a fitting peace laureate. But, as a former committee chairman remarked to me, there will always be those who are left out. That's how it goes in the prize-giving business.

Consider, now, some impossible laureates: people of the past who could never have won the Nobel Peace Prize, and people today who could never win it, owing to the nature of the committee. "Nature"? I am referring to a philosophical or political disposition (although the committee is certainly capable of surprises). Ronald Reagan, we have seen, is not the type of American president who wins the prize. For many in the world, he is a champion of democratization, liberalization, freedom, and, indeed, peace. For the Nobel Committee, and Scandinavian political elites in general—and Western political elites in general—he was more like a nuclear cowboy. The committee was much more likely to give its prize to Mikhail Gorbachev. (And lo . . .) Similarly, many people regard George W. Bush as a champion of democratization, liberalization, and freedom, and the peace that comes with those things. For the Nobel Committee, however, Bush was not just a cowboy—nuclear or not—but a cowboy from Texas.

In his second inaugural address, delivered on January 20, 2005, Bush said, "The best hope for peace in our world is the expansion of freedom in all the world." He also said,

> We will persistently clarify the choice before every ruler and every nation: the moral choice between oppression, which is always wrong, and freedom, which is eternally right. America will not pretend that jailed dissidents prefer their chains, or that women welcome humiliation and servitude, or that any human being aspires to live at the mercy of bullies. . . .
>
> We do not accept the existence of permanent tyranny because we do not accept the possibility of permanent slavery. . . .
>
> All who live in tyranny and hopelessness can know: The United States will not ignore your oppression, or excuse your oppressors. When you stand for your liberty, we will stand with you. Democratic reformers facing repression, prison, or exile can know: America sees you for who you are: the future leaders of your free country.

Many American conservatives hated this address, believing it to be pie-in-the-sky idealism, an expression of what they regard as "Wilsonianism" (as in Woodrow). Those on the left had nothing good to say about the address either—which led to a wry remark by Tony Blair, the Labour prime minister of Britain, who was speaking at a forum in Davos, Switzerland, days after the address. He said that Bush's speech was taken as "evidence of the 'neoconservative' grip on Washington." But "I thought progressives were all in favor of freedom over tyranny."

Edward Teller, the Hungarian-born physicist, could never have won the Nobel prize. (Do you recall that Chairman Gunnar Jahn chastised him at the ceremony for Linus Pauling in 1963?) But he would have been an understandable winner. He was the foremost scientific advocate of a defense against nuclear weapons—"a shield, not a sword," as he put it. Like Reagan and Philip Noel-Baker, our 1959 laureate, he was, at a minimum, deeply uncomfortable with Mutual Assured Destruction, or the "balance of terror," in a once-common phrase. Lester Pearson, in his Nobel lecture of 1957, spoke of this balance of terror and said that peace "must surely be more than this trembling rejection of universal suicide." Teller, with his scientific wits, worked for a better way.

In the world at any given time, there are fashionable causes and unfashionable causes. It can be hard to account for fashion. For 20 years, the regime in Sudan committed genocide in the south of that country. The victims were Christians and animists, mainly. Elie Wiesel referred to this killing as a "slow-motion genocide." Very few in the world paid attention or cared. But then, the regime turned to Darfur in the west, committing genocide there—and the whole world woke up, shocked. "Darfur" was on everyone's lips. On the streets of New York, to take one city, you could see people—especially young people—in T-shirts saying "Save Darfur" (not that any Darfurians were ever saved). Strange, the fashion of causes in the world.

Elite opinion around the world was almost unanimous against apartheid South Africa. Consider merely the realm of sports: From 1964 to 1992, South Africa was banned from the Olympic Games. And athletes from other countries paid a penalty if they competed in South Africa. (Musicians, too, were discouraged from performing there.) The United Nations kept a list of athletes who traveled to South Africa; this was the U.N. Register of Sports Contacts with South Africa. The list was compiled mainly through accounts in the South African press. For example, if Billie Jean King played in a tennis tournament, the news-papers could be expected to report that. And then King would get put on the list (as she was). This register was kept to shame and correct the straying athletes.

We might debate whether individual citizens, such as ath-letes, should be punished for the policies of the governments that rule them. And we might debate whether any country should be off-limits to athletes or others. But what about the fact that, from 1964 to 1992, athletes governed by other beastly regimes were allowed to compete in the Olympics? What about the fact that countries with regimes at least as beastly as South Africa's were not made pariah states? The world can be extraordinarily selective.

Many would like to anathematize and ostracize Israel the way apartheid South Africa was—we had a taste of this in our section on Desmond Tutu. In 2006, former president Jimmy Carter, the 2002 peace laureate, wrote a book called *Palestine: Peace Not Apartheid*. Israeli athletes have been harassed and hounded through-out the world. In 2010, the Jerusalem Quartet was harassed and disrupted as it attempted to play a concert in London's Wigmore Hall. The same thing happened the next year to the Israel Phil-harmonic, at the BBC Proms. Anti-Israel boycotts of all types are proposed or instituted all over and constantly. Norway and Scan-dinavia are no exception to an anti-Israel rule.

Could Natan Sharansky win the Nobel Peace Prize? As you know, he started out as Anatoly Shcharansky and was a guest in the Soviet Gulag for nine years. For much of the world, he repre-sented defiance, perseverance, and hope. He wrote that stunning memoir about his experiences, *Fear No Evil*. Then, he entered Israeli politics and became a champion, almost an apostle, of democracy: democracy as an answer to many of the world's ills. He put his arguments in a 2004 book, *The Case for Democracy: The Power of Freedom to Overcome Tyranny and Terror*. In a differ-ent world, he would be Nobel material, but the chances that the committee would consider Sharansky, who is associated with the Israeli Right, are negligible.

Much of the world has taken on the Palestinians as a pet cause. Accepting an award from the PLO in 2009, Carter said, "I have been in love with the Palestinian people for many years." I once lunched with an arts administrator from England who used a telling phrase: "my Palestinians." "The Israelis have been so awful to my Palestinians," she said. She uttered the words "my Palestinians" as she might have "my doggies and kitties."

The cause of Tibet, as I suggested earlier, has become rather popular in the world—almost no one excuses the Chinese government's persecution and oppression there. But the cause of human rights and democracy in China proper has been far less popular. In the run-up to the Olympic Games in Beijing, staged in 2008, there was much criticism of China, and talk of boycotts. But this had mainly to do with Beijing's treatment of Tibetans, not of Chinese. For many decades—six—Chinese democracy activists and dissidents were passed over for the Nobel prize (although there was that 1989 award to the Dalai Lama). They were often on the shortlist, but never came out on top. Wei Jingsheng, in particular, was repeatedly an also-ran. In the mid-1990s, he was mentioned in three straight Nobel lectures. Why? Laureates sometimes feel obliged to pay tribute to those who lost out, in the manner of Oscar winners who, clutching the precious statuette, praise or mention the other nominees. In 1999, a week before the Nobel announcement, the Norwegian newspaper *Dagbladet* reported that it had learned who would win: Wei and a second Chinese dissident, Wang Dan. This prompted Chinese officials in Oslo to issue a strong protest to the government (never mind that the Nobel Committee is independent from that government). But the report was wrong: The prize went to the French humanitarian group Médecins Sans Frontières (Doctors Without Borders).

In 2010, it was at last China's turn, as the Nobel Committee honored the political prisoner Liu Xiaobo. He was a leader of the Charter 08 campaign, the effort for freedom and democracy that drew its inspiration from Charter 77 in Czechoslovakia. It turned out that Chinese dissidents were not "impossible laureates" after all. The Nobel to Liu gave China's democracy movement a big boost.

Cuba's democracy movement could use a similar boost, and could have used one long ago. The cause of Cuban democracy and human rights has never been popular around the world; indeed, the Cuban dictatorship, which came to power in 1959, has been more popular. There are any number of Cubans to whom the Nobel prize could go, or could have gone, over the 50-plus years of the dictatorship's existence. It could have gone to Armando Valladares, the poet and dissident who is sometimes known as "the Cuban Solzhenitsyn." He spent 22 years in the Cuban gulag and wrote a classic memoir, *Against All Hope*. After Valladares came to America, President Reagan made him the U.S. ambassador to the U.N. Human Rights Commission. Today, the prize could go to Juan Carlos González Leiva, the blind lawyer who has endured much and is at the center of the Cuban democracy movement. Or it could go to Óscar Elías Biscet, who was released from prison in 2011 after twelve years. He is an Afro-Cuban physician and activist whose models include Gandhi and Martin Luther King. In 2007, George W. Bush awarded him the Presidential Medal of Freedom (in absentia, of course). Would the Nobel Committee ever give the peace prize to Biscet, or to a current prisoner of conscience? It would rock Cuba as maybe nothing else could.

In March 2003, the regime cracked down viciously on dissidents, in what is known to Cubans as the "Black Spring." Observing this, José Saramago made a noteworthy statement. He was the Communist Portuguese writer who had won the Nobel Prize in Literature for 1998. He said, "This is my limit. . . . Cuba has

lost my trust; it has damaged my hopes; it has defrauded my illusions." Forty-four years would seem rather a long time to maintain illusions—but some will not let them go ever.

In March 2009, the government of South Africa refused to
allow the Dalai Lama to enter that country. He had been invited to
a peace conference by three of his fellow laureates: Tutu, Nelson
Mandela, and F. W. de Klerk. The government denied him a visa
because it feared to offend Beijing. At the very same time, the government gave its highest honor—the Order of the Companions
of O. R. Tambo—to Fidel Castro. The Nobel Committee would
never honor Castro, or his brother-successor. But would they ever
dishonor them? Valladares once remarked to me, with a trace of
contempt, "If the Cuban dictatorship were right-wing instead of
left-wing, we would have won two or three Nobel prizes already."

A PARADE OF LAUREATES,
1991 *to* 2000

In 1991, the Nobel Committee shone its spotlight on Burma, then as now one of the darkest places on earth. The winner was Aung San Suu Kyi, symbol of Burma's democracy movement. She was under house arrest at the time of her award, and has been under house arrest, off and on, ever since. (At this writing, she is not under house arrest; about next month, no one can say.) Beautiful, poised, brainy, spiritual, and very brave, she is one of the world's most admired women, one of its most admired people—even if she is seldom heard from, owing to the conditions in which she has lived.

And perhaps we should pause to consider the pronunciation of her name: It can be approximated to "Awn Sahn Soo Chee."

She was born in 1945 in her capital city of Rangoon. Her father was Aung San, hero of Burmese independence. He was the country's de facto prime minister when he was assassinated by political rivals. (Six colleagues, including his brother, were killed with him.) This occurred in 1947, when Aung San Suu Kyi was two. Her mother, Khin Kyi, was a diplomat. In 1960, Khin Kyi was appointed ambassador to India, and her daughter went with her. Then, for university, the young woman went to Oxford, where she read "PPE": philosophy, politics, and economics. She met her future husband, Michael Aris, a scholar of Himalayan culture. After Oxford, she went to New York, where she worked in the U.N. Secretariat—led by a Burmese, U Thant, who had succeeded Dag Hammarskjöld. On New Year's Day 1972, Aung San Suu Kyi and Michael Aris were married.

During their courtship, she had written him, "Sometimes I am beset by fears that circumstances and national considerations might tear us apart just when we are so happy in each other that separation would be a torment." Aung San Suu Kyi asked Aris to take a vow before the vows. As he explained it later, she asked him to promise that he would not "stand between her and her country."

They had two sons, Alexander and Kim. Then, in the spring of 1988, Aung San Suu Kyi's mother, in Burma, fell ill. The daughter went to care for her—and has not since left Burma. That year, 1988, great political turmoil took place, and the country was seized by a military junta, calling itself the State Law and Order Restoration Council. This gave it the villainous-sounding acronym SLORC. The SLORC made so bold as to change the name of the country: to Myanmar (generally not used by those who support Burmese democracy). In 1997, the SLORC changed its own name to the State Peace and Development Council—Orwellian, but resulting in the nicer-sounding initials SPDC.

A week after the SLORC took power, Aung San Suu Kyi and her allies formed the National League for Democracy, and she had the title of general secretary. The daughter of Aung San was newly enlisted in politics, in the Burmese national struggle. In a famous incident, she was walking with a group of her associates when soldiers lined up in front of them and told them to stop. Otherwise they would shoot. Aung San Suu Kyi asked the others to step aside, and she went forward by herself. After what must have been some heart-stopping seconds—for all concerned—the commanding officer ordered the soldiers not to fire. Aung San Suu Kyi later said, or quipped, "It seemed so much simpler to provide them with a single target than to bring everyone else in."

In July 1989, the SLORC placed Aung San Suu Kyi under house arrest, cut off from the world: No communications were permitted. The SLORC was willing to let her leave the country, long has been: But they would not let her return, making her an exile forever. And she feels a commitment. She is determined not to leave the country until civilian rule is established and political prisoners are released.

In May 1990, the SLORC did something unusual: They held free elections. The National League for Democracy won in a landslide, taking more than 80 percent of the national-assembly seats. Consequently, the SLORC ignored the elections. The Nobel chairman would do some musing about this at the 1991 prize ceremony. He was a new chairman, Francis Sejersted, a history professor associated with the Conservative party. He said, "Why did the SLORC allow free elections? Probably because they expected a very different result, a result which would somehow have provided the legitimacy they needed to retain power. The dilemma of such regimes was demonstrated—trapped in their own lies." The same can be said of the Sandinistas, who held an election three months before the SLORC. Unlike the SLORC, the Sandinistas were unable to ignore the results, thanks to a large U.N. and international presence on the scene.

The world noticed Aung San Suu Kyi and her predicament, and Burma's predicament. In October 1990 she won a lustrous Norwegian award, the Rafto Human Rights Prize. The next summer, she won the Sakharov Prize, from the European Parliament. And, that October, word came that she had won the Nobel Peace Prize. The press reported that she had been nominated by Havel, the former dissident who was then serving as the first president of a free Czechoslovakia. He may never have been a laureate himself, but he did show a talent for nomination: He was a nominator for the 2010 winner, Liu Xiaobo, too.

Going to Oslo to represent Aung San Suu Kyi were her husband and sons. On their arrival, Michael Aris said, "We are very sorry we have not succeeded in bringing this year's laureate with us." An acceptance speech was given by their elder son, Alexander, age 18. He stood next to a large picture of his mother. And he said, "The Burmese people can today hold their heads a little higher in the knowledge that in this far-distant land their suffering has been heard and heeded." That night, the younger son, Kim, age 14, lit the first torch in the torchlight parade.

On the day of the ceremony, there was a rally for Aung San Suu Kyi at Rangoon University, broken up by the police. And, in front of her house, fully 300 soldiers were deployed. The SLORC seemed spooked.

Michael Aris died in March 1999, on his 53rd birthday. He had last seen his wife at Christmas 1995. The Nobel Peace Prize can be a powerful weapon against a tyrannical regime—as Walesa, for one, knows. But, despite that spooking in December 1991, the prize has not had much of an impact on the SLORC/SPDC. The cause of Burmese democracy is known, however—and we can say essentially what we said, or I said, about the Dalai Lama and Tibet: The cause is known because of the Nobel prize, coupled with the persistent efforts of the laureate. A member of the Nobel Committee managed to go to Burma and see Aung San Suu Kyi—who said that, when she is free to travel abroad and then return, the first country she will visit is Norway.

∼

The year 1992 marked the 500th anniversary of Columbus's discovery of America—or "encounter with America," as it had become more acceptable to say (because America was no discovery to the people already present). The Nobel Committee picked this year to give its prize to the most famous indigenous person America had to offer: Rigoberta Menchú Tum. Actually, she was the most famous indigenous person the Americas, as a group, had to offer. She was a Mayan from Guatemala. More specifically, she was a Quiché, a member of a particular Mayan people. She was also a young laureate, just 33. In its announcement, the committee said it was giving her the Nobel "in recognition of her work for social justice and ethno-cultural reconciliation based on respect for the rights of indigenous peoples."

Why was she famous, even before she was bathed in Nobel glory? In 1983, a book came out under the title *I, Rigoberta Menchú*. It told the story of the future laureate, or purported to do so. (More on that in a moment.) It talked about life during Guatemala's long-running civil war, in which terrible things were done to Menchú's family by government forces. It also depicted ongoing discrimination against indigenous people by wealthier, more powerful, European-descended Guatemalans. And it portrayed the Communist guerrillas as the friend of the indigenous, and of justice.

The book became canonical in the West, certainly throughout the United States. It was required reading at practically all levels. As Charles Lane remarked, *I, Rigoberta Menchú* was "scripture," shaping what millions thought of Latin America. In a 1999 essay for *The New Republic*, Lane wrote that "the book's vision of simple, virtuous peasants and evil, blood-drenched landlords is the sort of political cartoon" that proved "irresistible." Menchú went around the world as a celebrity of social justice, a small woman in her native garb, usually with a cheerful countenance. In the spring of 1992, months before her Nobel, she was in Norway, participating in a women's conference and meeting the prime minister, Gro Harlem Brundtland.

In December, at the presentation ceremony, Sejersted said, "Welcome to this little wintry country in the far north, so far from your own country and your own world." He also remarked, "It is 500 years this year since Columbus 'discovered' America, as we have been brought up to say, or since colonization began. The celebration of the anniversary has at least produced one benefit, in the spotlight it has so effectively focused on the worldwide problem of the rights of aboriginal peoples." Was Menchú being given the award specifically because this was the "Columbus year" (meaning that some sort of rebuke of Columbus was in order)? Sejersted put it this way: "For the Norwegian Nobel Committee it was a happy coincidence that it was precisely in the year of Columbus that she emerged as such a strong candidate for the Nobel Peace Prize."

I, Rigoberta Menchú was a project of the Guerrilla Army of the Poor, to which Menchú belonged. Known by its Spanish initials EGP, the group was part of the Communist insurgency against the Guatemalan dictatorship. It was founded in 1972 by Ricardo Ramírez, an old comrade of Che Guevara's. In the early 1980s, the international branch of the EGP brought Menchú to Paris. There, she was introduced to Elisabeth Burgos, a Venezuelan anthropologist and the wife of Régis Debray, the French "revolutionary" intellectual. Like Ramírez, both Debrays had been comrades of Guevara's. Menchú told her story to Burgos, who wrote the book: the international sensation. Ramírez and the EGP were in complete control of the product. As Burgos said later, the book was "intended to serve a political campaign."

Years later, in 1998, an American anthropologist, David Stoll, published a book called Rigoberta Menchú and the Story of All Poor Guatemalans. It demonstrated that much of the Menchú book was false. For instance, Menchú claimed—on the very first page—that she was denied an education and could not speak Spanish until she was an adult: until a few years before the publication of I, Rigoberta Menchú. In fact, she had been taken under the wing of

Belgian nuns, who had seen the intellectual promise in the girl. She was given an education at private boarding schools. More broadly, Menchú claimed in her book that the Communist guerrillas enjoyed wide support among the Mayans: which was far from the case.

Despite the falsehoods—and there were many, large and small, of varying types—it was indisputably true that terrible, savage things had been done to Menchú's family, several of whom were killed by government forces. Menchú was a survivor of violence.

Reaction to Stoll's book was furious, of course. It was truly iconoclastic: He had broken, or damaged, an icon by knocking her off her pedestal. In her own defense, Menchú said that she had spoken "my truth." She had "a right to my own memories." She also blamed any problems with the book on Burgos, claiming that *I, Rigoberta Menchú* was really the work of the Paris-dwelling anthropologist, not the Guatemalan peasant who was the subject of the book. Later, she said just the opposite: that the book was all her own, with no interference from outsiders.

Others had their own defenses of Menchú. Her publisher, Verso, cited the peculiarity of "oral cultures," saying that "the distinction between what has happened to oneself and what has happened to close relatives or friends can be easily lost." Others said that the book was meant to represent all Guatemalans, to be a portrait of the suffering of Indians at large. The response of American academia was typified by Marjorie Agosín, the chairman of Wellesley's Spanish department. She told the *Chronicle of Higher Education*, "Rigoberta Menchú has been used by the Right to negate the very important space that multiculturalism is providing in academia. Whether her book is true or not, I don't care. We should teach our students about the brutality of the Guatemalan military and the U.S. financing of it."

And the brutality of the guerrillas (financed by Castro)? That was not so much discussed. And the fact that the Nobel Committee had given its prize to an advocate of the guerrillas and their violence—a committee for whom even Gandhi might not have been pure enough in his pacifism? That was not so much discussed either. (The committee was concentrating on the "native rights" angle.)

In the wake of Stoll's book and its revelations, some people thought that the Nobel Committee should revoke the prize for Menchú: According to this view, it had been given under a misunderstanding. The committee would not hear of it. Geir Lundestad, the secretary, said, "All autobiographies embellish to a greater or lesser extent." He also said that Menchú's prize "was not based exclusively or primarily on the autobiography." Furthermore, the Nobel Institute likes to point out that David Stoll himself approves of the prize to Menchú. He believes that the laureate's book, and the prize conferred on her, focused attention on the Guatemalan conflict in a helpful way.

For 20 years now, Menchú has been a familiar kind of Nobel laureate. She has a foundation. She is a UNESCO goodwill ambassador. She does the "peace circuit." She talks about the gaps between rich countries and poor countries, ascribing the condition of the latter group to the greed, exploitation, and indifference of the former. During the Nobel centennial symposium, she said, "The most important achievement of the last 100 years for human coexistence was doubtless the establishment of the United Nations." There could be no sweeter music to Norwegian, and to Nobel, ears.

Menchú has been staunchly supportive of Castro and his dictatorship, and they have been staunchly supportive of her: Like the Nobel Committee, Castro pinned a medal on her. Elisabeth Burgos, who broke in some fashion with Communism, wrote the foreword to the 2008 edition of Stoll's book. She said of Menchú, "Sadly, she continues to extol Fidel Castro and his regime in ways that under-mine her avowed commitment to human rights." In this, she is very much like Adolfo Pérez Esquivel, with whom she often collab-orates (as she does with Tutu, Maguire, and some other laureates).

In 2007, Menchú entered the arena of electoral politics: She ran for president of Guatemala. She received just 3 percent of the vote—but that was more than Gorbachev in 1996, wasn't it? The press noted that Menchú had long been more famous abroad than at home. Here is the *Chicago Tribune*, for instance: "While Menchú is a favorite of intellectuals in and out of Guatemala, many indigenous voters complain that she is more likely to give a speech in Sweden than toil in a small Mayan village."

In any event, Menchú is the very symbol of the Latin Ameri-can Indian for the world at large. And she made the Nobel Peace Prize a very big deal in her corner of the world. Shortly after she won, a campaign was launched to get the prize for Samuel Ruiz, the bishop of Chiapas, known as a champion of the aboriginal cause in Mexico. Arriving in Oslo were 40 big boxes containing the signatures of 750,000 people. They weren't valid Nobel nomi-nators; but they were three-quarters of a million strong nonethe-less. This is a record for Nobel nominations, valid or invalid.

~

In 1993 came the last of the three South African Nobels: and it went to two men, Nelson Mandela and F. W. de Klerk. The tran-sition to full, multiracial, universal democracy had not yet been completed. But it was very close to its end. Mandela was widely regarded as the first black South African president—a president-in-waiting—and de Klerk as the last white one. The Nobel Com-mittee's announcement said that the men were being honored "for their work for the peaceful termination of the apartheid regime, and for laying the foundations for a new democratic South Africa."

Many thought that Mandela should be winning this award on his own, without the apartheid president, whether that president was a reformer and transitional figure or not. Mandela and de Klerk's relations were tense just then. At a news conference after the announcement from Oslo, Mandela was asked what de Klerk had done to merit the prize. He answered—"snapped," some press reports said—"Just ask the Nobel Peace Prize committee." One who welcomed the joint award was Tutu, who said, "I hope that it will work to weld us together as a people."

Mandela was an interesting kind of peace warrior (and de Klerk was too, but we will concentrate on Mandela, the far larger figure). He joined the African National Congress in 1944, when he was 26. This was eight years before Chief Lutuli became the organization's president. In 1960 came the Sharpeville Massacre and the banning of the ANC. Mandela turned militant, helping to found Umkhonto we Sizwe, or Spear of the Nation—this was the ANC's military wing. He went to Ethiopia and Algeria for training in the guerrilla arts. He returned to South Africa to apply them. He was arrested on August 5, 1962, and sentenced approximately two years later: to life in prison. He narrowly escaped the death penalty.

Writers about Mandela frequently say that he had no choice: that the apartheid government left him no choice but to turn militant, to take up the armed struggle. He himself says this. Of course, everyone had a choice: Lutuli did, Tutu did, countless people whose names we don't know did. Walesa had a choice, we could say, and so did other peace laureates. We may well say that Mandela's was the right choice, or the better choice, or a defensible choice, or a great one: The point is, it was a choice. Amnesty International could not count Mandela as a prisoner of conscience; it supported him, pressing his case, nonetheless.

In 1976, the apartheid government offered to release him, on the condition that he go to a Bantustan—to Transkei, a separate area for Xhosa-speaking South Africans. He refused. In 1985, the apartheid government again offered to release him: on the condition that he give up the armed struggle. Again, he refused. That government, under President P. W. Botha, began to negotiate with him anyway. In 1989, a new president came to power: de Klerk. A few months before, he had said—in words he would quote in his Nobel lecture—"Our goal is a new South Africa: a totally changed South Africa . . . ."

In February 1990, the government released Mandela and unbanned the ANC. Mandela's release was unconditional. And he said, "The factors which necessitated the armed struggle still exist today. We have no option but to continue. We express the hope that a climate conducive to a negotiated settlement would be created soon, so that there may no longer be the need for the armed struggle." Negotiations took place between Mandela and de Klerk, with many vicissitudes, as could have been expected. In the summer of 1993, a transition agreement was worked out. In October, as we know, the Nobel prize was announced.

Both men gave excellent Nobel lectures—truly excellent ones. Mandela saluted the previous South African winners. Then he said, "It will not be presumptuous of us if we also add, among our predecessors, the name of another outstanding Nobel Peace Prize winner, the late Rev. Martin Luther King Jr."—who had given his all for racial harmony and justice. Mandela praised his co-laureate, de Klerk, for having had "the courage to admit that a terrible wrong had been done to our country and people through the imposition of the system of apartheid." And at the end of his speech, he said, "Let a new age dawn!" That line figured in many headlines the next day.

And de Klerk? As the occasion invites, he meditated on "the nature of peace." He noted the importance of a free market in bringing both prosperity and peace—not a common observation at all, for a Nobel ceremony in Oslo. He made the more familiar

point that democracies—"genuine and universal democracies"—
don't make war on each other. And he said, "Five years ago, people
would have seriously questioned the sanity of anyone who would
have predicted that Mr. Mandela and I would be joint recipients
of the 1993 Nobel Peace Prize." At this, the audience chuckled
appreciatively.

The next April, all-inclusive elections were held, and the ANC
was voted into power. A government of national unity was formed:
with Mandela as the president, and de Klerk the second deputy
president. The inauguration on May 10 was one of the great political occasions of the age, attended by some 45 heads of state.

In 2002, George W. Bush presented Mandela with the Presidential Medal of Freedom, citing the South African's "immense
moral authority." He said, "It is this moral stature that has made
Nelson Mandela perhaps the most revered statesman of our
time." Bush could have done without the "perhaps." The United
Nations has declared July 18—Mandela's birthday—Nelson Mandela International Day. In Oslo, the Nobel Institute and the Nobel
Peace Center make sure to use Mandela's visage in their assorted
literature: A beautiful and cherishable visage it is, too. It represents an extraordinary character and spirit.

Have there been departures from this character and spirit?
Some of us say yes, and this is a painful topic. During his long
imprisonment, Mandela and the ANC were of course supported
by some of the worst dictators and regimes on the planet: Castro,
Qaddafi, the Soviets. They showered Mandela with awards. (Did
you know that Libya had a Qaddafi International Prize for Human
Rights?) They did not support Mandela because they were kind-
hearted democrats; it was all part of the war against the West,
broadly speaking. It was only natural for Mandela to be apprecia-
tive of support, wherever it came from, and whatever the motivation. But it also should have been natural for him to recognize,
especially after his release, that these dictators, who were so kind

to him, were monstrous to their own citizens; that they, too, ran "jailer-regimes." That's how Mandela referred to the apartheid government: a "jailer-regime."

But he evinced no such understanding. On the contrary, he praised Qaddafi's "commitment to the fight for peace and human rights in the world." Qaddafi's commitment, of course, was to terrorism, oppression, and dictatorship. One of Mandela's grandsons was named for Qaddafi, incidentally. And Mandela said the following about Castro's Cuba: "There's one thing where that country stands out head and shoulders above the rest. That is in its love for human rights and liberty." The Cuban people may love those things; their rulers for all this time, no.

Bear in mind that Mandela was indeed the most revered leader on the planet; that his moral authority was something like supreme. One word from him, in behalf of Libya's political prisoners, or Cuba's, could have done a world of good. Could have put unprecedented pressure on those regimes. Many of the prisoners were suffering under much worse conditions than Mandela ever faced. (He had regular visits from the Red Cross.) And their only crime might have been to write a poem or request an exit visa. Mandela never said a word for them. Keeping silent would have been bad enough, but he heaped praise on the jailers and persecutors, strengthening them with his moral authority. John F. Kennedy said, "Sometimes party loyalty asks too much." So does political loyalty in general.

There was one prisoner, a Libyan prisoner, whose cause Mandela took up. He was Abdelbaset Megrahi, the Libyan agent convicted in the Lockerbie bombing—the downing in 1988 of the Pan Am plane over Lockerbie, Scotland. Two hundred and seventy people were killed in that bombing. In 2002, Mandela visited Megrahi in his prison cell at Glasgow. He pleaded for better conditions for this prisoner. "He says he is being treated well by the officials, but when he takes exercise he has been harassed by a number of prisoners. He cannot identify them because they shout at him from their cells through the windows and sometimes it is difficult even for the officials to know from which quarter the shouting occurs."

During this same period, Qaddafi and Libya were imprisoning five Bulgarian nurses and one Palestinian doctor, whom they had falsely accused of infecting children with AIDS. The prisoners were not shouted at through windows: They were tortured beyond human description, with rape, dogs, electricity, and so on. One of the nurses, in her desperation, tried to kill herself by chewing the veins in her wrist. She had no other recourse.

As you know, Mandela is one of three Nobel peace laureates to have won the Lenin Peace Prize as well. Earlier in this book, I quoted from his acceptance speech—which, you remember, he gave twelve years after the fact, in the same year as his Presidential Medal of Freedom, and his visit to Megrahi: 2002. The next year, he opposed the Iraq War, as of course many did. But his words contained a special poison.

Two months before the war began, speaking of the United States and Bush, Mandela said, "What I am condemning is that one power, with a president who has no foresight, who cannot think properly, is now wanting to plunge the world into a holocaust." He accused Bush and his main ally, Britain's Blair, of thumbing their nose at the United Nations. "Is it because the secretary-general of the United Nations is now a black man? They never did that when secretary-generals were white." He said, "All that [Bush] wants is Iraqi oil." Apparently, that was not quite true, because Mandela also said that Bush was "trying to bring about carnage." The great South African saw no moral imperative in the removal of Saddam Hussein. He said, "If there is a country that has committed unspeakable atrocities in the world, it is the United States of America. They don't care."

Many people cheered these remarks, for they were wonderful fodder against Bush. Consider the source! CBS News reported excitedly that Mandela had "let the Bush administration have it right between the eyes." But at least a few admirers of Mandela were sickened.

That was all years after the Nobel, however. Why not conclude this section on an unquestionably positive note? Think back to 1961: At the end of his Nobel lecture, Lutuli broke out into song, treating the audience to "God Bless Africa," in Zulu. When the new South Africa dawned, this song became one of two official national anthems, the other being the old anthem, "The Call of South Africa." Then, in 1997, the two anthems were blended, to make one national anthem. The first verse is in Xhosa and Zulu; the second is in Sesotho; the third is in Afrikaans; and the fourth and final is in English. Musically and in other ways, the new, democratic South Africa—free at last from apartheid—has worked out.

～

It was in 1994 that Yasser Arafat came to Oslo to accept his Nobel Peace Prize—or one third of a peace prize. Yitzhak Rabin and Shimon Peres came with him. Arafat was chairman of the Palestine Liberation Organization, of course, and Rabin and Peres were the prime minister and foreign minister of Israel. The year before, the PLO and Israel had signed the Oslo Accords, inaugurating what has for all these years been known as the "Oslo peace process," or, simply, "Oslo." As the committee pointed out, the Middle East trio was really and truly being honored for work done in the previous year, just as Alfred Nobel's will stipulated. (The same can be said of the 1993 honorees, the South Africans: They were awarded for work done in the previous year.)

Nineteen ninety-four's was a prize in which Norwegians could take particular satisfaction—for what was being honored was an agreement and a process named after their own capital. Secret talks had taken place there between representatives of the PLO and Israel. They lasted from January to August 1993, and were conducted under the Norwegian wing: with Norwegian coaxing, cajoling, consoling—prodding. Once the parties were ready to unveil a plan to the world, they went to the White House lawn. There, on September 13, 1993, they signed the Oslo Accords. President Clinton was the smiling master of ceremonies. Rabin and Arafat shook hands (with Rabin obviously, visibly reluctant).

What were the accords supposed to do? In brief, establish peace: peaceful coexistence between Palestinians and Israelis. The PLO would recognize Israel and give up terrorism. Israel would recognize the PLO as "the sole legitimate representative of the Palestinian people," to use the hoary phrase. At the end of the rainbow would be that peaceful coexistence, no more terror or war.

The result seemed a long way off, if not chimerical altogether. But the Nobel Committee, in its announcement, said it was hoping that "the award will serve as an encouragement to all the Israelis and Palestinians who are endeavoring to establish lasting peace in the region." The outcome for South Africans was in the bag, at the time of that award in 1993; the situation for the Israelis and Palestinians was different.

Naturally, there was a storm of reaction to the 1994 prize—a storm that began even before the announcement, when the prize was expected to go to Arafat and Rabin, the two sides' chiefs. When a triumvirate was announced—two Israelis and one Palestinian—there was complaint about lopsidedness: Why two versus one? Why this advantage to the Israelis? Chairman Sejersted explained that half the prize was for the Israeli contribution and half for the Palestinian; it was just that the Israeli half was being shared, by two men who deserved equal credit. Some contended that the man who amounted to Arafat's foreign minister, Mahmoud Abbas, should have been included in the prize, making it even-steven: two and two. (Upon Arafat's death, Abbas would succeed him as PLO chairman.) Other considerations aside, we run up against Nobel rules here: A committee can't give a prize to more than three.

Rabin and Peres were old Labor lions, and old rivals. Each was claiming credit for the breakthrough with the Palestinians. It seemed sure that the prime minister would have a part of the Nobel, because he was, after all, prime minister. But Peres's friends campaigned for the foreign minister's inclusion in the prize. After the announcement, a *Washington Post* report noted with some slyness, "Last month, on the anniversary of the [Oslo Accords], Peres managed to spend the day in Oslo, where he met with Norwegian legislators." The Nobel Committee reached its final decision only on October 7, a week before the announcement: The peace prize would, for the first time, be three-way.

On the day of the announcement, something extraordinary took place: a second press conference in Oslo, not just the usual one with the committee chairman. The second press conference was held by Kåre Kristiansen, a committee member who was resigning in protest of the award—in protest of Arafat's share in it. Kristiansen was a veteran politician of the Christian Democratic party. The son of a Salvation Army pastor, he was a devout Christian himself, and a devout friend to Israel. After the 1973 war, he started a Friends of Israel group in the Storting. During the 1994 deliberations, he told his fellow committeemen that he could not stomach an award to Arafat: that he would resign if it came to that. He asked them to wait at least a year, to see how the Oslo Accords were working out. His colleagues would not wait— Kristiansen was the only member to oppose the decision.

At his press conference, he said of Arafat, "His past is too filled with violence, terrorism, and bloodshed, and his future too uncertain, to make him a Nobel Peace Prize winner." What's more, "it will give the wrong signal to other violent organizations in the Middle East and other parts of the world." Kristiansen asked, "Can there be any doubt that this award is going to downgrade the prize and weaken respect for it?" Never before had there been something like a minority report, or dissenting report, from the committee—even from the members who resigned in the wake of the "Vietnam" Nobel, to Kissinger and Le Duc Tho.

Announcement Day—October 14, that year—ended tragically in Israel. Five days before, a soldier named Nahshon Waxman had been kidnapped by Hamas terrorists. He had been seized while hitchhiking in central Israel to visit his girlfriend. On the night of the 14th, Rabin ordered a raid on the terrorist redoubt. The terrorists killed Waxman, and one of the rescuing soldiers. On that Friday evening, Rabin commented, "I would happily give back the Nobel Peace Prize to bring back the lives of the soldiers who fell."

In December, the three laureates and their camps got themselves to Oslo. In a concession to Norwegian and Nobel sensibilities, Chairman Arafat removed his sidearm, a .357 Magnum. He gave the first lecture—because the laureates were going in alphabetical order. He was not known as a religious soul, but he began with a quote from the Koran: "Then if they should be inclined to make peace, do thou incline towards it also, and put thy trust in Allah." The speech he gave was full of sweetness and light. This was a typical speech for him, in the West. Speeches back home were a different matter. Peres gave an address of really arresting beauty. And he made this direct statement: "I believe it is fitting that the prize has been awarded to Yasser Arafat. His abandonment of the path of confrontation in favor of the path of dialogue has opened the way to peace between ourselves and the Palestinian people."

Rabin was a famously taciturn and contained man—these are unusual qualities in a politician, particularly in a successful one. But, in Oslo, he gave an intensely personal and emotional speech. He talked about what it was to be a military commander and make decisions that would surely result in death: the death of your own people, and other people. And he began his speech with the following reflection:

> At the tender age of 16, I was handed a rifle so that I could defend myself—and also, unfortunately, so that I could kill in an hour of danger. That was not my dream. I wanted to be a water engineer. I studied in an agricultural school and I thought that being a water engineer was an important profession in the parched Middle East. I still think so today.

But life had other plans for him. I might note here that Rabin has a connection to the 1950 prize, won by Ralph Bunche. Rabin, then in his mid-twenties, was a member of the Israeli delegation that went to Rhodes for armistice talks with Egypt. (They were mediated by the U.N.'s envoy, Bunche, of course.) He left before the signing because he objected to the draft agreement.

The course of the Oslo peace process need not be rehearsed in these pages. There are shelves of books on the subject. Many people wanted the Nobel Committee to revoke Arafat's prize, or his third of it, because of the terror he was unleashing. He simply refused to make peace with Israel, and to allow Palestinians their state. Israel and the West bent over backward for him: In the eight years of Clinton, he was the most frequent foreign visitor to the White House. He would not "take yes for an answer." Arafat reverted to terror like an uncured drunk to the bottle. Kåre Kristiansen observed that his former colleagues on the committee had hoped "to motivate him to stay on track. That, of course, didn't happen, but the committee will never acknowledge that."

Speaking on Palestinian TV in 2009, Mohammed Dahlan, an old Arafat lieutenant, said proudly that the late chairman had always been a terrorist, no matter what he thought it advantageous to say to the West. "Arafat would condemn operations by day while at night he would do honorable things," said Dahlan—and by "honorable things," he meant the planning and approving of the very terror operations he condemned "by day." Many other former Arafat lieutenants have testified to Arafat's consistency in terror. This particular Nobelist died in 2004. Rabin was murdered by an Israeli extremist in 1995—murdered at a peace rally. Like Sadat, it was widely said, he paid the ultimate price for his peacemaking. Peres, ever more a lion, was elected to the largely ceremonial post of Israeli president in 2007.

When I bring up the Nobel Peace Prize with people, in casual conversation, they often say, "Didn't they give it to Arafat?" (I am speaking mainly of Americans.) Their tone suggests that they think, "What more is there to say?" Many people simply "checked out" when Arafat won the prize: stopped taking the prize seriously, thinking it irrevocably damaged. It is indeed a little weird to go into the Nobel Peace Center, encounter the display of postcards depicting the laureates through the decades, and see Yasser Arafat's smiling face, wrapped in his keffiyeh. Theodore Roosevelt, Fridtjof Nansen, Albert Schweitzer, Mother Teresa . . . Arafat. When the 1994 Nobel was announced, a cheeky editorialist for the *Washington Times* asked what Mother Teresa and Arafat had in common: "Is it the unusual headgear?" And you remember what Elena Bonner said in her 2009 speech to the Oslo Freedom Forum: ". . . to this day, I cannot understand and accept the fact that Andrei Sakharov and Yasser Arafat . . . share membership in the club of Nobel laureates."

Surely, we all have our opinions about the merits of the 1994 prize. I will give mine. It is almost certainly true that Arafat is the worst man ever to win the prize—although he is perhaps tied with Le Duc Tho. The 1973 co-laureate earned a reputation as a hard-liner even in a totalitarian dictatorship. That is a feat. But

Arafat's character does not mean that the 1994 prize is the worst ever. It doesn't even mean that the prize was a bad one. I believe it was defensible. Arafat did not win the prize by himself; he won it as part of a troika; he won it in concert with the two Israeli statesmen. Evidently, they didn't mind sharing the prize with Arafat. And Peres, as we have seen, took the step of declaring that Arafat's part in the prize was "fitting." Furthermore, the award was given at a time when the Oslo peace process was quite young. The fraudulence of it was not yet apparent, at least to most. The Nobel Committee wanted to encourage the process along, and hold the participants to it. That was a reasonable impulse and desire.

At the time of the award, an Israeli writer, Meir Shalev, noted the difference between the Nobel Peace Prize and the other Nobels. He said, "They don't give out Nobels for half a [scientific] study or a quarter of a book. But peace, so it seems, is another matter." Yes, and that can be justified.

What would you have done if you had been a member of the Norwegian Nobel Committee in 1994? It's hard to say at a distance, because a decision is of the moment, but I do not believe that I myself would have voted to give the prize to Arafat. I don't think I would have voted to let Arafat have a piece of the prize even if it meant not honoring the Oslo peace process. In his presentation speech, Sejersted said that the committee's role was not to "hand out certificates of good conduct" but to "reward practical work for peace," in accordance with the testator's guidelines. We can all appreciate that. And the Oslo Accords were practical work for peace. Yet I believe that Kristiansen was right: that Arafat was too grotesque a man, and his terrorist record too ample, to let him be a Nobel peace laureate—certainly at that stage. Someone like that should have been held to a greater, longer test of conversion. But, again, the committee had a case in 1994. And the committee in Kristiania/Oslo, over a century and a decade, has made many worse decisions.

∽

One of them came in 1995, I believe. In that year, the prize was given to Joseph Rotblat and the Pugwash Conferences on Science and World Affairs. That is, the prize was split: between Rotblat, a Polish-born British physicist, and Pugwash, the organization in which he was central. He was the secretary-general of Pugwash from its founding in 1957 to 1973; he was later president, from 1988 to 1997. Pugwash was essentially an anti-nuclear group, holding conferences that brought together scientists from the Free World (as some used to call it) and the Communist world. Obviously, some scientists had more freedom of action than others: The scientists from Communist states were all "official," meaning that they were carefully vetted, monitored, and compelled to serve a party line.

Pugwash grew out of the Russell-Einstein Manifesto of 1955, the great anti-nuclear declaration of the age. It was signed, not just by Bertrand Russell and Albert Einstein (in his dying days), but also by some others who are familiar to us: including Linus Pauling and Rotblat. These two were birds of a feather, and "great friends," as Pauling's son said after Rotblat's death. The money behind the Pugwash Conferences was Cyrus Eaton, an American industrialist who started out in Canada: in the village of Pugwash, Nova Scotia. The first conference was held at his estate there, in July 1957. The weather in eastern Canada must have been lovely.

Eaton was a curious figure: the capitalist mogul as friend of the Soviet Union. (Armand Hammer, better known than Eaton, was another such mogul.) He was born in 1883 and founded the Republic Steel Corporation in 1930. The Soviets had few more determined apologists. And he had much contempt for the country in which he had become rich and influential. At the time the

Pugwash group was set up, he gave an interview to Mike Wallace, who was becoming one of the most famous journalists in America. Eaton said, "There is more spirit of war in the United States than in any other country in the world." He also said that the U.S., stupidly fearing Communism, had built up a terrible police state. "Hitler in his prime never, through the Gestapo, had any such spying organizations as we have in this country today." When Wallace pressed him about the lack of freedom in the Soviet bloc, Eaton said, "If you take a vote in those countries, you might be surprised"—surprised at the people's support for the regimes. And yet, such votes somehow never took place. As was only natural, the Soviet government honored Eaton with the Lenin Peace Prize. He died in 1979 at the grand age of 95.

Rotblat lived to a grand age too: He was born in 1908 and died in 2005, at 96. A significant moment in his life occurred in 1944. He went to Los Alamos, to work on the Manhattan Project. His reason was, the Nazis were trying to get an atomic bomb, and the Allies needed to counter them. But soon the picture changed, in his eyes. As he told it later, he discovered that the Nazis had abandoned their nuclear efforts. What the Americans were doing was building bombs to use as leverage against Japan—and against a post-war Soviet Union. That, Rotblat could not abide. In disgust, he quit the Manhattan Project. Deterring Hitler's Germany was one thing, but deterring Tojo's Japan or Stalin's Russia was another. Rotblat would always be celebrated for his quitting of the Manhattan Project: It was seen as a great act of conscience.

At home in Britain, Rotblat was a founding member of CND, the Campaign for Nuclear Disarmament. But he focused most of his attention on Pugwash and its events. They were held all around the world, and their participants were stars of the antinuclear scene. Among the countries hosting the conferences were Romania, Czechoslovakia, Poland, and, of course, the Soviet Union. Dictators were happy to pin medals on the Pugwashers, and freely did. The conference in Poland was held in 1982, after General Jaruzelski had imposed martial law. Some suggested that the Pugwashers go elsewhere that year, in a gesture of solidarity, to Solidarity and to the Polish people in general; the organization was unmoved. The year before, Pugwash had denounced Israel for its destruction of Saddam Hussein's nuclear facility. You might have thought that an anti-nuclear group would be at least partly pleased.

One of the things the Nobel Committee was doing in 1995 was indulging its love of anniversaries—for there were two that year, as the committee noted: 50 years had passed since the atomic bombing of Japan; and 40 years had passed since the issuing of the Russell-Einstein Manifesto. Furthermore, the committee, through Sejersted, said that it wished to send a message against nuclear testing. Special criticism was reserved for the French, who had been testing in the South Pacific. The government in Paris responded to the committee in Oslo—and to Rotblat and Pugwash—with Gallic cool, even insouciance. A former adviser to President Chirac, Pierre Lellouche, felt free to slam the committee's decision: "I am personally and as a specialist in these matters perfectly scandalized by the fact that an organization that one knows was openly manipulated by the Soviets should be honored in this way."

Presentation Day saw two lectures—Rotblat's and one given on behalf of Pugwash, as an organization. The latter was delivered by the "Chair of the Executive Committee of the Pugwash Council," John P. Holdren. An American scientist and activist, he would later serve as chief science adviser to a Nobel peace laureate, President Obama. In his own lecture, Rotblat said, "The Cold War is over, but Cold War thinking survives. Then, we were told that a world war was prevented by the existence of nuclear weapons. Now we are told that nuclear weapons prevent all kinds of war."

The 1995 Nobel, as you can see, was another in a line of anti-nuclear Nobels. It was similar to a couple of awards in the 1980s: the one to Myrdal and García Robles, and the one to IPPNW, the physicians group. What made the 1995 prize especially galling, to some of us, was the claim that Rotblat and Pugwash had helped bring about a world of greatly reduced tension and danger—the post–Cold War (and pre-9/11) world. In his Nobel lecture, John Holdren said that neither "hawks" nor "doves" should congratulate themselves: Frankly, we were all a little lucky. An entirely just point. But, as some of us see it, Rotblat and the Pugwashers opposed virtually every step that made this better world possible.

They had nothing but scorn for deterrence, thinking it a snare and a delusion. They were for the unilateral disarmament of the West. They thought containment was a joke. They fought like tigers against anti-missile defenses. They opposed just about any attempt to resist the Soviet Union and its aggressive expansion.

Why were the unilateralists and accommodationists being honored instead of the tough-minded and freedom-minded leaders who, against heavy anti-nuclear propaganda, persevered to counter the Soviet Union, and see it out? In its 1995 announcement, the Nobel Committee said that it was rewarding Rotblat & Co. "for their efforts to diminish the part played by nuclear arms in international politics and, in the longer run, to eliminate such arms." The same commendation could have been made—would more sensibly and plausibly have been made—of Reagan, Weinberger (his defense secretary, Caspar Weinberger), Thatcher, Kohl, and the rest of the gang whom the Pugwashers detested and accused of warmongering.

Rotblat, as I have said, was the oldest person to have won the Nobel Peace Prize, and he remains that: He was 87 on Presentation Day. In 1998, the British government knighted him, meaning that he spent his last several years as "Sir Joseph." And his ideology remained intact to the end. In an interview, he was asked about the nuclear threat from North Korea and Iran. He would not really address the question, except to say that these regimes "feel they are vulnerable." He concentrated his fire on the United States, ever and always.

∼

As in 1991 the Nobel Committee had shone its spotlight on Burma, in 1996 it shone its spotlight on East Timor—a very far and obscure corner of the world (from the perspective of most Westerners, that is). East Timor lies on the eastern tip of the Malay Archipelago, within shouting distance of Darwin, Australia. Sejersted said to the laureates at the prize ceremony, "To reach this peaceful winterland Norway, you have come about as far from your home country as it is possible to travel on this earth." The laureates were Bishop Carlos Filipe Ximenes Belo and José Ramos-Horta. In their own ways, they were leaders of the opposition to the Indonesian occupation and brutalization of East Timor. Indonesia invaded in 1975, after the Portuguese departed. Sejersted said, "Of a population of between 600,000 and 700,000, nearly 200,000 have died as the direct or indirect result of the Indonesian occupation": through killing, famine, and disease.

Bishop Belo was the spiritual leader of East Timor, a very brave man who stuck his neck out for peace and (genuine) justice. Ramos-Horta was part of Fretilin, the guerrilla resistance. Its military commander was Xanana Gusmão, jailed in Jakarta. Ramos-Horta was in exile, traveling the world as the spokesman for the East Timorese cause. Sejersted called him "one of the moderates" of Fretilin, a man "whose ideal was social democracy." When the 1996 Nobel was announced, Ramos-Horta said that, while he was grateful, the prize should have gone to Gusmão, "our true leader."

We saw that in 1989 the Nobel Committee praised the Tibetan exiles for refusing to "set up any militant liberation movement." The East Timorese had such a movement, and José Ramos-Horta was very much a part of it, "moderate" social democrat or not. The Norwegian Nobel Committee has not been perfectly consistent, but then, neither have most institutions or individuals, and everyone agrees that life is messy.

Ramos-Horta was the son of a native Timorese woman and a Portuguese man. The elder Ramos-Horta had been deported to East Timor after participating in a revolt against Salazar. You remember how Amnesty International started: when Peter Benenson was provoked by the jailing of two student opponents of that same dictator. During his years of exile, the younger Ramos-Horta acquired a master's degree in peace studies at Antioch University: the radical institution in Yellow Springs, Ohio, where Irwin Abrams, the leading historian of the Nobel Peace Prize, taught. In 1993, Ramos-Horta received the Rafto Human Rights Prize in Norway—more specifically, he received it "for the people of East Timor," as the prize-giving organization said. The Rafto is sometimes a precursor to the Nobel.

As he explained in 2001, at the Nobel Institute's symposium, Ramos-Horta went to Oslo many times in 1994 and 1995. His "main concern," he said, was to put Bishop Belo and the East Timorese church "on the map" in Norway. He had been warned not to do any lobbying of the Nobel Committee, as this would only backfire. So "I was always extremely careful, discreet," in making the East Timorese case. A very promising moment came when a member of the Nobel Committee, Gunnar Stålsett, visited him in his hotel room. "For me," Ramos-Horta recalled, "it was like meeting with some top official in the Vatican." Ramos-Horta took care not to bring up Belo—but the committeeman brought him up, asking direct questions.

Ramos-Horta thought that 1995 would be the big year. He was fielding questions from the Norwegian press about a win for Belo, a win expected by many. He learned that Norwegian parliamentarians were supporting Leyla Zana, a Kurdish leader in Turkey, then in prison. As he recounted in 2001, Ramos-Horta thought, "Well, we have a serious competitor here." It's a little sad when just causes—when various persecuted peoples and their representatives—are in competition, hoping and trying to hit the jackpot of the Nobel Peace Prize. In 1995, when Rotblat and Pugwash were announced, Ramos-Horta was surprised: Like most of the world, he had never heard of them.

The next year, a friend and supporter asked him who he thought would win. Ramos-Horta answered, "I don't care. After what we went through last year, I don't care. They can give it to Leyla Zana, they can give it to Richard Holbrooke [the American diplomat who had shaped the Dayton Agreement, ending the Bosnian war]. I don't care." Zana had already won two awards: Rafto in 1994 and the Sakharov Prize the next year. In any event, the 1996 award was given to Bishop Belo—and to Ramos-Horta himself. "I was embarrassed," he said, "because I didn't think that I really fit the criteria." But he seized "the chance to further promote the cause of peace for East Timor. The doors that were closed were thrown open around the world. Pressure increased on Indonesia." Back in Dili, the East Timorese capital, Belo said something poignant: "Better that I had not won. It makes my responsibilities heavier."

Outwardly, the Indonesians played it cool. The deputy governor of East Timor said he did not "take Nobel prizes seriously. . . . This is just a conscience massage for the liberal West. It is just one of those things. The Nobel prizes are like the Oscars, and, as with Hollywood, they are partly removed from reality." In truth, however, as one expert noted, the Indonesians were "in a panic." The Nobel Peace Prize had been turned on them, like a gigantic gun.

At the prize ceremony, Sejersted celebrated an anniversary—a centennial, in fact: It had been a hundred years since the death of the testator, Alfred Nobel. The first of the two lectures that day was given by Belo. As befitted his position, this resembled a sermon, in some portions. Ramos-Horta gave a quite interesting address, containing at least one strange, clangorous sentence. Setting the Cold War "context" of the Indonesian invasion, he talked about the American departure from Vietnam—and, in particular, the famous photo of the helicopter on the embassy roof, with the desperate people snaking up the ladder. Ramos-Horta said that helicopter had come "to rescue remaining diplomats, CIA operatives, and a few privileged South Vietnamese stooges." One can think of better, less disgusting descriptions of those fleeing for their lives, as murderous, totalitarian forces closed in.

Many, probably most, people thought that East Timor had no chance of freedom from Indonesia. After the Nobel announcement in October 1996, a writer for the *Globe and Mail* began a column this way: "The winners of this year's Nobel Peace Prize . . . are by all accounts brave and honourable men. But they are linked to a lost cause . . . ." He ended that column by saying, "Even the Nobel Peace Prize will not change that"—will not change the futility of the cause. But Francis Sejersted, in his presentation speech, took a different line: "It has been said that Indonesia's annexation of East Timor is a historic fact. But history has never established anything as a fact forever. History always moves on."

In 1999, Indonesia allowed a referendum in East Timor, to determine the territory's future. People voted overwhelmingly for independence—and they would get it. For three years, the United Nations supervised this territory, and in May 2002 East Timor became the first new nation-state of the 21st century. Xanana Gusmão was president, and later prime minister (the head of government); Ramos-Horta was foreign minister, then prime minister, then president. In the years following the referendum and independence, East Timor has experienced great tumult, including violence. In 2006, an international force led by Australia had to come in and restore order. In 2008, Ramos-Horta was the victim of an assassination attempt. He was seriously wounded but survived.

There were several reasons for East Timor's surprise winning of independence. In 1997, Asia was hit with a terrible economic meltdown, and Indonesia was one of the countries hit hardest. Suharto, the longtime dictator, lost his hold on the government. Indonesia was in a weakened position, needing international cooperation, not as able as before to withstand international pressure. And, of course, the Nobel Peace Prize helped considerably. Many partisans of East Timorese independence say it was the key factor. The Nobel Committee may not have been able to make a dent in the Burmese dictatorship; but it dealt a serious blow to the Suharto-led Indonesian government, and for East Timor.

~

In 1997, the committee honored a notable and unusual achievement: the preparation and signing of the Mine Ban Treaty. The signing took place exactly a week before the prize ceremony. It was, and is, a treaty banning "anti-personnel" mines: mines designed to kill or maim people, as distinguished from "anti-tank" mines, which take much more pressure to explode. You will recall that mines figure in our general Nobel story: Sea mines were a specialty of old Immanuel Nobel, who made them for the czar, who was trying to win the Crimean War. What did Admiral Napier say? That "the Gulf of Finland is full of infernal machines."

The Mine Ban Treaty was the handiwork of the International Campaign to Ban Landmines and its leader, Jody Williams. They shared the 1997 Nobel prize: the organization and the woman, half the money going to each. Williams was an American, a Vermonter, born in 1950. Like a great many on the left, she spent the 1980s working against the Reagan administration's policies in Central America. In 1992, she took up the anti-landmine cause, eventually getting more than 1,000 NGOs from around the world to sign on (NGOs being "non-governmental organizations," as you know). The cause attracted many celebrity activists, one of whom was Diana, Princess of Wales. With her companion and their driver, she was killed in a car crash on August 31, 1997. This was about six weeks before the Nobel prize for the landmine banners was announced. Final negotiations for the Mine Ban Treaty took place in September—in Oslo, home of so much international activity, and Nobel-winning activity. But the treaty was signed in Ottawa—signed on December 3, by more than 120 nations. In fact, the process leading to the signing is known as the "Ottawa process," and the treaty itself is sometimes called the "Ottawa Treaty."

What was extraordinary about this treaty was that it sprang from NGOs, pressuring and eventually partnering with governments. In its announcement, the Nobel Committee said that, "as a model for similar processes in the future," the Ottawa process "could prove of decisive importance to the international effort for disarmament and peace."

Who could be against a treaty banning landmines? The United States, for one nation. One of the issues was the demilitarized zone between the two Koreas. As President Clinton explained, about a million mines were planted in that zone, protecting American and South Korean soldiers alike. (I suppose you could argue that a zone with a million mines is not truly demilitarized.) Also, the Pentagon was saying that, without the mines, North Korean forces could overrun Seoul quickly. The DMZ minefields were an indispensable buffer. The United States wanted to join the Mine Ban Treaty and asked for exceptions. The movers behind the treaty said, "No exceptions."

When the 1997 Nobel was announced, the heat was on Clinton to give up his objections and climb aboard. But his spokesman immediately said, "The president is absolutely rock-solid confident" in his position. For her part, Jody Williams said Clinton was "outside the tide of history" and "on the wrong side of humanity"—and, for good measure, a "weenie." Many people thought that Clinton should have phoned his congratulations to Williams; instead, he wrote them to her. The press got rather a kick out of the new laureate, who had a home in Vermont with a beaver pond out back, and who was often seen barefoot. She was celebrated as natural in her appearance and her speech. But she told a *Washington Post* "Style" writer what she planned to wear for the prize ceremony: "I have a glittering black pantsuit. It sparkles. It came from Lord & Taylor. I got it on sale in New York when I was there with my sister."

At the ceremony, Sejersted did not mention Immanuel Nobel but did mention Alfred: "It is a paradox that what we find inside landmines is Nobel's brilliant invention, dynamite." Williams, in her lecture, had a lovely line. She said that she was very pleased that she and her organization had won the Nobel Peace Prize. But "the real prize is the treaty."

Like so many others, she spoke at the centennial symposium, four years later. And she used her time to decry the United States, for its response to the terrorist attacks on it. She was dismayed that people were saying that 9/11 had "changed everything." Because the world—and the U.S. in particular—was still militaristic. "They immediately have gone to war," said Williams, referring to the U.S. and its allies. They had gone to war in Afghanistan (to see what they could do about al-Qaeda, and its patron, the Taliban). Moreover, said the laureate, "we see a rise of McCarthyism in the United States. We're told that all of this is done to protect civilization everywhere, and to protect our freedom. At the same time, Draconian laws are being passed in the United States of America to take away our freedom. . . . Supposedly this great war against

evil, Satan, and terrorism is being fought to protect us all . . . ."
The scorn in her voice could not have been heavier.

Williams continued, "I wonder, also, when the line is going
to be crossed where the patriotism in the United States becomes
xenophobia. When is the increased surveillance and repression in
the United States going to become state terrorism? I hope never.
It's entirely possible." The response of Jody Williams to the 9/11
attacks was the same as many others' (Dr. Lown's, for instance):
that the true danger came from the United States. America always
wore the black hat, even when it was down and bleeding.

She said that Americans were whining and wailing about
Ground Zero, but what about the other ground zeroes in the
world? Who cared about them, huh? "Afghanistan, before this
bombing, was already a country of ground zero. And we're
bombing it more." (Is that all "we" were doing?) Williams also
pointed her finger at a general, overarching foe: the nation-state.
"I believe that the hope of the future is not the nation-state." Even
the beloved United Nations was culpable, she said, because it was
composed of nation-states. For Williams, true hope lay in what
she called "civil society" (i.e., groups like her own, and persons
like herself).

At the end of her remarks, she beseeched her audience to stop
saying that everything had changed after September 11. What we
had seen, she said, was "resurgence of the state, resurgence of
repression, resurgence of McCarthyism. Even the good guys are
cheering this great coalition [in Afghanistan]! Canada, Australia,
and countries that were great in the landmine campaign are clamoring to send troops. This is a new and fabulous coalition? Not in
my book."

Bear in mind that Williams's lamentations and denunciations
came less than three months after the 9/11 attacks, when bodies

were still being retrieved from the rubble. The Iraq War was more than a year away. To the "War on Terror," as it was once called, Williams would not get more sympathetic. A movie about her life was made, by the way. It was called *My Name Is Jody Williams*, and starred Naomi Watts, the British-Australian actress.

〜

In 1998, it was time for the second award concerning Northern Ireland—a successor to the 1976 award, which honored Betty Williams and Máiread Corrigan (as she was then known) for their Community of the Peace People. Northern Ireland had not seen much peace since then. "The Troubles" continued, killing and embittering people. But 1998 was promising—for this was the year of the Good Friday Agreement. And the Good Friday Agreement was supposed to end the Troubles once and for all.

It was a multi-party agreement that strove to build institutions for reconciliation and a lasting peace. The most notable such institution was a Northern Ireland assembly. The agreement was meant to alter relations between Protestants and Catholics in Northern Ireland; between Northern Ireland and the Republic of Ireland; and between the Irish and British governments. The agreement was signed on April 10, 1998—Good Friday, as it happened. And it was ratified by voters in both Northern Ireland and Ireland on May 22. It was natural for the Nobel Committee to bless this agreement—and further the chances of its fulfillment—later in the year.

The committee divided the award between two men, John Hume and David Trimble. Said Sejersted, speaking at the ceremony, "[They] are both from Northern Ireland, where they have lived with and in the conflict. They are both prominent politicians, leaders respectively of the two largest political parties in Northern Ireland, parties which represent the two groups in a divided population." And they "have both helped to build confidence that it is

possible to arrive at reasonable compromises by peaceful means."
The chairman spoke true words. Many people thought that Gerry
Adams, the head of Sinn Féin, the "political wing" of the IRA,
should have been a laureate. (Sinn Féin was a party to the talks
culminating in the Good Friday Agreement.) But the committee
was satisfied with Hume and Trimble.

Hume was a Catholic and nationalist—but a reform-minded,
democratic, and peaceable nationalist. The description usually
applied to him was "moderate nationalist." He was the leader of
the SDLP, the Social Democratic and Labour Party. Urging work
for peace instead of the old enmity and strife, he would tell schoolchildren, "We must spill our sweat together, not our blood." Trimble, a Protestant, was the leader of the UUP, the Ulster Unionist
Party. He had no tolerance of extremists and killers, wherever they
came from, but he was ready to deal when a deal was to be had.
Both Hume and Trimble were despised by extremists: seen as
compromised, because compromising.

The cool, practical, and skeptical nature of Trimble was illus-
trated in his response to the Nobel announcement. He said that
he was "a bit uncomfortable" about the prize. And "I hope very
much that this award doesn't turn out to be premature." Someone
should have told him—maybe someone did—that Nobel wanted
his prize to go for honorable work done in the preceding year,
plain and simple: whether that work was cinching or not.

Hume, in his Nobel lecture, noted that the prize ceremony was
taking place on the fiftieth anniversary of the Universal Declaration of Human Rights (that document dear to the Nobel Committee's heart). "To me," he said, "there is a unique appropriateness, a
sort of poetic fulfillment, in the coincidence that my fellow laureate and I, representing a community long divided by the forces of
a terrible history, should jointly be honored on this day." He ended
his lecture by saying he wished to quote one of his "great heroes,"
Martin Luther King: "We shall overcome." Actually, those words

come from an old gospel song, but King indeed made splendid use of them (as he did of everything).

Trimble gave a lecture that was smart, nimble, wise—and very funny. I count it one of the best in Nobel history. He said that many, many people had contributed to peace in Northern Ireland, and that many thousands of others were performing heroic work for peace around the world. "Having said that, I am at the same time anxious to allay any fears on your part that I might fail to pick up the medal or the check. The people of Northern Ireland are not a people to look a gift horse in the mouth." Toward the end of his lecture, he said, "What we democratic politicians want in Northern Ireland is not some utopian society but a normal society."

Since 1998 and the Good Friday Agreement and the Nobel prize, there have been many problems in Northern Ireland, including terrorism and killings. But the Troubles have not returned, full-blown. Northern Ireland is pretty much a normal society (one of the highest conditions a society can aspire to). Many years ago, the American political writer George F. Will said that there were two "intractable" problems in the world: Northern Ireland and the Arab–Israeli conflict. And he said this well before the Cold War wound down, and the Soviet Union expired. The Arab–Israeli conflict is still with us—but the intractability of Northern Ireland seems to have been cracked. The 1998 Nobel Peace Prize was a very good award: given to good people who had worked hard and well to solve a terrible problem (and who had done this work in the preceding year, textbook-style, or will-style). People in Northern Ireland and elsewhere can hope that 1998's will be the last Nobel prize concerning the Troubles.

∽

The 1999 Nobel was a humanitarian award—and a human-rights award. It went to Médecins Sans Frontières, which we know in English as Doctors Without Borders. (More generally, the organization is known by its French initials, MSF.) The doctors of MSF respond to disasters both natural and political—earthquakes, for example, and ethnic cleansing. They give medical treatment to victims, in the traditional fashion of humanitarian groups; but they also speak out against human-rights abuses. Chairman Sejersted made clear that the 1999 Nobel belonged to both the humanitarian and human-rights categories (for those keeping score).

MSF was born in 1971, when a group of French doctors, along with some journalists, decided they needed a different kind of organization. Different from what? From the Red Cross, principally. The doctors had worked for the Red Cross in Biafra, the territory that declared independence from Nigeria and was then brought brutally back into the fold. The doctors did what they could for the mangled and bleeding bodies. But it frustrated them that they could not speak out against the causes of the horror. They could only mend, not protest. The Red Cross had rules of political neutrality. The Red Cross needed green lights from all governments and other political entities. MSF would be willing to be kicked out of places, for their criticisms.

The main founder and presiding spirit of MSF was Bernard Kouchner, a romantic figure of our age (more romantic than Seán MacBride). Doctor, ex-Communist, humanitarian, playboy, intellectual, controversialist, politician—perhaps it is easier to say he is French. He fell out with his organization, MSF, in 1979. The issue, apparently, was how to help the Vietnamese boat people. Some at MSF felt that Kouchner's desired approach was too direct or sensational. Kouchner started a different group, MDM, for Médecins du Monde (Doctors of the World). In 2007, when Nicolas Sarkozy became French president, Kouchner became foreign minister.

Speaking for MSF at the 1999 prize ceremony was James Orbinski, a Canadian doctor who was president of MSF's international council. He gave a bracing, no-nonsense speech that began,

"The people of Chechnya . . . are enduring indiscriminate bombing by the Russian army." He lost no time in taking advantage of his platform. With Moscow's envoy to Oslo sitting in the audience, he said, "I appeal here today to his excellency the ambassador of Russia, and through him to President Yeltsin, to stop the bombing of defenseless civilians in Chechnya."

Orbinski had worked in Rwanda when midnight struck. He said, "I would like for a moment to acknowledge among our invited guests Chantal Ndagijimana. She lost 40 members of her family in Rwanda's genocide in 1994. Today she is a part of our team in Brussels." He described some of the savagery he had witnessed. And he said, "There are limits to humanitarianism. No doctor can stop a genocide. No humanitarian can stop ethnic cleansing, just as no humanitarian can make war. And no humanitarian can make peace. These are political responsibilities . . . ." He went on to say, "Srebrenica was apparently a safe haven in which we were present. The U.N. was also present. It said it would protect. It had blue helmets on the ground. And the U.N. stood silent and present—as the people of Srebrenica were massacred." Just as had happened in Rwanda. Needless to say, Orbinski called for "a reform of peacekeeping operations."

In this address, Orbinski spoke like a man with urgent things to say, who would not be stopped from saying them, as a significant percentage of the world listened.

~

Under different circumstances, the prize for 2000 might have been a special prize: a prize imbued with millennial glory. But the big year for the Nobel prizes—all of them, Norwegian and Swedish—would be the next year, for that was the year of the Nobel centennial. In any case, the peace prize for 2000 went to an extraordinary man, Kim Dae-jung of South Korea—an example of the political oppositionist and prisoner who emerges from his cell to be the leader of his country. Westerners sometimes called Kim "the Nelson Mandela of Asia." By that they meant that he had courage, moral strength, and magnanimity.

He led far more dramatic a life than anyone could really want. He was born in 1925, and was captured by the Communists during the war (the Korean War). He was sentenced to be shot, but managed to escape. In his life of South Korean politics, he would have to escape many more times. This is the way he put it in his Nobel lecture: "Five times I faced death at the hands of dictators, six years I spent in prison, and 40 years I lived under house arrest or in exile and under constant surveillance." A liberal democrat, he was always a threat or annoyance to the strongmen. In 1973, he was kidnapped by South Korean agents at a Tokyo hotel. They took him to sea and prepared to drown him. According to most reports—and stories vary—the U.S. government, through CIA agents, swooped in to save him.

In 1980, after an uprising in his home base of Kwangju, the government charged Kim with sedition and conspiracy. The sentence (once more) was death. The Carter administration, in its last days, seemed powerless to save him. Carter's leverage with the South Koreans had approached nil. The Carter team appealed to the incoming Reagan administration to do something for Kim. Reagan agreed. His soon-to-be national security adviser, Richard V. Allen, delivered a message to Seoul: "If you kill him, you will be struck as though by a lightning bolt from the heavens." The execution was stayed. South Korea's strongman, Chun Doo-hwan, was one of the first visitors to the Reagan White House. He visited on February 2, 1981, less than two weeks after the president was sworn in. Reagan took a great deal of criticism for this visit: It appeared that he was coddling dictators. But the visit had been a price of sparing Kim. Reagan, just taking the criticism, never said a word.

One of the people blasting Reagan for his alleged coddling of dictators, and his alleged indifference to human rights, was Kim himself. Years later, Allen told him the story of what had happened, at the end of 1980 and the beginning of 1981. This was indeed a revelation.

In 1982, Kim was released and exiled to the United States. He taught at Harvard, even while keeping a close watch over his homeland. In 1985, he returned there, to resume his political opposition: to resume it on Korean turf itself. He had run for president once before, and would run three more times—before winning on that fourth try, in 1997. Shortly before the election, South Korea was socked by the Asian financial crisis. The voters were ready for a change. Finally, at age 72, Kim Dae-jung was president.

The main feature of his presidency, certainly in the eyes of the world, was his "sunshine policy": a policy of engagement and reconciliation—détente, if you will—with North Korea. In June 2000, Kim Dae-jung and Kim Jong-il, the North Korean dictator, held a summit in Pyongyang. Kim Jong-il promised that he would reciprocate with a visit to Seoul. It never happened. The sunshine policy led to some heartrending reunions between relatives long separated by the peninsular and national divide: Old people wept uncontrollably; the North Koreans, even after some fattening up, were emaciated. But the sunshine policy did not produce much, beyond these emotional reunions. It was later revealed that there had been South Korean payments to the North, just before the summit: dubious business deals worth $500 million to the North Koreans. Was Kim Dae-jung trying to bribe Pyongyang, for the summit? Was he increasing his chances of winning the Nobel Peace Prize? A cloud appeared over the award. More than a few said, "The Nobel Peace Prize was purchased for the sum of $500 million."

In any event, Kim was a natural winner in 2000. He was known far and wide, of course, but the new committee chairman, Gunnar Berge (a veteran Labor politician), spoke of a special relationship. In his presentation speech, he said, "As a member of a delegation from the Norwegian Storting, I visited South Korea in 1979, a visit which among other things brought me into contact with supporters of Kim Dae-jung. I am glad I was able then to serve as a link to important connections in Scandinavia."

The committee was giving Kim the award for several reasons. First, he stood for democracy and human rights in South Korea. Second, he stood for these things throughout Asia as a whole. For instance, he was a strong supporter of the East Timorese and of Aung San Suu Kyi in Burma. (José Ramos-Horta attended the 2000 prize ceremony.) Third, there was the sunshine policy. Berge compared it to the *Ostpolitik* of an earlier laureate, Willy Brandt. Yes, there is always the danger of "reverses," said Berge, but the Nobel Committee "adheres to the principle, 'Nothing ventured, nothing gained.'" The world was spared the sight of Kim Jong-il in Oslo, as a co-recipient of the Nobel Peace Prize. That would have been too perverse even for the prize at its most strained. But Berge said, "North Korea's leaders deserve recognition for their part in the first steps toward reconciliation between the two countries."

When it was his turn at the lectern, Kim Dae-jung talked about his "breakthrough" with North Korea. And he talked about his decades-long "struggle" to refute the lie that human rights and democracy were for the West only: that they did not apply to Asia, which had its own traditions and values. Nonsense, said Kim: Human rights and democracy were universal, not alien to the Asian man and woman.

He left office in 2003 and died in 2009, age 83. The sunshine policy had already been extinguished. As Jeane Kirkpatrick said, North Korea is a "psychotic state," and the world has very little experience of psychotic states. Moreover, this one is nuclear-armed. The North seemed to punctuate its hostility in March 2010 when it blew a South Korean naval vessel out of the water (killing 46). Pyongyang denied this act, even while it celebrated it.

The presidency of Kim Dae-jung was not a roaring success: People went to jail for corruption, including two of the president's sons. The sunshine policy came to look foolish and even dangerous. But Kim had an overall greatness. He once said, "I used all my strength to resist the dictatorial regimes, because there was no other way to defend the people and promote democracy. I felt like a homeowner whose house was invaded by a robber. I had to fight the intruder with my bare hands to protect my family and property without thinking of my own safety." His first act on becoming president was to pardon the generals who had sentenced him to death. Once, while in prison, Kim wrote to a son, "Only the truly magnanimous and strong are capable of forgiving and loving."

In his Nobel lecture, he said he wished to offer a "personal note," which included,

> I have lived, and continue to live, in the belief that God is always with me. I know this from experience. In August of 1973, while exiled in Japan, I was kidnapped from my hotel room in Tokyo by intelligence agents of the then military government of South Korea. The news of the incident startled the world. The agents took me to their boat at anchor along the seashore. They tied me up, blinded me, and stuffed my mouth. Just when they were about to throw me overboard, Jesus Christ appeared before me with such clarity. I clung to him and begged him to save me. At that very moment, an airplane came down from the sky to rescue me from the moment of death.

Nobel lectures have featured many remarkable passages, probably none more remarkable than that.

# INTERLUDE

LEVERAGING THE NOBEL

Nobel laureates sometimes band together, or are banded together, outside Oslo. In fact, they don't appear in Oslo together at all, except for special occasions, such as the Nobel centennial in 2001. As I have mentioned, there is a Nobel Women's Initiative. It was founded in 2006. At the time, there had been twelve female peace laureates, and half of them came together to form this organization. They were the Northern Irishwomen, Williams and Maguire; Rigoberta Menchú; Jody Williams; Shirin Ebadi (the 2003 laureate, whom we will discuss shortly); and Wangari Maathai (2004). Collectively, the women say,

> It is the heartfelt mission of the Nobel Women's Initiative
> to work together as women Nobel Peace Prize Laureates to
> use the visibility and prestige of the Nobel prize to promote,
> spotlight, and amplify the work of women's rights activists,
> researchers, and organizations worldwide addressing the root
> causes of violence, in a way that strengthens and expands the

global movement to advance nonviolence, peace, justice and
equality.

How do these Nobelists go about doing what they do? "We accomplish this mission through three main strategies: convening,
shaping the conversation, and spotlighting and promoting."

Then we have World Summits of Peace Laureates, put together
by a Permanent Secretariat for such summits. The secretariat is
a "broadly based collaboration between the International Gorbachev Foundation and the City of Rome." (I am quoting from the
organization's own literature.) "The Permanent Secretariat, based
in Rome, is a non-profit association without political aims." Of
course, the Permanent Secretariat very much has political aims.
What the organization intends to say, probably, is that those aims
are nonpartisan. One purpose of the organization, aside from the
holding of the summits, is to support the work of laureates "as
mediators in various conflicts around the world."

The first summit was held in 1999, in the secretariat's home
city of Rome. It had a theme, and a grand one: "New Policies for
the 21st Century." Subsequent themes have included "Poverty
and Remission of the International Debt of Underdeveloped
Countries" and "Water Emergency and Other Emergencies of the
Planet." As at such conferences everywhere, there are panel sessions. In 2007, one of them was "The Next Generation: From the
Greenhouse Effect to Compatible Bioenergies," chaired by Betty
Williams. Often, Nobel peace laureates come to be seen as all-
purpose, global gurus.

At these summits, the summiteers give a special prize to "personalities selected within the culture and entertainment business
who have stood out in the defense of human rights and in the dif-
fusion of the principles of Peace and solidarity in the world." The
prize is called, simply, the Peace Summit Award, or sometimes

the Man of Peace award, or Woman of Peace award. Winners from the popular-music field include Yusuf Islam (formerly known as Cat Stevens), Peter Gabriel, and Annie Lennox. Winners from the acting field include Roberto Benigni and George Clooney. Even at gatherings of Nobel laureates, there is a felt need for a little glamour—glamour outside the laureate world.

In 2007, the laureates of these summits came up with a charter: a Charter for a World Without Violence. It has an epigram: "Violence is a preventable disease." And a couple of snippets will give a taste of the document as a whole. The signers say they recognize "the urgent need to develop an alternative approach to collective security based on a system in which no country, or group of countries, relies on nuclear weapons for its security." They further say, "All states, institutions and individuals must support efforts to address the inequalities in the distribution of economic resources, and resolve gross inequities which create a fertile ground for violence."

Who are the signers? Thirteen individual laureates, plus five institutional laureates (such as International Physicians for the Prevention of Nuclear War and the American Friends Service Committee). Some laureates are conspicuous by their absence. Was there something in the charter that Lord Trimble, for example, felt unable to put his name to? The signers are joined by "supporters of the charter," who are divided into categories. First come "institutions"—i.e., non-laureate institutions—including the "Basque Government." Then come "organizations," such as the International Federation of Humanist Parties and, out of Canada, Raging Grannies. Finally come "personalities." One of these is Clooney, and another is Dennis Kucinich, a famously left-wing member of the U.S. Congress.

To conclude this interlude, we will glance in on PeaceJam— "jam" as in "jamming," which is to say, making music in a joyous, freewheeling way. PeaceJam, based in Arvada, Colorado, is aimed at connecting young people with Nobel laureates. It was founded in 1996 by Dawn Engle and Ivan Suvanjieff—who were married five years later in Cape Town. Officiating at the wedding was Desmond Tutu, one of the couple's main jammers. Jody Williams was the maid, or matron, of honor.

PeaceJam, as an article in the *Chronicle of Philanthropy* summarized, "links 12 Nobel Peace Prize winners with children and teenagers to devise community-service projects and teach them about activism, using the lives and current work of the laureates as concrete examples." The organization says that its program "is built on a pyramid of three simple ideas: Education, Inspiration, and Action." The "action" may include the painting of a mural or the opening of a "fair trade" coffeehouse. The education, as indicated above, centers on a study of the inspirers, the laureates.

PeaceJam's founders want the peace laureates to have the celebrity appeal of actors and rockers—of the Clooneys and Gabriels. Suvanjieff has said, "I want the Nobel laureates to be icons," and "I want peace to be hip, sexy, and cool." He refers to the laureates as "the Nobels": Sounds almost like a rock group.

The biggest PeaceJam so far occurred in Denver in 2006, as the organization was celebrating its tenth year. Ten laureates were present, speaking to over 2,000 young people from over 30 countries. The event was indeed a kind of "jam," having the air of a rock concert—in part, it must be admitted, because there was rock music, live onstage. At one point, Tutu took the microphone and told the assembled youngsters, "You are real coooooool! . . . and you're going to change the world!" Then he raised his arms above his head and danced around, as the crowd cheered.

In the course of the jamming, the laureates issued a statement, a "Global Call to Action," listing ten "barriers to peace." These had to do with water, racism, poverty, a lack of "social justice," and so on. As the *Washington Times* reported, "Conspicuously absent from the list was global terrorism. Several laureates said that terrorism was an outgrowth of ignorance, prejudice and inequality, and that it cannot be eradicated until those underlying social issues are addressed." That sounds very much like "the Nobels": who may forget that plenty of people encounter injustice in life without ever thinking about killing innocents, much less doing so.

Denver was a grand opportunity for the Nobels to teach the kids the iniquity of the United States at war. For instance, Tutu said, "You are some of the most incredibly generous people. How about exporting your generosity instead of your bombs?" Even Tutu must know, in his more reflective moments, that few nations can match the United States in generosity to other nations. To take one interesting example: Before 9/11, the U.S. gave more humanitarian aid to Afghanistan, then ruled by the Taliban, than did any other nation in the world. You could say, too, that the toppling of the Taliban, and the toppling of Saddam Hussein, were "generous" acts. Certainly many Afghans and Iraqis do.

Adolfo Pérez Esquivel told the Denver kids, "Bush says he prays. But I think God covers up His ears when George Bush prays." Shirin Ebadi said, "When someone claims that he has a mission from God to bring war to Iraq and kill the people of Iraq, this is a kind of terrorism and a kind of fundamentalism." Where had Ebadi acquired this bizarre, and bizarrely false, view of Bush and his decisions and actions? Betty Williams, pleased with a girl in the crowd, said, "Eleven-year-old Ana has more intelligence than your president." This time, however, Williams did not express a desire to kill the president, at least according to reports of the jam. Back to Pérez Esquivel for a moment: As so many laureates have done, he contrasted the paltry 3,000 people who were killed on 9/11 with the children who are regularly dying of hunger. "I call that economic terrorism," he said.

The two Williamses, Betty and Jody, share not only a name, but also an ideology, and, to a degree, a style. According to the

Washington Times, Jody Williams "said the September 11 attacks were a response to U.S. aggression around the world, and that the White House should have tried to understand the reasons behind them before invading Iraq." The laureate was quoted as saying, "They do not like the aggressive policies of the country and they don't like that we're ignorant of that."

The impartation of such wisdom is one way in which laureates use, as the Nobel Women's Initiative puts it, "the visibility and prestige of the Nobel prize." There they were, in Denver, all lined up, seated on the stage like royals and oracles. They have a powerful platform, provided by those five committeemen in Oslo. What they do with it, of course, can be admirable and less so.

A PARADE OF LAUREATES, 2001 *to* 2008

In its centennial year, 2001, the Nobel Committee decided to award the United Nations—and, along with it, the incumbent U.N. secretary-general, Kofi Annan. Organization and man split the prize. The committee's heart has always lain with the U.N. and its forerunners. By now, you know this well. As soon as it could, the committee awarded the Inter-Parliamentary Union—in the person of its co-founder Frédéric Passy. (That was in the inaugural year of 1901, of course.) As soon as it could, the committee honored the League of Nations—in the person of Woodrow Wilson, its architect. As soon as it could, the committee honored the United Nations—in the person of Cordell Hull, for the drafting of its charter.

Recall the words of Johan Ludwig Mowinckel, as he presented the prize to Arthur Henderson in 1934: The League of Nations "is our only consolation, our best hope." Recall the words of Egil Aarvik, as he presented the prize to the U.N. Peacekeeping Forces in 1988: "Our determination has to be channeled into the United Nations. This is the best hope for the future of the world—indeed its only hope!" Over and over, the committee had honored U.N. agencies and U.N. people. Now, in 2001, it was honoring the U.N.

itself. In the words of the announcement, the committee wished "in its centenary year to proclaim that the only negotiable route to global peace and cooperation goes by way of the United Nations."

And the secretary-general? Annan, a son of Ghana, had worked for the U.N. virtually his entire career. It might be just as accurate to call him a son of the U.N. He was the first secretary-general to emerge from the U.N. bureaucracy. He began as a budget officer for the World Health Organization in 1962. He became the official in charge of peacekeeping operations in 1993—and was in charge during the Rwanda genocide and the Srebrenica massacre. In 1997, he was promoted to the top job. Jetting hither and yon, with a hand in everything, pronouncing on everything, he was called "president of the world," and "the secular pope." He was a total U.N. man, a totally devout son. He spoke U.N. language, thought U.N. thoughts. Asked about suicide bombers, he replied that "most people" would regard their attacks as "illegal."

A book on the peace prize has been written in close association with the Norwegian Nobel Institute. Called *The Nobel Peace Prize: One Hundred Years for Peace* (with an addendum for years beyond the hundredth), it is the product of three Norwegian historians. Each of them is responsible for different sections, different laureates, different years. The historian writing on the 2001 prize says that, after the attacks of September 11—which occurred a month before the prize announcement—Annan "reminded the world that all major religions and faiths embrace values such as tolerance and mutual understanding. These values must be defended against those who believe they have found the one and only truth." The historian continues,

> Given these points of view, it was not surprising that religious
> extremists disapproved of the Nobel Committee's prize-
> winners for 2001. Israeli parliamentarians sent a letter of

protest to the Committee, and although the Saudi Arabian terrorist Osama Bin Laden did not specifically mention the prize, three weeks after the announcement he described Kofi Annan as a "criminal" for having pressured the government of the world's most densely populated Muslim country, Indonesia, to pull out of East Timor.

With these exceptions, the announcement of Kofi Annan as winner of the Nobel Peace Prize was received with acclamation from every corner of the earth.

As you might suspect, that is not true. It is not true that Annan's victory was acclaimed by everyone except Israeli parliamentarians and Osama bin Laden—although that statement is a neat illustration of a mindset. It is a mindset you often see in Nobel folk. (Recall Tutu's grouping of bin Laden, Saddam Hussein, and George W. Bush.) A *Washington Times* report on the 2001 announcement said, "Conspicuous dissent came from survivors groups in Rwanda and Bosnia, two nations grievously failed by U.N. peacekeeping missions in the mid-1990s, when Mr. Annan was the head of that department." The chairman of a Rwandan group said, "He has a heavy responsibility in the Rwandan genocide. It is a pity, it is unfortunate—he should not have been awarded that Nobel prize." A spokesman for a Bosnian group said, "This award, to me, looks as if it has been commissioned by the U.N. itself to help them wash their hands of responsibility." And you remember the "Pillar of Shame," erected on the hills of Srebrenica on the 15th anniversary of the massacre: those shoes forming the letters "UN."

This is not to say that Annan or the U.N. should be judged guilty for failing to stop the genocide in Rwanda or the smaller slaughter in Srebrenica. That is another book, and, indeed, such books have been written. (Annan has expressed remorse over the carnage, bear in mind.) It is to say that Israeli parliamentarians and the world's number-one terrorist were not the only people unwelcoming of the 2001 Nobel.

Why were some Israelis unwelcoming? Here is one reason. In October 2000—a year before the Nobel announcement—three Israeli soldiers were kidnapped by Hezbollah terrorists. The terrorists had crossed the border into Israel wearing U.N. uniforms and driving vehicles with the U.N. insignia. U.N. peacekeepers— real peacekeepers—made a video that constituted evidence in this event. For months, U.N. officials denied to Israel that they had a video. Finally, in July 2001, they acknowledged possession. Annan's spokesman said, "It is clear that serious errors of judgment were made, in particular by those who failed to convey information to the Israelis which would have been helpful in an assessment of the condition of the three abducted soldiers," who were of course killed. "The secretary-general regrets this error." The Israelis wanted to see the video, and the U.N. showed it to them: but only heavily edited, with the faces of Hezbollah men obscured. The U.N. said it could do no other, as a neutral organization. The Israelis thought this neutrality was odd, between a member-state and a terrorist group.

There are many more details to this sordid, appalling story. The point here is that one might forgive Israelis for being less than thrilled with the 2001 Nobel Peace Prize. Some in that country, however, were quite pleased, including Shimon Peres, one of the 1994 laureates.

On Presentation Day, there was a parade of laureates, a literal such parade. Into Oslo's City Hall came Máiread Maguire, beaming; Tutu in a Nehru jacket; Rigoberta Menchú, in an array of purples; Jody Williams, looking almost royal, nodding to the cheering crowd. It was a Nobel extravaganza, honoring the prize as an institution, so to speak, and honoring the United Nations.

About the U.N., we all have our opinions. Some of us have trouble seeing it as a great force for peace, or even a minor force for peace. Earlier, I quoted an observation made by Solzhenitsyn: The U.N. is not so much the united nations, or peoples, as the united governments, or regimes. The body as a whole is only as good as its constituent parts. For many years, the Sudanese government has carried out a genocide in Darfur (and this government has sat on the U.N. human-rights panel). The U.N. has been able to do nothing about the genocide. One major reason is, Khartoum's biggest backers, China and Russia, are on the Security Council.

Then there is the corruption—the corruption that pervades the United Nations. An egregious instance was the "Oil for Food" program, in which Saddam Hussein enriched himself, consolidated his power, and bribed a host of officials: U.N. officials and other officials. Kofi Annan, as secretary-general, was implicated in that scandal.

The U.N. human-rights panel is a source of particular agony. What could be more exalted than a human-rights tribunal of the United Nations? This little body—a body within a body—was started by Eleanor Roosevelt, René Cassin, and their friends. And what became of it? On the human-rights panel have sat the worst human-rights abusers in existence. I repeat, Qaddafi's Libya once presided as president. Other members have included Mugabe's Zimbabwe, the Communists' China, the Baathists' Syria, the Sauds' Saudi Arabia, the Castros' Cuba, and, of course, genocidal Sudan.

No doubt, the U.N. is capable of good work, and it is a body with many agencies, some of which are better than others. But the U.N. can make a mockery of itself, and the grand claims for it. Consider the place of the mullahs' Iran. Even while it has violated every nuclear rule, and pledged to wipe a member-state, Israel, off the map, it has been "vice chairman" of the U.N. Disarmament Commission. (Later, North Korea, another flagrant nuclear violator, chaired the disarmament conference.) In 2010, Iran was elected to the U.N.'s women's-rights panel—formally, the U.N. Commission on the Status of Women. Iran is a regime that routinely uses rape as a means to oppress, punish, and silence women. Evin Prison in Tehran practically exists for this purpose. Iran is a regime that stones girls to death for the crime of having been gang-raped. And Iran graces the U.N. panel dedicated to women's rights. I think of hackneyed words: Orwellian, Kafkaesque. Really, is it any wonder that some have a hard time sharing the appreciation that Norwegians and others have for the United Nations, much less their reverence for it?

Those who revere the U.N., revere it for several reasons. The idea of a world community is attractive. The U.N. is as close to a world government as we have yet come. And the U.N. is a check on American power, as many see it. The Nobel Committee's award to the U.N. and Kofi Annan was widely interpreted as a warning to President George W. Bush, whose country had just been attacked so bloodily: *Don't you dare respond alone; don't you dare form your own coalition; the United Nations must have supremacy in any fight against Islamist terrorism.* In his presentation speech, Gunnar Berge said as much.

~

In 2002, he was very specific—specific in his comments to the press upon the announcement of the award. The award was going to Jimmy Carter, the former American president who had been a bridesmaid for many years. The committee, as you know, had wanted to honor him in 1978, along with Sadat and Begin; but he had not been nominated before February 1, and those were the rules. Out of office, he had been nominated repeatedly: He and his Carter Center were addressing themselves to a variety of world problems; his views were the kind most congenial to the Nobel Committee; he seemed a natural winner. As Secretary Lundestad said in an interview after the 2002 announcement, "He's been a hot candidate every year." So, what was different about this year? George W. Bush was president, and many were strongly opposed to what he was doing in the War on Terror: specifically, his warnings that Saddam Hussein could face war if he did not comply with U.N. resolutions.

And Chairman Berge said that the 2002 award "should be interpreted as a criticism of the line that the current administration has taken. It's a kick in the leg to all who follow the same line as the United States." "Kick in the leg" is a Norwegian way of saying "slap in the face," "poke in the eye." The chairman was making things unmistakably clear: The 2002 Nobel was not just an award to Carter; it was an award against Bush (and there would be others, arguably).

Other committee members were uncomfortable with Berge's remarks. One said that he agreed with them but wished they had been left unsaid. Others said that Berge should speak for himself, not the committee; the announcement was what spoke for the committee, not the chairman's embellishments to the press. And what did the announcement say? It, too, was clear enough, though not as blunt as Berge: "In a situation currently marked by threats of the use of power, Carter has stood by the principles that conflicts must as far as possible be resolved through mediation and international cooperation based on international law, respect for human rights, and economic development." When the committee spoke of "threats of the use of power," they apparently did not mean terrorists or terror states; they meant the United States and its allies.

The *New York Times* surely detested Bush as much as Gunnar Berge did. But even the *Times* was a little uncomfortable with the chairman's bluntness. The editors said, "The point would have been more eloquently made had the committee chairman . . . refrained from explicitly interpreting the prize as a criticism of America's current presidential administration. Jimmy Carter's achievements are big enough to stand on their own."

Bush, for his part, did not seem bothered. His first act that Friday—the Friday of the announcement—was to call Carter to congratulate him. That was at 7 A.M.; the laureate himself had been woken at 4, to be informed of his victory. The two presidents had a friendly conversation, in which Bush said that the award to Carter was "long overdue." (This according to Carter's own report.)

The 39th president, Carter, had for 20 years been a thorn in the side of his successors—a glorious thorn, thought his admirers. A *Time* magazine essayist, Lance Morrow, described him as "America's anti-president." He irked President Clinton with his interventions in Haiti and North Korea. He told the Haitian dictator Cédras, "I'm ashamed of what my country has done to your country." A few years before, in the administration of the first Bush, he had done something remarkable. The president was in the process of forming a coalition for the Gulf War: the effort to expel Saddam Hussein's army from Kuwait and prevent the invasion of other countries, especially Saudi Arabia. Carter wrote to members of the U.N. Security Council and other governments, asking them to resist Bush's efforts. The U.S. administration found out about it when the Canadian prime minister, Brian Mulroney, called the U.S. defense secretary, Dick Cheney, to ask what was going on.

While in office, Carter was billed as a "human-rights president." And he was indeed tough on American allies who abused human rights. But he could be perplexing when it came to leaders who were not American allies. For example, he hailed Tito as "a man who believes in human rights," a man who "has led his people and protected their freedom almost for the last 40 years." He said of Ceausescu and himself, "Our goals are the same: to have a just system of economics and politics . . . . We believe in enhancing human rights. We believe that we should enhance, as independent nations, the freedom of our own people." Carter's general outlook on human rights is in line with the general Nor-

wegian outlook. The Carter Center has said in a mission statement, "'Human rights' is a broad term, encompassing freedom
from oppression and freedom of speech to the right to food and
health." What I have stated before, I might state again: Those who
have liberty tend to have material well-being also. And those who
lack liberty tend to lack much else, too.

In 1997, Carter wrote an article for the *New York Times* headed
"It's Wrong to Demonize China." He said, "Westerners emphasize personal freedoms, while a stable government and a unified
nation are paramount to the Chinese. This means that policies
are shaped by fear of chaos from unrestrained dissidents or fear
of China's fragmentation by an independent Taiwan or Tibet."
The phrase "unrestrained dissidents" is interesting. "The result is
excessive punishment of outspoken dissidents and unwarranted
domination of Tibetans." The phrase "excessive punishment" is
interesting, too. Speaking about China and the United States,
Carter said that "ill-informed commentators in both countries
have cast the other side as a villain and have even forecast inevitable confrontation between the two nations." That is a Nobel-like
statement, implying a moral equivalence between a repressive
Communist state and a liberal republic. One more line, from this
piece: "Mutual criticisms are proper and necessary, but should
not be offered in an arrogant or self-righteous way, and each of us
should acknowledge improvements made by the other."

Even some Carter fans and defenders were unsettled by some
of the things he said in and about North Korea—specifically
about Kim Il-sung, the self-styled "Great Leader." Kim was one
of the most monstrous dictators in all history (and the son who
succeeded him, Kim Jong-il, the "Dear Leader," was no improvement). Carter said of Kim, "I find him to be vigorous, intelligent,
surprisingly well informed about the technical issues, and in
charge of the decisions about this country." You can expect them
to be in charge, absolute rulers of totalitarian states. Carter further

said, "I don't see that they," the North Koreans, "are an outlaw nation." He said that he had been able to "observe the North Koreans' psyche and their societal structure and the reverence with which they look upon their leader." Pyongyang, he enthused, was a "bustling city" where shoppers "pack the department stores." He was reminded of the "Wal-Mart in Americus, Georgia." In truth, North Korea was a starving and pulverized nation. A Potemkin village had apparently struck Carter as real.

It was in the Middle East that he made his greatest fame. And, in the Middle East, he was a fierce partisan—certainly after his presidency. I have mentioned an award he received from the PLO in 2009: It was the Palestine International Award for Excellence and Creativity. When he accepted this award, he made the statement, "I have been in love with the Palestinian people for many years." With the Israelis, he has been far less in love. His views of the Arab–Israeli conflict are little different from those of the PLO. The title of his aforementioned book, *Palestine: Peace Not Apartheid*, encapsulates the mindset.

Carter had a deep and close relationship with Yasser Arafat. After the Gulf War, Saudi Arabia was peeved at Arafat, because he had supported Saddam Hussein. Arafat asked Carter to fly to Riyadh to smooth things over with the princes: The PLO chief wanted Saudi funding restored to him. Carter obliged. The former president even acted as a public-relations adviser and speechwriter to Arafat. Douglas Brinkley reports on this in *The Unfinished Presidency: Jimmy Carter's Quest for Global Peace* (a very admiring book). Carter, writes Brinkley, "drafted on his home computer the strategy and wording for a generic speech Arafat was to deliver soon for Western ears . . . ." Carter told Arafat, "The audience is not the Security Council, but the world community. The objective of the speech should be to secure maximum sympathy and support of other world leaders . . . ." Here is the sort of line that Carter suggested Arafat use: "Our people, who face Israeli bullets, have no weapons: only a few stones remaining when our homes are destroyed by Israeli bulldozers."

In 1996, Carter monitored the elections in the Palestinian Authority, which Arafat had no trouble winning, naturally. Carter pronounced these elections "democratic," "open," "fair," and "well organized." They were unquestionably well organized. R. James Woolsey, a former CIA director (under Clinton), quipped that "Arafat was essentially 'elected' the same way Stalin was, but not nearly as democratically as Hitler, who at least had actual opponents." Arafat's opponent, an elderly woman, was a prop.

Carter's words and actions over these decades appalled a great many, making them wonder at his reputation for humanitarianism, idealism, and human rights. But some of his actions, along with his words, were unimpeachable, exciting universal applause: for instance, his fight against river blindness. In any case, in late 2002, Carter was ready for his Nobel moment. And Oslo was ready for him.

He arrived with an entourage of about 80 friends, relatives, and supporters. December 10 may have been cold, but the ceremony was very warm: an event of good feelings. Jessye Norman, the great American soprano, and Carter's fellow Georgian, sang. One of her offerings was "He shall feed his flock like a shepherd," from Handel's *Messiah*. Chairman Berge said, "Jimmy Carter should of course have been awarded the peace prize a long time ago." And "it became increasingly obvious that the bypassing of Carter had been one of the real sins of omission in peace-prize history. This year we can finally put all that behind us."

Then Berge showed that he fancied himself a sociologist of America—a second Gunnar Myrdal, perhaps? "Jimmy Carter only served one term as president of the United States. In a country where such importance is attached to outward success, that has cast a shadow." He also made a statement of undoubted truth, even perceptiveness: "Most of us become more conservative as we grow older. With Jimmy Carter the opposite seems to be the case. In this respect he is an atypical pensioner, growing with the years more and more radical and critical of society. His criticism of those in power in his own country and abroad has grown sharper."

At the end of his speech, Berge said, "Jimmy Carter will probably not go down in American history as the most effective president." That was somewhat nervy—even clumsy—to say in front of Carter himself. "But he is certainly the best ex-president the country ever had. And, most importantly for us: He is a most worthy recipient of the Nobel Peace Prize."

Carter, in his lecture, addressed the question of Iraq indirectly, but directly enough. You know that Ralph Bunche, giving his lecture in 1950, spoke of "preventive war"—what in later years we more commonly called "preemptive war." Carter quoted Bunche: "To suggest that war can prevent war is a base play on words and a despicable form of warmongering," etc. Then Carter said, "For powerful countries to adopt a principle of preventive war may well set an example that can have catastrophic consequences." Elsewhere in his speech, he paid a striking and humble tribute to Martin Luther King—calling him "the greatest leader that my native state has ever produced."

Later in the day, the laureate, his entourage in tow, returned to City Hall, for an interview with CNN. The interviewer, Jonathan Mann, talked about how Carter had missed out on a portion of the 1978 Nobel. And he said, "You've been very gracious about going 20 years without this prize." Actually, it had been closer to 25. "But in private, did you ever curse your fate, or stay up a night or two late, wondering how different life would have been, or just grousing about the injustice of it all?" Carter answered, "Yes. It was hard for me to understand, because I have to admit, I really wanted to earn the Nobel Peace Prize . . . ." Mann subsequently said to him, "Mr. President, you are arguably the most respected American on the planet today." The audience broke into applause.

Carter is no doubt the type of American, the type of person, greatly respected by the type of person who determines the Nobel Peace Prize. Gunnar Berge called him "certainly the best ex-president the country ever had." Others, as I have indicated, have a starkly different view—for example, Joshua Muravchik, the American scholar who wrote a long, damning essay on Carter called "Our Worst Ex-President." Carter is one of the several Nobel peace laureates who have warm relations with the Cuban dictator, Fidel Castro. Describing a visit with him in 2011, Carter said, "We welcomed each other as old friends."

Return, now, to that book about the peace prize, written by the three Norwegian historians, working closely with the Nobel Institute. The historian who writes about Carter ends, "Maybe he was too honest and too upright to lead a superpower." That is precisely the view of Carter's admirers, and quite possibly of Carter himself.

∾

In 2003, the Nobel Committee made a decision that surprised many people, not excluding the laureate. She was Shirin Ebadi, an Iranian lawyer who worked for human rights: particularly the rights of women and children. She did this in Iran, not in exile, and Iran had no shortage of those needing someone to defend them: someone like Ebadi. It would become no less true in following years, and perhaps even more true.

Ebadi was not completely unknown outside Iran in 2003. She was certainly known in Norway—for she had won the Rafto Prize two years before. Still, her Nobel came as a surprise. And here we have an example of someone who did not campaign for the award. Indeed, she had not even known she had been nominated. (She confirmed this to me in a 2011 interview.) The frontrunner for

2003 had been Pope John Paul II, nearing the end of his papacy, and his life—the pontiff died in 2005. At least his was the name most frequently mentioned in the press. Another name mentioned was Václav Havel's, as it so often was. In presenting the prize, the Nobel chairman noted that John Paul II had been "among the first to congratulate" Ebadi.

She was born in 1947, the daughter of an expert on commercial law, Mohammad Ali Ebadi. She herself became, not only a lawyer, but a judge—and a pioneering judge. Sketching out her life, she wrote, "I am the first woman in the history of Iranian justice to have served as a judge." Her judgeship came to an end in 1979, when the Khomeinist revolution triumphed. In the opinion of the new rulers, Islam forbade women to be judges; for one thing, they were too emotional.

In its announcement, the Nobel Committee made sure to say, "Ebadi is a conscious Muslim." She was also one who "sees no conflict between Islam and fundamental human rights." At the time of the announcement, Ebadi happened to be in Paris, attending a seminar. In short order, she held a press conference. It was widely noted—noted throughout the world—that she did not wear a headscarf. Her rule was, she wore such a scarf at home, in compliance with the law, but outside the country, no. Every woman should be free to make this choice herself, she believes. Conducting the press conference, she delighted many when she denounced what the United States and its allies were doing in Afghanistan and Iraq. She also warned against any similar activity in her own country: "The fight for human rights is conducted in Iran by the Iranian people, and we are against any foreign intervention in Iran." It was unclear exactly whom she meant by "we": Iranian democrats have long disagreed on the matter of foreign intervention, or help.

She had a memorable flight back home from Paris, with fellow passengers congratulating her excitedly. There were exceptions, however. She writes in her 2006 memoir, *Iran Awakening*, that "two very serious men" warned her that "I should be careful not to undermine the honor of those who had shed their blood for the people and Islam." When the plane landed in Tehran, she was accorded a hero's welcome. People swarmed the airport and its surroundings, hoping to catch a glimpse of the laureate. This was especially true of women, alive with new pride and hope.

Not all Iranian democrats and reformers were proud of Ebadi, or approving of her. She was known as a "soft" opponent, or critic, of the regime: a "moderate," even a "member of the loyal opposition." In the perception of many, she did not oppose the Khomeinist revolution wholesale; she worked "within the system." And this bothered many activists, particularly those in exile (who, of course, were much freer to speak). Some of them gathered in Oslo on Presentation Day, to protest the award to Ebadi. They accused her of being an apologist for "political Islam," which, in their opinion, was necessarily tyrannical. In our discussion eight years later, Ebadi made it clear that she favors a secular republic, not a religious one.

In 2003, the Nobel Committee had a new chairman, Ole Danbolt Mjøs, a professor of medicine, a university administrator, and a Christian Democrat. Addressing the laureate directly, and referring to the committee's announcement in October, he said, "I believe this announcement has already changed your life, Shirin Ebadi." He also said, ". . . now, of course, you have suddenly become quite a world celebrity!" The Nobel Peace Prize indeed tends to do that to recipients. Going to the heart of the 2003 Nobel, Mjøs said, "All people are entitled to fundamental rights, and at a time when Islam is being demonized in many quarters of the Western world, it was the Norwegian Nobel Committee's wish to underline how important and how valuable it is to foster dialogue between peoples and between civilizations." We might argue about who was more responsible for the "demonization" of Islam: Western reactionaries or Muslim extremists, committing atrocities in the name of Islam (and thereby blackening that name). In any case, Mjøs said it was "a great pleasure for the Norwegian Nobel Committee to award—for the first time in history—the Nobel Peace Prize to a woman from the Muslim world."

In her lecture, Ebadi—sans veil or headscarf, of course, and in an elegant suit—took her stand. She said, "I am an Iranian. A descendant of Cyrus the Great." And "I am a Muslim." Her rebuke of oppressive theocracy came as follows: "Some Muslims, under the pretext that democracy and human rights are not compatible with Islamic teachings and the traditional structure of Islamic societies, have justified despotic governments, and continue to do so." Yet the press reported that her harshest rebukes were for the United States and its allies. And the press was quite correct.

She said that, "in the past two years, some states have violated the universal principles and laws of human rights by using the events of 11 September and the war on international terrorism as a pretext." (Everyone had a pretext, she appeared to be saying in this speech: despotic and democratic countries alike.) She specifically denounced the American facility at Guantánamo Bay, housing terror detainees. And she brought Israel into the act—and much else into the act—in a remarkable sentence:

> Why is it that in the past 35 years, dozens of U.N. resolutions concerning the occupation of the Palestinian territories by the state of Israel have not been implemented promptly, yet, in the past twelve years, the state and people of Iraq, once on the recommendation of the Security Council and the second time in spite of U.N. Security Council opposition, were subjected to attack, military assault, economic sanctions, and, ultimately, military occupation?

In this sentence, Ebadi condemned both the Gulf War of 1991 and the Iraq War that had started earlier in 2003. And, like other laureates, before and later, she had nothing to say about what people had suffered under the Taliban or the regime of Saddam Hussein. (Neither, for that matter, did she have anything to say about Kuwaitis under Iraqi occupation—or about Palestinians under the PLO.)

After being honored in Norway, Ebadi led, in some ways, a typical Nobelist's life: She gave commencement addresses at American universities, joined campaigns against Israel, collected yet more awards. You have heard what she said about George W. Bush at the 2006 PeaceJam: "When someone claims that he has a mission from God to bring war to Iraq and kill the people of Iraq, this is a kind of terrorism and a kind of fundamentalism." She confirmed to me in 2011 that she said this, and meant it. So, again, this is typical laureate-ism.

But Ebadi was not really a typical laureate: because she worked in danger at home. She did not have the luxury of liberal-democratic surroundings. In 2008, the authorities raided her office and shut it down. The next year, they went into her safe-deposit box and took her Nobel medal and diploma, along with other items (her *Légion d'honneur*, for example). She eventually got her medal back, she told me—but her house, her money, and other assets, no. The regime took it all. Starting in 2009, a particularly bloody year for the Iranian people, Ebadi found it prudent to stay abroad, where she remains as I write. She has not done all that some Iranians would like. Some would like her to play a bolder, more aggressive, more heroic role. But that she has done a lot, sticking her neck out, no one can deny. She has been heroine enough.

What about the effect of her peace prize on Iran—or rather, on Iranians? "It has had an extremely positive effect," Ebadi said in 2011. "Up to that time"—the awarding of her prize in 2003—

"my NGO was the only one in Iran working on human rights. But now, fortunately, there are numerous people in the country who are focusing on human rights, and, in my view, that is one of the impacts of my winning the Nobel Peace Prize." Besides, the prize "demonstrated to the Iranian people that human rights are the best way of realizing democracy." (That is to say, I believe, that a persistent and thorough human-rights campaign is the best way.) And a final word: "The Nobel Peace Prize enabled me to raise my voice and make sure that more people around the globe hear me, which was naturally conducive to my work." This is an old and familiar theme: the peace prize as megaphone.

~

In 2004, the Nobel Committee performed one of its exercises in expanding the definition of peace—a definition that the committee through the years had already expanded a great deal. They gave the prize to a Kenyan woman who was dedicated to the planting of trees: She called her organization the "Green Belt Movement." And environmentalism and peace, the committee was thinking, went hand in hand.

Wangari Maathai, the 2004 laureate, had an extraordinary life, in common with so many other peace laureates, beginning with the first two in 1901. She was born in 1940. Twenty years later, she went to America, on a study program. This was the same program that had taken her fellow Kenyan Barack Obama to America the year before (1959). Of course, he would soon become Barack Obama, Sr., father to the future president—and Nobel laureate, we must say, in a book like this. Maathai and Obama were among hundreds of Africans who were taking advantage of American scholarships.

After arriving in New York (on the first flight of her life), Maathai took a Greyhound bus to Atchison, Kansas. There, she studied at Mount St. Scholastica College, graduating with a degree in biology in 1964. She then went to the University of Pittsburgh for a master's degree in the same subject. Her doctoral studies took place back home—at the University of Nairobi. She earned her Ph.D. in anatomy, and was said to have been the first woman in either East Africa or Central Africa to have a Ph.D.

With her degrees and drive, she did a variety of work, in academia and out. But the cause of her life came with the Green Belt Movement, which she started in 1977. Many years later, she wrote, "When I was growing up in Nyeri in central Kenya, there was no word for desert in my mother tongue, Kikuyu. Our land was fertile and forested." But much deforestation and desertification then set in. Maathai aimed to counter this by asking women to plant trees, trees in their millions. The women would receive a small sum for doing so. "We must pull together to save the land," Maathai told her countrymen, particularly her countrywomen. While she was leading this movement, she also became a force for democracy and women's rights. Her approach was "holistic," it was often said, by Maathai herself and her admirers around the world.

She did not have a favorable environment in which to work: the Kenya of Daniel arap Moi, who ruled dictatorially from 1978 until 2002. Maathai was hounded and persecuted many times, and she saw the inside of jail cells. When a democratic loosening came in 2002, she was elected to parliament. The following year, she was appointed the assistant minister for the environment. She was in that job when the Nobel Institute called.

Maathai had already won awards, and important awards: Seldom is the Nobel prize a person's first big honor; it is merely the biggest. In 1991, she won the Goldman Environmental Prize, sometimes called the "Green Nobel." Of course, what need is there for a Green Nobel, if the Nobel itself is going to be green? And Maathai, like so many of her predecessor laureates, had ties to Norway. An early supporter and partner of hers was the Norwegian

Forestry Society. Then, in 1997, she received an honorary doctorate from the Agricultural University of Norway. And in the summer of 2004, just months before her Nobel, she won the Sophie Prize, an environmental award set up by Jostein Gaarder, the Norwegian writer who scored a huge success with his philosophical novel *Sophie's World.*

In its announcement, the Nobel Committee said it was awarding Maathai for "her contribution to sustainable development, democracy, and peace." Borrowing a slogan—indeed, a verse—from a popular bumper sticker, the committee said, "She thinks globally and acts locally." The committee also took care to note that Maathai was "the first woman from Africa to be honored with the Nobel Peace Prize." It is also true that she was the first black woman to win.

Environmentalists were obviously delighted with the award, glad to have the Norwegian Nobel Committee so firmly in their camp. Norway's leading newspaper, *Aftenposten,* asked, "What does tree-planting have to do with peace?" A lot, the paper answered. And "there is something untraditional and exciting about this award." Others—even Nobel devotees—thought that the 2004 award went too far afield, stretching the definition of peace excessively. This view was neatly put by Espen Barth Eide, a Laborite who had been Norway's deputy foreign minister. He said that it falls on the Nobel Committee to provide a definition of peace for any given "epoch." And "if they widen it too much, they risk undermining the core function of the peace prize. You end up saying everything that is good is peace."

Maathai, who died in 2011, was an attractive, dynamic, instantly likable woman. A fellow environmentalist, an American, once said, "She has the widest and brightest smile of any human being I know." But there was a fly in the ointment of Maathai's Nobel. She had been quoted as saying that the AIDS virus was concocted in the West for the purpose of decimating black people.

(This charge, about the West and AIDS, is as widespread as it is deranged and damaging.) The virus had been cooked up by "evil-minded scientists," Maathai had been quoted as saying, and these scientists were intent on "biological warfare" against blacks.

Following the announcement of her Nobel, she gave an interview to *Time* magazine, as she sat under a tree outside her Nairobi offices. She said, "I have no idea who created AIDS and whether it is a biological agent or not. But I do know things like that don't come from the moon. I have always thought that it is important to tell people the truth, but I guess there is some truth that must not be too exposed." Asked to elaborate, she said, "I'm referring to AIDS. I am sure people know where it came from. And I'm quite sure it did not come from the monkeys. Why can't we be encouraged to ask ourselves these questions?"

The Nobel Committee had a problem: Had they given their prize to a kook? Just before Presentation Day, the problem was largely solved. The committee issued a statement from Maathai, which read, "I neither say nor believe that the virus was developed by white people or white powers in order to destroy the African people. Such views are wicked and destructive." The ceremony could proceed with less of a shadow.

It was a festive day, the laureate gaily dressed in an African outfit, Kenyan dancers performing for the crowd. Chairman Mjøs defended the committee's decision, as presenters are often called on to do. He proffered the traditional line that "there are many different paths to peace"—and "environmental protection has become yet another path to peace." When the environment degrades, he explained, there is greater competition for resources, which can lead to hostilities, including war. Mjøs also said that the 2004 award should be seen as a "special tribute" to African women in general.

For many years, the concept of "social justice" had been in vogue; increasingly, people were talking about "environmental justice." And the Nobel Committee tends to stay in vogue. At the 2010 World Social Forum—a counter-gathering to the pro-market Davos forum—a Brazilian intellectual named Candido Grzybowsky said, "Capitalism's unsustainability has never been so obvious. We need to create a system based on social and environmental justice." In just a few words, that expresses the spirit prevalent in recent years. Did Wangari Maathai deserve the Nobel Peace Prize for her "environmental" and related "justice"? In my view, she did as much for peace—peace broadly defined—as Alva Myrdal, Joseph Rotblat, and many other laureates. Probably more than they.

∾

In 2005, the committee gave a U.N. award. And an anti-nuclear award. Was it also a third kind of award—another "kick in the leg" to President Bush and the United States? Chairman Mjøs, announcing the award, denied it. He said, "This is not a kick in the leg to any country." There were many who were skeptical of that denial. The award went to the International Atomic Energy Agency and its director general, Mohamed ElBaradei. Agency and man had given the United States fits for years, opposing American policy, and seeking to thwart it, at nearly every turn. This was particularly true where Iraq and Iran were concerned. ElBaradei was a pretty much open foe of George W. Bush. You could forgive those who thought that the 2005 Nobel was maybe a kick in the leg.

The IAEA is a U.N. agency, resident in Vienna, established in 1956. Its inspiration was President Eisenhower's "Atoms for Peace" speech, delivered before the U.N. in 1953. Eisenhower wanted nuclear technology—this example of "the miraculous inventiveness of man"—to be tipped toward peaceful uses, not destructive ones. The IAEA is often called the U.N.'s "nuclear watchdog"; given its laxity on Iraq, Iran, and some other states, a few have derided it as a nuclear "watch-puppy." ElBaradei, like Kofi Annan, was a classic U.N. man. An Egyptian born in 1942, he had worked for the U.N. since 1980, and for the IAEA since 1984. He became director general in 1997 and stayed in that post three terms—till 2009.

Until recent times, the IAEA was essentially a technical agency, known mainly to specialists. It was far from a player on the world stage. Under ElBaradei, it became a political body: and it played—even strutted—upon the stage. ElBaradei was not especially embarrassed about this. He said, "You can't separate security from politics. We cannot be unaware of the political context in which we operate and the political ramifications of our work." He talked a lot about Iraq and Iran, of course. But he also talked about, for example, the Israelis and the Gaza Strip. If Annan was the "president of the world," ElBaradei was a vice president.

The IAEA's record makes an interesting story. On the eve of the Gulf War in 1991, the agency assured one and all that Iraq was in full compliance with the Nuclear Nonproliferation Treaty. (Here is another interesting story, or sub-story: Saddam Hussein's regime sat on the IAEA's board of governors from 1980 to 1991.) After the war, the director general of the time, Hans Blix, admitted, "It's correct to say that the IAEA was fooled by the Iraqis." On the eve of the Iraq War of 2003, the IAEA again said that Iraq was clean: Its weapons of mass destruction were a thing of the past. The U.S. was not prepared to accept the agency's word for it—and, with its allies, went into Iraq. They found no WMD. They certainly found no such weapons ready to use (and Saddam Hussein, of course, had used them before). ElBaradei and the IAEA felt sweet vindication.

How about Iran? Its nuclear ambitions loomed large, as they loom still. For almost 20 years, Iran fooled the IAEA. The world learned of the mullahs' nuclear program in 2002: not from the nuclear watchdog, but from an Iranian dissident group, which blew the whistle. You might have thought this would have instilled humility. It was not noticeable in ElBaradei. I recall seeing him with the Iranian foreign minister, Kamal Kharrazi, in January 2005. They were together on a panel at the annual meeting of the World Economic Forum in Davos. They seemed chummy, and they also seemed smug: They spoke as though Washington's concerns about Iranian nukes were silly. After all, Bush and his team had been wrong about Iraq.

For several years, ElBaradei had been mentioned as a possible Nobel laureate, and he was anxiously watching his television when the committee announced the 2005 award. Actually, he was grimly watching his television. He had not received a phone call from Oslo, so figured he had been passed over—"again," as he later put it to the press. "I was about to start grumbling about the choice and telling my wife that there are more important things in life than prizes." But then he heard his name. And "it was an absolutely delightful surprise. I was just hugging my wife in front of the television." The next day, a *New York Times* reporter expressed the general reaction: "The award was a vindication of a man and an agency long at odds with President Bush and his administration over how to confront Iraq and Iran."

Almost everyone likes the idea of the International Atomic Energy Agency. Its prescribed mission is unimpeachable. But we might ask the rude question, What has it done? What has it achieved? Galling to many people after the Nobel announcement was ElBaradei's claim, and that of others, that the IAEA was responsible for the ending of Qaddafi's WMD program. The reality was much different. And that reality unfolded something like this:

In March 2003, as the U.S.-led coalition was going into Iraq, Qaddafi started some serious negotiation with the U.S. and Britain over his WMD. The war was concentrating his mind. Then, in May, President Bush established the Proliferation Security Initiative: designed to do what the IAEA, in ideal circumstances, might have done. Under the PSI, about a dozen nations cooperated, free of the U.N. framework. In October 2003, two of those nations, Italy and Germany, stopped a ship en route to Libya: It was carrying nuclear goodies from the A. Q. Khan network. Qaddafi was a customer of both Khan, the renegade Pakistani scientist, and North Korea. The seizure of his shipment further concentrated his mind. And at the end of 2003—in December—his mind was really concentrated: The U.S. dragged Saddam Hussein out of his "spider hole," to be tried and, eventually, executed. Qaddafi gave up his WMD. Those materials now rest at the Oak Ridge National Laboratory in Tennessee.

The PSI had dealt a serious blow to nuclear proliferation; it took WMD out of the hands of a brutal and adventurous dictator. The U.S. military did its part, too, by its actions in Iraq. Would the PSI ever receive a Nobel Peace Prize? Would the president who established it? Would the American serviceman? Those questions are just rhetorical, as you know.

When Israel attacked and destroyed Syria's nuclear facility in September 2007—a facility supplied and staffed by North Korea—ElBaradei condemned Israel in his usual harsh terms, while casting doubt on the whole idea of Syrian malfeasance. It was left to his successor as director general, Yukiya Amano, to confirm that Israel had, indeed, destroyed a nuclear reactor. Under Amano, the IAEA resumed its original role of essentially neutral agency, providing technical judgments; it was no longer the political actor that ElBaradei had made it, with considerable flamboyance. ElBaradei was in the headlines for putting in a bid to lead his native Egypt, during the popular uprising that drove Hosni Mubarak, Sadat's successor, from power.

The country that occupied center stage during ElBaradei's IAEA tenure was, of course, Iran. And he had a tendency to defend, excuse, and protect this regime. In January 2009, an interviewer confronted him with Ahmadinejad's declaration that Israel must be "wiped off the map." (To be most precise, Ahmadinejad was quoting Khomeini, with approbation, needless to say.) ElBaradei, typically, was pooh-poohing: "There have been a lot of offensive statements, frankly, on the part of Iran, although from what I understand, Iran wants a one-state solution—not, as reported in the media, that Israel should be wiped off the map." By "one-state solution," he meant the proposal that all Palestinians should live together with Israelis (meaning, naturally, that there would be no Jewish state).

ElBaradei has always been strongly opposed to sanctions on Iran, regarding them as counterproductive. As director general, he openly lamented that, if he reported certain facts to the U.N. Security Council, those facts would trigger sanctions. Some people, including officials in the Bush administration, had trouble trusting him to report the facts, given his inclination to be a political player, and given his political and policy views.

Shortly before his third and final term expired, it was reported that the IAEA was sitting on a damning report about Iran: about the mullahs and their nuclear maneuverings. The U.S. and others wanted this report circulated; ElBaradei did not. The Associated Press said, ". . . although even some of his senior aides favor publication, ElBaradei has balked" (according to those same senior aides). The AP continued, "The agency chief has been keen to avoid moves that could harden already massive Iranian intransigence . . . ." He was also wary of "pushing the U.S. or Israel closer to a possible military strike on Tehran's nuclear facilities." Two years before, ElBaradei had made perfectly clear where he stood. He told the BBC, "I wake every morning and see 100 Iraqis, innocent civilians, are dying. I have no brief other than to make sure we don't go into another war or that we go crazy into killing each other. You do not want to give additional argument to new crazies who say, 'Let's go and bomb Iran.'" Traditionally, the IAEA's "brief" has been to ascertain and report facts, leaving political and military decisions to others: to member-states. But ElBaradei imagined and seized a much larger role for himself.

Over and over, he downplayed any danger coming from Iran. In July 2009, he said, "In many ways, I think the threat has been hyped." Two months later, it was discovered that Iran had a secret uranium-enrichment plant near Qom. ElBaradei pronounced this facility "nothing to be worried about." Strangely enough, people worried nevertheless. And we will have one more quotation from ElBaradei—this one from July 2010: "Of course I am very much in favor of a Middle East free of nuclear weapons, without Iranian, but also without Israeli, atomic weapons." (One of ElBaradei's persistent claims was that the Israeli nuclear deterrent was no more defensible morally than, say, the acquisition of nukes by Tehran.) "But in general, the danger of a nuclear-armed Iran is overestimated—some even play it up intentionally."

Perhaps ElBaradei is right that a nuclear threat from Iran has been "hyped," "overestimated," "played up." Perhaps his pooh-poohing will come to look wise. If it does not, however, the 2005 Nobel prize will look very unwise, to say the least.

～

Muhammad Yunus had a great many admirers and boosters, including Bill Clinton. In 2002, speaking at Berkeley, the former president called Yunus "a man who long ago should have won the Nobel prize." He added, "I'll keep saying that until they finally give it to him." They gave it to him in 2006. And, making his presentation speech, Mjøs said, "Now Clinton will no longer need to remind us."

Yunus was an economist who had an inspired and inspiring idea: "microcredit," or "microloans." As the name implies, these were very small loans, and they were given to very poor people, as a way of getting them on their feet, and established in an enterprise.

Yunus was called the "Banker to the Poor." Indeed, that was the title of his 2003 autobiography—whose cover showed a ladder, from the bottom up.

He was born in 1940, in the part of India that, about three decades later, became Bangladesh. When he was in his mid-twenties, he won a Fulbright scholarship, going to Vanderbilt University for his Ph.D. (Vanderbilt is in Nashville, Tennessee, about 135 miles west of Oak Ridge and Qaddafi's WMD program.) Surveying the Nobel laureates, we have a glimpse of the place of American education in the progress of the world: José Ramos-Horta studied at Antioch and Columbia; Kofi Annan studied at Macalester and MIT; Maathai studied in Kansas and Pittsburgh; ElBaradei took his Ph.D. at New York University.

Yunus taught for a while at Middle Tennessee State University, and later back home in Bangladesh. In 1974, the country was hit with a famine, and the economist was hit with something of a crisis of conscience. As he put it in his Nobel lecture,

> I found it difficult to teach elegant theories of economics in the university classroom, in the backdrop of a terrible famine . . . . Suddenly, I felt the emptiness of those theories in the face of crushing hunger and poverty. I wanted to do something immediate to help people around me, even if it was just one human being, to get through another day with a little more ease. That brought me face to face with poor people's struggle to find the tiniest amounts of money to support their efforts to eke out a living.

He started by lending $27 out of his own pocket to 42 villagers. In 1983, he founded the Grameen Bank, or Village Bank. Almost all of the borrowers were women, engaged in such enterprises as basket-weaving. And, almost invariably, they paid back. They were afforded the joy of financial self-sufficiency (and the variety of good that comes with it). Yunus has said, "Lend the poor money in amounts which suit them, teach them a few sound financial principles, and they manage on their own." His method—the Grameen model—has been copied around the world.

Yunus has received a great many awards and honors—awards and honors on the Tutu level, if not beyond. He received them before the Nobel and after. In 1994, he won Norman Borlaug's World Food Prize. The Nobel that came to him twelve years later was shared with his bank, the Grameen Bank. The committee's order was Yunus, then the bank, his child. In their announcement, the committee members said they were giving the prize to Yunus and Grameen "for their efforts to create economic and social development from below. Lasting peace cannot be achieved unless large population groups find ways in which to break out of poverty. Microcredit is one such means. Development from below also serves to advance democracy and human rights."

Muhammad Yunus was a performer of good deeds, unquestionably. But should he have won the peace prize—any peace prize? Was an award in economics more appropriate? There was a debate, unsurprisingly. *The Economist* magazine said, "The purpose of the prize has become muddled." The committee might be better off, said the magazine, if it withheld the prize, until a clearly meritorious candidate emerged: the ender of a war, to give a very high example. Others rejoiced at this broadmindedness concerning peace. And a libertarian writer, the American John Tierney, made a canny, provocative point. He wrote,

> I don't want to begrudge the Nobel Peace Prize won last week
> by the Grameen Bank and its founder, Muhammad Yunus.
> They deserve it. The Grameen Bank has done more than
> the World Bank to help the poor, and Yunus has done more
> than Jimmy Carter or Bono [the activist rock star] or any
> philanthropist.

> But has he done more good than someone who never got
> the prize: Sam Walton? Has any organization in the world
> lifted more people out of poverty than Wal-Mart?

Workers throughout the world made goods that were sold to this giant retailer, based in Arkansas. And Wal-Mart was a godsend to shoppers with little to spend. But Wal-Mart would be no likelier to win the Nobel Peace Prize than would the Proliferation Security Initiative, George W. Bush, or the American serviceman. The company is anathema to establishment Norway. In 2006— the very year of the Yunus-Grameen prize—the Norwegian state divested its pension fund from Wal-Mart. It complained that the company was exploiting the Third World poor and preventing unionization. Once, an official of the Progress party—Norway's classical-liberal party—showed me the paraphernalia in his office. They included a little Wal-Mart truck. He said that this was the most politically incorrect item imaginable.

There was not much debate in Bangladesh. Instead, there was sheer jubilation over the 2006 prize. People celebrated for three days. Some said this was the biggest national celebration since independence from Pakistan in 1971. The presentation ceremony in Oslo was a celebratory affair too: complete with Bangladeshi dancers. And the audience was adorned with actresses: Sharon Stone and Anjelica Huston; also Norway's own Liv Ullmann.

In his presentation speech, Mjøs was back on one of his themes from 2003: the "demonization of Islam" by the West. He said,

> Since the 11th of September 2001, we have seen a widespread
> tendency to demonize Islam. It is an important task for the
> Nobel Committee to try to narrow the gap between the West
> and Islam. The peace prize to Yunus and Grameen Bank
> is also support for the Muslim country Bangladesh and for

the Muslim environments in the world that are working for dialogue and collaboration. All too often we speak one-sidedly about how much the Muslim part of the world has to learn from the West. Where microcredit is concerned, the opposite is true: The West has learned from Yunus, from Bangladesh, and from the Muslim part of the world.

Not many would have thought that Yunus and microlending had anything whatever to do with Islam, or religion. Yunus did not mention Islam or religion in his lecture. And Amartya Sen had made an interesting comment to the *New York Times*, after the announcement of the 2006 award. (Sen, like Yunus, is a Bengali, an economist, and a Nobelist—the winner of the 1998 memorial prize in economics.) He said that the Yunus approach could compete with fundamentalist Islam: "It's a very secular movement, very egalitarian, market-friendly and socially radical."

As usual, there was music at the Nobel ceremony, including excerpts from Mozart's *Exsultate, jubilate,* sung by Renée Fleming, the great and starry American soprano. At the Nobel concert the next day, another American soprano appeared, this one much less known, and at the beginning of her career. She was Monica Yunus, one of the laureate's daughters. She sang the aria from Puccini's *Gianni Schicchi,* "O mio babbino caro"—"Oh, daddy dearest."

∽

In this period we are discussing—the 2000s—the global elites had no greater concern than global warming: a concern that topped terrorism, war, and nuclear proliferation. Global warming was a roaring passion. At the Davos meeting in 2006, Bill Clinton was asked to name his three foremost concerns for the world. The first words out of his mouth were "climate change." (He then cited inequality among peoples and cultural divides.) At the 2007 prize ceremony, Chairman Mjøs said, ". . . this year's award decision was not especially difficult. For it is rare for the world to be so concerned with a particular phenomenon or for that phenomenon to have such a decisive impact on our existence on earth. This year, a great deal is hinging on global warming."

To whom had the committee given the award? To the Intergovernmental Panel on Climate Change and Al Gore (in that order). The IPCC was an arm of the United Nations. Like the IAEA, it was supposed to be a technical agency, giving key information to member-states. Even more than the IAEA, it was a political body, even a crusading one, telling the member-states—particularly the democratic and prosperous ones—what they must do.

And Al Gore? He was probably the world's leading environmentalist politician. In his presentation speech, Mjøs said he was, "in the opinion of the Norwegian Nobel Committee, the single individual who has done most to prepare the ground for the political action that is needed to counteract climate change." Born in 1948, Gore grew up in Washington, D.C., because his father, Albert Gore, Sr., was a senator. But the Gores' hometown was Carthage, Tennessee (about 50 miles east of Nashville). This was Cordell Hull country too, as Gore noted in his Nobel lecture. Gore became a U.S. representative, then a senator, then vice president—for the eight years of Clinton. In 2000, he was the Democratic nominee for president, and he won the popular vote over George W. Bush—but lost in the Electoral College. This was probably the most disputed and bitterest election in American history.

Well before it became the great global concern—the leading concern of global elites—Gore was a red-hot on the environment. In a 1989 article for the *New York Times*, he warned of "an environmental holocaust without precedent." He liked to use the language of the Holocaust. That article was headed "An Ecological Kristallnacht. Listen." Gore wrote, "Once again, world leaders waffle, hoping the danger will dissipate. Yet today the evidence is as clear as the sounds of glass shattering in Berlin."

About global warming, Gore and his allies had no time for doubts, and they had no time for debate. For them, the case was closed. "The science" had determined that man had caused alarming, perilous global warming, and that was that. Governments and societies needed to change their ways drastically in order to counter this threat. Gore likened his critics—those who questioned his theories and prescriptions—to "people who believe that the earth is flat," and to people who "believe the moon landing was staged on a movie lot in Arizona." The chairman of the IPCC, Rajendra Pachauri, was of the same disposition. He said of the skeptics, "They are people who deny the link between smoking and cancer. They are people who say that asbestos is as good as talcum powder. I hope that they apply it to their faces every day."

Skeptics or critics were called "deniers," in a parallel to "Holocaust deniers." Gore is one who regularly uses this term. A reporter for America's most important television news program, *60 Minutes*, was asked why he did not include skeptics or dissenters in his global-warming reports. The reporter, Scott Pelley, said, "If I do an interview with Elie Wiesel, am I required as a journalist to find a Holocaust denier?"

In 2004, Pachauri attacked Bjørn Lomborg, a Danish scientist who, while he accepted global warming, argued against radical and possibly bankrupting measures to counteract it. The IPCC chairman thought it appropriate to compare Lomborg to Hitler. He said to *Jyllands-Posten*, the Danish newspaper, "What's the difference between Lomborg's way and Hitler's way of viewing humanity?" He concluded, "If you follow Lomborg's way of thinking, it might be right, what Hitler did."

The global-warming crusade reached its apogee in 2007, the year of the global-warming Nobel. In January, the Davos meeting was almost entirely taken up with climate talk. There were 17 separate sessions on the subject, bearing such titles as "The Security Implications of Climate Change," "The Economics of Climate Change," and "The Legal Landscape Around Climate Change." After hours, there was a Climate Change Nightcap, hosted by, among others, Shimon Peres and Claudia Schiffer, a German supermodel. Traditionally, Prince Charles had taken a skiing vacation in neighboring Klosters—but he canceled it in 2007, explaining that he wanted to reduce his "carbon footprint." Charles has called global warming "the biggest threat to mankind."

Days after the Davos meeting, the lights went out all over Europe—not as Sir Edward Grey meant, but in environmental protest: Frenchmen made the Eiffel Tower go dark, Italians made the Colosseum go dark, and Greeks made their parliament go dark. They were making some statement about climate change. *The Journal of Affective Disorders* published an article entitled "Global warming possibly linked to an enhanced risk of suicide: Data from Italy, 1974–2003."

This was the climate, politically, psychologically, and emotionally. At the Davos meeting, a Bush-administration official was accosted about global warming wherever she went. "Why is the United States letting the rest of the planet burn?" people would say to her. (The U.S. was judged the main offender.) The official was openly and unapologetically skeptical of the crusaders' claims. One lady said to her, "But haven't you seen Al Gore's movie?" The official said no. The lady replied, not with malice, but with sweet sympathy, as though talking to an ignorant child, "Oh, you must learn, dear. I'll send the movie to you."

That movie was called *An Inconvenient Truth*, and it was a documentary version of Gore's standard talk on global warming. In February 2007—a few weeks after the Davos meeting—it won the Academy Award, for Best Documentary Feature. Seven and a half months later, the Nobel Committee delivered another big award. Gore was in San Francisco. In anticipation of victory, he was watching the Nobel announcement live on television at 2 A.M. So, Gore won the Oscar and the Nobel Peace Prize in the same year. Think of that: the world's two most glamorous awards (you could argue) in the very same year. That will probably happen to no one else ever.

In Oslo, the press had a question for Mjøs—a by-now standard question: Was this another kick in the leg? It was not an unreasonable question. Bush was anathematized by environmentalists, as he was by the Left in general. Once more, the chairman denied that this was a kick. And once more, some people were disbelieving. The *Washington Post* editorialized, ". . . these denials are hard to take seriously from a group that has handed the peace prize to adversaries of President Bush." The three Norwegian historians who collaborated in *The Nobel Peace Prize* write jointly about the 2007 award. They say, "The Committee hoped the prestige that comes with the Peace Prize would give Gore an even greater standing in the media and strengthen the Democrats' fight for a new, eco-friendly USA." That sounds quite right.

And, as people called the 2005 award a "vindication" for Mohamed ElBaradei, people called the 2007 award a "vindication" for Gore. The *Washington Post* editorial was titled "Gore v. Bush: The Nobel Peace Prize committee hands a victory to Al Gore." In their first sentence, the editors said that Gore's prize meant "vindication." A *New York Times* headline read, "With Prize, Gore Is Vindicated Without Having to Add President to Résumé."

On December 10, Pachauri, the IPCC chairman, gave the lecture for his agency. An Indian, he wore a sleek, smart black kurta. Appropriately for one of the world's foremost greens, he adorned that garment with a striking green handkerchief. His lecture was on the perishing of peoples from environmental degradation. Then Gore was up. His own speech was rather beautifully written. And, apparently, it was indeed his own. Before he gave it, he told an interviewer that he had written it himself, "with the help of Mr. Google."

In this speech, he reflected on his life since his presidential defeat. The defeat, he said, was an "unwelcome verdict" that had "also brought a precious if painful gift: an opportunity to search for fresh new ways to serve my purpose." As he often did, he mixed environmentalism and religion, saying, "The distinguished scientists with whom it is the greatest honor of my life to share this award have laid before us a choice between two different futures—a choice that to my ears echoes the words of an ancient prophet: 'Life or death, blessings or curses. Therefore, choose life, that both thou and thy seed may live.'" And over and over, he conveyed urgency, a sense of crisis. "We, the human species, are confronting a planetary emergency—a threat to the survival of our civilization . . . ." We "have begun to wage war on the earth itself. Now, we and the earth's climate are locked in a relationship familiar to war planners: 'mutually assured destruction.'" "Once again, it is the eleventh hour." And so on.

In the next couple of years, global-warming concerns continued to grip and, in some cases, addle the world. A U.S. senator, Debbie Stabenow, talked of a new volatility in the weather. "You can see it in the storms that we have. I feel it in flying." In December 2009, the U.N. held a big climate conference in Copenhagen. Secretary-General Ban Ki-moon, speaking in August of that year, said, "We have just four months. Four months to secure the future of our planet." That was the tone, unrelentingly apocalyptic.

It was a good thing that the IPCC and Al Gore won the Nobel Peace Prize when they did—because, at the end of 2009, around the time of the Copenhagen conference, the roof fell in on them. There was a global scandal dubbed "Climategate," centering on research scientists who fed information to the IPCC. These men were shown to be conniving, dissembling, stonewalling, bullying, deceiving—very far from scientists, as we like to think of them. They were more like ideological crusaders and political operatives. The IPCC's report for 2007, issued shortly before the glory of the Nobel, was shown to be full of holes. In a particular rebuke to Pachauri, the Indian government decided to create its own climate panel. The environment minister, Jairam Ramesh, said, "There is a fine line between climate science and climate evangelism. I am for climate science."

Some of the IPCC-associated scientists were chastened and humbled; others were defensive, defiant, and mad. Pachauri belonged to the latter camp, and Gore was of a similar temper. A question: Would the Nobel Committee have honored the IPCC and Gore after 2009? It is highly unlikely. And future generations will likely render a verdict on the 2007 Nobel. Was it a masterstroke, far-seeing and constructive? Or was it an embarrassment, symbolizing a period of mass hysteria? I said in my introduction that I suspected this Nobel would come to be seen as "silly." I also said, "I may be wrong."

∿

In this decade of the 2000s, the committee had given the award to a number of celebrities: Annan, Carter, ElBaradei, Gore. Yunus was a near-celebrity—he became a full-fledged one after the Nobel. In 2008, the committee took a break from celebrities, and also from "expansive" prizes—ones that stretch (and stretch) the definition of peace. They gave a traditional prize, one that was almost a throwback to the first years of the Nobel: when "mediation" and "arbitration" were bywords of the peace movement. When there was, in fact, a peace movement. Moreover, the committee gave its 2008 prize to a fellow Northerner—not quite a Scandinavian (though that depends on how you define "Scandinavian"), but a Northerner all the same. He was Martti Ahtisaari, a longtime peace negotiator and internationalist from Finland.

He was born in 1937 in Viipuri, a town that soon became a Soviet property called Vyborg. In his Nobel lecture, Ahtisaari explained what happened, also describing the impact of these events on his life:

> I . . . was a child affected by a war. I was only two years old when, as a result of an agreement on spheres of interest between Hitler's Germany and Stalin's Soviet Union, war broke out, forcing my family to leave soon thereafter . . . . Like several hundred thousand fellow Karelians, we became refugees in our own country as great-power politics caused the borders of Finland to be redrawn and left my hometown as part of the Soviet Union. This childhood experience contributed to my commitment to working on the resolution of conflicts.

You may recall that Alexandra Kollontay came as close as any Soviet Communist, probably, to winning the Nobel Peace Prize. (Pre-Gorbachev, that is.) A campaign was launched for this diplomat and glamour girl in 1946. The argument was that she should be honored for her role in the negotiations that led to the conclusion of Soviet–Finnish hostilities. You may also know that we have a tribute to Karelia in music—from Jean Sibelius, the Finnish national composer, who in 1893 wrote the music that would be fashioned into the beloved *Karelia Suite*. The music was commissioned by the Viipuri Students Association, which was planning a fundraiser.

Ahtisaari was not only a Northerner, he had Norwegian roots: via a great-grandfather, who came from Tistedalen, in the southeastern county of Østfold. Ole Danbolt Mjøs, in his presentation speech, had some fun:

> I see that Ahtisaari . . . wondered in an interview whether it might be held against him that he was allegedly "12.5 percent Norwegian." It may well be that we have treated Norwegian

candidates especially restrictively in recent decades. In 1921 and 1922, however, the Norwegian Nobel Committee was bold enough, awarding the prize first to Christian Lange and in the following year to Fridtjof Nansen. So two Norwegians have received the peace prize, as against five Swedes and one Dane. Not until today has the prize gone to a Finn. But in that connection we have listened to Alfred Nobel. He urged that the worthiest candidate should receive the prize "whether he be Scandinavian or not."

In 1960, when he was in his early twenties, Ahtisaari went to Pakistan to work for the YMCA. One of the initial laureates, Henry Dunant, was a pioneer in this organization and movement. And John R. Mott, the YMCA executive, was a laureate in 1946 (beating out Kollontay). Note too that, in the same year Ahtisaari went to Pakistan, Father Pire, the 1958 laureate, was there as well, doing the work that would lead to his "Islands of Peace."

In 1965, Ahtisaari joined his country's ministry of foreign affairs, eventually concentrating on development aid. And in 1973, he was appointed ambassador to Tanzania. Africa would become an important component of his career. In 1977, he was named the U.N.'s high commissioner for Namibia, taking over from Seán MacBride, the 1974 co-laureate. In due course, Ahtisaari helped Namibia secure its independence from South Africa. Some referred to him as "Namibia's midwife." After the coming of independence in 1990, he and his wife, Eeva, were given honorary Namibian citizenship. And Mjøs said this in his presentation speech: "Many boys in Namibia have been named after Martti. That must be at least as great an honor as being awarded the Nobel Peace Prize."

Ahtisaari played many another part. He was a U.N. undersecretary-general. He was the Social Democrats' candidate for the presidency of Finland, and won. He served one term (from 1994 to 2000). He performed diplomatic work in Kosovo, Northern Ireland, Indonesia, and elsewhere. Mediating between the Free Aceh Movement and the Indonesian government, he asked each side a pointed, memorable question: "Do you want peace or do you want to win?"

Announcing for Ahtisaari, the Nobel Committee said they were honoring him "for his important efforts, on several continents and over more than three decades, to resolve international conflicts." This was a classic lifetime-achievement award. There was no pretense about heeding the testator's words concerning the "preceding year." Mjøs said, "It is not easy to take every sentence in Nobel's will absolutely literally."

In his lecture, Ahtisaari sounded one of the great themes of his career: No conflict is beyond resolution. He said, "Peace is a question of will. All conflicts can be settled, and there are no excuses for allowing them to become eternal." This is reminiscent of something said in another lecture, almost a hundred years before. Do you remember Elihu Root? "There is no international controversy so serious that it cannot be settled if both parties really wish to settle it. There are few controversies so trifling that they cannot be made the occasion for war if the parties really wish to fight." Ahtisaari said that even the Middle East was amenable to conflict resolution. And he took note of an election in America, held the month before. "I hope that the new president of the United States, who will be sworn in next month, will give high priority to the Middle East conflict during his first year in office."

Ahtisaari had already expressed his enthusiasm for this new president. Shortly after the election, he remarked to the press that the world had witnessed "a sea change in the United States." The election had shown that "the U.S. is capable of change." (Has that ever been in doubt?) Ahtisaari, of course, meant change of the most positive kind. As it transpired, this sea-changing president was the next laureate. And we will turn to him after one more interlude.

INTERLUDE

A STROLL THROUGH THE
NOBEL PEACE CENTER

Near Oslo City Hall, where the Nobel ceremony takes place, and hard by Oslo Harbor, is the Nobel Peace Center. This grand building is an old train station, erected in 1872. It is splendidly restored. The building is rather beautiful, in addition to grand, and a pale yellow. The Storting voted in December 2000, just before the Nobel centennial was to begin, to establish this peace center. It would open in June 2005: to be part of another centennial celebration, the one marking Norway's independence from Sweden. King Harald was on hand to give the Peace Center its launch. The center is meant to "spur reflection and debate on issues relating to war, peace and conflict resolution."

There is a relationship between the Nobel Peace Center and the Norwegian Nobel Committee—to wit, "The Nobel Peace Center's governing board is appointed by the Nobel Foundation on the recommendation of the Norwegian Nobel Committee." (I have been quoting official literature.) As of 2011, the chairman of the Peace Center board was Geir Lundestad, the director of the Norwegian Nobel Institute, and secretary to the committee. (Those jobs go together, you remember.) His deputy chairman was a committee member.

When I visited the center in 2010, there was something off-beat at the gates: a large neon sign, saying, "LAUGHTER." But not quite. Because, to the left of the "L," there was another letter, "S." It flickered occasionally, giving you "SLAUGHTER." This was political art, or point-making art, or at any rate something to catch the eye, and play with the brain. At the front doors was a poster of President Obama, with the words "A Call to Action." Obama was captured in a heroic, "iconic" pose, similar to the ubiquitous image of Che Guevara.

Inside, there was an exhibition devoted to Obama, as the latest laureate: It is customary for the center to feature laureates in this way. This particular display was maybe half exhibition and half shrine. The Peace Center people were keen to associate Obama—or the Nobel Committee's selection of Obama—with Alfred Nobel's will. Visitors were informed that the exhibition showed "the connection between Nobel's three criteria for receiving the Nobel Peace Prize and Obama's visions and work for fraternity, disarmament, and diplomacy." Many around the world were wondering why Obama, this rookie president, was awarded the grand prize. The overriding point of the exhibition was that this award was traditional, deserved, and right. Were the Nobel people a touch defensive? It seemed so.

Another exhibition paid tribute to the South African laureates: Lutuli, Tutu, and Mandela & de Klerk (in chronological order). There were music videos, showing Tutu and Mandela, in particular, as rock stars: peace-and-humanity stars. The old shots of Winnie Mandela, the middle of Mandela's three wives, made one a little wistful. At one time, she, too, was a peace-and-humanity figure—a star—before she descended into murderous extremism. The Nobel people seem quite proud of their South African laureates, eager to wrap their arms around them. Indeed, the anti-apartheid cause was one of the most popular ever in the West.

One of the permanent features of the Peace Center is the Electronic Wallpaper, where you can call up all sorts of information related to the Nobel prize and its winners. Of course, human beings write these articles and nuggets: so there is almost inevitably a bias. This is especially glaring where Middle Eastern matters are concerned. Materials about the Arab–Israeli conflict are written from a Palestinian point of view—as though a PLO spokesman were the author. An example: "In 2001, Arafat's longtime enemy Ariel Sharon became Israeli prime minister. Israeli forces re-occupied large areas of Palestinian territory, bombing Arafat's headquarters in Ramallah and isolating him there." And why might that have been? Was Sharon merely feeling beastly? Did it have anything to do with the incessant murder of Israeli civilians, ordered or sanctioned by the PLO chief? If you listen to the Electronic Wallpaper, Arafat is a simple victim.

Be that as it may, the "wallpaper" is a good idea, taking advantage of some recent bells and whistles. The Peace Center quotes an encomium from the *Guardian*: "The Nobel Peace Center is a triumph of technology and MTV style, and could become a pacifist pilgrimage site for the world."

The restaurant is, naturally, the Café de la Paix. And there is, naturally, a gift shop—in which you meet a giraffe, the mascot of the center. His name is Fred, which is no accident: "Fred" means "peace" in Norwegian. Children are invited to "come join Fred's fabulous journey!" They receive a "peace passport," learn about "people who work for peace," and "place a wishing star in the sky." The shop sells assorted items, including sponge cloths "for more peaceful cleaning." With these, you can "wipe away your fear," and "wash for peace." The cloths bear quotations from various peace laureates—e.g., "Happiness is not something ready-made. It comes from your own actions" (the Dalai Lama).

And there are books, as in most any museum gift shop. I saw several biographies of Obama, and hagiographies. This is not a place for much criticism of that laureate. The other books for sale had a particular flavor—a political flavor: Edward Said's indictment of the West, *Orientalism*; Al Gore's *The Assault on Reason* (the assaulters being, in his view, George W. Bush, Republicans, and conservatives); and so on. I had the feeling that I was looking at "official books." There is more political diversity in Norway itself than in the shop, at the time of my visit.

Then there are the postcards I mentioned earlier: postcards showing the laureates from Dunant & Passy on. What you choose to buy is, of course, a matter of taste. Arafat, smiling in his keffiyeh, may make you gag—or you may snap him up, smilingly. Fridtjof Nansen seems particularly at home in this shop: a Norwegian hero, and a world hero, on Norwegian soil.

 OBAMA'S HOUR

Was Barack Obama not an American president after the committee's own heart? He was practically a soulmate of theirs, sharing basically the same worldview. If the Norwegian Nobel Committee—if Scandinavian political elites—could design an American president, he would look a lot like Obama. He was virtually the committee's dream president, just as his predecessor, George W. Bush, had been their nightmare president. The 2009 Nobel Peace Prize was an expression of relief that Bush was no longer president. It blessed a new day.

Indeed, this prize could be construed as the fifth anti-Bush Nobel. There was the prize to Annan and the U.N. in 2001, shortly after 9/11. (To be sure, this was also the centennial Nobel, and the committee most values the U.N.) There was the prize to Carter the next year: when the Nobel chairman said, candidly, Yes, we are kicking him in the leg (the "him" being Bush). In 2005, the award went to ElBaradei and the IAEA. Two years later, there was the global-warming award, to Gore and the IPCC, fierce foes of the president. Now there was this award to Obama, the un-Bush, even the anti-Bush. We might say, at a minimum, that Bush figured in several Nobels, in a negative way. There were Nobels in reaction to Bush.

Obama had been in office less than two weeks when nominations came due: from January 20 to February 1. Obviously someone had thought to nominate the new president—perhaps a committee member or members themselves did so. And he had roughly eight and a half months, until the announcement in October, to show the committee his stuff. Obama became the third sitting U.S. president to win the prize, after Theodore Roosevelt in 1906 and Wilson in 1920 (when that president won the prize for the previous year). And Obama was the third leading Democrat in a decade to win the prize, along with Carter and Gore. The time when Nobel prizes were awarded to Republicans—TR, Root, Dawes, Kellogg, Butler—had long since passed. (There was, it is true, the anomalous award to Kissinger in 1973.)

Probably the president Obama most resembled was Carter, another man dear to the Nobel Committee's heart. In June 2010, *Der Spiegel* was to ask, "Will Obama Be the 'Jimmy Carter of the 21st Century'?" To many people, the comparison was no compliment; to others, it was. Carter believed that America had committed much wrong in the world and needed to atone. America was guilty of supreme arrogance and needed to learn humility. Obama judges in the same way. In the United States, there was a T-shirt, not complimentary. Picturing Obama, it said, "Welcome Back, Carter" (a play on the title of an old TV show, *Welcome Back, Kotter*).

In 2004, Obama was a state senator in Illinois. In November of that year, he was elected to the U.S. Senate, and he almost immediately started running for president. Many people, particularly on the left, of course, viewed him as a salvific figure. In the summer of 2008, a writer for *New York* magazine said that Obama was "our national oratorical superhero—a honey-tongued Frankenfusion of Lincoln, Gandhi, Cicero, Jesus, and all our most cherished national acronyms (MLK, JFK, RFK, FDR)." Never mind that those are not acronyms: The writer's sentiment was widespread.

Campaigning for president, Obama had a strong sense of what his tenure would mean. In November 2007, he said, "I truly believe that the day I'm inaugurated . . . not only does the country look at itself differently, but the world looks at America differently. . . . The world will have confidence that I am listening to them, and that our future and our security is tied up with our ability to work with other countries in the world." In late October 2008, he said to a cheering crowd in Missouri, "We are five days from fundamentally transforming the United States of America." What would that fundamental transformation involve? For one thing, it would involve moving the United States in a more social-democratic—in a more Norwegian—direction. I happened to be in Oslo right after the passage of what some call "ObamaCare." Discovering that I was American, a hotel worker said, "Oh, congratulations on your new health-care system. This is a happy time for you." The Norwegian media would unlikely have told her anything else.

When Obama was elected, many people said that, after an eight-year hiatus, America would rejoin the world. In their view, Bush was an insular, nationalistic, chest-thumping cowboy who had turned his back on the world. Obama would be just the opposite. In the weeks before the election, I debated a professor at Yale, who stressed that "the world" wanted Obama to be president. Polls had shown that "they," "the world," would elect Obama in a landslide. What more was there to say? Well, you could say this: that the election, for better or worse, was national.

In 2004, Senator John Kerry, the Democratic presidential nominee, said something interesting in a debate versus Bush. He said that American foreign and defense policies should "pass the global test." Obama was nothing if not a passer of the global test; indeed, he could ace that test. And the Nobel Peace Prize was his A+. There are presidents more likely to win the approval of the Rotary Club in Butte, Montana, than the approval of the Norwegian Nobel Committee. Reagan and Bush—both Bushes, really, but especially George W.—fall into that category. Carter and Obama fall into the opposite category. Sometimes, a president can please both Butte and Oslo. Sometimes, he cannot. As Reagan famously said in the 1960s, there comes "a time for choosing."

When Obama won the peace prize, French president Nicolas Sarkozy said, "It confirms . . . America's return to the hearts of the people of the world." Back in the U.S., David Ignatius, a foreign-policy columnist, wrote, "The Nobel committee is expressing a collective sigh of relief that America has rejoined the global consensus." Being of roughly the same mind as Obama and the committee, Ignatius added, "They're right. It's a good thing." In its announcement, the committee said this: "[Obama's] diplomacy is founded in the concept that those who are to lead the world must do so on the basis of values and attitudes that are shared by the majority of the world's population." It is a most perspicacious panel that knows the values and attitudes, the minds and hearts, of the world's population (some 7 billion). These five Norwegian politicos, unlike the insular George W. Bush, must contain multitudes.

The likes of the committee prized Obama for any number of reasons. He strongly opposed the Iraq War. He thought Guantánamo Bay a disgrace (though he decided he could not shut it down). He canceled anti-missile defenses in Eastern Europe. Poland and the Czech Republic were unnerved, but the Russian government was comforted. And he curtailed the anti-missile-defense program at home. When democratic protesters massed on Iran's streets, he stayed largely silent. He was keen to work with the Iranian government. He had sent them a message at Nowruz, the Iranian new year, saying that the United States now sought "engagement that is honest and grounded in mutual respect." In this message, he twice referred to the country as "the Islamic Republic of Iran," as the mullahs do.

He eagerly put "daylight" between the United States and Israel—"daylight" being the administration's word for "distance." He was showily cold to Benjamin Netanyahu, the Israeli prime minister. He gave the Medal of Freedom to Mary Robinson, the Irish politician who had presided over the U.N.'s Durban conference in 2001—a conference that dissolved into an anti-Israel and anti-Semitic jamboree. When some complained about the medal, she said, "There's a lot of bullying by certain elements of the Jewish community." He yukked it up with Hugo Chávez, the Venezuelan strongman, giving him a soul-brother handshake and calling him "mi amigo." When a constitutional crisis occurred in Honduras, Obama sided unequivocally with a Chávez ally and the would-be Chávez of Honduras, Manuel Zelaya. At the U.N., he had the United States join the Human Rights Council, despite its domination by murderous dictatorships.

The stylistic touches mattered—such as the language in the Nowruz message, and the handshake with Chávez. Obama bowed to the king of Saudi Arabia—then to the emperor of Japan, then to Wen Jiabao, the Chinese premier. Under Obama, the U.S. government—at least the executive branch—would no longer say "War on Terror." Instead, they would say "overseas contingency operations." They would no longer say "terrorism." Instead, they would say "man-caused disaster." Also, Obama was quite happy to disparage his predecessor, including on foreign soil. For example, he told a group of students in Turkey, "George Bush didn't believe in climate change [a highly debatable statement, as everyone acknowledges that climate changes]. I do believe in climate change. I think it's important." Often, he positioned himself between the United States and its adversaries, as a neutral explainer or arbiter. In a comment that attracted a lot of attention,

Evan Thomas of *Newsweek* magazine said, ". . . in a way, Obama's standing above the country, above the world—he's sort of God." One conservative sardonically remarked that Obama was America's first "non-aligned president."

In the words of Archbishop Tutu, he had "lowered the temperature in the world." Those words were quoted by the Nobel chairman in his presentation speech. Whereas Bush was belligerent, the Nobel people thought, Obama was pacific, or soothing. One way to interpret "lowering the temperature" is that Obama was easier on tyrants and bullies, more willing to give them a pass, on the grounds of "realism." He did not make such a fuss over freedom. Remember, though, that when Tutu et al. were struggling against apartheid, they wanted the "temperature" hot, not low.

The committee had a new chairman, Thorbjørn Jagland, a senior Labor man. Indeed, he had been prime minister—and foreign minister and president of the Storting. He had also been a vice president of the Socialist International and was now secretary-general of the Council of Europe. It was he, of course, who walked through the doors into Nobel Hall to make the 2009 announcement. When he spoke the name of Barack Obama, there were oohs, ahs, and maybe a gasp or two from the assembled press. The announcement said that the American president was being honored "for his extraordinary efforts to strengthen international diplomacy and cooperation between peoples." Obama, the committee stated, had "created a new climate in international politics." The statement continued,

> Multilateral diplomacy has regained a central position, with emphasis on the role that the United Nations and other international institutions can play. Dialogue and negotiations are preferred as instruments for resolving even the most difficult international conflicts. The vision of a world free from nuclear

arms has powerfully stimulated disarmament and arms-
control negotiations. Thanks to Obama's initiative, the U.S.A.
is now playing a more constructive role in meeting the great
climatic challenges the world is confronting. Democracy and
human rights are to be strengthened.

Only very rarely has a person to the same extent as Obama
captured the world's attention and given its people hope for a
better future.

The line about democracy and human rights, and their being
strengthened, was puzzling. George W. Bush had pursued a "freedom agenda," particularly in his first term. He had preached and
promoted democracy and human rights at every turn. And for
this, he was widely scorned as a "neoconservative," determined
to "impose American values" on reluctant others. Obama, by contrast, was soft-pedaling democracy and human rights, if nodding
to them at all. He was more interested in harmonious relations
between governments.

Take the case of Iran. Like Obama, Bush had sent Nowruz
greetings to that country—but to its people, wholly apart from
the government. Obama had made sure to address his greeting
to "the people and leaders of Iran." As they massed in the streets,
democratic protesters chanted, "Obama, Obama! Either you're
with *them* [meaning the regime] or you're with *us*!" In a 2011
interview with the *Wall Street Journal*, Natan Sharansky called
Obama's stance during the Iranian tumult "maybe one of the biggest betrayals of people's freedom in modern history." He continued, "At the moment when millions were deciding whether to go
to the barricades, the leader of the Free World said [in effect], 'For
us, the most important thing is engagement with the regime, so
we don't want a change of regime.'" Bush was a different cat. At
Nowruz 2008, he gave an interview to the Voice of America's Per-
sian service, saying, "My thought is that the reformers inside Iran

are brave people," and "they've got no better friend than George W. Bush." It was a boast, but not an empty one.

How about the U.N. Human Rights Council? Bush had shunned it, because it was dominated by those dictatorships—whose main purpose, in any case, was to defame Israel. He thought that U.S. membership could not improve the panel, only legitimize it. Obama had a different view. And the matter of Medals of Freedom? You can learn a lot from a president's selections. Bush was the type to give the medal to Dr. Óscar Elías Biscet, the Cuban prisoner of conscience (who was unable to travel to Washington to accept). Obama, when he took office, made to conciliate the Cuban government. When the peace prize to Obama was announced, Fidel Castro said that he had often disagreed with the committee's choices. But he could commend the 2009 choice: "I must admit that, in this case, in my opinion, it was a positive step."

None of this is to say, with absolute or cocky certainty, that Bush was right in his approach and Obama wrong in his own. That is a foreign-policy debate, and a debate about tactics. There are arguments on both sides. But the Nobel Committee's line, "Democracy and human rights are to be strengthened," was puzzling.

When Chairman Jagland finished his announcement, some of the assembled press applauded. Then there were questions. In answer to one of them, Jagland said that the committee's vote had been unanimous. Further into the press conference, a man raised his hand. He was apparently a reporter, like the others around him. But he did not have a question. When Jagland called on him, the man said, "As an American citizen, I'd like to thank the Nobel Committee for recognizing our president for the work he's doing for peace in the world." The chairman said, "Thank you."

At the White House, Obama walked into the Rose Garden and said, "Well, this is not how I expected to wake up this morning."

Many thought that Obama looked and sounded embarrassed. He said,

> I am both surprised and deeply humbled by the decision of the Nobel Committee. Let me be clear: I do not view it as a recognition of my own accomplishments, but rather as an affirmation of American leadership on behalf of aspirations held by people in all nations. To be honest, I do not feel that I deserve to be in the company of so many of the transformative figures who've been honored by this prize—men and women who've inspired me and inspired the entire world through their courageous pursuit of peace.
>
> But I also know that this prize reflects the kind of world that those men and women, and all Americans, want to build—a world that gives life to the promise of our founding documents. And I know that throughout history, the Nobel Peace Prize has not just been used to honor specific achievement; it's also been used as a means to give momentum to a set of causes. And that is why I will accept this award as a call to action—a call for all nations to confront the common challenges of the 21st century.

That was a graceful handling of an awkward situation into which the president had been put.

In Norway, there was a bit of embarrassment at what the committee—probably the most consequential Norwegians—had done. Nils Butenschøn, director of the Norwegian Center for Human Rights at the University of Oslo, said, "It seems like the committee wanted to award the prize to the American president to confirm the status of the prize rather than the worthiness of the candidate." He also worried, as others did, about the "integrity" of the prize. Had the Nobel Committee merely summoned this superstar of a president to Oslo, to bask a little in his glory?

In various public remarks, Chairman Jagland said two different things: that Obama was getting the prize for what he had already accomplished, not for what he might accomplish in the future; and that he was getting it in order to receive strength for the future. The Nobel prize has long been awarded for both reasons, of course. Lech Walesa spoke of the Obama award in his interview with me the next year. Said the 1983 laureate, "The wise men of the committee gave the award to Obama for his potential merit, and to encourage him not to stray from a path of peace." Then, with his characteristic twinkle, he said, "Well, we could all get a Nobel prize for our potential merit—and in order to be encouraged. For example, every journalist could get the Nobel prize to be encouraged to write better."

In America, conservatives were scornful, as could well be imagined. Many said, in essence, "What else do you expect from a group of Scandinavian lefties who have already given their prize to Gore, Carter, ElBaradei, and Annan?" The writer Mark Steyn put it pithily and pointedly: The award to Obama was "an exquisite act of condescension from the Norwegians, a dog biscuit and a pat on the head to the American hyperpower for agreeing to spay itself into a hyperpoodle." Yet even some people on the left—Obama supporters—were taken aback. Joe Klein of *Time* magazine wrote, "Let's face it: this prize is premature to the point of ridiculousness." Ruth Marcus of the *Washington Post* wrote something similar: "This is ridiculous—embarrassing, even. I admire President Obama. I like President Obama. I voted for President Obama. But the peace prize? This is supposed to be for doing, not being—and it's no disrespect to the president to suggest he hasn't done much yet. Certainly not enough to justify this prize."

Mockery was heard throughout the land. The spirit was encapsulated by a sign outside a North Carolina restaurant, a picture of which went around the Internet. The sign said, "Free Nobel Peace Prize with an Order of Shrimp Tacos."

There were suggestions that Obama turn the prize down, in a display of humility and realism. And there were suggestions that he do something creative—unprecedented—in his accepting of the prize. Thomas L. Friedman, the *New York Times* columnist, said that Obama should go to Oslo and make a surprise announcement in his lecture: He, the president, would accept the award "on behalf of the most important peacekeepers in the world for the last century—the men and women of the U.S. Army, Navy, Air Force and Marine Corps." Many expressed the opinion that the Nobel prize was, in fact, a poisoned chalice for Obama: because it would restrict his freedom of action as American commander-in-chief. For example, how could a peace laureate make, or escalate, war? How could he attack Iran's nuclear facilities? Did he not have a peace prize—a Norwegian vision—to live up to?

As it happened, Obama made a decision about the Afghan War less than two weeks before traveling to Oslo to accept the peace prize: He announced that he was sending 30,000 additional troops to the country, in a "surge" of the kind that Bush had ordered for Iraq (though Obama shrank from making this comparison). At the same time, he announced a date certain for American withdrawal, or at least the beginning of that withdrawal: July 2011. Nevertheless, the surge left some devotees of the Nobel prize aghast: What kind of warmonger was the committee awarding? Why, he was practically as bad as Bush! But that was not a majority opinion, among devotees: Most of them were thrilled that this gifted young "progressive" president—who was African-American, to boot—was going to stand in City Hall, and throughout the world, as the laureate.

In Oslo, Obama did not do the full slate of events: He did not do all that is expected of, let's say, an ordinary laureate. For example, he declined to hold a press conference or to attend the Nobel concert. These departures from tradition irked more than a few Norwegians. They were particularly miffed that Obama turned down a lunch with King Harald. But most people, probably, were understanding of the president's truncated schedule. Obama said, "I still have a lot of work to do back in Washington, D.C., before the year is done." The way Secretary Lundestad put it was, "Obama has to govern the U.S."

He was certainly at the prize ceremony, the main event. After the dignitaries, including the laureate, had paraded in, a Norwegian soprano with the Christmassy name of Solveig Kringelborn sang songs of Grieg. The first was "God morgen"—"Good Morning"—whose words are by Bjørnson. After these songs, Jagland gave his presentation speech. And he lost no time in citing the will:

> The committee always takes Alfred Nobel's will as its frame of reference. We are to award the Nobel Peace Prize to the person who, during the "preceding year," meaning in this case since the previous award in December 2008, shall have done the most or the best work "for fraternity between nations, for the abolition or reduction of standing armies, and for the holding and promotion of peace congresses" . . . .
>
> The question was actually quite simple. Who has done most for peace in the past year? If the question is put in Nobel's terms, the answer is relatively easy to find: It had to be U.S. president Barack Obama.

We see how flexible the committee is. Only twelve months before, the Nobel chairman, giving that lifetime-achievement award to Ahtisaari, was shrugging, "It is not easy to take every sentence in Nobel's will absolutely literally."

The present chairman, Jagland, hailed Obama both in general terms and in specific ones. Getting specific, he said, "The new administration in Washington has reconsidered the deployment in Eastern Europe of the planned anti-missile defenses and is instead looking at other multilateral options to secure the region. This has contributed to an improved atmosphere in the negotiations on strategic nuclear weapons between the U.S.A. and the Russian Federation." Jagland also praised Obama's conciliatory attitude toward China. (The president had recently postponed a visit with the Dalai Lama, in order to respect Beijing's sensitivities.) He said, "The rise of new great powers often leads to war and conflict. There are those in America who fear that history may repeat itself in that respect. The Obama administration's cooperation with Beijing means that we have little reason to fear such a repetition." You can praise an administration or a president for his "cooperation with Beijing," or you can praise him on the grounds that—as the committee put it in its announcement—"democracy and human rights are to be strengthened." It is odd to do both.

Jagland next made a statement that was odd—very odd—from several angles. Echoing the announcement, he said,

> Obama's diplomacy rests on the idea that whoever is to lead the world must do so on the basis of values and attitudes that are shared by the majority of the world's population. That was how they put it, those earlier American presidents who, above all others, were seen as world leaders also outside the United States: Woodrow Wilson and Franklin D. Roosevelt, John F. Kennedy and Ronald Reagan. America's ideals were the world's ideals: They lived, in Reagan's words, "not only in the hearts and minds of our countrymen but in the hearts and minds of millions of the world's people in both free and oppressed societies who look to us for leadership."

As you know, George W. Bush, the Nobel Committee's bête noire, spoke constantly of American values as universal ones: not particular ones or national ones. As you also know, it was precisely for this reason that many American conservatives criticized and scorned him: scorned him as a fuzzy-minded "Wilsonian." And it was amazing to hear a Nobel chairman praise and quote Reagan, another committee bête noire, at least during the time of his presidency. Remember what Óscar Arias said: "Reagan was responsible for my prize." The committee had told him he was receiving the prize in order to have a club against Reagan. In future Nobel ceremonies, will chairmen be praising and quoting George W. Bush?

After Jagland finished his speech, Lang Lang, the young Chinese pianist, came out to play a Chopin étude: the quiet, lulling one in E major, Op. 10, No. 3. He wore a white tunic, to which he had attached, near the throat, a dove of peace. Then, the chairman presented Obama with the medal and diploma—after which, the laureate's chosen performer took the stage. Remember, the recipient of the Nobel prize gets to choose a musician for his Nobel ceremony. Obama chose the American jazz singer Esperanza Spalding, who appeared with her ensemble. Then it was time for the lecture.

Obama had given his address some serious thought, as the occasion deserved. Some of his words were mere undergraduate reflections on war and peace. But some of his words reached a considerably higher level. One feature of his speech was a defense of American power—the kind of defense not heard at a Nobel ceremony since George C. Marshall received the prize in 1953.

At the outset, Obama said, "I would be remiss if I did not acknowledge the considerable controversy that your generous decision has generated." The audience laughed appreciatively. The president continued, "In part, this is because I am at the beginning, and not the end, of my labors on the world stage. Compared to some of the giants of history who've received this prize—Schweitzer and King; Marshall and Mandela—my accomplishments are slight."

Soon after, he said, "But perhaps the most profound issue sur-
rounding my receipt of this prize is the fact that I am the commander-in-chief of the military of a nation in the midst of two
wars. One of these wars is winding down. The other is a conflict
that America did not seek; one in which we are joined by 42 other
countries—including Norway—in an effort to defend ourselves
and all nations from further attacks."

At no point in his lecture did Obama utter the word "Iraq."
Iraq was nothing more than a war that was "winding down." And
this was a "war of choice," Obama was saying, by implication—
a war of choice rather than a "war of necessity," as the Afghan
War was. That had been Obama's mantra during the presidential
campaign, too: Iraq the bad and unnecessary war, Afghanistan
the good and necessary one. He mentioned, as we have just seen,
that Norway was part of the coalition in Afghanistan. He did not
mention that there had been an equally big coalition in Iraq, of
which Norway was part.

Obama quoted from Martin Luther King's Nobel lecture,
delivered 45 years before: ". . . violence never brings permanent
peace. It solves no social problem: It merely creates new and more
complicated ones." The president then remarked, "As someone
who stands here as a direct consequence of Dr. King's life work,
I am living testimony to the moral force of nonviolence. I know
there's nothing weak—nothing passive, nothing naive—in the
lives of Gandhi and King." You knew there was a "but" coming:

> But as a head of state sworn to protect and defend my nation, I
> cannot be guided by their examples alone. I face the world as it
> is, and cannot stand idle in the face of threats to the American
> people. For make no mistake: Evil does exist in the world. A
> nonviolent movement could not have halted Hitler's armies.
> Negotiations cannot convince al-Qaeda's leaders to lay down
> their arms. To say that force may sometimes be necessary is

not a call to cynicism—it is a recognition of history; the imperfections of man and the limits of reason.

Obama noted that "in many countries there is a deep ambivalence about military action today, no matter what the cause. And at times, this is joined by a reflexive suspicion of America, the world's sole military superpower." And here he came to the part of his speech that was most unlike a Nobel lecture.

> But the world must remember that it was not simply international institutions—not just treaties and declarations—that brought stability to a post–World War II world. Whatever mistakes we have made, the plain fact is this: The United States of America has helped underwrite global security for more than six decades with the blood of our citizens and the strength of our arms. The service and sacrifice of our men and women in uniform has promoted peace and prosperity from Germany to Korea, and enabled democracy to take hold in places like the Balkans. We have borne this burden not because we seek to impose our will. We have done so out of enlightened self-interest—because we seek a better future for our children and grandchildren, and we believe that their lives will be better if others' children and grandchildren can live in freedom and prosperity.

George W. Bush and Ronald Reagan could have said the exact same things—and they did, repeatedly. In fact, such language was the theme music of their presidencies. After Obama ended this interesting lecture, Lang Lang returned for one more piece: the *Liebestraum No. 3* of Liszt. And that was the end of the ceremony.

Obama did not immediately jet back to Washington. He attended the Nobel banquet that night—and made a remark that got a big laugh. Referring to Chairman Jagland and his presentation speech, he said, "I told him afterward that I thought it was an excellent speech—and that I was almost convinced that I deserved it."

AFTERWORD

Come to the land of peace!
Come where the tempest hath no longer sway,
The shadow passes from the soul away,
The sounds of weeping cease!
(Felicia Hemans, "The Angels' Call")

It is not really possible to write a history of the Nobel Peace Prize: a complete history, that is. Because the prize keeps going, and you, the writer, must stop. I will stop with President Obama and 2009. But shall we have a peek at 2010, plus 2011? These were good and interesting awards. In my view, the 2010 award was one of the best ever. An award to a Chinese freedom figure was overdue, but, 61 years after Mao and his gang took control of that vast country, it came.

The award went to Liu Xiaobo, the aforementioned prisoner of conscience. In 2009, the Nobel Committee, through its chairman, had praised Obama for his "cooperation with Beijing." But the next year, the committee was willing to infuriate Beijing. And furious they were. In reaction to the naming of Liu, the government did a number of things, larger and smaller. They placed the laureate's wife, Liu Xia, under house arrest. No one could attend the prize ceremony for him. They launched a cyber-attack on the Norwegian Nobel Institute. They warned governments around the world to keep their ambassadors in Oslo away from the ceremony. Shamefully, many of them complied. And, in a poetic touch, they created their own prize, an alternative Nobel: the Confucius Peace Prize. Who else created their own prize, out of pique at the Nobel Committee? The Nazis in the 1930s, and the Soviets in the 1940s. The Chinese Communists were in fine company.

Liu Xiaobo, incidentally, managed to get word out that he was dedicating his Nobel prize to the victims of the Tiananmen Square massacre in 1989.

In 2011, the prize went to three individuals "for their non-violent struggle for the safety of women and for women's rights to full participation in peace-building work." Two of the laureates were Liberian, and the other was Yemeni. One of the Liberians, Leymah Gbowee, rallied women to put an end to the Second Liberian Civil War (which lasted from 1999 to 2003; the first had gone from 1989 to 1996). They pressured the combatants relentlessly, in any way they knew. One of their tactics came out of *Lysistrata*: They staged a sex strike. In 2008, Gbowee was featured in a documentary called *Pray the Devil Back to Hell*. The Liberian peace movement led to the election of Ellen Johnson Sirleaf in 2005. She was the first woman ever elected head of state in Africa. And she was another of the 2011 laureates. The daughter of a pioneering politician in Liberia, she had a bold and reforming spirit. She was also a canny practitioner of politics. Like Margaret Thatcher, she was known in her country as "the Iron Lady."

The Yemeni laureate was Tawakkul Karman—and she, too, was known in her country as "the Iron Lady," or "the Iron Woman." Also as "the Mother of the Revolution." Karman was a leading figure in the Arab Spring (whether hoped for or real), which began in early 2011. Like Johnson Sirleaf, she was the daughter of a prominent politician. She became a journalist, an activist, and a politician herself. She stuck her neck out in opposing Yemen's traditional dictatorship. If the history of the liberalization of the Arab world is ever written, her name will have a place.

Here we will end our parade of laureates, having looked at a great many—about 120 of them. We have traversed miles and miles of history, much of it pivotal, almost all of it turbulent. We have done the 20th century and made a dent in the 21st. What do you suppose will happen in the future—the near future, specifically? Who do you suppose will win the peace prize?

I'll give you an obvious candidate: Bill Clinton. He is said to want the prize—who doesn't?—and he works in a high-profile way through his Clinton Global Initiative. Such an organization, or endeavor, is virtually Nobel bait (not that the prize is Clinton's motivation). The committee may well honor the 42nd president, but they will probably have to wait a decent interval: Only in 2009 did they give a prize to an American president. Seven years before that, they gave a prize to a former president (Carter). Five years later, and two years before Obama, they gave a prize to a former vice president (Gore). How many presidential Americans can you pile on? Shouldn't there be some top Democrat without the Nobel Peace Prize?

We can expect that Liu Xiaobo will someday be out of prison and free to go to Oslo, to collect his prize and give his lecture. We can expect that Aung San Suu Kyi, too, will find herself in Oslo, giving her lecture. In 1991, her son Alexander spoke for her.

A hundred and one years before that, Alfred Nobel said something I wish to quote—at least he was reported as saying it, and it sounds like him: "I intend to leave after my death a large fund for the promotion of the peace idea, but I am skeptical as to its results. The savants will write excellent volumes. There will be laureates. But wars will continue just the same until the force of circumstances renders them impossible." I don't say that the book you are reading is an excellent volume. But there have certainly been laureates, and wars have certainly continued just the same. When will the force of circumstances render them impossible?

In 1947, a woman named Margaret A. Backhouse spoke in Oslo for the Friends Service Council. She said,

> War will not cease until mankind has learnt the positive nature of peace. We speak of the present and the between-the-war period as "peace-time," but we all know that it would be truer to describe the condition as the period when there is no official warfare. There is not peace in the minds of men, and there will not be until we have replaced misunderstanding by sympathy, fear by trust, jealousy and hatred by love.

In the meantime, the Nobel Committee has a job to do (as do we all, in our different ways). And we may ask—as we have asked throughout this book, really—how they have done it. Listen to Ferdinand Buisson, that estimable Frenchman—"the world's most persistent pacifist"—as he gives his Nobel lecture in 1927:

> Since the beginning of this century, gentlemen, you . . . have always kept your hopes alive. While awaiting the time when humanity will justify you, as it surely will, you have steadfastly continued to mark milestones reached along the way to victory.

Has humanity justified the Nobel Committee? There are awards we embrace, and awards we recoil from, or at least disapprove of. It depends on our individual beliefs, our understanding.

Peace is not a simple matter, as every thinking and experienced person knows. And, as I noted earlier, there are few subjects about which people are glibber or cheaper. In 2008, the *Guardian* published an article about Chairman Ole Danbolt Mjøs. Accompanying the article was what the paper labeled a "curriculum vitae," giving a few basic facts about him. These included his "likes" and "dislikes." His "likes" were his "wife and family," "peace," and "the Arctic Cathedral of Tromsø." His "dislikes" were "wars" and "nuclear weapons." Well, thank you very much. Are there lovers, or even likers, of wars and nuclear weapons? Apart from some psychopaths, no. There are those who think that war is sometimes necessary, and those who think that nuclear weapons are needed for the maintenance of peace, until lions lie down with lambs, all cuddly.

The cause of peace is not to be confused with the cause of pacifism—at least of pacifism foolishly practiced. Neither is the cause of peace the same as the cause of disarmament. One of the Nobel Committee's greatest errors has been to treat weapons as bad in and of themselves, without regard to who possesses them and why. Presenting the prize to the IAEA and Mohamed ElBaradei in 2005, Mjøs said,

> It is hypocritical to go on developing one's own nuclear weap-
> ons while doing everything in one's power to prevent others
> from acquiring such weapons. As ElBaradei himself has put
> it, it is like "some who have . . . continued to dangle a cigarette
> from their mouth and tell everybody else not to smoke."

A cute line—but it can be tantamount to saying, "Israel's nukes, Ahmadinejad's nukes, what's the big diff?" Nearly everyone knows there is a big difference; even those who deny it must know, somewhere. At a prize ceremony long ago, Prime Minister Mowinckel did something that, to me, causes a chill. Do you remember? First, he quoted Holberg: "Everybody says that Jeppe drinks, but nobody asks *why* Jeppe drinks." Then he said, "Let us all who now complain that Germany also is arming look into our own consciences and ask *why* Germany is arming." That was in 1934. I hope it is not too glibly retrospective to say that the Reich would have armed and militarized no matter what—and that the weakness, rather than the strength, of other nations invited aggression.

I think, too, of Ludwig Quidde, Buisson's co-laureate in 1927. He was an enlightened pacifist. And he took as the theme of his Nobel lecture the relationship between security and disarmament. He said,

> The popular, and one may say naive, idea is that peace can be secured by disarmament and that disarmament must therefore precede the attainment of absolute security and lasting peace. This idea prevailed in the early days of the organized peace movement. "Lay Down Your Arms!" was the title that our great pioneer, Bertha von Suttner, gave her famous book . . . . This title was generally understood to mean: "Lay down your arms and we shall have peace."

But that, of course, was an idiocy. As Quidde went on to say, "To a great extent, disarmament is dependent on guarantees of peace. Security comes first and disarmament second."

Not long ago, I had a conversation with a young Norwegian historian in Oslo. With real indignation, he spoke of Norway's helplessness before the Nazi onslaught of 1940. The dictum had always been, *Si vis pacem, para bellum* ("If you want peace, prepare for war"). Clever, sanctimonious, and self-congratulatory people had changed this into *Si vis pacem, para pacem* ("If you want peace, prepare for peace"). That was the inscription on the box containing a gold pen, you may recall, given to Frank Kellogg in Le Havre. My Norwegian friend was contemptuously angry about this notion, saying, "When the Nazis came here, we were defenseless, and Nazis are very bad people to be occupied by." It was moving to see this kind of emotion—well-informed emotion—in a man born decades after the events in question.

He further pointed out that the Socialist Left party was now in government: and that this party declares, in its platform, that the United States is the number-one threat to peace in the world. That, too, earns his angry contempt.

I have called a reflex opposition to arms one of the Nobel Committee's "greatest errors." What about other errors (now that I have donned the robe of judge)? There is the unwavering faith in the U.N., and, before that, the League of Nations. No matter how feckless, corrupt, laughable, or sinister the "world body" is, the Nobel Committee showers it with awards, declaring it man's last, best hope. This does not, in my view, comport with reality. I also think of errors made in the Cold War. There were two of those, primarily. And they both fall under the heading "Moral equivalence."

First, there was the weird insistence on saying that the Communists had something to contribute on the subject of human rights. Had something to teach us. You know this attitude: *Here, we may be able to go to church or write an article, but there, they have a right to food and health!* Chairman Lionæs had a penchant for citing the Soviet constitution and Bolshevik slogans ("Bread and Peace"). And her reference to "the Eastern European viewpoint," when she meant Communist ideology, was grotesque. She was a better woman than that, much—as she proved when she protested Dr. Evgeny Chazov's moment of Nobel glory in 1985. Second, there was the insistence that the United States and the democratic West, and the Soviet Union and the undemocratic East, were basically two reckless players, endangering the world with their arms games.

In the 45 years of the Cold War, the committee sometimes did well, as when it honored Sakharov and Walesa. (Those were the only figures in the 75-year history of the general anti-Soviet struggle to win the Nobel prize.) Sometimes, the committee did not so well.

Recently, the committee has taken to linking poverty to terrorism—saying that the former causes the latter. The committee has said it, and their laureates have said it. This, too, is an error, I believe. Plenty of terrorists have been well off, most prominently bin Laden. And we should take care not to insult poor people, most of whom have never had a murderous thought in their lives. We should also take care not to succumb to excuses for terrorism, however subtle they are. At the centennial symposium, held three months after 9/11, Elie Wiesel was a rare laureate who would have no excusing of terrorism whatsoever. (In this, he distinguished himself from Dr. Chazov's friend Dr. Lown, among many others.) And, as people like to stretch the definition of peace, they like to stretch the definition of terrorism: Adolfo Pérez Esquivel, you have heard, refers to poverty as "economic terrorism."

Then there is the problem of "Peace, peace; when there is no peace." You may remember what Tony Blair said to George W. Bush, when embarking on his diplomacy in the Arab–Israeli conflict: "If I win the Nobel Peace Prize, you will know I have failed." This was just a quip, sure, but embedded in it was a deadly criticism. It must have stung the Norwegian Nobel Committee, if they learned about it. They have sometimes mistaken a pretend peace—a sham peace—for the real thing. They have sometimes mistaken mischief-makers, or clever aggressors, or other sophists, for real peacemakers. Of course, we have all been guilty of something like that, in our various spheres, at one time or another.

Maybe we could have a parlor game. It will be one, I'm afraid, in which there is only one player, me. But others can play along in their own fashion. The question is, What have been the best and worst Nobel prizes? To start with the negative, I believe that some of the worst have been those given to disarmers, both before World War II and during the Cold War. That will hardly surprise the reader, I know. The laureates I have in mind are the unilateralists, the freezers, the accommodationists—the Arthur Hendersons and Alva Myrdals and Joseph Rotblats. (Recall the harsh words of Lenin: "The fool Henderson and Co.") I do not believe that their ideas and actions were peace-tending. They believed so, however—and, in almost all cases, I don't question their sincerity.

The very worst award? Which one was that? I think a case can be made for 2005's, to the IAEA and ElBaradei. The agency was terribly wrong about Saddam Hussein and nukes before the Gulf War. And for almost 20 years they were clueless about Iran. Once that program was revealed, by Iranian whistleblowers, ElBaradei seemed more interested in protecting the regime from economic sanctions or military attack than in holding the regime to nuclear account. The agency, under his leadership, was grossly politicized. You may not think that the IAEA and ElBaradei were as culpable, bumbling, or harmful as I do. But the Nobel Peace Prize to them? Why? Was the committee merely taunting the United States and its allies for finding no WMD during the Iraq War?

Now to the positive side, and the question of what have been the best Nobels. Allow me to leave aside the heroes of democracy, human rights, and freedom—the Lutulis, Sakharovs, and Lius. Allow me also to leave aside the humanitarians and saints. Mother Teresa is simply an argument-stopper. For sheer, clear peacemaking, it's hard to beat Sadat and Begin. In essentially the same category lie the Good Friday boys, Hume and Trimble. Again, this was good, solid, clear peacemaking and conflict-ending. (I should probably insert the caveat that conflicts are subject to re-eruption.) And how about Carlos Saavedra Lamas, the lead mediator in a cessation of the Chaco War?

The committee has made a few gutsy choices, with the gutsiest of them probably being the award for 1935 to Ossietzky. In 1946, Albert Einstein said that "the bestowal of an honor of this magnitude on this simple martyr" would be forever to the credit of the Nobel Committee. The award to Liu was fairly gutsy too. But the committee has often shown a weakness for fashion, fads, political correctness. The award to Rigoberta Menchú, in the "Columbus year" of 1992, had its comic aspects. And, in honoring Gore and the IPCC, the committee looked, to me and others, like bandwagoneers.

I suppose I consider George C. Marshall something like the ideal peacemaker. He confronted evil when it appeared, and fought it, with arms. Then he went about bolstering the peace—through, for example, the Marshall Plan, or the European Recovery Program, as he was the only one to call it. He understood demilitarization and disarmament to be a peace-destroying disaster, for his country and its allies. He warned and worked against these things. And here we run into the problem of Nobel's will.

Oh? What problem is that? I have mentioned it before. As you well know, the testator wanted his peace prize to go to "the person who shall have done the most or the best work for fraternity between nations, for the abolition or reduction of standing armies, and for the holding and promotion of peace congresses." The middle of those three "criteria," as some call them, is the problem: "the abolition or reduction of standing armies." Would Nobel have stuck with this criterion if he had seen what Marshall saw, and many others saw, in the 20th century? I don't claim to speak for him. But I feel I know him a bit—and I suspect not.

From time to time, there are calls to end the Nobel Peace Prize, on the grounds that it cannot be responsibly given—that the notion of peace is too slippery. In 1994, the British historian Max Beloff published an article in the *Daily Mail* headed "Has the Nobel Prize become an insult to peace?" (I think of the *Life* magazine headline about the award to Linus Pauling: "A Weird Insult from Norway.") Beloff wrote this article just before the announcement of the 1994 prize, which was expected to go to Arafat and Rabin. (In the end, Peres was added.) Beloff said, "Perhaps this is the moment to abolish the Nobel Peace Prize altogether. I have often wondered about the wisdom of offering 'prizes' for so grand

and subtle a thing as peace." The scientific prizes—the Nobels in chemistry, physics, and physiology or medicine—will always be less controversial, because more objective, relatively speaking. The literature prize is quite subjective. And the peace prize: virtually a plaything.

One afternoon, I bought a book from a vendor outside the Vigeland Sculpture Park in Oslo. I said—as I often did in that period—"What do you think of the Nobel Peace Prize?" He answered, first, as a Norwegian: "It placed Norway on the map." Then he said, "I don't agree with many of the committee's choices. But a prize for peace is a good thing." I believe I agree with him, on the whole. Chairman Fredrik Stang wound up his 1927 presentation speech—the one devoted to Buisson and Quidde—as follows:

> To work for the cause of peace is to clear a path for honest and just relations between peoples, for recognition of the intrinsic worth of human beings and of the equal right of all people to live here on earth, and for the success of the greatest political idea ever conceived: the supplanting of war by peace.

Well and good. But how should one go about awarding a peace prize, specifically the Nobel Peace Prize, the king of them all? (There are more than 300 peace prizes in the world, by the way.) The Nobel Committee has wandered into some distant fields: microlending, for instance, and global-warming campaigning. I rather like what Hjalmar Branting, "the father of Swedish socialism," said in his Nobel lecture, delivered in June 1922. He cited those three criteria in Nobel's will. And he commented,

> "Fraternity between nations" is placed first. It sets forth the great goal itself. The other points cover some of the prerequisites and methods of attaining this end, expressed in the light

of the striving and longing which prevailed at the time the testament was drawn up. The formulation itself mirrors a particular epoch in history. Fraternity between nations, however, touches the deepest desire of human nature.

Say what you will about the abolition or reduction of standing armies or the holding and promotion of peace congresses: "Fraternity between nations" is a rugged and enduring principle, and desire. It should be the guiding star, I believe, in the awarding of the Nobel Peace Prize. If I were a committeeman—there's a far-fetched concept!—I would ask, "Who has done the most or best work in the preceding year for fraternity between nations? By whatever means, who has done the most or best work?" Of course, that would rule out the human-rights awards, the freedom awards: Lech Walesa would not have received the prize, and you recall how he said that, in his opinion, without this gift from the Norwegian Nobel Committee, Solidarity would not have succeeded. And we cannot have a Sadat and Begin every year. They appear only every now and then. We can't even have a Saavedra Lamas every year.

I would not rule out human-rights awards, and I would not even rule out a far-afield, or "imaginative," award once in a great while: a microlender, or certainly a multitudes-feeding agronomist. But "fraternity between nations" would still be my guiding star, and I would want to make most choices on that basis. Where possible, I would respect the "preceding year" stipulation. I would not rule out lifetime-achievement awards—but I believe that the preceding year should be uppermost in the committee's mind. Also, I think the committee should beware celebrityitis: Nobelprize winners need not be celebrities. Let the award go to some quiet, barely known people, of the Ahtisaari type. The Nobel prize will make them celebrities, or quasi-celebrities, in any case. And if the Nobel Peace Prize is boring, rather than flashy? So be it.

One Oscar ceremony is enough. Hollywood does Hollywood better than Oslo does.

One more thing: The prize need not be given every year. The statutes say it must be given at least once in five years. The committee has not skipped a year since 1972. And, as I've said, people now expect the prize to come every year, like Christmas. For some, canceling the prize, or holding off on it, would be like canceling or postponing Christmas—or the Oscars. But a less frequently given prize might mean more. And the committee could be surer that a worthy recipient is found.

Peace! A glorious concept, however much abused. The peacemakers really *are* blessed. The land of peace, true peace, is the brightest land there is. But what is peace, true peace, real peace? (Have I asked that before?) To declare someone a "champion of peace," in Alfred Nobel's phrase, is a bold act. To declare him the greatest such champion in all the world is an even bolder one. With all the humility we can muster, we must try to be sure we know what we're talking about.

A NOTE ON SOURCES

As the reader can imagine, this book was built on a wealth of materials: books and articles by the hundreds. It was also built on the author's own interviews, with a tremendous variety of people. These people include Nobel laureates, their spouses, their friends and associates, former members of the Nobel Committee, relatives of such people, scholars, and experts of other types. There are no footnotes in this book (as the reader may or may not have noticed). Where I think a particular thought, fact, or story should be attributed, I do so, right in the text. This happens frequently. Other information is generally findable, and not with difficulty.

Indispensable to anyone interested in the Nobel Peace Prize are two websites: that of the Nobel Foundation in Stockholm and that of the Norwegian Nobel Institute in Oslo. I have of course used them liberally, as a person uses water and air. These sites have presentation speeches, acceptance speeches, lectures, banquet toasts, biographies, photographs, films, essays, articles, statistics, and more.

There are a few general histories of the prize, and various papers and essays on it. As a rule, those who write about this subject are broadly supportive of the whole enterprise: the Nobel

Committee and its selections. (They will occasionally jab a selection, finding Theodore Roosevelt preposterous, for example.) As I say in my text, the leading historian of the peace prize—certainly in English—is Irwin Abrams. An American, he was born in 1914 and died in 2010. He was a man of the Left, a Quaker, a pacifist. As a conscientious objector in World War II, he worked with the American Friends Service Committee (co-laureate for 1947). For over 60 years, he was a professor at Antioch College, in Yellow Springs, Ohio. He was a regular guest of the Nobel Institute at the prize ceremonies. For twelve straight years, he nominated Jimmy Carter for the prize. Carter finally grabbed the brass ring—or the gold medal—in 2002. An obituary in the *Yellow Springs News* tells us something about that year's Nobel banquet: "President Carter came up to Irwin, his wife Rosalynn at his side, to take his hand and express his thanks. Irwin later said it was one of the high points of his life." Abrams was a man of strong opinions, and he was not shy about voicing them, or writing them. My own opinions are very different. What is inarguable is that Abrams was an excellent historian and a superb writer.

Of the laureates, there are many biographies, and from the laureates, there are many autobiographies—as well as other books. I have used cartloads of histories, memoirs, and other volumes. Each year of the Nobel Peace Prize sends you scurrying off to find information, and perhaps opinions, too. What did the Locarno Treaties say? What happened after the Sharpeville Massacre? Why did Kouchner fall out with MSF? What was the relationship between the IAEA and the PSI, if any? Each section of this book required some combination of materials: some combination of books, articles, interviews, etc.

A history of the Nobel Peace Prize is, in a sense, a general history of the world from 1901 on. To sum it up—maybe too grandly—I have availed myself of the numberless resources needed to write such a book.

ACKNOWLEDGEMENTS

My gratitude to the dedicatees of this book is made obvious by the fact of the dedication. I would also like to thank *National Review* colleagues, past and present. These include Adam Bellow, Rick Brookhiser, Jack Fowler, Rich Lowry, Chris McEvoy, Mike Potemra, David Pryce-Jones, and Amy Tyler. The last (but not the least) of these served as research assistant for the book. A graduate of Providence College, a Dominican institution, she knew exactly who Father Pire was (the Nobel peace laureate for 1958).

In Norway, my friend Kristian Norheim was a great help, and so was the staff of the Nobel Institute. That certainly includes the director, Geir Lundestad. Particular thanks go to the longtime librarian, Anne Kjelling. If there is a more knowledgeable, more capable, more considerate librarian in all of Europe, I would be very surprised.

I salute the people at Encounter Books. My editor was Carol Staswick, a brilliant woman. You know how writers always say, in their acknowledgements, "Any mistake is my own"? I know just what they mean. And this same editor made the index, which you will find a wonder.

In my Note on Sources, I said I had talked to "a tremendous variety of people." Yes, I conducted hundreds of interviews, whether brief or lengthy, with Nobel laureates, scholars, and anyone else who could help me understand and tell the story. Not a page went by that did not prompt a consultation or two. I will not name my consultants, or interviewees, here, for three reasons: one of them pretty good; one of them okay; and one of them weak.

Some number of these people would not want their assistance known, and some other number might gulp a little. That is the good, or pretty good, reason. The okay reason is this: If I listed my sources in general, that list would resemble a small-town phonebook. The weak reason is, I'm mortified at the thought of failing to include someone. My old friend Bill Buckley often said (some version of), "Inclusio unius est exclusio alterius"—Start naming names, and you're bound to leave someone out.

At any rate, I thank my host of helpers for what they have made possible.

LIST OF NOBEL PEACE LAUREATES

1927 Ferdinand Buisson and Ludwig Quidde

1929 Frank Kellogg

1930 Nathan Söderblom

1931 Jane Addams and Nicholas Murray Butler

1933 Norman Angell

1934 Arthur Henderson

1935 Carl von Ossietzky

1936 Carlos Saavedra Lamas

1937 Robert Cecil

1938 The Nansen International Office for Refugees

1944 The International Committee of the Red Cross

1945 Cordell Hull

1946 Emily Greene Balch and John R. Mott

1947 The Friends Service Council and the American Friends Service Committee

1949 John Boyd Orr

1950 Ralph Bunche

1951 Léon Jouhaux

1952 Albert Schweitzer

1953 George C. Marshall

1954 The Office of the U.N. High Commissioner for Refugees

1957 Lester Bowles Pearson

1958 Father Dominique Pire

1959 Philip Noel-Baker

1960 Albert John Lutuli

1961 Dag Hammarskjöld

1962 Linus Pauling

1963 The International Committee of the Red Cross and the League of Red Cross Societies

1964 Martin Luther King, Jr.

1965 The United Nations Children's Fund (known by its original acronym UNICEF)

1968 René Cassin

1969   The International Labour Organization

1970   Norman Borlaug

1971   Willy Brandt

1973   Henry Kissinger and Le Duc Tho

1974   Seán MacBride and Eisaku Sato

1975   Andrei Sakharov

1976   Betty Williams and Máiread Corrigan

1977   Amnesty International

1978   Anwar Sadat and Menachem Begin

1979   Mother Teresa

1980   Adolfo Pérez Esquivel

1981   The Office of the U.N. High Commissioner for Refugees

1982   Alva Myrdal and Alfonso García Robles

1983   Lech Walesa

1984   Desmond Tutu

1985   International Physicians for the Prevention of Nuclear War

1986   Elie Wiesel

1987   Óscar Arias Sánchez

1988   The U.N. Peacekeeping Forces

1989   The 14th Dalai Lama

1990   Mikhail Gorbachev

1991   Aung San Suu Kyi

1992   Rigoberta Menchú Tum

1993   Nelson Mandela and F. W. de Klerk

1994   Yasser Arafat, Shimon Peres, and Yitzhak Rabin

1995   Joseph Rotblat and the Pugwash Conferences on Science and World Affairs

1996   Carlos Filipe Ximenes Belo and José Ramos-Horta

1997   The International Campaign to Ban Landmines and Jody Williams

1998   John Hume and David Trimble
1999   Médecins Sans Frontières (Doctors Without Borders)
2000   Kim Dae-jung
2001   The United Nations and Kofi Annan
2002   Jimmy Carter
2003   Shirin Ebadi
2004   Wangari Maathai
2005   The International Atomic Energy Agency and Mohamed
       ElBaradei
2006   Muhammad Yunus and Grameen Bank
2007   The Intergovernmental Panel on Climate Change and Al
       Gore
2008   Martti Ahtisaari
2009   Barack Obama
2010   Liu Xiaobo
2011   Ellen Johnson Sirleaf, Leymah Gbowee, and Tawakkul
       Karman

INDEX

International Labour Organization, 134, 173, **203–4**; on "social justice," 99–100

International Peace Bureau, 61, **79**; Seán MacBride Peace Prize, 221

International Physicians for the Prevention of Nuclear War (IPPNW), 161, **257–62**, 265; and Charter for a World Without Violence, 335

International Space Station, 96

International Women's Peace Conference, 231

International Workingmen's Association, 63

Inter-Parliamentary Union, 77, 149; and Cremer, 63; and Gobat, 61, 79; and Lange, 110; and Norway, 26, 33; and Passy, 58, 63, 339

Iran: democracy movement in, 352–53, 386, 389–90; and Ebadi, 351–56; Evin Prison, 344; nuclear program, 361–65, 393, 409; Obama on, 386–87, 389; U.N. role, 343–44; women's rights in, 343–44

Iran Awakening (Ebadi), 353

Iraq: WMD in, 361, 362–63, 409; *see also* Hussein, Saddam; Iraq War

Iraq War, 34, 230, 324; Carter on, 350; Ebadi on, 352, 354–55; Mandela on, 304–5; Obama on, 386, 393, 397; Pérez Esquivel on, 242–43; Tutu on, 256

Ireland, Republic of: Easter Rising, 220; Good Friday Agreement, 324–25

Irgens, Johannes, 65

I, Rigoberta Menchú, 295–98

Irish Republican Army (IRA), 220–21, 228–29, 231; Sinn Féin, 220, 325

Islam: "demonization" of, 353–54, 368–69; and human rights, 352; and microcredit, 368–69; in Norway, 38

Islam, Yusuf, 335

Israel: Amnesty International on, 233; "apartheid system," 230; boycotts of, 287–88; Camp David Accords, 50–51, 234–38; Ebadi on, 354; El-Baradei on, 363–64; founding, 170–71, 235; and Norway, 36–37, 38; nuclear weapons, 221, 365; and Obama, 387; Oslo Accords, 36, 305–11; and Saddam's nuclear facility, 314; and Sinai, 235, 238; Six-Day War (1967), 184, 235; Stern Gang, 171;

Norwegian Nobel Institute,
24, 49, 205, 380; announcement in, 86; centennial
symposium, 200, 260, 317;
Chinese cyber-attack on,
402; funds from, 122; on
"globalized" prize, 55; and
Mandela, 302; and Nazi
invasion, 146–47; and Nobel
prize history, 340, 351
Norwegian People's Peace
Prize, 216, 244
Nuclear Nonproliferation
Treaty, 246, 361
nuclear weapons, 18; and anti-
missile defense, 187, 247,
394–95; and deterrence,
193, 248–49, 314–15; freeze
movement, 91, 98, 246–47,
248; Hiroshima & Nagasaki,
178, 219, 260; and IAEA,
360–65; and IPPNW, 257–
62, 265; Japan's rejection
of, 219; and Latin America,
246; Manhattan Project, 313;
and Nazis, 313; and North
Korea, 331; Pugwash Conferences on, 160, 312–16; and
Reagan, 248–49; Schweitzer
on, 176; Soviet physicians'
oath on, 260; in Syria, 363;
and weapons "apartheid,"
261

Obama, Barack, 3, 4, 54,
383–99, 403; Ahtisaari
on, 378; and Carter, 384;
music for, 87; and Norway,
37–38, 40, 383, 385; in Peace
Center, 380, 382; and peace
sign, 207; prize critics, 230;
as salvific, 384–85; as un-
Bush, 383–84, 385; "world's"
choice, 385–86
Obama, Barack, Sr., 356
ObamaCare, 385
Oftedal, Christian, 163
Olaf Haraldsson (Olaf II),
31–32
Olav V, King, 182, 263
Olympic Games: Beijing, 288;
founder of, 166; Noel-Baker
in, 4, 186; Norwegians
in, 30; South Africa ban,
286–87
Orbinski, James, 327–28
Ordeal of Woodrow Wilson, The
(Hoover), 166
Orientalism (Said), 382
Ortega, Daniel, 268
Orwell, George, 103
Oscar II, King, 27, 171
Oscars. See Academy Awards
Oslo Accords, 36, 305–11
Oslo Freedom Forum, 37, 227
Ossietzky, Carl von, 3, **136–39**,
251; and Brandt, 212, 213;